Julian Hanebeck
Understanding Metalepsis

Narratologia

Contributions to Narrative Theory

Edited by
Fotis Jannidis, Matías Martínez, John Pier,
Wolf Schmid (executive editor)

Editorial Board
Catherine Emmott, Monika Fludernik, José Ángel García Landa, Inke Gunia,
Peter Hühn, Manfred Jahn, Markus Kuhn, Uri Margolin, Jan Christoph Meister,
Ansgar Nünning, Marie-Laure Ryan, Jean-Marie Schaeffer, Michael Scheffel,
Sabine Schlickers

Volume 56

Julian Hanebeck

Understanding Metalepsis

The Hermeneutics of Narrative Transgression

DE GRUYTER

ISBN 978-3-11-076461-1
e-ISBN (PDF) 978-3-11-051692-0
e-ISBN (EPUB) 978-3-11-051525-1
ISSN 1612-8427

Library of Congress Cataloging-in-Publication Data
A CIP catalog record for this book has been applied for at the Library of Congress.

Bibliographic information published by the Deutsche Nationalbibliothek
The Deutsche Nationalbibliothek lists this publication in the Deutsche Nationalbibliografie;
detailed bibliographic data are available on the Internet at http://dnb.dnb.de.

© 2021 Walter de Gruyter GmbH, Berlin/Boston
This volume is text- and page-identical with the hardback published in 2017.
Illustrations: Martina Bangel
Language editing: Joseph Swann
Printing and binding: CPI books GmbH, Leck
♾ Printed on acid-free paper
Printed in Germany

www.degruyter.com

Für Hedwig

Acknowledgements

This study was accepted in March 2016 as a doctoral degree thesis at the Faculty of Humanities of the University of Wuppertal. It has been minimally revised for publication.

My thanks are due first and foremost to my supervisor, Roy Sommer, who supported my work in an ideal way. Thank you for your time, inspiration, suggestions and critical perspectives, which improved not only this book but also, I would like to think, its author. I have profited at many levels from the staff and programmes of the University of Wuppertal's Center for Graduate Studies and Center for Narrative Research, and I am indebted to the members of this latter institute – in particular my second assessor Katharina Rennhak, Matías Martínez, and Sandra Heinen – for valuable comments and feedback. To Janine Hauthal and the team at the Graduate Center I am deeply grateful for continued support and fruitful cooperation. And I must especially thank Rüdiger Imhof, without whose encouragement, support and – perhaps even more crucially – without whose seminar on *Tristram Shandy* which I attended all those years ago, this study would almost certainly not have come about. I am indebted to the editors of *Narratologia* for accepting the volume into their series, and to Stella Diedrich and Antonia Schrader of De Gruyter's for their support and assistance in preparing the book for publication.

At various points in its development I was invited to present aspects of my work for discussion in colloquia at my home university and at ISSN conferences in Washington, Las Vegas and Manchester. For their critical comments I would like to thank my fellow participants in the narrative research working group and doctoral colloquium at the Department of English and American Studies of the University of Wuppertal. I have many close colleagues to thank for their special support in the final phase of my PhD project, most of all Daniel Becker, Meike Dreiner, Carolin Gebauer, Bettina Hofmann, Monika Kieslich, Maria Leopold, Lukas Preuss, Remus Racolta and Antonius Weixler. My heartfelt thanks are also due to Joseph Swann for his excellent proof-reading and to Martina Bangel for the design of the graphics in this book.

Most of all I must, however, thank my family, Hans and Amalberga Hanebeck, Alexander Hanebeck and Kara Preedy, Calvin Hanebeck and Cosima Hanebeck. And last of all my mind turns to Björn Krüger and Thorsten Sala, with whom I recorded the album *The Manufacture of Madness* just before completing the first version of my thesis. Thank you, Björn and Thorsten – *I wanna do it again.*

Table of Contents

1 **Introduction** —— 1

2 **Framing the Structure of Narrative Metalepsis** —— 11
2.1 Rhetorical Metalepsis and Narrative Metalepsis: From Rhetorical Trope to Narratological Category —— 11
2.1.1 Historical Background: The Rhetorical Trope Metalepsis and Its (Narratological) Reception in the Late Twentieth Century —— 11
2.1.2 Genette's Concept of Narrative Metalepsis (1972) —— 17
2.1.3 New Nuances of Meaning: A Minimal Definition of Metalepsis and the Metaleptic Dynamic —— 23
2.2 A Critical Reassessment of Metalepsis —— 31
2.2.1 Metalepsis and the Diegetic Universe —— 33
2.2.2 Metalepsis and Narrational Acts —— 47
2.2.3 A Transmedial Definition of Metalepsis —— 71
2.2.4 Metaleptic Types —— 81
2.2.4.1 Figurative Metalepsis —— 84
2.2.4.1.1 Figurative Metalepsis I: Epistemological Metalepsis —— 85
2.2.4.1.2 Figurative Metalepsis II: Rhetorical Metalepsis —— 87
2.2.4.2 'The Marked Case': Ontological Metalepsis —— 93
2.2.4.2.1 Immersive Metalepsis —— 94
2.2.4.2.2 Recursive Metalepsis —— 100
2.2.5 Metaleptic Effects —— 108

3 **Breaking the Frame: Metalepsis as Hermeneutic Experience** —— 121
3.1 Narratology and Hermeneutics —— 121
3.1.1 Drawing the Boundaries of Narratology: The Practice that Conceives of the Experience of Narrative Teleologically —— 124
3.1.2 A Hermeneutic Perspective on Narratological Practice: The Hermeneutics of Distanciation and the Hermeneutics of Belonging —— 136
3.1.3 The Negativity of Hermeneutic Experience —— 146
3.2 The Metaleptic Transgression: 'Impossible Narration' —— 152
3.2.1 'Impossible Narration' I: Aporia and Paradox in the Establishment of Diegetic Levels —— 157
3.2.2 'Impossible Narration' II: The Mimetic Presence of the Represented —— 165
3.2.3 'Impossible Narration' III: Realist Aporias —— 174

3.2.4	'Impossible Narration' IV: Metaization and the Self-Reflexive Paradox —— 181
4	**The 'Model' Case: 'Impossible Narration' and Metaleptic Transgressions in Laurence Sterne's *Tristram Shandy* (1759–1767)** —— **191**
4.1	"Any One Is Welcome to Take My Pen, and Go on with the Story for Me That Will": Tristram Shandy's 'Impossible Narration' —— 191
4.2	"Get My Father and My Uncle Toby off the Stairs and Put Them to Bed": Metaleptic Transgressions in *Tristram Shandy* —— 203
4.2.1	Figurative Metalepses in *Tristram Shandy* and the Uncontrollability of Time —— 204
4.2.2	Ontological Metalepsis: Immersive Metalepsis and the Question of Reality —— 218
4.2.3	Ontological Metalepsis: Immersive (Second Person) Metalepsis and Hermeneutic Experience —— 230
4.3	"And Now, You See, I Am Lost Myself!–––": Instead of a Conclusion on Metalepsis and Laurence Sterne —— 238
5	**Beyond Sterne: The Potential of Metaleptic Experience** —— **243**

References —— **263**

Index —— **283**

1 Introduction

> Everything which distinguishes man from the animals depends upon this ability to volatilize perceptual metaphors in a schema, and thus to dissolve an image into a concept. For something is possible in the realm of these schemata which could never be achieved with the vivid first impressions: the construction of a pyramidal order according to castes and degrees, the creation of a new world of laws, privileges, subordinations, and clearly marked boundaries – a new world, one which now confronts that other vivid world of first impressions as more solid, more universal, better known, and more human than the immediately perceived world, and thus as the regulative and imperative world.
>
> — *Friedrich Nietzsche, "On Truth and Lies in an Extra-Moral Sense"*

Angela Carter's short story "The Loves of Lady Purple," written in Japan in the early 1970s, challenges the conventional construction of spatiotemporal and logical distinctions created by narrative embedding: the embedded tale (the metadiegetic story told by a puppeteer) deals with the grotesque career of Lady Purple, a prostitute who kills her male clients. One evening, the puppet with which the puppeteer narrates this story comes alive, kills the puppeteer and enacts the metadiegetic story in the diegesis. Seemingly, and in violation of representational logic, the character Lady Purple literally leaves the world of which the puppeteer tells and enters the world in which he tells. Gérard Genette's *Discours du récit* (1972), which was written at the same time, offers a simple yet ingenious model for such a phenomenon: 'Narrative metalepsis' designates a disruption of the hierarchical structure of diegetic levels of narratives, that is, any violation of the boundary that separates the world of the narrating from the world of the narrated. Metalepsis is based on and questions one of the most fundamental assumptions that govern the understanding of narrative: according to representational logic, narrational acts and the events of the story they tell are situated in spatiotemporally distinct contexts. This is how we conventionally make sense of narrative: the space and time of narrated events cannot coincide with the space and time of the narration.

Yet the metaleptic denial of conventional narrative sense-making belongs to the conventions of narrative: ever since the publication of Laurence Sterne's *The Life and Opinions of Tristram Shandy, Gentleman* (1759–1767), metalepsis has been part of the repertoire of narrative techniques employed by novelists. In one of the initial chapters of Sterne's novel, Tristram, the narrator, claims that his narration is guided by the expectations of his narratees. Supposedly obliging those "who find themselves ill at ease, unless they are let into the whole secret from first to last" (I.iv)[1], the narrator justifies the excessively detailed account of his birth by a "backwardness in [his] nature to disappoint any one soul living" (ibid.). The ensuing suggestion of the narrator has often been read as a metaleptic move across diegetic levels:

> To such, however, as do not choose to go so far back into these things, I can give no better advice, than they skip over the remaining part of this Chapter; for I declare before hand, 'tis wrote only for the curious and inquisitive.
> ————————————————Shut the door.————————————————
> I was begot in the night, betwixt the first Sunday and the first Monday in the month of March, in the year of our Lord one thousand seven hundred and eighteen. I am positive I was.— (Ibid.)

Monika Fludernik cites this passage from *Tristram Shandy* as a *bona fide* example of metalepsis, claiming that "the narrator in Book 1.4 orders the narratee to shut the door (on the story level!)" (2003b, 386), which would constitute the literal movement of the extradiegetic narratee into the diegesis. According to Werner Wolf, on the other hand, this passage, in which "the extradiegetic narrator asks the – equally extradiegetic (!) – fictional reader to 'Shut the door' [...], does *not* fulfil the criterion of transgression" (2005, 90; emphases in the original) which is the defining characteristic of metalepsis. Both Fludernik and Wolf follow Genette's definition, and both agree that speaker and addressee belong to the extradiegetic level, but they differ when it comes to judging on which diegetic level the door to be closed can effectively be *located*.

There are good reasons for both Fludernik's and Wolf's structural analyses of this excerpt – reasons which substantiate their respective decisions whether or not to regard this as an instance of metalepsis. Even though their accounts disagree, they share a tendency that is typical of narratological approaches to metaleptic narratives; metalepsis is usually presented, if not conceptualized, as a possibility of narrative that is independent of individual acts of understanding. Taken together, however, Fludernik's and Wolf's analyses suggest that metaleptic transgressions neither invoke some deep-structure logic that precedes and may become manifest in the structural analysis of given narratives nor are they a place of stable meanings that transcend the hermeneutic situation in which they come into being.

---

[1] All references to Laurence Sterne's *The Life and Opinions of Tristram Shandy, Gentleman* (1759–1767) are, in accordance with common practice, to volume (capitalized Roman numerals) and chapter (small Roman numerals) in the Florida edition (1997).

One way to account for this is the elusive nature of the circular metaleptic form. Like all taxonomies and categories of narratology, metalepsis is based on a structural relation: it presupposes what Nietzsche has termed the "construction of a pyramidal order [...] and clearly marked boundaries" (Nietzsche 1992 [first German ed. 1896], 84) that exist beyond the contingent historical attempt to make sense of a particular narrative. But unlike all taxonomies and categories of narratology, metalepsis *per definitionem* denies the very structural relations that are the phenomenon's prerequisite. Metalepsis is thus not only a structuralist category that presupposes a structural form that emerges unchanged in contingent attempts to understand, say, a passage from *Tristram Shandy*, but also the very category that challenges – but at the same time extends and enriches – narratology's "pyramidal order."

The various analyses, explications and reconceptualizations of metaleptic transgressions and their effects that have been developed in narratological monographs and articles since the 1980s are indicative of how metalepsis functions as a nodal point in a system of narratological categories. What 'metalepsis' denotes in narratological parlance is often subtly different from Genette's initial account; analyses of metalepses are often contradictory (as in the case of Fludernik's and Wolf's description of the metaleptic form of the passage from *Tristram Shandy*) and there is no general consensus about the phenomenon's scope or theoretical implications. Its unique position in a system of narratological distinctions and categories makes metalepsis indeed, as John Pier puts it, "a threshold of discovery" (2011, 275). A threshold which, as a narratological category, defies definition: in the introduction to the volume *Metareference Across Media: Theory and Case Studies* (2009), Wolf concedes that "metalepsis does not (yet) have a generally accepted definition" (50–51). More recently, Jeff Thoss has maintained that "one cannot but wonder whether, when we talk about metalepsis, we always talk about the same thing" (2015, 1–2).

The problem of narratological accounts of metalepsis, I maintain, lies in the relationship of tension between a simple definition of structural relations and a complex event of understanding[2] which playfully questions and calls attention

---

[2] The characterization of understanding as an 'event' implies that (from the perspective of philosophical hermeneutics) the understanding subjectivity does not take precedence over the various elements of the hermeneutic situation. Jeff Malpas describes the historical situatedness of an understanding subjectivity as "the complex and interwoven character [...] that is central to the hermeneutical – a situatedness that involves time and space, self and other, 'practice' *and* 'theory'" (Malpas 2010, 274; emphasis in the original). The traditions of understanding narrative, the categories which make traditions possible, the narrative in question, author and recipient, etc., all belong to an event that is not shaped by a single agency that approaches an

to the various elements of the hermeneutic situation in which it comes into being: the structuralist category relies on a complex set of historically situated prerequisites (which can never be defined once and for all). Wolf rightly points out that "the defining paradoxicality of metalepsis [...] can refer to logical impossibilities (the contamination of the ontologically different realms of 'nature' and 'art'/'artefacts') or to what goes beyond, and is therefore impossible according to reigning 'doxa' (e.g., the 'orthodox' idea that the present cannot influence the past)" (2013, 117). I would like to add that what Wolf terms "doxa" is not only incidental to but the very basis of the construction of a metaleptic contamination of "ontologically different realms" (ibid.). A close analysis of the realization of metaleptic potential makes visible what the structuralist category models: The construction of "ontologically different realms" (ibid.) relies on manifold relations (past and present, representation and represented, subject and object, cause and effect, etc.) which in turn rely on whole bundles of 'orthodox' ideas that specify what it means, say, that a past event is the cause for an effect in the present.

Considered as a dynamic, as an event of understanding, metalepsis foregrounds what narratological analyses conventionally bracket and what can be described from a Nietzschean perspective as the genesis of "the more solid, more universal and better known [...] world" (Nietzsche 1992 [first German ed. 1896], 84) of narratological categories: "A continuum stands before us from which we isolate a pair of fragments, just in the same way as we perceive a movement as isolated points and therefore do not properly see but infer it [...]. There is an infinite set of processes in that abrupt second which evades us." This comment from *The Gay Science* (Nietzsche 2006 [first German ed. 1882], 112) is taken up again by Nietzsche in *Beyond Good and Evil*:

> One should not wrongly reify [verdinglichen] "cause" and "effect," as the natural scientists do (and whoever, like them, thinks naturalistically) [...] One should use "cause" and "effect" only as pure concepts, that is to say, as conventional fictions for the purpose of designation and communication – *not* for explanation. [...] [T]he effect does *not* follow cause, there is no rule of "law." It is *we* alone who have devised cause, sequence, for-each-other, relativity, constraint, number, law, the freedom, motive, and purpose; And when we project and mix this symbol world into things as if it existed "in itself," we act once more as we have always acted – *mythologically*. (1989 [first German ed. 1886], 29)

---

isolated object: "Hermeneutics proposes to make subjectivity the final, and not the first, category in a theory of understanding. Subjectivity must be lost as radical origin if it is to be recovered in a more modest role according to which, far from beginning, the subject has to respond to the proposals of meaning the text unfolds" (Ricœur 1991 [first French ed. 1986], 37).

Along these lines, it could be argued that to designate a certain narrative as metaleptic does not offer an explanation, but constitutes a conventional fiction "for the purpose of designation and communication." If we bracket the metaleptic dynamic (the event of understanding metalepsis) and consider metalepsis a formal property of a narrative object, we "act once more as we have always acted – mythologically" (ibid.) – that is, we think the category and its "symbol world" (ibid.) into the (narrative) continuum before us. This is a decidedly Nietzschean reading of narratological practice. Yet whoever thinks 'naturalistically' (or narratologically in the sense of restrictive theorists) is hard pressed to provide a sound basis for thinking, in Nietzsche's words, the 'myth' of narrative structure into the 'thing' read or understood. As the radically different findings by Fludernik and Wolf demonstrate, the 'causes,' the 'after-one-anothers,' etc., are dependent on a complex hermeneutic situation in which a given narrative emerges.

I propose to answer this Nietzschean challenge to narratology by offering an account of how the narrative structuring that is the prerequisite of metalepsis can be traced back to the conditions and possibilities of the hermeneutic situation in which metaleptic transgressions come into being. Even though a Nietzschean denial of structuralist thought is an epistemological quandary that is relevant to understanding the metaleptic 'form,' this approach is based on the assumption that the (narrative) structuring of the continuum in which understanding takes place is inevitable, albeit a conventional fiction "for the purpose of designation and communication" (Nietzsche 1989 [first German ed. 1886], 29). Thus, this book is concerned with the intricate relation between a structuralist category and the event of understanding to which it belongs; it describes metalepsis narratologically; it explores the limits of structuralism; it offers an explanation of why and how metalepsis resists (but at the same time enhances) the narrative structuring of understanding; and it offers an account of the complexities that narratological categories cannot model.

As a 'threshold of discovery,' metalepsis offers a perspective on narrative that is dialogical: metalepsis can be taken to exemplify how hermeneutic experience and structural description depend upon one another. Ricœur claimed in a contribution to the French magazine *Esprit* in 1963 that 'it will never be possible to do hermeneutics without structuralism' (cf. 622; this is a loose translation offered by Alison Scott-Baumann in 2009, cf. 22). Acknowledging that a consideration of the event of understanding metalepsis begins with a precise outline of the structure of narrative, Chapter 2 considers the history of narratological contributions that describe the metaleptic form, discusses their merits and problems, and offers, very much in a structuralist tradition, a reduction of complexity that provides a heuristic framework for understanding certain representational possibilities and phenomena: I propose a transmedial model of metalepsis, a scalar model of the metaleptic denial of diegetic properties, and a tree diagram of metaleptic types. This tree diagram introduces a new systematization of preceding types and offers new distinctions and terms. The new terms I propose are 'figurative metalepsis' (a category that subsumes what in narratological parlance is referred to as 'epistemological' and 'rhetorical' metalepses) and 'immersive' and 'recursive' metalepsis (a new distinction between types of 'ontological' transgression).

If we think of narratological categories as the structures established from an analytical distance, then twentieth-century hermeneutics offers the reintegration of those structures into an act of understanding that belongs ontologically to that which it understands. Proceeding from a structuralist account, this book traces the metaleptic dynamic from a hermeneutic perspective, based on the insight (to turn Ricœur's quip on its head) that 'it will never be possible to do structuralism without hermeneutics.' The experience of metalepsis has hermeneutic repercussions that throw light on the conditions and limitations of narratological analysis; metalepsis sheds light on narratology in general. Chapter 3 therefore considers the hermeneutics of narratology (a lacuna of narratological research) and argues that narratological practice and its explanatory paradigms still tend to be informed by a hermeneutics of 'distanciation,' a hermeneutics that strives for the methodological distance of the understanding subject. From this distance the object of narrative is seen in terms of a methodological reflection that allows the description of what is untouched by the contingency of the historical event of an understanding subjectivity. Such an analysis is, in other words, based on and directed towards what is common to the experiences of many (if not all) recipients of a given narrative (if not narrative *per se*). I assume that narratologists (no matter whether they think of their approach as restrictive or postclassical) generally do not expect the students they teach to consider the famous instance in chapter 55 of John Fowles' *The French Lieutenant's Woman* (1969) as non-metaleptic (at least not once they are familiar with the concept). In view of this, I describe narratology (and this includes postclassical narratologies) as a practice that conceives of the experience of understanding narrative *teleologically* – that is, narratology is structured towards, and outlines, the *unity* of experiencing narratives from an analytical distance.

Yet, and this is one of the central arguments of this book, understanding metalepsis foregrounds how the conceptual prerequisites of narratological categories rely on unstable acts of understanding: Following Gadamer and Ricœur, Chapter 3 argues that it is the dialectic between the hermeneutics of distanciation and the hermeneutics of belonging that characterizes the understanding of (metaleptic) narratives. What follows from this is that in the event of understanding metalepses one potentially encounters what Hans Georg Gadamer has termed the 'negativity of hermeneutic experience,' the experience of a self-reflexive, dynamic and dialogical structure that results in an oscillating openness. This is the second aim of Chapter 3: to show in how far the negativity of hermeneutic experience can be described as belonging to the hermeneutic situation in which metalepsis is understood; how the frameworks with which narrative is approached are subjected to an aporetic movement in the event of understanding metalepsis. Metalepsis, considered in the context of the conceptual frameworks with which narratives are approached (and, from a hermeneutic perspective, shaped), is characterized as the 'impossible' narration that highlights the limitations of these conceptual frameworks.

These insights into the hermeneutics of narratology and the event of understanding metalepsis inform the readings of metaleptic narratives in this book. The narratological concept of metalepsis has been applied to phenomena in a wide variety of genres and media, from drama (Landfester 1997, Fludernik 2003b, Genette 2004, Klimek 2009/2010) to pop lyrics (Ben-Merre 2011), from film (Genette 2004, Limoges 2008, Klimek 2009, Thoss 2011a, Sarkhosh 2011, Thoss 2015) to videogames (Harpold 2008, Ryan 2006) and comic books (Kukkonen 2011a, Thoss 2015). The transmediality of metalepsis is undisputed today. There is also consensus about the proliferation of metaleptic phenomena in postmodern literature and art. However, explanations of this proliferation usually correlate the metaleptic form with generic features or philosophical thought. Metalepses have often been discussed with reference to Gödel's theorem as "the problem [...] of maintaining distinct levels through avoidance of self-reference by elaborating meta-levels ad infinitum" (Pier 2009, 196). Read in this way, metalepses are one of many manifestations of a decidedly philosophical quandary. In her discussion of Russell, Gödel and Tarski, Sonja Klimek (2010) argues that the epistemological crisis of modernity is concerned with paradoxes in mathematical logic and philosophy of language, which are prefigurations ("Präfigurationen") of the sheer quantity of metalepses evident in fantasy literature today (cf. 2010, 330–344). This interesting argument offers one explanation for the ubiquity of metaleptic phenomena in contemporary (fantasy) narratives.

However, metalepsis typically allows and resists such correlations. There are many instances of metalepsis that have nothing in common with the logical and mathematical paradoxes of twentieth-century philosophy. Metalepsis can have "reconstructive effects" (Malina 2002, 133) and be "compatible with immersion" (Wolf 2013, 116), compatible with constructions of meaning that disagree with mathematical and philosophical paradoxes. Moreover, such an argument does not take into account that metalepsis has been a structural possibility at least since Ancient Greek narrative[3] and that Laurence Sterne, the phenomenon's early master, has been influenced – from a conventional historical viewpoint – by John Locke, but hardly by twentieth-century philosophers. In view of the amount of narratological attention lavished upon the forms and functions of metalepsis in the past thirty years, it seems striking that Laurence Sterne's *The Life and Opinions of Tristram Shandy, Gentleman*, a novel which offers one of the most radical explorations of the metaleptic potential of narrative, has not yet received more than a few cursory mentions. Chapter 4 is intended to close this research gap; it traces many interpretative possibilities that emerge from a hermeneutic dialogue that approaches *Tristram Shandy* with the narratological concept of metalepsis. From a structuralist perspective, Laurence Sterne's *The Life and Opinions of Tristram Shandy, Gentleman* is one of the earliest narratives that systematically challenge the conventional construction of spatiotemporal distinctions created by narrative embedding. More than two hundred years before Genette introduced metalepsis as a narratological category, Laurence Sterne's novel contains the metaleptic potential for the realization of all the metaleptic types I shall offer – with the notable exception of recursive metalepses.

From a hermeneutic perspective, metalepsis in *Tristram Shandy* is an application in the Gadamerian sense – forcing the concepts that temporally and logically precede the category into a dialogical openness that thwarts all attempts at final interpretation. Such an investigation moves beyond narratological attempts to reconcile the metaleptic dynamic with the text-internal structure of narrative. Equally, it moves beyond the "contextualist dimensions of contemporary 'postclassical' narratological scholarship" (Darby 2001, 423) in which the attempt is made to correlate textual phenomena with, say, cognitive or sociolinguistic phenomena. Understanding metalepsis in *Tristram Shandy* will thus be described as a hermeneutic experience – unstable, manifold and self-referential, forcing the concepts that temporally and logically precede metalepsis into a dialogical openness that resists objectification and 'finalization.' In

---

[3] Irene de Jong's book article "Metalepsis in Ancient Greek Literature" (2009) supplies a surprisingly large number of examples in Homer and Pindar that can be read as metalepses. More recently, the collection *Über die Grenze: Metalepse in Text- und Bildmedien des Altertums* (2013) has established the prevalence of narrative metalepsis in a wide variety of works from classical antiquity.

this sense, metalepses are similar to Dostoevsky's dialogical characters, who, according to Mikhail Bakhtin, are defined by the "sense of their inner unfinalizability, their capacity to outgrow, as it were, from within and to render untrue any externalizing and finalizing definition of them" (Bakhtin 1984 [first Russian ed. 1929/1963], 59).

Choosing *Tristram Shandy* as the model case challenges the notion that metalepsis is inherently connected to modernist or postmodernist sensibilities, poetics or philosophical positions. A hermeneutic consideration of metaleptic narratives from various centuries does not yield a clear historical development of metaleptic possibilities of meaning. Metalepsis, I maintain, does not have a particular place in a conventional history of ideas. Accordingly, the final chapter discusses a comic book, movies and the *Tibetan Book of the Dead* and argues that the state of the art of metalepsis is not the acme of historical development. Chapter 5 does not describe the most recent or, in terms of media technology, most sophisticated metalepses – but offers the outline of a movement towards what I take to be the most radical metaleptic potential of narrative. The fact that I find this potential in a non-fictional religious narrative from the seventh century and in a comic book from the twenty-first century may be taken to exemplify that metalepsis cuts across the typical distinctions that inform historical genealogies.

One tentative conclusion that can be drawn from the metaleptic narratives presented in Chapter 5 is that radical metalepses potentially serve as a bridge connecting the understanding of narrative with the beginning of human representation in the cultic enactment of divinity. These metalepses perform what Gadamer terms 'the original mimetic relation' that offers the unmediated presence of the represented. In "Poetry and Mimesis" (1986a [first German ed. 1972]), Gadamer argues that in the cultic event "the act in which something is recognized [...] is not an act of distinction, but of identification. However ineliminable it may be, and however we may emphasize it, the distance between the image and the original has something inappropriate about it as far as the real ontological meaning of mimesis is concerned" (ibid. 120). Understanding narrative relies on the construction of this distinction, on the spatiotemporal, logical and ontological distance between the 'original' and its image or narrative representation: here and now we understand the there and then. The cultic event, on the other hand, does not represent divinity as something external or beyond (belonging to the there and then), it does not refer to that which is not present. The cultic event enacts divinity as *presence*: "It is a matter neither of there and then, nor of here and now, but it is encountered as the very self-same" (ibid.). Metalepsis encourages addressees to perform an act of recognition that realizes "the real ontological meaning of mimesis": transcending the ontological distance of narrational acts, anchoring the recognized presence to the world in which it is understood, metalepsis invites us to experience then and now as 'the very self-same.'

2 Framing the Structure of Narrative Metalepsis

2.1 Rhetorical Metalepsis and Narrative Metalepsis: From Rhetorical Trope to Narratological Category

Gérard Genette's account of the narrative phenomenon he termed 'metalepsis' can be located between the long history of a rhetorical trope and nearly thirty years of narratological reception and application. This chapter first delineates the rhetorical history of the concept (which can be traced back to the first century BC) and offers an account of how the genesis of the rhetorical trope 'metalepsis' sheds light on Genette's influential (re)conceptualization of narrative metalepsis in 1972 (2.1.1.). Genette's structuralist account of metalepsis in *Discours du récit* is the focus of Chapter 2.1.2.; this chapter offers a detailed account of his definition of metalepsis and considers its formal logic, as well as the model of narrative on which it is based. Narratologists have been offering definitions of the form(s) of the narratological category 'metalepsis' for more than 30 years and have debated its functions as well as its theoretical implications, thus creating an extensive body of writing. Even though this body of writing argues for shifts in emphasis, a widening or narrowing of the phenomenon's scope or a reconceptualization of one or more of its constituent parts and/or field(s) of reference, there is a common ground that agrees with the formal logic of Genette's definition of 1972. In Chapter 2.1.3. I propose a minimal definition of metalepsis and argue that it offers a potent heuristic that makes visible how such hierarchical relations have been part of understanding metaleptic narratives for many decades.

2.1.1 Historical Background: The Rhetorical Trope Metalepsis and Its (Narratological) Reception in the Late Twentieth Century

The earliest definition of the rhetorical trope of metalepsis can be found in a catalogue of rhetorical terms attributed to the Alexandrian grammarian Tryphon in the first century BC, which classifies metalepsis as the synonymy that refers to the synonymy's homonym (cf. Cummings 2007, 221; and Burkhardt

1992, 1089).⁴ Roughly 2000 years later, Gérard Genette cites the eighteenth-century rhetorician Fontanier as the source for his concept of metalepsis. Fontanier calls the "narrative figure" (Genette 1980 [1972]⁵, 234) which consists of the pretence that the poet "himself brings about the effects he celebrates," (Fontanier, qtd. in Genette 1980, 234) *author's metalepsis*. Genette supplies three well known examples of this pretence: one by Laurence Sterne, one by Diderot, and the general linguistic usage that attributes the cause of the diegetic events to the author, "as when we say that Virgil 'has Dido die' in Book IV of the *Aeneid*" (Genette 1980, 234). Obviously, the last example involves neither synonyms nor homonyms.

The story of the rhetorical trope 'metalepsis' which unfolded between Tryphon and the eighteenth century has been told in various and contradictory ways. Whether or not the trope originated in a 'faulty interpretation' of a few lines in Homer, as the nineteenth-century German scholar Richard Volkmann claimed (cf. 1885, 427), the various uses (and definitions) of the rhetorical trope 'metalepsis' to which Genette alludes are complex and riddled with subtle differences in meaning. There are, of course, Renaissance predecessors for Fontanier's version of the rhetorical trope: Philipp Melanchthon defines metalepsis in his *Elementa Rhetorices* (2001 [1531]) effectively as a kind of metonymy, i.e. as the substitution of a cause for an effect or an effect for a cause (cf. Burkhardt 1992, 1092–1093). In subtle contrast to this, the standard analysis of metalepsis in classical rhetoric, offered by Quintilian in the eighth book of his *Institutio Oratoria* (95 CE), describes metalepsis as the transitional stage of such a substitution: "It is the nature of Metalepsis to be a sort of intermediate step between the term transferred and the thing to which it is transferred; it does not signify

---

4 Both Cummings and Burkhardt supply modern-day equivalents to Tryphon's analysis of a Homerian trope. Burkhardt chooses "Die Mahlzeit beschließt" (which can be roughly translated as 'the meal has ruled...') as an example of the rhetorical trope in Tryphon's sense (cf. 1992, 1089). The homonymy of the German words *Gericht* (court of justice) and *Gericht* (meal) is the first prerequisite for metalepsis. The second prerequisite is that *Mahlzeit* (meal) is synonymous with *Gericht* (in the sense of meal). The replacement of *Gericht* with *Mahlzeit* in the sentence "Die Mahlzeit beschließt" (the meal has ruled...) instead of "Das Gericht beschließt" (the court of justice has ruled...) employs the synonym of a homonym that does not 'fit.' Thus, *Mahlzeit* (meal) obliquely evokes *Gericht* (court of justice). Strikingly, and this is indicative of the rarity of this figure, the homonyms in Cumming's example are not strictly homonymic: "In everyday language-use, the closest analogy may be in rhyming slang, where *have a butcher's* (from *have a butcher's hook*) means 'have a look'" (Cummings 2007, 221).

5 The French original *Discours du récit* was published in 1972. Here and in the following I cite the English edition which was first published in 1980 (foreword by Jonathan Culler, translated by Jane E. Lewin).

anything in itself, but provides the transition" (2001, 447).⁶ According to Quintilian, then, metalepsis consists in an intermediate step in the structural relations of the terms (or tropes) involved, connecting what would not belong together without the trope: "The commonest example is *cano* ('I sing') equals *canto, canto* equals *dico* ('I say'), therefore *cano* equals *dico; canto* is the middle term" (ibid.). Defining metalepsis as *transumptio* (which can be translated as 'a taking or assuming of one thing for another'), Quintilian suggests that a polyseme is replaced by a synonym that is equivalent to (one of) the polyseme's meaning(s) but which does not agree with the context. The order of presentation of the tropes in Book VIII of *Institutio Oratoria* (metalepsis follows metaphor, synecdoche, metonymy, antonomasia, onomatopoeia, and catachresis) suggests that metalepsis is not only the last of the figures that involve a change of meaning, but also in a certain sense an inferior kind of trope (cf. ibid.).

Renaissance rhetoricians have closely followed the definition of Quintilian and incorporated metalepsis into Renaissance theory. However, at least two distinct types of metalepsis emerged in the sixteenth century⁷: on the one hand, Desiderius Erasmus (in close alignment with Quintilian) characterized metalepsis as a movement "by stages towards what we mean to say" (qtd. in Cummings 2007, 220) in the first book of *De Duplici Copia Verborum ac Rerum Commentarii Duo* (1512). This definition has been elegantly paraphrased by Brian Cummings: "We could call this a kind of metaphorical ellipsis, in which one or more middle terms are excluded" (ibid.).⁸ This is largely congruent with the notion of metalepsis as a polyseme replaced by a synonym that is equivalent with (one of) its meaning(s) but does not agree with the context. On the other hand, Melanch-

---

6 Quintilian's account of metalepsis has been accused of conceptual ambiguity (cf. Burkhardt 1992, 1090). One explanation provided for this is connected to textual scholarship: "In a sentence which gave his sixteenth-century editors some difficulty, Quintilian compares metalepsis to a process of transition, perhaps even transition from one trope to another: 'quae ex alio [tropo] in aliud velut viam praestat' ['which, as it were, makes a path from one thing [one trope] to another']. The Aldine edition of 1512 and sixteenth-century editions of Quintilian thereafter, deleted the word *tropo*. [...] It was therefore hard for a sixteenth-century reader to see the difference between metalepsis and any other kind of metaphor" (Cummings 2007, 226). Yet even without the deletion of the word *tropo*, it is still difficult to establish how precisely metalepsis could connect what kind of tropes as a 'path.'
7 Burkhardt (1992, 1087–1088) argues that there are *three* types of metalepsis. One connected to Tryphon and Quintilian (as a special form of synonymy), one associated with the grammarian Donatus, and one with Melanchthon (both offer metalepsis as a special kind of metonymy).
8 Lanham, in agreement with Cummings, cites Quintilian's example and argues that the "main element would thus seem to be the omission of a central term in an extended metaphor" (Lanham 1968, 66).

thon defined metalepsis as a special kind of metonymy, which is the tradition followed by Fontanier and quoted by Genette.

The twentieth-century interest in metalepsis by critics such as Harold Bloom (1975), Hillis Miller (1976), Paul de Man (1979), John Hollander (1981) or Judith Butler (1997) introduces further complications and subtleties, as it moves away from the definitions of classical rhetoric in an attempt to explore the trope's theoretical implications. Brian Cummings argues that this modern interest in metalepsis "has been as it were a digression or transumption from its classical and Renaissance origins. Metalepsis in modern theory has become a figure of the figure, a figure of literary influence or legacy (in Bloom and Hollander) or of the presence of authorship in narrative (in Genette)" (2007, 220). Strangely enough, it seems that (a genealogy of) metalepsis would resist any attempt to offer a unifying or progressive account of the concept's genesis, since the term haunts all present discussions with a seemingly unparalleled range of meanings and uses (of which the rhetorical tradition is only a part), from ancient legal discourse to the question of fiction and 'reality.'

The intention of the present chapter, however, is not to reconstruct the development of the concept (or concepts) from antiquity through the Renaissance to the present day,[9] but to survey the (narratological) reception of the rhetorical trope in the late twentieth century in order to uncover the ways in which the rhetorical tradition has crucially influenced the genesis of the narratological category – if, that is, the rhetorical tradition has shaped the narratological category at all. Predictably enough, there is disagreement in narratological discussions on the precise meaning of metalepsis as a rhetorical term, as well as on the extent of Genette's indebtedness to the rhetorical tradition.

In view of these subtle differences of meaning and various definitions of the rhetorical trope of metalepsis and the complex history of its reception, it comes as no surprise when Werner Wolf concludes that metalepsis as defined by Genette is an "originally narratological concept" (2005, 88).[10] While a definition

---

9 See Hollander (1981, 133–149) for an insightful examination of the rhetorical trope's "confused but revealing history" (ibid., 134) from antiquity to the Renaissance.

10 Werner Wolf traces the discontinuities of meaning between the rhetorical trope and the narratological category and argues that the narratological concept can neither be derived from nor traced back to the trope's various uses in rhetorical literature (cf. 2005, 88). Following Hollander's and Fletcher's entry "Metalepsis or Transumption" in *The New Princeton Encyclopedia of Poetry and Poetics* (1993), Wolf maintains that this is due to the fact that metalepsis occurred in rhetorical contexts "with rather imprecise meanings" (2005, 88). The entry "Metalepsis or Transumption" reads like a very condensed rendition of Hollander's argument (presented at length in his study *The Figure of Echo* [1981]) that the trope of metalepsis is allusive as

such as "that trope by which later *effects* covertly substitute for earlier causes" (Hawes 2005, xvi) can be used to describe a range of phenomena that in Genette's definition are clearly metaleptic, it seems impossible to establish a coherent framework that incorporates rhetorical and narratological conceptions of metalepsis. The few narratologists who have commented on the relationship between the rhetorical trope and the narratological concept have at best – more often than not *implicitly* – acknowledged a point of intersection between those concepts: Marie-Laure Ryan for instance argues that the metaleptic transgressions she describes (following Genette) are "not coextensive with all the uses of metalepsis in rhetorical literature" (2006, 246). Typically, those narratological analyses trace Genette's rhetorical heritage to one of the conceptions that emerged in the Renaissance and attempt to distinguish the "simple figure" (Kukkonen 2011b, 2) from Genette's appropriation, without mapping the area of intersection between the rhetorical and narratological uses.[11] However, the various conceptions of metalepsis as (a) a kind of metaphorical substitution ('a movement by stages towards what we mean to say'), (b) a metonymical operation, or rather (c) an inappropriately used synonym have led to subtle differentiations in the twentieth-century which not only mirror the earlier divide (originating in the Renaissance), but also fail to offer a "simple figure" as a stable point of departure for tracing the connection between the rhetorical tradition and the narratological category.

While Genette originally considers the rhetorical trope of metalepsis *implicitly* as a metonymy (1980, 234), he seems to argue in 2004 that it is structurally similar to a kind of extended substitution. This is corroborated by John Pier's comment on Genette's (2004) reassessment of rhetorical metalepsis: "Metalepsis shares with metaphor and metonymy the principle of transfer of sense" (Pier 2009, 195). Explicitly connecting the metonymical conception of the rhetorical trope (following Dumarsais and Fontanier) and metalepsis, Genette expands

---

well as elusive (cf. Hollander 1981, 115–116; 140) and that rhetoricians "from Augustine through the English Renaissance critic George Puttenham [...] are in confused disagreement about its [metalepsis'] function" (ibid.). One of the reasons for this 'elusive allusiveness' is that metalepsis is a trope that "seems to involve a temporal sequence" (ibid., 134) and can accordingly be considered synchronically as well as diachronically (cf. ibid., 114–116; 135–136).

11 The narratologists who connect metalepsis to a rhetorical tradition preceding the Renaissance include Klaus Meyer-Minnemann (2005), Sabine Schlickers (2005), and Philippe Roussin (2005). Jan Christoph Meister (2003), in his discussion of metalepsis as a rhetorical concept, "counts metalepsis under the tropes characterized by the use of synonyms. More precisely, [...] metalepsis refers to a contextually inappropriate use of synonyms" (Meister 2003, no pagination). Thus, Meister reiterates Quintilian's definition.

this principle beyond single rhetorical figures (cf. Genette 2004, 7–16). Not only is each rhetorical trope or figure already a 'little fiction' ("une petite fiction" [ibid., 17]), but what Genette terms "métalepse *fictionnelle*" (ibid., 17) is also the extension of figurative and/or tropical language use to all fiction. In loose agreement with Fontanier's example above, metalepsis ("that trope by which later *effects* covertly substitute for earlier causes" [Hawes 2005, xvi]) has been widened in scope to include and define fictional narration in general. "Tout fiction est tissée de métalepses" (2004, 131), Genette concludes – 'all fictions are woven through with metalepses.' This 'transfer of sense' structurally resembles Quintilian's definition of metalepsis. However, John Pier rightly argues that Genette does not consider metalepsis "in Quintilian's sense as the intermediate step or transition between a term which is transferred and the thing to which it is transferred, resulting in an inappropriate synonym" (2009, 194).

The most convincing example of any attempt to delineate the theoretical overlap between the rhetorical trope and the narratological category and, what is more, to derive the latter from the former, was offered by William Nelles in his *Frameworks* (1997). Strikingly, he conceptualizes the rhetorical trope as a kind of process ('a movement by stages towards what we mean to say') which he derives from Quintilian (and, in contrast to Genette, not from one of the Renaissance versions)[12]. He begins his outline of the metaleptic phenomenon (indebted to Genette) by discussing the classical rhetorical term, or, to be more precise, by discussing what he terms the "admittedly cryptic example" by Quintilian. He argues that "the metalepsis has no independent meaning as 'content' but produces significance by purely structural means, making it particularly amenable to structural description" (1997, 153). Analogous to the rhetorical figure of metalepsis that provides a particular transition between two terms, Nelles argues that narratological or narrative metalepsis provides a transition between two "narrative levels" (ibid.). Accordingly, he still refers to metaleptic transgression, which he expounds and typologizes as a "trope" (ibid., 157). Genette's claim (2004) that fictional narration 'transfers sense' from the real diegesis ("la diégèse réelle") to the fictional diegesis ("la diégèse fictionnelle") and vice versa (cf. Genette 2004, 131), not only reiterates William Nelles' assessment that narrative has "at least the potential for narrative metalepsis" (1997, 152), but also the manner in which Nelles arrives at this conclusion.

---

[12] Needless to add, the question of whether the rhetorical trope metalepsis described by Renaissance rhetoricians can be neatly analyzed into distinct types or versions is certainly debatable (cf. the slightly differing accounts of Burkhardt and Cummings briefly mentioned above).

Likewise, it could be argued that the notion of metalepsis described above – (following Quintilian) as a polyseme replaced by a synonym that is equivalent with (one of) its meaning(s) but does not agree with the context – exhibits another conceptual overlap with Genette's redefinition in *Narrative Discourse*. The various possible contexts of person, space and temporal deixis are typically employed in fictional narration to create metalepses. In a sense, the 'polysemy' of certain deictic terms is used in a similar manner when these deictic expressions are metaleptically employed in a way that does not agree with the context. When "I," "you," and "this moment" refer to extra-, meta- or intradiegesis in a manner that contradicts representational logic, we are very close to Tryphon's classification as mentioned at the beginning of this chapter. The continuities of meaning between the rhetorical trope and the narratological category are perhaps as surprising as its discontinuities.

This sub-chapter has demonstrated that there are a number of (subtly different) definitions of the rhetorical trope and that some of these definitions can indeed be meaningfully aligned with Genette's delineation of metalepsis. Thus, even though the existence of different notions of metalepsis (by Quintilian, Erasmus, etc...) and the (lack of) precision with which they are employed, as well as the complex etymology of the word metalepsis, "seem to generate [...] 'a semantic field' [...] crowded with hermeneutical blossoms" (Hollander 1981, 134), such blossoms may still elucidate (the genesis of) the narratological category outlined by Genette.

2.1.2 Genette's Concept of Narrative Metalepsis (1972)

When Gérard Genette introduced the rhetorical term 'metalepsis' into narratological terminology in his seminal *Narrative Discourse*, he defined it as "any intrusion by the extradiegetic narrator or narratee into the diegetic universe (or by diegetic characters into a metadiegetic universe, etc.), or the inverse" (1980, 235). This definition is perfectly straightforward if one accepts its premise that there are indeed distinct (textual) 'universes' or 'worlds' that can be unambiguously distinguished by their relation to what Genette refers to as 'the diegesis'[13],

---

[13] Gerald Prince offers a succinct definition of the term *diegesis* corresponding to Genette's use of the term: "The (fictional) world in which the situations and events narrated occur (in French: *diégèse*)" (2003, 20). Chapter 2.2.1 offers an analysis of narratological conceptions of the notion of 'diegesis.' To what extent this notion, which is the fundamental conceptual pre-

that there is, in other words, an ahistorical structural make-up of the narrative text that obliges all readers to construct 'universes' – separate and hierarchically structured ontological levels – whose boundaries can be paradoxically and illegitimately 'crossed' (or negated) by narrators, narratees or characters in a movement named 'narrative metalepsis.' Accordingly, the meaningful application of the narratological category initially presupposes the allocation of narrators, characters (and, possibly, by implication, existents[14], events, and utterances) to one distinct diegetic level[15] in an unambiguous spatiotemporal structure of 'universes' with clear boundaries – and then the allocation of the very same entities to another diegetic level, the (implied) movement being either from the world of the telling to the world of the told or vice versa.

Genette's examples of metalepsis are strictly fiction-internal phenomena taken from novels by Cortázar, Diderot, Sterne, Balzac, Proust, and Robbe-Grillet, as well as from a play by Pirandello (cf. 1980, 234–236), all of which illustrate the 'impossibility' involved in metalepses:

> All these games, by the intensity of their effects, demonstrate the importance of the boundary they tax their ingenuity to overstep, in defiance of verisimilitude – a boundary *that is precisely the narrating (or the performance itself)*: a shifting but sacred frontier between two worlds, the world in which one tells, the world of which one tells. (Ibid., 236)

---

requisite for metaleptic phenomena, implies a stratification of narrative (diegetic levels) introducing aporia and paradox will be discussed in Chapter 3.1.1.

14 Existents are "the objects contained in story-space" (Chatman 1990, 107) which can be an "actor or an item of setting" (Prince 2003, 28).

15 It is common practice among narratologists to use 'narrative level' and 'diegetic level' interchangeably (cf., for instance, Herman 1997, 132; or Didier Coste and John Pier 2009, 295) to denote the level "at which an existent, event or act of recounting is situated with regard to a given diegesis" (Prince 2003, 20). 'Narrative level,' moreover, is regularly used to metaphorically characterize the "three distinct notions" (Genette 1980, 25) of *histoire*, *récit* and *narration* in the 'three-level model' of narrative or any similar distinction such as Chatman's 'two-level model' which, subsuming *récit* and *narration* under one heading, consists of story and discourse. This practice is problematical. First of all, these levels do not correspond. While the *narration* (of the primary narrative) is always and by necessity extradiegetic, the *histoire*, the 'what' of a narrative usually extends over various 'diegetic levels.' Moreover, the third 'narrative level' in Genette's model, the *récit*, cannot be distinguished by its relation to diegesis in the same way, since it is "a physical object directly accessible to analysis" (Nelles 1997, 111) and thus dissimilar from diegetic levels. For convenience, 'narrative levels' will be exclusively used here to denote any of the three-level or two-level models of narrative (which can imply "the level of the narrative act situated outside the spatiotemporal coordinates of the primary narrator's discourse" [Coste and Pier 2009, 295]), whereas the designation 'diegetic levels' will be reserved for those artefact-internal levels that are distinguished by their relation to a diegesis alone.

In Genette's definition of metalepsis, the boundary separating the levels in that hierarchical structure is decisive: *acts of narration* create and hierarchically connect diegetic levels. The transgressive nature of metalepsis consists in crossing the boundary or boundaries instigated by narrative acts. This is modelled on – or at least agrees with – the representational logic of everyday lived experience: the past of the 'reality' in which someone tells a story and the evocation of a fictive world are, from the perspective of the addressee, both physically inaccessible. According to this paradigm, neither characters nor narrators can thread their way through the semiotic signs (narrative discourse) that evoke the (logically subordinate) narrative world and arrive in the past, or in a fictive world, as the same character/narrator. Whether one tells tales of the past, the present or the future, whether these tales are fiction or not, one cannot physically interact with such a *discursive* (or discursively evoked) world. Yet the metaleptic transgression violates such prerequisites in a (playful) disruption of the representational logic of narrative. Accordingly, the transgressive metaleptic movement produces "an effect of strangeness that is either comical (when, as in Sterne or Diderot, it is presented in a joking tone) or fantastic" (Genette 1980, 235).

A shift or mediation from one diegetic level or 'world' to another can only be instigated by the narrator on the 'higher' level: "The transition from one narrative level to another can in principle be achieved only by the narrating, the act that consists precisely of introducing into one situation, by means of a discourse, the knowledge of another situation" (ibid., 234).[16] Whether the relationship of the narrator to the 'universe' (created by the 'narration of another situation') can be characterized as homo- or heterodiegetic, as fictional of 'factual,' Genette's notion of diegetic levels considers the world of which one tells as 'a recounting' – as such, it does not exist independently of the act of narration: structurally, the diegesis comes into being through (the reception of) the semiotic signs that the extradiegetic narrator employs in order to create that (diegetic) 'universe.'[17]

---

[16] Thus, the spatiotemporal difference between the events recounted and their recounting in (conventional) narrative representations can only be assessed by the one who recounts the events – characters conventionally do not exhibit any knowledge of their being in a narrative (let alone in a hierarchical structure of diegetic levels) in fictional narrative.

[17] Genette offers an example that seems to go against the grain of this analysis. He cites the following sentence by the narrator in *Jacques le fataliste* as metaleptic: "What would prevent me from *getting the Master married* and *making him a cuckold*?" (Diderot, qtd. in Genette 1980, 234). This can be interpreted as a violation of the conventional pretence that what the discourse is relating is, from the perspective of the narrator, the 'literal' truth. As such, I would argue that

If one accepts the notion of 'diegetic levels' and their boundaries, Genette's definition has a simple and sound logical form. In the following, I would like to offer a brief analysis of the propositional logic of Genette's model of metalepsis.[18] I consider the following sentences a complete account of metalepsis according to Genette (1972):

(1) In this narrative, no narrator or existent literally moves across or negates the boundary between diegetic levels in a paradoxical violation of representational logic.
(2) In this narrative, no character displays knowledge of superordinate diegetic levels in a paradoxical violation of representational logic.[19]
(3) In this narrative, no diegetic levels coincide temporally or spatially in a paradoxical violation of representational logic.[20]
(4) This narrative is metaleptic.

Each of the sentences (1), (2) and (3) can be combined with sentence (4). The following (admittedly unwieldy) sentence (5), which combines (1) and (4), is a conditional whose antecedent is a negation:

(5) *If it is not the case that*, in this narrative, no narrator or existent moves literally across or negates the boundary between diegetic levels in a paradoxical violation of representational logic, *then* this narrative is metaleptic.

If 'P' stands for sentence (1) and 'Q' for sentence (4), then sentence (5) could be abbreviated with the help of the logical symbols '~' (*tilde*, abbreviation of 'it is

---

this has little or no metaleptic potential (otherwise all fictional narratives would be metaleptic). Only the assumption that the narrator 'moves' into the diegesis to effect these changes would make this example metaleptic. Incidentally, Genette's model implies that time-travelling is not metaleptic. The past and a diegetic rendering of the past are distinct – even though it may be argued that the past is only accessible by "the act that consists precisely of introducing into one situation, by means of a discourse, the knowledge of another situation" (Genette 1980, 234).

18 For this purpose, I follow the second edition of *Logic: Techniques of Formal Reasoning* (1980) by Kalish, Montague and Mar and use the logical symbols they advocate.

19 Even though Genette does not explicitly mention this, this is the implication of the following statement: "The transition from one narrative level to another can in principle be achieved only by the narrating, the act that consists precisely of introducing into one situation, by means of a discourse, the knowledge of another situation" (Genette 1980, 234).

20 This is the implication of Genette's examples that narrate "as if the narrating were contemporaneous with the story and had to fill up the latter's dead spaces" (Genette 1980, 235).

not the case that') and '→' (*arrow*, abbreviation of 'if..., then') in the following manner:

(6) (~P → Q)
 – i.e. the negation of sentence 'P' entails 'Q.'

This is the formal structure of Genette's account of metalepsis. It is simply, as I have stated, a conditional whose antecedent is a negation. This logical form is based on the following premise: all narratives are objects that have hierarchically organized diegetic levels, each of which is created by an act of narration. This structuralist prerequisite defines the scope and limitations of Genette's model of metalepsis. In order to use Genette's category as a heuristic, it is decisive to have a clear outline of this prerequisite – yet what narratologists mean by 'diegetic level' is often subtly different from Genette (1972). Genette himself (2004) supplies an interesting example of this when he considers the question whether it is an instance of metalepsis if an extradiegetic narrator refers to Napoleon in a novel (as does the narrator of Tolstoy's *War and Peace*): expressing what I take to be narratological consensus, I would argue that this 'Napoleon' is the fictional *homologue* of the historical Napoleon. Only the first of the two is diegetic, only the one created by the extradiegetic narrator can be involved in a metaleptic transgression in which Napoleon becomes fully and 'physically' immersed in a story within a story. The assumption is that 'reality' is not diegetic. When Genette widens the scope of metalepsis in 2004, he claims precisely that Napoleon has metaleptically entered the diegesis of *War and Peace* from the 'historical extradiegesis' (*extradiégèse historique*), thus arguing that 'reality' is just another diegesis (which he refers to as *diégèse réelle*) (cf. 130–131).[21] This widening of the scope does not change the logical form of Genette's definition – it simply changes the premise.

Genette's account of metalepsis in 1972 introduces the categorical distinction between a fictive context of narrating (extradiegesis) and the 'real' world in which a historical author writes (extratextuality). In the chapter "Implied Au-

---

21 The moment it is assumed that there is nothing outside our diegetic (or discursive) constructions of 'reality,' the metaleptic game enters the world of historical authors and readers with a vengeance. Genette's example of a metaleptic 'reality' is the following sentence: "Cet homme-là est un véritable Don Juan" (ibid., 131). Leaving aside the question whether acting like or being referred to as Don Juan supplies any of the 'diegetic' qualities, the assumption that 'reality' is diegetic, has serious consequences: the category 'metalepsis' simply becomes much too inclusive. In other words, if Napoleon's 'appearance' in *War and Peace* is metaleptic, then which narrative is not?

thor, Implied Reader?" of *Narrative Discourse Revisited* (1988), he explicitly excludes "from the narratological field [...] the real author" (Genette 1988, 137) and maintains that "a narrative of fiction is produced fictively by its narrator and actually by its (real) author" (ibid., 139). It is on this basis that Genette considers the implication of the 'real' world as a potential metaleptic effect: "The most troubling thing about metalepsis indeed lies in this unacceptable and insistent hypothesis, that the extradiegetic is perhaps always diegetic, and that the narrator and his narratees – you and I – perhaps belong to some narrative" (Genette 1980, 236).[22] The idea that metalepsis suggests that the extradiegesis is always diegetic – and, by implication, that the 'real' world is someone else's narration, does not fall within the definition or its premise as outlined above.

To sum up, Genette's definition of metalepsis (1972) can be broken down into four major aspects (three of which describe the premises of the propositions above). Firstly, and most importantly, the boundary/boundaries transgressed in metalepsis are instigated by the (multiple) act(s) of narration. This very act itself, the narrating (re-enacted by the reader) constitutes the boundary (which, according to Genette's implied paradigm of the representational logic of conversational storytelling, continually necessitates the construction of at least two 'worlds': the world of the telling and the world of the told). Secondly, each entity created by such 'boundaries' is conceived of as part of a 'world' or 'universe' (which is constructed in analogy to the spatiotemporal conditions of real-world experience). There is a hierarchical relation between these worlds, which are, therefore, referred to as diegetic 'levels.' Thirdly, a literal movement of a character or narrator from one diegetic level to another constitutes, according to narrative logic, a (logically) 'impossible' violation of the structure of narrative. And, lastly, such transgressions often have a playful and comical character. This last point is certainly not part of the logical form of the narrative phenomenon, but is one of its potential effects. Accordingly, for Genette, this playful quality is

---

22 I understand "you and I" (Genette 1980, 236) in the quote above as a reference to real readers. In his diagram(s) of narrative agents, Genette distinguishes between extradiegetic narratee, implied readers (or, as Genette prefers, potential readers) and real readers (cf. 1988, 139–150). Since he is of the opinion that "the extradiegetic narratee merges with the implied or potential reader" (ibid., 138), his writing may at times suggest a denial of this distinction. Richard Walsh lucidly comments on the "equivocal status of the extradiegetic level" (2010, 39): "[I]s the extradiegetic a diegetic level? Genette needs it to be such, because the primary narrating instance may be fictional, and so represented (as with Marcel's narration, or Pip's, or Huck's). At the same time he also needs it not to be diegetic, because the primary narrating instance is directly addressed, he says, to 'you and me' (1980, 229)" (2010, 39).

neither a necessary consequence nor a condition of metalepsis, but rather an interpretative possibility.

One of the classic narratological examples[23] of metalepsis is "The Kugelmass Episode" (1980), a short story by Woody Allen, in which the protagonist Kugelmass is transported by means of his psychiatrist's machine into Gustave Flaubert's novel *Madame Bovary*, where he has an affair with Emma. Emma is in this case the heroine of the fictional homologue of *Madame Bovary* and belongs to the metadiegetic level of Woody Allen's short story. Subsequently, diegetic (i.e. fictive) readers of *Madame Bovary* encounter Emma making love to Kugelmass instead of eloping with Léon or Rodolphe. This example is a negation of the sentence (1) above and can be analyzed with the help of Genette's criteria: Kugelmass's metaleptic transgression violates the boundary created by the act of narration that produces the fictional homologue of *Madame Bovary*. The short story thus demonstrates that any storyworld[24] is (physically) inaccessible to entities apart from the (fictional) characters that 'inhabit' it. The "Kugelmass Episode" constitutes a violation of that premise and consequently runs counter to what readers conventionally expect to be possible in (fictional) story-telling. Physical contact of the diegetic character Kugelmass with the metadiegetic character Madame Bovary can thus be conceptualized as an *illicit* move between ontologically distinct universes. Lastly, the playful quality and comical effects of metalepsis in "The Kugelmass Episode" are clearly evident.

2.1.3 New Nuances of Meaning: A Minimal Definition of Metalepsis and the Metaleptic Dynamic

Taking into account the various uses of the notion in the anthology *Métalepses: Entorses au Pacte de la Représentation* (Pier and Schaeffer 2005), Werner Wolf maintains that "metalepsis does not (yet) have a generally accepted definition" (2009, 50–51). It is undoubtedly narratological consensus that the varying accounts of metalepsis are indicative of the challenge that the phenomenon poses to narrative theory. This challenge is documented not only by the contributions

---

23 Among others, Ryan (cf. 2006, 208) and Roberta Hofer (cf. 2011, 247) have quoted "The Kugelmass Episode" as a paradigmatic example of metaleptic narration.

24 David Herman (2002) defines *storyworld* as the cognitive result of a process of imaginative relocation which narrative comprehension necessarily entails: "Storyworlds are mental models of who did what to and with whom, when, where, why, and in what fashion in the world to which recipients relocate – or make a deictic shift – as they work to comprehend narrative" (9).

to the *Métalepses* anthology, but also by the many accounts of metaleptic transgressions by critics such as Douglas Hofstadter (1979), Robyn Warhol (1986), Brian McHale (1987), Patrick O'Neill (1994), William Nelles (1997), David Herman (1997), Klaus Hempfer (1999), Debra Malina (2002), Frank Wagner (2002), Monika Fludernik (2003b), Gérard Genette (2004), Marie-Laure Ryan (2004, 2005, 2006), Werner Wolf (2005, 2009b, 2013), Jan Christoph Meister (2005), Bernd Häsner (2005), Gerald Prince (2006), Françoise Lavocat (2007, 2016), Sonja Klimek (2009, 2010), John Pier (2009, 2011), Matei Chihaia (2011), Erwin Feyersinger (2011, 2012), Jeff Thoss (2011, 2013, 2015), Thomas Morsch (2012), Jan Alber and Alice Bell (2012), Liviu Lutas (2015), Alice Bell (2016), or the collection of essays *Metalepsis in Popular Culture* (2011). What unifies all these accounts of metalepsis is that they build on, expound and develop the narratological category outlined by Genette in 1972. Genette's model supplies the *sine qua non* for all narratological discussions of metaleptic transgression in the diverse field(s) of classical and postclassical narratologies.

Unavoidably, each of the many reformulations and subtle theoretical reconceptualizations of metaleptic phenomena introduces *new* nuances of meaning. This holds true even for simple paraphrases of Genette's definition: Herman, for instance, who, according to Jan Christoph Meister, "has perhaps best expressed the narratological consensus" (2003, no pagination), succinctly paraphrases Genette's definition as "the interplay of situations, characters or events occupying diegetic levels that are *prima facie* distinct" (Herman 1997, 132). This paraphrase shifts the emphasis of Genette's original definition somewhat, since it refrains from metaphorically verbalizing the very act of breaching the boundary between the diegetic levels (Genette variously calls it an intrusion and a transgression) and, by choice of vocabulary, highlights the trope's playful character. This emphasis is no doubt congenial to another aspect of metalepsis highlighted by Genette in the very sentence in which he defines it: metalepsis "produces an effect of strangeness that is either comical (when, as in Sterne or Diderot, it is presented in a joking tone) or fantastic" (1980, 235). However, Herman's definition does not capture the importance Genette attached to the fact that the boundary between diegetic levels is *violated* by metalepsis: "All these games," Genette claims, "demonstrate the importance of the boundary they [...] overstep' (ibid., 236) in "the deliberate transgression of the threshold of embedding (Genette 1988, 88). Similarly, my own attempt to render Genette's account (Chapter 2.1.2.) may have unduly shifted the emphasis towards a structuralist paradigm with an analysis of a premise (consisting of three aspects) and the propositional logic of the definition – a decidedly structural analysis of a structuralist category.

Yet while each redefinition of Genette's outline of metalepsis involves a shift in emphasis, a widening (or narrowing) of the phenomenon's scope, or a reconceptualization of one (or more) of its constituent parts or of its field of reference, each redefinition at the same time reiterates important aspects of the original concept. In other words, there are core elements that unite all narratological accounts of metalepsis and supply a common ground for the application of the narratological category despite the controversies. A minimal definition of metalepsis that unites these elements and which agrees with Genette's original conception might look like this:

> Metalepsis designates (the construction of) a narrative entity or entities (e.g. a character or existent, etc.) that literally moves across or denies the boundary separating the world(s) of the representation from the world(s) of the represented. Moving from either of these worlds to the other, it thus belongs (at least temporarily) to distinct spatiotemporal frames of reference, which results in a fiction-internal paradoxical transgression defying representational logic.[25]

This definition employs the propositional logic of Genette's definition and broadens the premise in order to make it transmedially applicable[26]. Even though such a minimal definition introduces new nuances of meaning, it offers sufficient conditions[27] for metalepsis – I argue that all narratological accounts of metalepsis consider everything that falls under the definition above as metaleptic.[28] Woody Allen's "The Kugelmass Episode" is a case in point. No nar-

---

[25] This attempt to supply a minimal definition of metalepsis consciously evades 'locating' metalepsis as the structural property of an object, the construction of a recipient, a semantic possibility intentionally created, etc. It offers a minimal set of defining attributes that emerge in the hermeneutic situation in which metalepsis is understood; a set of attributes that occur in all accounts of metalepsis. As such, it agrees with Genette's definition, which implies that metalepsis is a structural feature of narrative, as well as with a recent account by Feyersinger (2012), which describes metalepsis as a cognitive blend.

[26] Thus, I follow Richard Walsh who suggests that "a narrating instance may be considered as any particular use of any medium for narrative purposes. Narration [...] is essentially a representational act, not just a verbal one" (2010, 37).

[27] For a distinction between sufficient and necessary conditions of definitions, see Peg Tittle (2011, 196–200).

[28] It is, however, not the case that this definition offers *necessary* conditions accepted by all narratologists. While Alber and Bell (2012), for instance, would consider everything that falls within the above definition as metaleptic, they would also include cases of 'horizontal metalepsis' as metaleptic – which do not fall within the above definition (for a detailed discussion of horizontal metalepsis, see Chapter 2.2.). Other examples of metalepses that would not fall within the minimal definition of metalepsis are transgressions that involve the 'reality' in which flesh-and-blood humans live and understand narrative (cf. for instance Werner Wolf

ratological discussion of this short story denies that (a) this is an instance of metalepsis or that (b) we need a refined model that moves beyond this consensus to analyze this short story's structure.

If it is relatively simple, following Genette, to devise a definition with sufficient conditions for metalepsis, why then is the concept of metalepsis so controversial? Why is there no generally accepted definition? What, in other words, is the problem of metalepsis? The first problem is the premise itself: Genette's notion of diegetic levels is deceptively simple, a fiction-internal (set of) structural relation(s) that coincide(s) with distinct 'universes,' often visualized geometrically with the help of the Chinese boxes (or similar) model. What is considered as metaleptic relies on the distinction of the artefact-internal spatiotemporal relations created by narrative acts. Yet what 'diegetic levels' and acts of narration and their spatiotemporal conditions exactly are, especially in various media, is far from undisputed.[29] Moreover, the metaphorical locus of a 'boundary' that separates these levels adds further possibilities of meaning and complexity to an analysis of metalepsis.

The second problem concerns the relationship between the model, the narrative phenomenon described by the model and the hermeneutic situation in which the model is applied. Typically, analyses of metalepses seem to imply, in agreement with the structuralist bent of Genette's original conception, that the particular narrative phenomenon examined has an unchanging and essential structural make-up. Yet metalepsis is not some narrative deep structure existing independently of the individual attempt to make sense of a particular narrative. "The Kugelmass Episode" may be one of the few uncontentious cases, but – as the following discussion will demonstrate – most potentially metaleptic narratives refuse unequivocal analyses of their structure.

The problem of metalepsis is thus rather the complex dynamic that unfolds when 'diegetic levels' (or the worlds of the representation and the represented) are negated or destabilized in the metaleptic transgression. Typically, understanding metalepsis involves the construction of changing and vanishing spatiotemporal frames of reference and the attempt to 'stabilize' semantic instabilities (who speaks to whom, what are the spatiotemporal conditions of the narrated/narration etc.). In the complex metaleptic dynamic that ensues, mean-

---

2009b or Debra Malina 2002), or the transgressions I would term 'figurative metalepsis' (cf. Chapter 2.2.4.1.).

29 Cf. Genette's own revision of what he considers diegetic in the preceding chapter. For a recent critique of the logical incoherence of typologies based on person and level (both of which are defined by their relation to the diegesis), see Walsh (2010).

ings proliferate as spatiotemporal dimensions (temporarily) collapse. Since metalepsis is the 'narrative structure' that *per definitionem* denies its own prerequisites, such constructions and reconstructions consist in complex readerly ascriptions of meaning that are characterized by an element of negativity. The notion of diegetic levels implies that a fictive reader cannot physically join the world of the characters of which he reads; yet in the case in point a fictive reader does physically join the world of the characters of which he reads. These two propositions negate and thus *destabilize* each other.

What are the spatiotemporal and logical properties of metaleptic narration? In the negation, meanings proliferate; the negativity of the metaleptic dynamic consists in an oscillation of conflicting possibilities of meaning that throws into relief how we make sense of narrative (worlds). This, I would argue, is why narratological definitions of metalepsis have so far proven problematic: because they can only offer an abstract and static model (of the starting point) of the metaleptic dynamic. An acknowledgment of the scope and limitations of the model yields the insight that it can neither account for its own prerequisites nor for the complexity instigated by the negativity of the metaleptic dynamic. While the metaleptic structure may be an integral part of the hermeneutic situation in which the metaleptic dynamic emerges, it can neither account for the hermeneutic situation on which it relies nor trace the hermeneutic consequences engendered by metalepsis. This, in turn, allows the insight that metaleptic texts, performances or artefacts (typically) have a metaleptic *potential* that needs to be *realized* by a reader or viewer.

From this perspective, it is not surprising that even some of the instances that are usually considered unambiguous paradigms of metalepsis can be read as non-metaleptic. A good example is Chapter 55 of John Fowles' *The French Lieutenant's Woman* (1987 [1969]), in which the extradiegetic narrator seemingly enters the diegesis as a figure "that unmistakably refers to Fowles himself" (Wolf 2005, 102). It seems to be narratological consensus that this part of Fowles' novel is metaleptic.[30] In the glossaries of *A Companion to Narrative Theory* (2005), edited by James Phelan and Peter J. Rabinowitz, and of *The Narrative Reader* (2000), edited by Martin McQuillan, this chapter is even cited as a paradigmatic example of metalepsis. However, the German narratologist Sonja

---

30 Among those who consider John Fowles' novel metaleptic are Nelles (1992, 1997), Heise (1997), Cohn (2005/2012), Wolf (2005, 2009b), Ryan (2006), Abbott (2008 [2002]), Langemeyer (2010), Kukkonen (2011b), and Thoss (2011b).

Klimek challenges this reading in her dissertation *Paradoxes Erzählen: Die Metalepse in der phantastischen Literatur* (2010).[31]

Klimek argues that flesh-and-blood authors who use their name to create literary figures that are part of the narrative's fictional world(s) – like "John Fowles," who is of course to be distinguished from the historical John Fowles – can be grouped among a variety of paradoxical phenomena.[32] Yet not all such phenomena violate the representational logic of diegetic levels (and thus, according to Klimek, and in agreement with the minimal definition above, not all such phenomena constitute metaleptic transgressions). It could be argued, with Klimek, that a diegesis populated by the fictional homologues of its historical author is not metaleptic, because no diegetic levels need to be transgressed. Another example of this is the following scene from Martin Amis' *Money*:

> Oh yeah, and a writer lives round my way too. A guy in a pub pointed him out to me, and I've since seen him hanging out in Family Fun, the space-game parlour, and toting his blue laundry bag to the Whirlomat. I don't think they can pay writers that much, do you? [...] He gives me the creeps. 'Know me again would you?' I once shouted across the street, and gave him a V-sign and a warning fist. He stood his ground and stared. This writer's name, they tell me, is Martin Amis. Never heard of him. Do you know his stuff at all? (1984, 71)

This passage does not necessarily cue the construction of a metaleptic transgression because Martin Amis (the flesh-and-blood human being in the extrafictional world) can create his extradiegetic narrator and his fictional homologue

---

31 "Wenn z.B. innerhalb des im 19. Jahrhundert spielenden fiktionalen Textes *The French Lieutenant's Woman* (1969), den John Fowles im 20. Jahrhundert geschrieben hat, eine literarische Figur mit dem fiktionalen Namen „John Fowles" – logikwidriger Weise ein Jahrhundert verfrüht – auftaucht, so ist das keine narrative Metalepse. Zwar handelt es sich bei diesem [...] Beispiel durchaus um eine Paradoxie der Kohärenz (und nicht um eine Paradoxie der Zeit, denn dann müssten sich John Fowles und „John Fowles" auf derselben ontologischen Ebene befinden). Eine Paradoxie der Darstellung (und somit eine Metalepse) liegt jedoch nicht vor" (Klimek 2010, 44).

32 Klimek distinguishes paradoxes of time, paradoxes of space and paradoxes of coherence (cf. 2010, 42–44). Among her examples of narrative paradoxes is the narrator who narrates events that he or she could not have witnessed (which, according to Klimek, amounts to a paradox of space [cf. ibid., 43]). In Klimek's example *Tristram Shandy*, this paradox is complicated by the fact that the act of narration not only creates an event that Tristram could not witness (Tristram time and again highlights the fictive narrative situation), but also the narrator Tristram (as we all know, Tristram is a character-narrator in a novel). Thus, Tristram's story is recounted by an act of narration that generates the story. For a detailed discussion of this narrative paradox, see Chapter 3.1.1.

who populates the diegesis of *Money* without metaleptic consequences – Martin Amis, the extradiegetic narrator and 'Martin Amis,' the character, are distinct and belong to different spatiotemporal frames of reference. The author Martin Amis can also situate his diegetic story in 'London,' the fictive homologue of the city he lives in without metaleptic implications. Since Klimek (in agreement with the minimal definition above) conceives of metalepsis as a fiction-internal phenomenon[33], she does not pursue the question whether such instances demonstrate the discursive construction of both 'reality' and fiction and the metaleptic potential this may imply. A more obvious possibility of meaning, which Klimek in this particular instance does not consider, is the construction of a fiction-internal extradiegetic world of telling from which the extradiegetic 'author' metaleptically descends.

It has also been argued that metaleptic transgressions occur in *Money* and in *The French Lieutenant's Woman* because the fictional extradiegetic narrator has literally moved into the diegesis (cf. *A Companion to Narrative Theory* [2005] and *The Narrative Reader* [2000]). As maintained above, narratologically informed readings typically evoke the notion that an analysis of this much-quoted chapter can yield only one valid result. The implication of the brief analysis in *A Companion to Narrative Theory*[34] is that the text-internal ahistorical structure of Chapter 55 of *The French Lieutenant's Woman* is metaleptic. The implication of Klimek's analysis is that it is non-metaleptic. Among the reasons why narratologists are divided in such basic questions such as whether a given text is metaleptic or not is the semantic instability that arises when the model is applied, and the question of the establishment of the model's prerequisites – and not, I would argue, because there is disagreement about the logical form of metalepsis outlined above.

---

33 Klimek argues that Chapter 55 of *The French Lieutenant's Woman* is not metaleptic because metaleptic transgressions are fiction-internal phenomena that cannot involve extrafictional reality: "Es steht jedem empirischen Autor frei, neben den üblichen motivischen und sprachlichen Versatzstücken seiner Wirklichkeit auch Elemente seines eigenen Charakters [...] oder eben seinen Namen im fiktionalen Text zu erwähnen. Das bedeutet jedoch nicht, dass er selbst als Mensch in die Diegese seines Werks eintreten könnte. [...] John Fowles als Mensch in der Wirklichkeit war nie in einem Roman, so wie auch literarische Figuren wie Schneewittchen oder Rotkäppchen nie in die Wirklichkeit kommen können. Es ist gerade das Besondere an Metalepsen, dass sie nur *innerhalb* von literarischen Texten möglich sind" (Klimek 2010, 44).

34 The *Companion to Narrative Theory* offers the following definition of metalepsis: "the breaking of the conventional barriers between diegetic levels, as, for example, when John Fowles has his extradiegetic narrator in *The French Lieutenant's Woman* enter the diegesis (narrative world) of his protagonist Charles Smithson" (2005, 547–548).

In the following, I will attempt to demonstrate that a close reading of the (at least potentially non-metaleptic) passage from Chapter 55 of Fowles' *The French Lieutenant's Woman* yields semantic instabilities (which each particular reading struggles to stabilize): After giving a simple-past third-person account of a bearded man who stares at the diegetic character Charles with unusual intensity (cf. Fowles 1987 [1969], 346–347), the seemingly extradiegetic narrator addresses a seemingly extradiegetic narratee (and, possibly, by implication, the extratextual reader) in the present tense: "You may one day come under a similar gaze" (ibid., 347). What follows is a curious kind of metafictional meditation:

> In my experience there is only one profession that gives that particular look, with its bizarre blend of the inquisitive and the magisterial; of the ironic and the soliciting. Now could I use you? Now what could I do with you?
> It is precisely, it has always seemed to me, the look an omnipotent god – if there were such an absurd thing – should be shown to have. Not at all what we think of as a divine look; but one of distinctly mean and dubious (as the theoreticians of the *nouveau roman* have pointed out) moral quality. I see this with particular clarity on the face, only too familiar to me, of the bearded man who stares at Charles. And I will keep up the pretence no longer.
> Now the question I am asking, as I stare at Charles, is not quite the same as the two above. But rather, what the devil am I going to do with you? (Ibid., 348)

The present tense suggests that the extradiegetic narrator literally stares at the diegetic figure his words evoke. The implied movement of the narrator into the world of which he tells is usually considered a prime example of a metaleptic transgression. Yet on the very same page, the narrator declares that the diegetic figures are "figments of my imagination" (ibid., 348), which, of course, has implications for the construction of the narrative situation. First of all, it constitutes a violation of the conventional pretence that what the discourse relates is the literal truth (which is not necessarily metaleptic). Among other things, Fowles' narrator is a parody of the omniscient narrators of Victorian fiction, a parody which he contrasts here with a first-person perspective that is explicitly unreliable. Nothing prevents such a narrator from inventing a narrative 'world' in which a fictional homologue of himself asks questions in the first person. The last sentence in the quotation above could be read as a kind of interior monologue, which would imply that the 'levels' involved in the narrative situation remain basically intact. Or, although a "John Fowles" has entered the compartment, the 'staring' could be understood as metaphorical (and thus belonging to the extradiegesis). This reading does not seem misguided, as the (possibly extradiegetic) narrator is capable of 'looking' at the face of the 'bearded and familiar man' three sentences before.[35]

In short, even though such a reading is highly unlikely, nothing could prevent readers from conceptualizing the narrative situation and its spatiotemporal make-up as unchanged. All of this could be further complicated by the fact that decisions of whether this passage is metaleptic or not rely on the boundaries constructed according to representational logic. Yet the boundaries between diegetic universes (a construction cued by an act of narration) become unstable when the status of diegetic entities is questioned as 'figments' in Fowles writing. What is the basis for the assumption that, 'impossibly,' the narrator 'literally' stares at the character his words create in an instance of metalepsis? It is typical for texts with metaleptic potential that the questions 'who speaks?' and 'who sees?' can only be answered with some difficulty. Even if Chapter 55 of Fowles' novel is understood as a paradigmatic example of metalepsis, the structure of diegetic levels on which such an understanding relies has become unstable; an instability that, in turn, questions the possibility of metaleptic narration (for metaleptic narration presupposes *and* denies a categorical distinction between diegetic levels). One possible conclusion of this short analysis is that the metaleptic potential of a given narrative is not solely the result of semantic aspects of a narrative, but has to be realized in the complex and potentially interminable hermeneutic situation in which it arises.

2.2 A Critical Reassessment of Metalepsis

In Chapter 2.1. it has been argued that Genette's concept of metalepsis consists of four major aspects, which are (a) the narrative act that marks the boundary between (b) diegetic and extradiegetic 'universes.' Any (c) (literal) 'movement' by one of the narrative *dramatis personae* or some other entity from one universe to another is a transgression of narrative logic. The (d) effect of metalepsis is often playful. In what follows, these aspects of Genette's definition will be reconsidered – a reconsideration which is based on the premise that the problem of defining metalepsis lies in the relationship of tension between a simple definition of structural relations and a complex operation that playfully questions and calls attention to the various elements of the hermeneutic situation in

---

[35] The question whether focalization is a matter of the diegesis or the extradiegesis (or both) is still very much disputed. For a recent survey of positions, see Hühn, Schmid and Schönert (2009).

which it comes into being. It is indicative of this relationship of tension that metalepsis can be (and of course has been) approached either as a simple structuralist narratological category, or as a "short circuit" (McHale 1987, 119) that collapses the structuralist narrative system, a logical paradox resembling Hofstadter's concepts of 'strange loops' and 'tangled hierarchies' (cf., for instance, Ryan 2006). Definitions and models of metaleptic transgression cannot, however, include or delineate in its entirety the hermeneutic situation in which metalepses come into being; they can only supply an abstract conceptualization of the operation's starting or turning point. Thus, this chapter offers, very much in a structuralist tradition, a reduction of complexity that provides a heuristic framework for understanding certain representational possibilities and phenomena. Considering metalepsis in this sense from a structuralist perspective (and drawing on the different explications and reconceptualizations of metaleptic transgressions and their effects that have been developed in the field of narratology since the 1980s), this chapter proposes a transmedial model of metalepsis, a scalar model of the metaleptic denial of diegetic properties, and a typology of metaleptic transgressions.

While Chapter 2.1. delineated a minimal definition that offered sufficient conditions for metalepsis, Chapters 2.2.1. and 2.2.2. offer detailed analyses of what I take to be the main prerequisites of, and thus *necessary* conditions for, metalepsis: metalepsis violates the boundary between the domain of the signifier and that of the signified (the domains of the signifier/signified are largely equivalent to diegetic levels/universes), both of which are created and hierarchically related by acts of (narrative) representation. I argue that a clear outline of these prerequisites is decisive – yet what narratologists mean by 'diegetic level' is often subtly different. Chapter 2.2.1. offers a precise delineation of the logic and properties of diegetic levels. Attempting to structure the possibilities of meaning that emerge in the metaleptic dynamic, this chapter suggests four scales that can be used to describe the extent to which the properties of the 'diegetic universes' involved in a metaleptic transgression are 'invalidated.' Chapter 2.2.2. introduces a model that visualizes how metalepsis denies the logical and pragmatic rules governing the very *act* of narration or production of signs (words, gestures, images, etc.) that creates the narrative in the first place. I propose the violation of the logic of this act of (narrative) representation as a necessary condition for metalepsis.

The delineation of necessary conditions of metalepsis and the precise analysis of the structuralist prerequisites of the phenomenon are foundational for the transmedial model of the act of representation and the transmedial model of metalepsis offered in Chapter 2.2.3., as well as for the proposal of metaleptic types (Chapter 2.2.4). The latter is partly a summary of typologies by William Nelles, Monika Fludernik, Sonja Klimek and Marie-Laure Ryan – yet it also introduces a new systematization of preceding types and offers new distinctions and terms: the new terms I propose are 'figurative metalepsis' as a category that subsumes epistemological and rhetorical metalepses as well as the new opposition between 'immersive' and 'recursive' types (which are both 'literal' transgressions of the logic of the act of representation). While Chapters 2.2.1. to 2.2.4. seek to trace the metaleptic form, and supply models for metaleptic narrative structure, Chapter 2.2.5. considers some of the potential effects that structure can elicit.

2.2.1 Metalepsis and the Diegetic Universe

To be human is to be embedded and immersed in a physical and tangible world: the relations of human experience rely on the construction of a coherent spatiotemporal frame in which that experience is embedded. Moreover, whatever is understood presupposes networks of relatedness that are not restricted to spatiotemporal conditions. This is reflected in narrative, which, as Fludernik has argued in *Towards a 'Natural' Narratology*, essentially communicates human experientiality and accordingly relies on "cognitive parameters based on man's experience of embodiedness in a real-world context" (Fludernik 1996, 17). The very beginning of *Tristram Shandy* establishes the world of which Tristram Shandy tells as a world that closely resembles the 'real-world context' in which Sterne's novel was first read:

> On the fifth day of November, 1718, which to the aera fixed on, was as near nine calendar months as any husband could in reason have expected,—was I Tristram Shandy, Gentleman, brought forth into this scurvy and disastrous world of ours.—I wish I had been born in the Moon, or in any of the planets, (except Jupiter or Saturn, because I never could bear cold weather) for it could not well have fared worse with me in any of them (though I will not answer for Venus) than it has in this vile, dirty planet of ours,—which, o' my conscience, with reverence be it spoken, I take to be made up of the shreds and clippings of the rest. (I.i)

The narrator clearly means 'this world of ours' as the spatiotemporal continuity in which his narration, the narrated event and the act of reading take place. Yet there is, of course, a distinction between the world in which the novel was and is published and read by flesh-and-blood human beings on the one hand and the mimetic evocation of a fictive 'world' of which (and in which) the narrator writes (even though both can be referred to as 'this vile planet of ours') on the other. Genette's notion of diegetic levels[36] can be conceptualized as the positionality of narrative representations according to representational logic, which introduces crucial distinctions into *Tristram Shandy's* fiction-internal 'scurvy world' and separates it categorically from the world in which his flesh-and-blood readers read. The worlds in which (extradiegesis) and of which (diegesis) Tristram tells are not only separated by a temporal hiatus, but also connected by a logical and hierarchical relation. Thus, Genette maintains that "any event a narrative recounts is at a diegetic level immediately higher than the level at which the narrating act producing this narrative is placed" (1980, 228). I would argue that Genette's description of written narrative mirrors the structural relations of what Fludernik terms the "prototype of natural narrative" (1996, 57). Since Fludernik traces written narrative back to "oral narrative's referential mimetic mode" (ibid., 37), she argues that writing is understood analogously to what she terms 'real-world experience,' and that narrative understanding cognitively relies on frames and schemata of 'real-world experience.' This phenomenon she calls 'narrative mimesis':

> Narrative mimesis evokes a world, whether that world is identical to the interlocutors' shared environment, to a historical reality or to an invented fictional fantasy. And in so far as all reading is interpreting along the lines of a represented world, it necessarily relies on the parameters and frames of real-world experience and their underlying cognitive understandings. Mimesis is therefore here conceived in radically constructivist terms. (Ibid.)

This elemental construction of 'worlds' in 'natural narratives' is arguably the frame on which Genette's narrative structure relies. As the beginning of *Tristram Shandy* demonstrates, the novel in particular can be seen in the tradition of writing that exemplifies the 'evocation of world,' a tradition influentially characterized by Ian Watt's seminal study *The Rise of the Novel* (1967). It comes as no surprise that Fludernik (1996, 37–38) loosely relates her concept of 'narrative mimesis' to Watt's often quoted definition of "formal realism [...]: the premise, or primary convention, that the novel is a full and authentic report of human experience" (Watt 1967, 32). Realism in this sense 'evokes a world' and is thus no longer linked to the nineteenth-century movement of Realism, but refers to the novel's "mimetic evocation of reality both from a sociological and psychological perspective" (Fludernik 1996, 37). According to Fludernik, this notion of realism is paradigmatic for the understanding of human experientiality. Thus, it could

---

36 The notion of diegetic level is perhaps most succinctly defined by Gerald Prince as "the level at which an existent, event or act of recounting is situated with regard to a given diegesis" (2003, 20).

be argued that even the most unnatural narratives and their (physically or logically) impossible and/or ephemeral storyworlds share basic spatiotemporal conditions; or, more precisely, are (re-)constructed with cognitive parameters that are shaped by 'real-world experiences.'

Genette's 'diegetic universe' and its extradiegetic genesis are seemingly based on a model of narrative competence that is basically 'experiential' in Fludernik's sense. I maintain that Genette's notion of diegetic levels can be described as the result of the process that Fludernik terms 'narrative mimesis'; the process by which human beings create narrative worlds ("whether that world is identical to the interlocutors' shared environment, to a historical reality or to an invented fictional fantasy" [ibid., 37]). The diegesis is the world readers need to construct when they understand the "mimetic representation of individual experience that cognitively and epistemically relies on real-world knowledge" (ibid., 38) – a construction logically distinct from and hierarchically subordinated/dominant[37] both to the world in which that diegesis is created (extradiegesis) and to the world in which it is understood (the extratextual world).

What becomes apparent in this discussion is that Genette (in his original delineation of metalepsis) does not explicitly distinguish between the hierarchical properties of the structure of narrative's communicative situation(s) and the semantic properties of the discourse that creates the worlds presupposed by this communicative situation.[38] This 'conflation' is suggested by the very term Ge-

---

[37] Fludernik's and Genette's accounts suggest different hierarchical relations between the 'worlds' involved. While Fludernik's 'radically constructivist' approach implies that a narrated world is logically subordinated to the (narrative) world in which it is created, Genette's structuralist model implies that the creation of a narrative world is logically subordinated to the world recounted (the event is situated at a diegetic level 'higher' than its recounting [cf. Genette 1980, 228]). What unites these accounts is the fact that both conceptualize the relationship between the text-internal world of the telling and the world of the told as hierarchical. Chapter 3.1.1 offers an analysis of the relationship of tension between the notion of a story recounted by an act of narration and the notion of an act of narration that generates the story, and argues that this is a narrative paradox potentially laid bare by metaleptic transgressions.

[38] This insight is indebted to Herman's article "Toward a Formal Description of Narrative Metalepsis" (1997). David Herman argues that the different nuances of meaning suggested by the various accounts of metalepsis all result from a conflation of what he has identified as the "two dimensions" (Herman 1997, 133) along which metalepsis can be characterized: "The first dimension centers on the formal profile of metaleptic narration, in particular, the formal features attaching to distinct yet interactive diegetic levels; the second dimension centers on the semantic or world-creating (and -destroying) functions performed by metaleptic technique in narrative contexts" (1997, 133). However, since I consider both 'dimensions' of diegetic uni-

nette uses: on the one hand, 'diegetic universe' refers to 'worlds' understood within the cognitive parameters shaped by human experientiality (e.g. the fictive world in which Tristram Shandy tells – which in many ways resembles 'this vile planet of ours'); on the other, it refers to the diegetic geometry of the logic of narrative representation (whose hierarchical relations are often represented in narratological accounts by the 'Chinese boxes' model). The number of narratologists who (implicitly) reiterate Genette's concept of the 'diegetic universe' (the hierarchical structural relation of ontological domains) in their discussions of metalepsis suggests that these approaches or conceptualizations are inextricably linked – in other words, one cannot meaningfully talk about the transgression of diegetic levels without the (implied) concept of a 'world' according to a realist paradigm that mirrors human sense-making capabilities.[39] Strikingly, these notions remain largely unreflected in narratological discussions of metalepsis. Even though they are intrinsically related (one presupposing the other), it is, I contend, valuable for heuristic reasons to clearly distinguish one from the other.

In his discussion of Genette's account of metalepsis, Bernd Häsner has made a similar point. He criticizes Genette's delineation of metalepsis as 'transgressive' (cf. 2005, 15) because it moves from the narrative situation (*Erzählmodell*) to the 'worlds' that are part of understanding narrative (*Weltmodell*) without clearly distinguishing between the two.[40] Häsner's example of

---

verses as the prerequisites of metalepsis, I do not distinguish them in terms of a form/function dichotomy.

39 In line with this, most narratologists use the terms Genette supplies or some synonymous terms in order to trace the narrative worlds and structural relations presupposed by metalepsis. Like most critics, William Nelles does not distinguish between the structural relations (diegetic level) and the construction of a world: in typical narratological fashion, Nelles speaks of "the worlds of the different levels" (ibid.). Malina, too, has stressed the importance of Genette's conceptualization of the transgression of that frontier "as an entry into another universe," a conceptualization which assumes the "theoretical independence and distinct ontological status of diegetic realms" (2002, 4). Werner Wolf (2009b) has referred to "different 'worlds' or (onto)logical levels" (51), David Herman prefers to talk about "narrative frames" and "storyworlds" (cf. 1997, 134ff.), Marie-Laure Ryan resorts to the "metaphor of the stack," the "notion of diegetic levels" (2006, 204) and the "stacking of realities" (ibid., 443), Jan Christoph Meister (2003) speaks of a symbolic system consisting of three representational and discursive layers" and refers to "existential levels in worlds" (Meister 2003, no pagination). And Patrick O'Neill maintains that metalepsis derives from "the conception of nested narrative worlds" (1994, 115).

40 "Vor allem scheint Genettes Darlegung selbst in gewisser Weise transgressiv zu sein, insofern sie nämlich recht umstandslos vom Erzählmodell zum Weltmodell überwechselt" (Häsner 2005, 15).

this 'conflation' is Genette's reference to "Sterne" (instead of to 'the fictive narrator' [cf. Häsner 2005, 15][41]). Häsner argues that the 'real' world (which is seemingly part of what Häsner calls *Weltmodell*) needs to be distinguished from the textual 'levels' comprising the narrative situation. It is highly unlikely, however, that Genette was unaware of this ("Sterne" in this instance can be read as a reference to the creation of a fictive narrator by the historical author – this is not necessarily a terminological imprecision) because the very notion of 'diegetic level' establishes that distinction: even though they cognitively rely on 'real-world' world-making, diegetic universes are never extratextual.

Häsner's own delineation of metalepsis can be taken to corroborate the underlying equation of hierarchical diegetic levels and 'worlds.' In the case of *Tristram Shandy*, there are not only the world in which Sterne writes, the textual 'worlds' of the narrator Tristram, but also the world in which one reads (or listens to the reading of *Tristram Shandy*). Strikingly, and somewhat against the grain of his own critique of Genette, Bernd Häsner describes this relationship between the extratextual world of a flesh-and-blood reader (the world in which one reads) and the narrative text from a systems theoretical perspective as a structure reiterated by the 'worlds' of the narrative situation.[42] This text-internal reiteration of the structural relation between the narrative and its flesh-and-blood reader or listener is, according to Häsner, a prerequisite for metalepsis. Häsner rightly maintains that this structural relation constitutes the hierarchy of levels (*Ebenenhierarchie*, cf. Häsner 2005, 16) presupposed by metalepsis. Yet this relation also mirrors the 'world-making' which is shaped by the cognitive parameters described above: Häsner maintains that the 'sphere of production and reception' (*Sphäre der Produktion und Rezeption*) is reiterated by the system (in this case, the narrative) – yet the 'sphere of production and reception' presupposes the construction of a world beyond a simple structural relation. In other words, it could be argued that the logical differentiation and the semantic (world-creating) characteristics described by Genette with his terms *extradie-*

---

41 "Ohne kleinlich sein zu wollen, scheint mir die Identifizierung von Autor und Erzähler, die Genette in diesem Zusammenhang mehrfach unterläuft, symptomatisch für diese Extrapolation zu sein. Anläßlich entsprechender Metalepsen in Sternes *Tristram Shandy* erklärt er [Genette], daß ‚Sterne' den Leser auffordere, die Tür zu schließen [...], tatsächlich ist es natürlich der fiktive Erzähler Tristram, der dies tut" (Häsner 2005, 15).
42 "[W]enn man den einzelnen narrativen oder dramatischen Text als ein 'System' auffassen will und die Sphäre seiner Produktion und Rezeption als seine 'Umwelt', könnte man sagen: eine systeminterne Ebenendifferenzierung, die die Relation von 'System' und 'Umwelt' im Innern des Systems wiederholt" (Häsner 2005, 16).

gesis and *diegesis* are a possible conceptualization of the text-internal reiteration of the communicative situation in which the narrative is read.

Approaching Genette's diegetic relay from the perspectives of Häsner's structural analysis and Fludernik's 'narrative mimesis' offers the insight that the diegetic prerequisites of metalepsis are twofold and inextricably linked: the semantic (world-creating) properties of discourse and the hierarchy of structural relations are both presupposed by Genette's original concept of metalepsis. Some more recent narratological discussions of metalepsis have moved away from Genette and given up the structural relation (between different hierarchically organized levels) implied by the notion of diegesis as a prerequisite for metaleptic transgressions. It was Frank Wagner (2002) who first introduced the notion of 'horizontal metalepsis,' a transgression between two 'parallel' worlds situated on one diegetic level. More radically, Alber and Bell (2012, 169) argue that "terminology that describes the domains of existence as 'worlds' rather than 'levels' more accurately represents what [...] happens during the course of ontological metalepses."[43]

Such bracketing of the structural and hierarchical relations of diegetic levels (and the possibility of their metaleptic transgression) allows the widening of the scope of the category 'metalepsis.' Alber and Bell maintain that the "transmigration of a character or narrator into a different fictional text is metaleptic because [...] it involves the transgressive violation of storyworld boundaries through jumps between ontologically distinct zones or spheres" (2012, 168). This is not restricted to certain kinds of storyworlds (for instance, storyworlds that are incompatible for specific reasons):

> A fictional entity that originates in another text [...] will always belong to another storyworld. For example, the first-person narrator of Gilbert Sorrento's [sic] *Mulligan Stew* is Martin Halpin, a minor character from James Joyce's *Finnegan's Wake*. Irrespective of which diegetic level Halpin occupies in each text, however, he certainly inhabits more than one storyworld or, to express it another way, moves from one ontological domain to another. (Ibid., 169–170)

Alber and Bell argue that the concept of metalepsis should include such "horizontal transmigrations" (ibid., 169) that "represent cases of [...] 'transfictionali-

---

[43] Such an argument implies that Genette's concept does adequately account for the semantic (world-creating) properties of discourse. Jeff Thoss (2015) presents a similar argument. As he sees it, Genette's concept of metalepsis needs to be augmented by possible-worlds theory, a theory that offers a framework in which "narrative levels are thought of not so much as levels but as separate worlds each possessing a distinct and fully realized ontology" (ibid., 9).

ty'" (ibid., 168).⁴⁴ Among their examples is a quote by John Pier who offers the following phenomenon as a metalepsis in his article on metalepsis in the *Handbook of Narratology*: "Sherlock Holmes appears in the fictional universe of *Madame Bovary*" (2009, 199). Even though there is a certain similarity between transfictional phenomena and metaleptic transgressions (in Genette's sense), an approach that does not make the transgression of the hierarchical relation between diegetic levels a prerequisite for a definition of metalepsis may generate problems and make the definition of metalepsis too inclusive. For instance, it may prove exceedingly difficult to establish what precisely induces readers or viewers to construct a 'transgressive' movement between distinct 'ontological domains.' Does this only apply to single characters such as Martin Halpin or also to species (such as elves and orcs), technology (for example spaceships travelling faster than light) or even types of situations or genre conventions (e.g. the plot formulae of popular genres). In other words, when are recognizable elements constructed as metaleptic (that is, according to Alber and Bell, from another ontological domain) and when are they not? Are postmodern rewrites such as Jean Rhys's *Wide Sargasso Sea* metaleptic? Is Henry Fielding's *An Apology for the Life of Mrs Shamela Andrews* a metaleptic narrative?⁴⁵ Because of such problems, a distinction between metalepsis and transfictionality seems to offer greater analytical clarity and precision. Whereas recognition of transfictionality relies on the construction of various storyworlds (Martin Halpin exists

---

44 It should be added that this widening of the scope of 'metalepsis' is far from undisputed. While the transmedial applicability of the narratological concept is consensus today, transgressions 'between parallel worlds' and/or between 'work and the world of the author or recipient outside it' have not yet been generally accepted as metaleptic phenomena: Sonja Klimek, for instance, argues for a more restrictive use of metalepsis that applies to "strictly fiction-internal vertical transgressions of different levels of representation [i.e., fictitious (sub-) worlds])" (2009, 171), a use which, according to Klimek, entirely coincides with Genette's 1972 definition (cf. Klimek 2009, 2010 and 2011).
45 Jeff Thoss follows a suggestion by Bareis (2008) "as to how one could theorize lateral metalepsis" (Thoss 2015, 12) and argues that "a narrative needs to specify that one of its entities originates from a different fictional world before this entity's presence in the narrative can be qualified as metaleptic. This appears to be a workable criterion that may allow us to do without the notion of hierarchy while still being able to clearly pinpoint whether, let us say, a novelist's use of the character Sherlock Holmes can be qualified as metaleptic or not" (ibid., 13). Thoss is careful to point out that "metalepsis between parallel worlds does not operate along such clear-cut lines as metalepsis between worlds arranged hierarchically" (ibid., 27) – which is why, I would argue, the notion is problematic: since the establishment of horizontal metalepsis is dependent on imprecise criteria (how does a narrative specify that one of its entities originates from a different fictional world?), its inclusion makes the concept of metalepsis heuristically less valuable.

in the storyworlds created by Joyce and Sorrentino) as well as their reception, understanding metalepsis additionally relies on the artefact-internal hierarchies established by representational logic.

Following Fludernik, I argue that understanding narrative involves hierarchical relations modelled on mental or cognitive representations of the 'worlds' in which the understood (or communicated) and the understanding are both embedded. In other words, understanding narrative is inevitably situated – not only in the sense that, from a hermeneutical perspective, it is necessarily historical and belongs to traditions of knowledge, but also in the most literal sense. The spatiotemporal situatedness of understanding narrative is mirrored by the spatiotemporal dimensions of the worlds of which narratives tell. The representational logic of narrative demands at the very least a distinction between the space and time of the worlds in which we understand and the space and time of the worlds that are represented within it. Most (if not all) cultural artefacts that relate a story reiterate that crucial spatiotemporal and logical distinction within the artefact. I argue that precisely this artefact-internal reiteration is a necessary precondition for metalepsis. Metaleptic phenomena rely on the conceptualization of a (communicative) situation in which represented existents and human experientiality are understood as embedded within a coherent spatiotemporal framework that is distinct from the spatiotemporal 'world' in which the representation is located.

To sum up, I maintain that diegetic geometry is modelled on the representational logic of the relation of lived experience, which presupposes a nonlinguistic *conceptualization* of a spatiotemporal frame of reference distinct from the 'unmediated' spatiotemporal conditions of the 'world' in which that experience is represented. This dichotomous relatedness is conventionally hierarchical: one spatiotemporal frame logically 'contains' the other. I argue that these are the necessary prerequisites of metalepsis. Even though, from a hermeneutic perspective, the notions contained in Genette's term "diegetic universe" presuppose each other and are inextricably linked, I believe it can be helpful for heuristic reasons to distinguish and isolate the fundamental temporal and spatial dimensions of metalepsis; moreover, a distinction between the representational logic that connects diegetic levels (the hierarchical structure of diegetic levels) and the semantic characteristics of the worlds that are the prerequisite of this geometry can likewise prove beneficial in analyses of metaleptic artefacts. While it is true that all metalepses (at least implicitly) violate these prerequisites, not all metalepses violate in the same way and to the same degree the different notions contained in the term 'diegetic universe.' As John Pier (2009) has it, "theories of metalepsis discriminate between minimally and conspicuously transgressive changes of level" (197). Attempting to structure the possibilities of meaning that emerge in the metaleptic dynamic, I suggest four scales that can be used to describe the extent to which the properties of the 'diegetic universes' involved in the metaleptic transgression are 'invalidated':

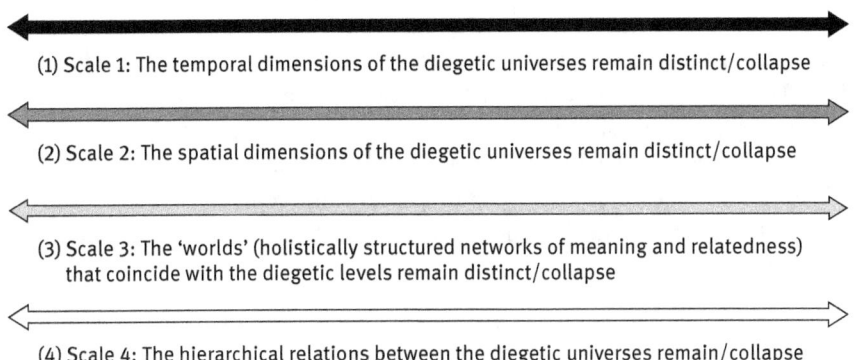

Figure 1: Four Scales

First of all, these scales allow the distinction between minimal and conspicuous transgressions of what I take to be the properties of diegetic universes. Scale 4 refers to the text-internal reiteration of the communicative situation in which the narrative is understood, a structural relation that is hierarchical. While scales 1, 2 and 3 are intimately related, the conspicuous transgression of one of these properties does not necessarily entail the conspicuous transgression of the others. The following short analyses of metaleptic transgressions are test cases that may (hopefully) demonstrate the heuristic value of the isolation of the above-mentioned criteria. One of the examples of metalepsis offered by Genette in *Narrative Discourse* comes from Honoré de Balzac's *Lost Illusions* ("While the venerable churchman climbs the ramps of Angoulême, it is not useless to explain..." [Balzac, qtd. in Genette 1980, 235]), a serial novel originally published between 1837 and 1843. This passage can be analysed according to my criteria in the following manner: While the temporal dimensions of the extradiegetic telling and the diegetic events have seemingly been collapsed, the other aspects of the dichotomy of relatedness outlined above remain. The spatial dimensions (the spatial constraints of the diegesis do not concern the narrator), the hierarchical relation (apart from the projected simultaneity of diegesis and extradiegesis the narrator is still very much in control of the world he tells), as well as the 'worlds' (the narrator and the narratees do not physically interact with the world of the diegesis and – more importantly – do not consider themselves as part of the story) remain distinct. I by no means contend that this is the only possible reading of this particular collapse of diegetic structure. One could also understand it as a transgression in which the narrator has literally descended into the diegesis. Yet I would argue that readers of this passage are more likely to construct a narrative situation in which the diegesis and the extradiegesis have *one* temporal dimension, apart from which they remain distinct. The transgression of the temporal logic of the diegetic universes in this passage *implicitly* questions the spatial and hierarchical properties of extradiegesis and diegesis as well as the 'worlds' of the telling and the told. With the help of the 4 scales, this could be visualized in the following manner (the dot shows to what extent the diegetic properties are denied in the metaleptic transgression).

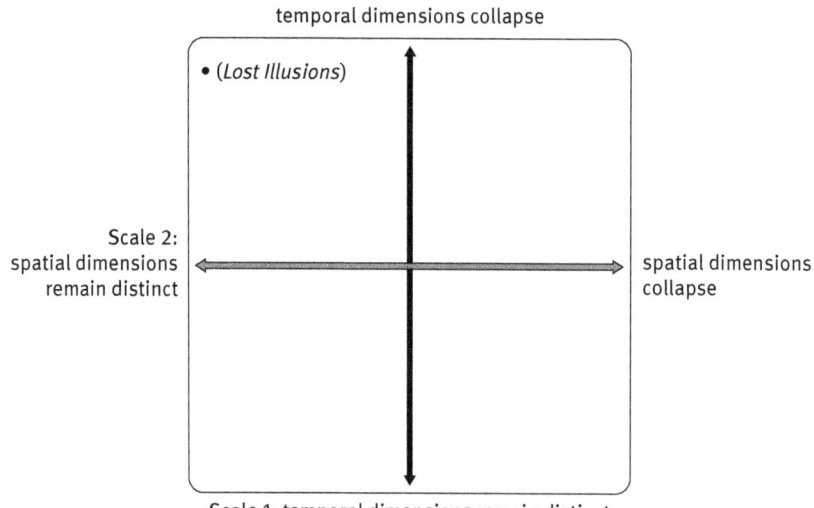

Figure 2: The Temporal and Spatial Dimensions of the Diegetic Levels in the Metaleptic Transgression by Honoré de Balzac (Lost Illusions)

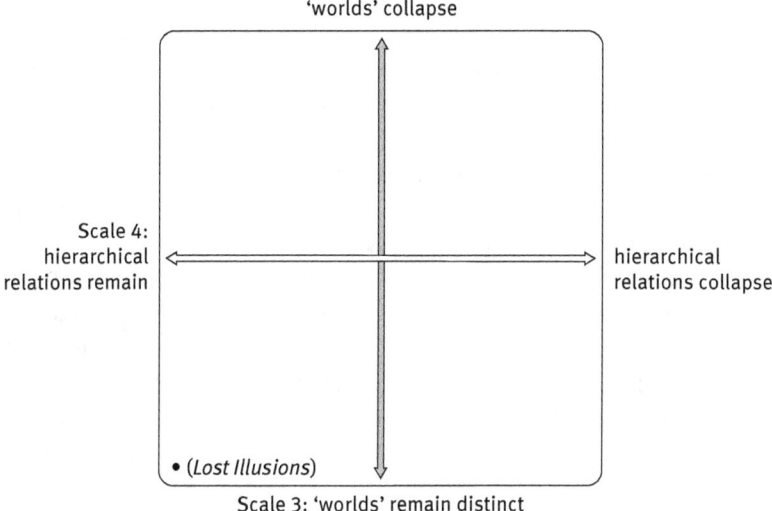

Figure 3: The 'Worlds' and Hierarchical Relations of the Diegetic Levels in the Metaleptic Transgression by Honoré de Balzac (Lost Illusions)

Even though this model has scalar axes, it can only represent a static model of metaleptic transgressions (more precisely, a static model of how the metaleptic transgression violates the properties of the diegetic levels involved). I want to briefly discuss other well-known examples of metalepsis and structure my readings with the help of this scalar model. "The Kugelmass Episode" by Woody Allen arguably leaves the spatial dimensions of the diegetic levels intact (the diegesis and the metadiegesis retain their distinct spatial dimensions, as Kugelmass and Madame Bovary experience first the former and then the latter, but never both at the same time). Thus it could be argued that with the exception of the metaleptic travellers Kugelmass and Madame Bovary, the spatial properties of the diegesis and metadiegesis remain distinct in the metaleptic transgression. The fact that this distinction is questioned by Kugelmass' entry into *Madam Bovary* presumably does not induce readers to construct diegetic and metadiegetic space as a continuum. The distinction between diegetic and metadiegetic time seems to be more radically questioned: while Kugelmass 'spends' time inside *Madame Bovary*, diegetic time in New York passes in his absence. Yet this seems to apply only to Kugelmass when he is inside *Madame Bovary* – and not to any other existent of either the diegesis or the extradiegesis (the implied logic is that it takes diegetic time to spend time in a metadiegesis).

The hierarchical relations between the diegetic levels involved are violated to a certain degree as well: Kugelmass is transported into *Madame Bovary* and is able to change the metadiegetic events from 'within' the metadiegetic novel by meeting and seducing Madame Bovary (afterwards, diegetic students reading the novel wonder about the bald Jew who sleeps with the novel's heroine). This is a violation of the hierarchical relation between diegetic levels: "The transition from one narrative level to another can in principle be achieved only by the narrating, the act that consists precisely of introducing into one situation, by means of a discourse, the knowledge of another situation" (Genette 1980, 234). In "The Kugelmass Episode," metadiegetic events literally shape the diegetic discourse that relates them. Yet, at the same time, the metadiegetic events are (mostly) subjected to the diegetic narrative act that created them. Madame Bovary, for instance, retains the character supplied by the diegetic narrative act. In a similar manner, there is also a contamination of worlds. The world of *Madame Bovary* (metadiegetic France) and the world of Kugelmass (diegetic New York) are altered by visits from existents who come from another diegetic level. These contaminations, however, are not extensive. Thus, the metadiegetic and diegetic worlds seem to remain distinct, with the exception of the two narrative agents who cross the boundary between them. This holds true, I would argue, even though Kugelmass is accidentally (and permanently) transported to the 'metadiegesis' of a vocabulary book in the short story's ending.

Flann O'Brien's *At-Swim-Two-Birds* (1966 [1939]) offers more radical negations of the properties of diegetic levels. In this famous metaleptic narrative, a metadiegetic novelist is tortured by his characters in a limbo that seems to cut across various diegetic levels. As is well known, *At-Swim-Two-Birds* stars a diegetic (and unnamed) college student who writes a novel about the metadiegetic writer Dermont Trellis, who, in turn, narrates a meta-metadiegetic story containing characters 'hired' from other works, as well as the female character Sheila Lamont. Sheila Lamont is supposed to be assaulted and betrayed by the meta-metadiegetic character Furriskey – yet Dermont Trellis is so enamoured of his own creation that he assaults her himself. The characters in Trellis' (meta-metadiegetic) fictional story are not only exasperated by Trellis' poor storytelling abilities, but also resent the fact that he controls their destinies (an example of epistemological metalepsis). Wanting autonomy from the story written by Trellis, they drug him into sleep so that he cannot exert control by writing his book (thus determining the meta-metadiegetic existence of his characters). The moment Dermont Trellis is asleep, his characters enjoy absolute freedom – which leads to the question who narrates this freedom from their narrator? Complicating matters further, the meta-metadiegetic Sheila Lamont gives birth to Trellis' son Orlick, who is then a hybrid being (cf. Malina 2002, 12) whose parents belong to different diegetic levels. Orlick has inherited his father's power of storytelling and, after long discussions with the characters in his father's story (to which he seems to belong), narrates the torture of Dermont Trellis. Even though this narrative is meta-meta-metadiegetic, is has a direct effect on the metadiegetic Dermont Trellis. The limbo in which the devilish Pooka MacPhellimey tortures the seemingly metadiegetic Dermont Trellis includes characters such as Finn MacCool, Cowboys and mad King Sweeney – characters plagiarized by Trellis from other works. The diegetic levels involved seem to have collapsed into a limbo which not only conflates the temporal and spatial dimensions of the diegetic levels involved, but also destroys the hierarchical relation and the semantic characteristics of the worlds involved. All of this comes to an end when a metadiegetic character burns the pages on which Trellis wrote his story, thus freeing Trellis from the clutches of his characters and restoring a conventional diegetic hierarchy.

In the short story "Tlön, Uqbar, Orbis Tertius" by Jorge Luis Borges on the other hand, the metadiegetic fiction displaces diegetic reality for good when the narrator explains in a postscript that "a secret and benevolent society" has created a "methodical encyclopedia of the imaginary planet [...] *Orbis Tertius*" (1964 [1962], 15). This metadiegesis (alternatively called Tlön) replaces the diegesis in which it was created: "The contact and the habit of Tlön have disintegrated this world" (ibid., 18), the narrator asserts. Leaving aside the question of the narrator's unreliability (a possibility the narrator considers on the first page), the diegetic structure can be read in the following manner: The metadiegesis literally and metaleptically replaces the diegetic 'reality' – and becomes the reality in which the narrator and the other characters literally 'live,' whereas the diegetic 'reality' (which resembles the world in which Borges wrote) is relegated to the metadiegetic position of fictive accounts in books. As a fiction, the short story implies, the diegetic reality will persist for some time. Thus the metaleptic structure of "Tlön, Uqbar, Orbis Tertius" can be read as an exchange of the metadiegesis and the diegesis (an inversion of their hierarchical relation), which otherwise, and apart from a short transitional period, remain distinct.

46 — Framing the Structure of Narrative Metalepsis

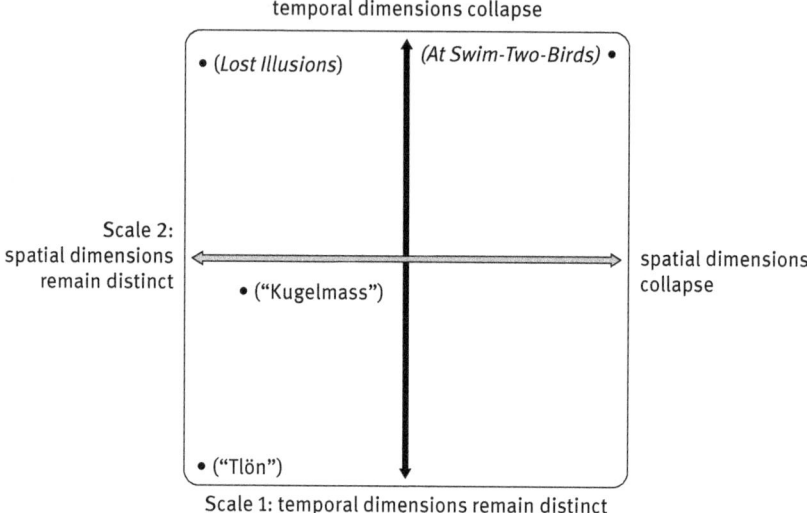

Figure 4: The Temporal and Spatial Dimensions of the Diegetic Levels in Various Metaleptic Transgressions

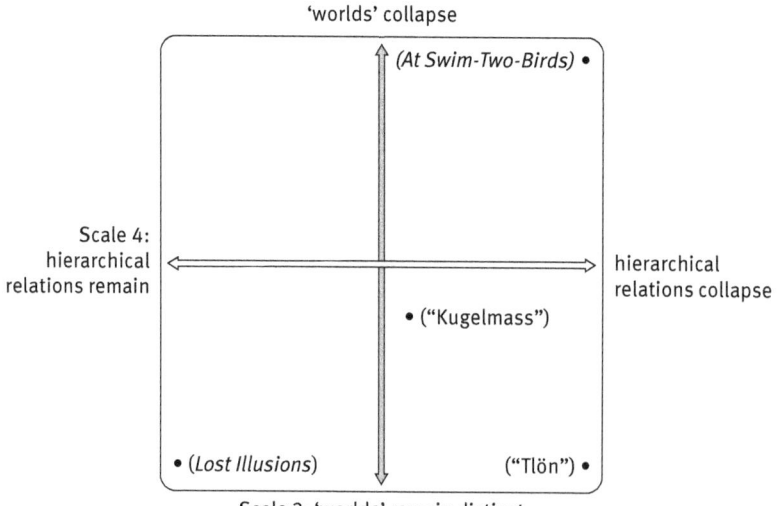

Figure 5: The 'Worlds' and Hierarchical Relations of the Diegetic Levels in Various Metaleptic Transgressions

Hopefully, these analyses have demonstrated the heuristic potential of this scalar model of the denial of the diegetic prerequisites in metaleptic transgressions. It should be added that these visualizations are not intended to suggest that the analyses on which they are based are the only possible readings of the narratives discussed, in their metaleptic denial of diegetic structures. Yet they allow a precise description of what the (reading of a) particular metaleptic movement denies. Moreover, I would argue that the model can be employed to visualize the properties of Genette's notion of diegetic levels and, accordingly, can show if, and how, the conceptual basis of narratological accounts of metalepsis departs from it. The one notable departure is the notion of 'horizontal metalepsis,' which relies on scales 1–3 but does not consider the hierarchical relations created by the artefact-internal reiteration of the communicative situation in which narrative is understood as a necessary prerequisite for metalepsis. While Wolf (2009b) and Wagner (2002) restrict this to horizontal transgressions "within a work" (Wolf, 2009b, 52), Alber and Bell consider 'transmigrations' from one work to another as metaleptic. This widening of the scope of the category entails that metalepsis is no longer connected to a violation of representational logic. The following chapter argues that this widening of the scope also entails that metaleptic transgressions are no longer connected to the logic of the narrational acts that create diegetic universes, and that this may lead to a loss of precision and heuristic value.

2.2.2 Metalepsis and Narrational Acts

In *Narrative Discourse*, Genette considers the effects of metalepsis in the following manner: "All these games, by the intensity of their effects, demonstrate the importance of the boundary they tax their ingenuity to overstep, in defiance of verisimilitude – a boundary *that is precisely the narrating (or the performance itself)*: a shifting but sacred frontier between two worlds, the world in which one tells, the world of which one tells" (1980, 236). It is striking that he conceives of what he metaphorically refers to as the 'boundaries'[46] of his static model of 'diegetic universes' as *dynamic* acts of narration. More striking, perhaps, is the fact that Genette, apart from this one sentence, does not consider how 'the narrating' can function as a 'boundary' that separates diegetic levels. The 'narrating' is defined by Genette as "the producing narrative action and, by extension, the

---

46 This is a literal translation of the French original. The boundary crossed or violated is the "frontière mouvante mais sacrée entre deux mondes" (1972, 245).

whole of the real or fictional situation in which that action takes place" (ibid., 27). Though it may seem counterintuitive at first sight that such 'action' should function as a metaphorical boundary, there are, I would argue, very good reasons for this; for as this 'shifting' (temporal) performance connects signs from a given semiotic system (images, words, gestures, etc.), a 'world' emerges that is distinct from the world in which that particular connection is established, thus distinguishing the worlds of the telling and the told.

Contrary to Genette, I will not only maintain that the narrating supplies a metaphorical 'boundary' between the world of the telling and the told, but also theorize how combinations of signs (and, by extension, how represented combinations of signs) cue the construction of a categorical distinction between the domain(s) of the signifier and the domain(s) of the signified. Such distinctions rely on the rhetorical dimension of narration: I maintain that a basic contextual assumption of the communicative situation of narrative (and thus a basic interpretative assumption of its recipients) is that the combination of signs that results from a narrational act[47] not only communicates a storyworld (domain of the signified), but is also situated in the world in which that combination of signs is produced and received (domain of the signifier). In a literary context, the situatedness of the combination of signs is usually constructed as either the world in which a historical author writes or, in the case of fictional narrative, the world in which a fictive narrator narrates. This distinction (between the domains of the signifier and the signified) guides the production and the reception of narrational acts – and as such, I maintain, is a *necessary* condition in my definition of metalepsis.

Narratological discussions of metalepsis have for the most part used the notion of a 'boundary' as metaphorically as Genette. Yet Genette's specification that the boundary "*is precisely the narrating (or the performance itself)*" (1980, 236) has not elicited detailed discussions. There is one notable attempt by Marie-Laure Ryan (2006) to classify two different kinds of boundary (that can be metaleptically 'crossed') in her typological differentiation between rhetorical and ontological metalepses. Strikingly, even though the distinction between

---

[47] I follow the terminology of Herman (2012, 44–45) who maintains that narrational acts "result in textual performances on the basis of which reasons for acting – reasons for producing a narrative that has a particular plot structure, mode of temporal sequencing, thematic focus, etc. – can be ascribed to those who engage in narrational conduct. Narration, in other words, does involve behaviour that that is explicable in causal terms; yet it cannot be exhaustively described as behaviour but rather falls in the subcategory of behaviours that constitute actions and that are engaged in for reasons. Interpreters impute these reasons to narrating agents to make sense of their behaviours as communicative actions in the first place."

ontological and rhetorical metalepsis has become widely accepted, the initial conceptual basis for that distinction has not been taken up in narratological discussions. Ryan's original differentiation rests on the assumption that "the border between levels may be of two kinds: illocutionary or ontological. The first type occurs when a text-internal storyteller presents a story as true fact [...]. Here the boundary marks a change of speaker, but the represented world remains the same" (ibid., 205). The ontological boundaries, on the other hand, divide the story presented as fiction from the 'factual' world of diegetic narrating. According to Ryan, this "change of world" (ibid., 205) – in Genettian terms the fact that a heterodiegetic narrator relates a 'fictive' event – is the prerequisite for the transgression termed ontological metalepsis (cf. ibid., 205ff.). Yet can there be a meaningful text-internal distinction between fiction and non-fiction within a work of fiction that employs metalepses?

Ryan's account suggests that the fictive existent (which, therefore, does not literally exist) in the world of the narrator should be distinguished from the 'real' existent which exists in the world of the narrator, a world, which, in turn, is a fictive world evoked by the fictional text. What, in other words, is 'real' from the perspective of a fictive narrator constructed by flesh-and-blood readers? This is connected to the argument that the occurrence of metaleptic transgressions renders the distinction between intrafictional reality and fiction obsolete: Jeff Thoss' article "Unnatural Narrative and Metalepsis: Grant Morrison's *Animal Man*" considers the intrafictional relationship between reality and fiction and argues that "metalepsis inevitably blurs the line between reality and fiction – at least within the fiction – if it does not abolish it altogether" (2011b, 193).[48]

---

[48] This question can be further complicated by the argument that equates narrativity and fictionality, an argument that "derives from the [...] claim [...] that very little of the meaningfulness of narrative can be seen as independent of the artifice of narrativization" (Walsh 2007, 39). Taking into consideration the discursive nature of non-fictional narratives from a Nietzschean perspective, it could be asked whether it is not possible to relate non-fictive events with the help of metalepses in such a way that recipients would assume they are dealing with factual narration. Such questions necessitate the embedding of the text in the contexts of its reception. The elusive 'distinction of fiction' (cf., for instance, Schmid 2010, 29ff.) very much relies on the hermeneutic situation in which the fictional and the non-fictional, the fictive and real are distinguished according to the conceptual prerequisites and hermeneutic assumptions of writer and reader, traditions of reading, etc. Richard Walsh's *The Rhetoric of Fictionality* (2007) argues similarly – in what I would term a hermeneutic fashion – that fictionality is "a contextual assumption by the reader, prompted by the manifest information that the authorial discourse is offered as fiction. This contextual assumption is a preliminary move in the reader's effort to maximize relevance" (36).

Bracketing such questions, Ryan's distinction implies that rhetorical metalepsis consists in a transgression of diegetic level(s) that belong to a continuous given world (for instance the past of the world in which a narrator relates that past). Ontological metalepsis, on the other hand, transgresses the boundary that originates in a narrative act generating an ontologically discontinuous world (for instance a narrator in twenty-first century New York relating a fairy tale). Yet the distinction between what could be termed 'homodiegetic' and 'heterodiegetic' metalepses respectively (these are not Ryan's terms) has to my knowledge never been discussed by narratologists.[49] One reason for this may be that the represented is always physically inaccessible and thus, in this respect, not different in kind – it is not clear why the narrated past of the world in which someone narrates should be more or less accessible than a world of fiction (in the present of the act of narration, both are storyworlds evoked/created by signs and 'exist' as the domain of the signified). All subsequent narratological discussions of rhetorical and ontological metalepses have excluded the distinction between various *kinds* of boundary and followed Ryan's argument that rhetorical metalepsis consists in a "temporary breach of illusion" which "does not threaten the basic structure of the narrative universe" (Ryan 2006, 207).[50] Subsequent narratological discussions of Ryan's distinction rely on the structural relations of 'narrative universes' and consequently on a static model of levels or worlds.

In the following, I offer a model that visualizes a fundamental contextual assumption of the communicative situation which I take to be a prerequisite of metalepsis: dynamic narrational acts cue the construction of hierarchically related, yet categorically distinct spatiotemporal domains. This model is based on the premise that all narration consists in a combination of signs from a conventional semiotic system (language, images, gestures, etc.) put together "for narrative purposes" (Walsh 2007, 89). Thus, following Herman (2012 and 2013) and Walsh (2007), I assume that all narratives are the product of acts of narrative 'representation' – acts which presuppose, and belong to, a communicative situation. The most basic element of this model is a combination of signs:

---

[49] This does not amount to the contention that the distinction between 'homodiegetic' and 'heterodiegetic metalepses' has no heuristic potential. The metaleptic potential in *Being John Malkovich* could be described as belonging to the 'homodiegetic' kind. Controlling Malkovich like a puppet could be argued to constitute a metaleptic narrative act that creates a 'narrative' that belongs to the 'world' in which it is told.

[50] For a detailed discussion of rhetorical and ontological metalepses, see Chapter 2.2.4. below.

The narrational act combines signs from a semiotic system

Figure 6: The Narrational Act

The white rectangles represent what I consider (from a semiotic perspective) the result of a narrational act: a chain or combination of signs. The arrow below these signs represents the fact that both the creation and the understanding of a combination of signs are dynamic acts and that an atemporal combination of signs is an abstraction. The white rectangles (the combination of signs) here represent the "physical object directly accessible to analysis" (Nelles 1997, 111); in the case of literary narrative, Genette's 'recít.' What are, from a rhetorical perspective, the contextual assumptions which are relevant for the prerequisites of metaleptic transgressions? How is (the result of) the dynamic narrational act turned into a hierarchy of diegetic levels? The following figure takes into account that the signs always belong to a communicative situation and cue the fundamental construction of the spatiotemporal domains of that situation.

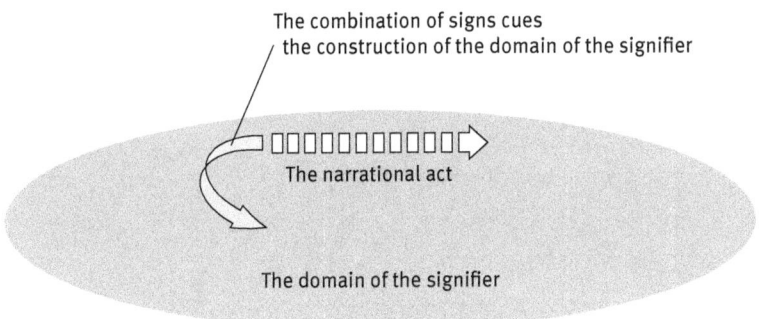

Figure 7: The Construction of the Domain of the Signifier

A narrative combination of signs from a semiotic system implies a communicative situation in which a narrational act creates that particular combination. This is how narratives are offered and received: a basic contextual assumption of narrative is that narrational acts are situated in a spatiotemporal domain; they presuppose the domain of the signifier. Each sign is a physical entity (images, gestures, sound waves in the air, written words, etc.) that presupposes the spatiotemporal realm of its production. The construction of this domain relies on the semantic aspects of the combination of signs, (generic) conventions and the context in which it is received. In the case of oral storytelling, the domain of the signifier is the world in which the story is told (in which the signs are combined), which, in turn, may or may not coincide with the 'world' in which it is understood (if such a narrative is encountered as a recording, then the domain in which these signs are put together is inferred). Some narrational acts are collaborative efforts and/or have been created over long periods of time and in various locations. The domain of the signifier can thus be subdivided in as many ways as the spatiotemporal sphere(s) in which the physical entities of signification are produced and/or received: the spatiotemporal conditions of the communicative situation. If, for instance, a narrational act quotes the narrational act of someone who is not present ("This is the amazing story I was told by my colleague…"), then this communicative situation cues the construction of a further distinction, and recipients can situate the narrational act in two domains: they can situate the narrational act in the here and now of the spatiotemporal domain they share or, alternatively, in the original situation which is related (e.g. the situation in which the colleague tells her story). The domain of the signified, on the other hand, is the mental construction of the spatiotemporal domain that embeds what is related.

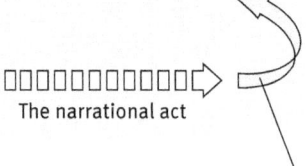

The domain of the signified

The narrational act

The combination of signs cues the construction of the domain of the signified

Figure 8: The Construction of the Domain of the Signified

The combination of signs that results from a narrational act cues the construction of a storyworld: the domain of the signified. This domain does not exist without the signs that 'create' it. A very basic contextual assumption of participants of a communicative situation in which a narrative is created and understood is thus the construction of a double spatiotemporal relation: the domain of the signifier is the spatiotemporal frame in which the narrational act is embedded and the domain of the signified is the distinct spatiotemporal frame of the storyworld. The following model visualizes how this static relation (in Genette's terms, the worlds in which and of which a narrator tells [cf. 1980, 236]) depends on dynamic acts of narration/understanding. If signs are put together 'for narrative purposes,' then that temporal act of creation (mirrored by an act of understanding) is approached by the assumption that the domain of the signifier and the domain of the signified are categorically distinct.[51]

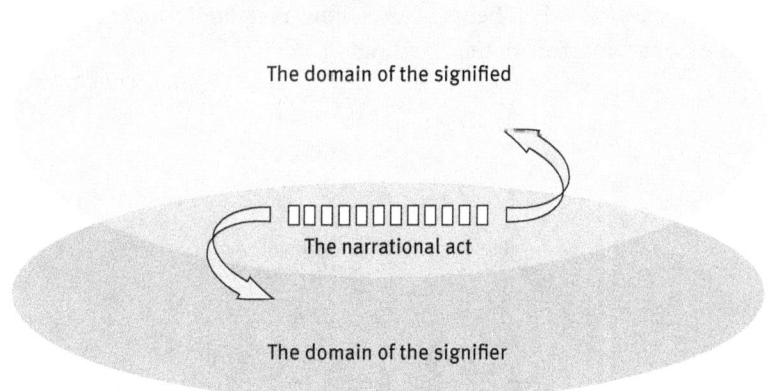

Figure 9: Narrational Acts Cue the Construction of the Domains of the Signifier/Signified

Drawing on semiotics and rhetorical approaches to narrative, this model visualizes the fundamental interpretative assumption that categorically distinguishes the domain(s) of the signifier and domain(s) of the signified in narrational acts. This agrees with the fact that, as Didier Coste and John Pier maintain in their

---

51 It may be argued that this also holds true for simultaneous or 'real-time' non-fictional oral narration. Even though the 'telling' may be almost contemporaneous with the 'told,' there is nevertheless always a temporal hiatus between, for instance, the sports broadcast and the event which precedes it logically and temporally – the event the broadcast has just reported.

contribution ("Narrative Levels") to the *Handbook of Narratology*, "the narrative act necessarily takes place in a spatiotemporal universe which is external to that of the events related" (2009, 301). While the narrational act is spatiotemporally external to the related events, the signs that are the result of this narrational act have a position that is both external and 'internal' (to the 'world' of the events). As physical entities, the signs belong to the universe in which they are produced/combined. As mental concepts, the signs 'create' the storyworld (which would not exist if it were not for the signs). The domains of the signifier and the signified are both inextricably linked to the sign. The combination of signs in this sense offers a point (or rather a plane) of osculation, where the domains of the signifier and the signified are hierarchically connected. It is this very 'boundary,' I maintain, that is transgressed in metalepsis. In other words, the metaleptic transgression is the violation of the assumption that narrational acts create a spatiotemporal bifurcation (that comes into being *while* the signs are understood). The following figure shows how metaleptic narratives cue the construction of a 'violation' of this 'boundary':

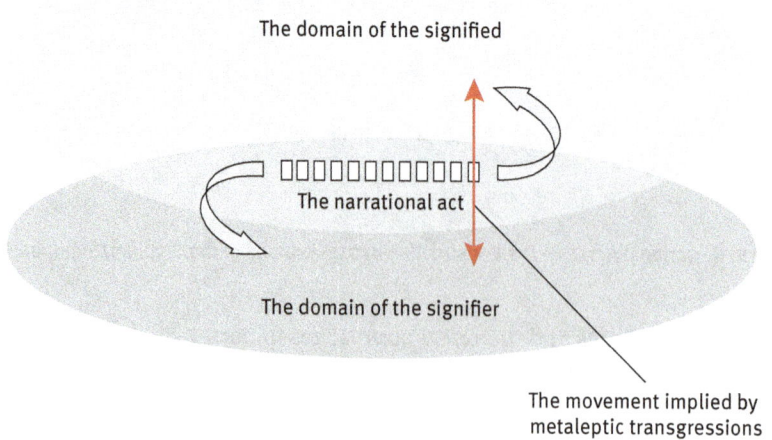

Figure 10: A Model of Metalepsis

The transgression of what one could metaphorically term the 'boundary' instigated by such acts thus relies not only on semantic aspects of the narrative in question, but also on the rhetorical dimensions of the communicative situation.

I argue that the violation of the assumption that the domain of the signifier and the domain of the signified are categorically distinct is a *necessary* condition in a definition of metalepsis: Metalepsis designates the narrative phenomenon which, in a paradoxical violation of representational logic, triggers the construction of a narrator, existent, event or utterance that 'literally' moves across this very 'boundary' or negates (a part of) the relation of the domains of the signifier/signified. It should be added that any 'literal' movement across this boundary has to be inferred. Metaleptic narratives cannot show the movement of an existent which shoves away signs in order to travel from the domain of the signified to the domain of the signifier (or vice versa), but only the *result* of such movement.

The domains of the signifier and signified are often, especially in the case of fictional narratives, further subdivided. A description of such subdivisions can profit from Richard Walsh's (2007) account of the narrative instance as a 'representational act':

> The most elementary and irreducible distinction among narrative instances is not symmetrical but hierarchical: it corresponds to Plato's distinction between diegesis and mimesis, formulated as, on the one hand, a first-degree act of narrative representation (Genette's extraheterodiegetic category); and on the other hand, a second-degree narrative representation of a narrative representation (all Genette's other categories). (2007, 92)

Most metaleptic narratives rely on these 'second-degree narrative representations' and the hierarchies they generate.

> [W]hile it is possible in nonfiction for a narrative instance to be transmitted within a framing instance (that is, for one narrative to be quoted within another), the appearance of such hierarchies of transmission within fiction is itself a product of representational rhetoric. The various transgressions of level Genette classifies as metalepsis [...] are answerable only to that rhetoric; their significance is to be evaluated in relation to the discernible import of representational discourse, rather than to the iron law of noncontradiction. Beyond the pragmatic, contextual circumstances of actual communication (including actual fictive communication), the structure of narrative instantiation does not exist except as a product of representation, and the logic of represented narrative transmission has no priority over the rhetorical emphases of the representational act itself. (Ibid., 92–93)

In the following pages the attempt will be made to model "various transgressions of level." I locate the basis of such transgressions not only in the semantic content of the respective narratives, but also, following Walsh, in the communicative situation in which the combinations of signs (which result from narrational acts) are received. This process of reception relies on "pragmatic, contextual circumstances of actual communication" (ibid., 92) which guide the construction of the hierarchies of transmission that Genette terms diegetic levels.[52] Thus, in what follows, diegetic levels will not be seen as structural properties of an ahistorical object of narrative that exists beyond the hermeneutic situation in which it is understood. The following figures visualize, rather, how "the structure of narrative instantiation" (ibid.) presupposed by metalepses relies on the basic interpretative and contextual assumption that categorically distinguishes the domains of the signifier and signified. Metalepses highlight that this assumption conventionally guides not only the production and reception of what Walsh terms the "first-degree act of narrative representation" (ibid.), but is also extended to *represented* narrational acts (which cue further subdivisions of the domains of the signifier and signified).

A potential further subdivision of the domain of the signifier consists in the additional creation/evocation of a fictive context of the production of the signs (the extradiegesis or exegesis[53]) – a construction that is often implied by fictional narratives. While it is the case that Laurence Sterne wrote *Tristram Shandy*, the very same signs imply a fictive context of production (that of the narrator Tristram). This representation of a narrational act is described by Wolf Schmid (2010) as 'author communication' and 'narrative communication,' in what he refers to as the "doubling of the communication system" (Schmid 2010, 33), which defines fictional narrative.[54] Yet this 'doubling' can only emerge when

---

[52] The representation of narrative instances in fiction is not, according to Walsh, a transmission – at least not in the strict sense: "Properly speaking, media cease to function transmissively (i.e., as technological conduits for independently semiotic content) as soon as they themselves become semiotic – which is to say, here, representational" (ibid.).

[53] For the purposes of this model, I use Schmid's (2010) term exegesis instead of extradiegesis (both, I assume, refer to the same thing, the fictional context of the production of the signs; that is, both are established by their relation to the diegesis) because in the recursive structure of narrative, there can be an exegesis 'contained' within a diegesis (which I think is preferable to the terminological distinction between an extradiegesis within a diegesis).

[54] "The *narrated world* is the world created by the narrator. The *represented world* created by the author is not limited to the narrated world. The represented world includes the narrator, his or her addressee and the narration itself. The narrator, the listener or reader whom the narrator assumes and the act of narration are represented in the fictional work and are fictive entities. Therefore a narrative work does not just narrate, but represents an act of narration. The art of narrative is structurally characterized by the doubling of the communication system: the *narrator's communication* in which the narrated world is created is part of the fictive represented world, which is the object of the real *author's communication*" (Schmid 2010, 32–33). Whether this is an accurate description of how all readers approach fictional narratives is, however, a debated area of narrative theory. Herman argues that such accounts and the way they inform the narrative communication diagrams are heuristic concepts that may become reified, "ob-

readers approach the narrative as fictional (thus, the recognition/construction of the author's communication relies, for the most part, on pragmatic competence). Without further paratextual or other contextual information, fiction and non-fiction may often be indistinguishable – Daniel Defoe, the father of the novel, managed to convince his contemporary readers that the events in *Robinson Crusoe* (1917) had actually taken place (cf. Mayer 1997, 197). Accordingly, Robinson Crusoe was constructed as the author of the narrative that was read and the possible distinction between the author's and the narrator's communication became moot. Yet there are more ways in which the domain of the signifier can be subdivided by represented narrational acts. I would argue that, since the metadiegetic narrative act of representation is also (and similarly) 'represented,' the domain of the signifier undergoes a further subdivision in embedded narration. Using an often cited example, Joseph Conrad's *Heart of Darkness* can be taken to exemplify a conventional subdivision of the domain of the signifier:

---

scuring how the constructs at issue are ways of describing phases or aspects of the inferential activities that support the co-construction of narrative worlds (2013, 599).

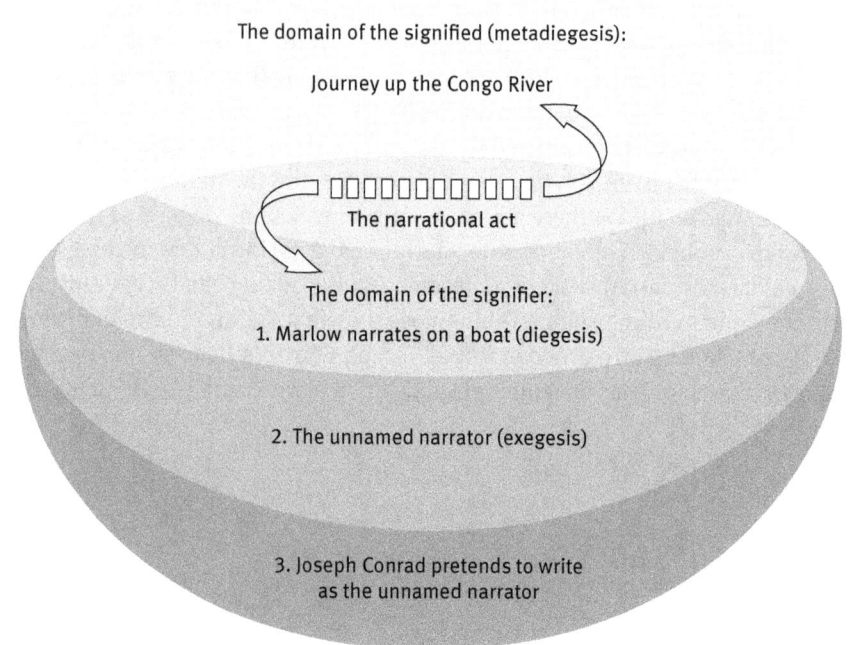

Figure 11: A Construction of Narrative Instances in Joseph Conrad's *Heart of Darkness*

This figure visualizes how diegetic levels can be, in the words of Richard Walsh, "latent contexts of the current narrative situation" (2010, 43) and shows how the largest part of the narration can be situated: the white rectangles represent the signs (words) actual readers encounter when they open a copy of *Heart of Darkness*. As is well known, the largest part of the novel consists in Marlow's diegetic account of his metadiegetic voyage up the Congo River (which is, as the frame tale makes clear, mediated by an extradiegetic or exegetic narrator). I would argue that the 'production' of the particular combination of words which offers the metadiegetic storyworld (the search for Kurtz) can be 'placed' in three spatiotemporal domains and be approached as three distinct, but hierarchically related, acts of narrative representation: Marlow's act of representation, the act of representation of an unnamed narrator (who may have invented Marlow, who may supply a reliable or unreliable account of Marlow's narration), and the writing of the author Joseph Conrad. While the first two can be inferred on the basis of the text, the third relies on paratextual and contextual information.

Thus, this example demonstrates how narratives represent narrational acts and how the domain of the signifier can be constructed.[55] A potential further subdivision of the domain of the signifier is the world in which readers read the novel – which may or may not be constructed as the world in which Conrad writes.

Complementing this, I would like to offer a visualization of a potential subdivision of the domain of the signified, using the example of Jasper Fforde's *The Eyre Affair* (2001). Here, an important distinction highlighted by the model is the notion of a diegetic exegesis:

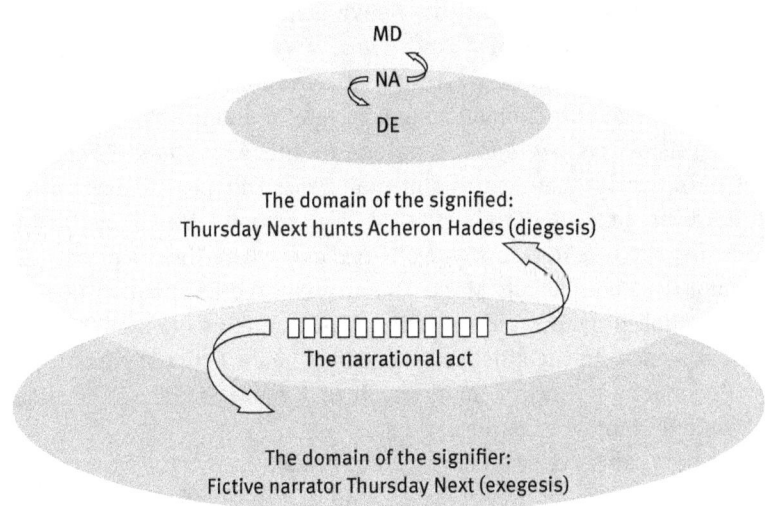

Figure 12: A Visualization of Narrational Acts in Jasper Fforde's *The Eyre Affair*

The white rectangles represent the combination of signs that are a "physical object directly accessible to analysis" (Nelles 1997, 111), Genette's *récit*. 'DE' stands for diegetic exegesis, 'NA' for the diegetic narrational act, and 'MD' for

---

55 This account has been influenced by Marie-Laure Ryan's model of the stack: "The pushing of a new story to on the top of the stack interrupts the current story and divides the cognitive activity of the reader between the tale of the highest level, which always occupies the center of attention, and the unfinished stories of the lower levels, which remain present in the back of the mind. This division of attention explains why narrative stacks rarely reach more than three or four levels" (2004, 205).

metadiegesis. Figure 12 visualizes how the particular combination of signs of *The Eyre Affair* can cue the construction of a recursive narrational act which represents another narrational act. This structure follows logically from the assumption that the domain of the signifier and the domain of the signified are categorically distinct – an assumption that is extended to represented narrational acts. The fictive extradiegetic (or exegetic) narrator Thursday Next narrates the diegetic story in which she hunts the master criminal Acheron Hades (Figure 12 does not consider the possibility of situating the combination of signs in the world in which the historical author writes). The storyworld, a parallel universe in the year 1985 (the novel is partly detective story, partly sciencefiction, partly fantasy), contains (the fictive homologue of) a novel written by 'Charlotte Brontë': '*Jane Eyre*.' Since '*Jane Eyre*' is a work of fiction, this metadiegetic story is created by an act of narration that *implies* the fiction-internal "doubling of the communication system" (Schmid 2010, 33). In the past of the diegesis of *The Eyre Affair* 'Charlotte Brontë' wrote '*Jane Eyre*.' This is a diegetic narrative act that creates a metadiegesis. The diegetic exegesis of this novel, however, consists in the fictive act of narration 'written' by 'Jane Eyre,' the homodiegetic narrator. In *Heart of Darkness*, where the act of narration of the narrator does not mediate Marlow's narration, there is no diegetic exegesis ("[Marlow] paused again as if reflecting, then added..." [Conrad 1995 [1899], 39]). Recursiveness in the strict sense occurs when a fictional narrative represents a fictional narrative that implies a diegetic exegesis ("The Kugelmass Episode" would be another example of this).

This model can serve as a heuristic that visualizes how the assumption that the domain of the signifier and the domain of the signified are categorically distinct is 'violated' by metaleptic implications. This applies to narrational acts as well as to represented narrational acts, as the following example from *The Eyre Affair* may elucidate:

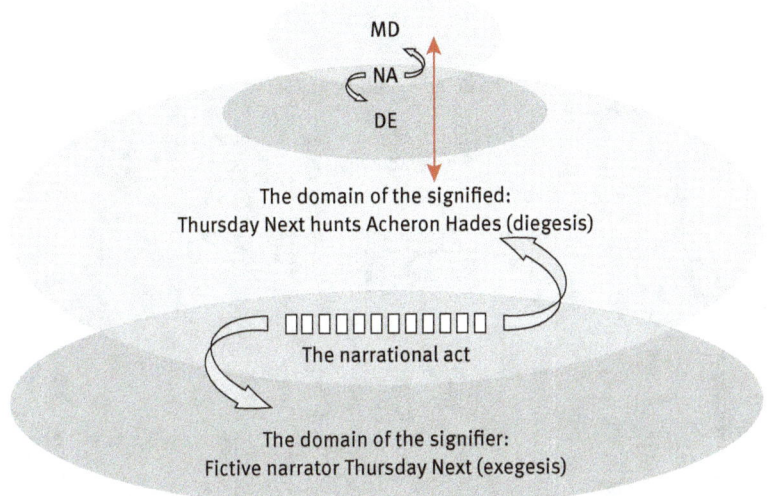

Figure 13: A Model of a Metaleptic Transgression in Jasper Fforde's *The Eyre Affair* I

Figure 13 visualizes the metaleptic implications of the moment when the product of the narrational act (represented by the white rectangles) describes the metadiegetic character Jane Eyre as an abducted prisoner in the diegesis – all because, the narrative implies, Acheron Hades manages to travel into the metadiegesis of '*Jane Eyre*' to kidnap the novel's heroine and bring her back into the diegesis; a metaleptic denial of the assumption that represented narrational acts are governed by the same spatiotemporal bifurcation and representational logic as narrational acts whose combinations of signs are directly accessible. It remains unclear whether these changes affect the diegetic exegesis ('DE,' the world in which the fictive 'Jane Eyre' writes) – yet it leads to a change in what diegetic characters read when they open their copies of '*Jane Eyre*.' The metadiegesis ('MD') is changed by this metaleptic abduction. The model shows how the presentation of diegetic events implies a metaleptic transgression 'across' the 'boundary' instigated by a narrational act (which can be interpreted as a diegetic act of narration ['NA'] by 'Charlotte Brontë' representing the act of narration of 'Jane Eyre' in the diegetic exegesis) that creates the metadiegesis. This metaleptic transgression relies on a reader's subdivision of the domain of the signified of the 'extraheterodiegetic' (cf. Walsh 2007, 92) act of narrative representation. Yet the same novel presents metaleptic potential that presupposes the construction of a subdivision of the domain of the signifier:

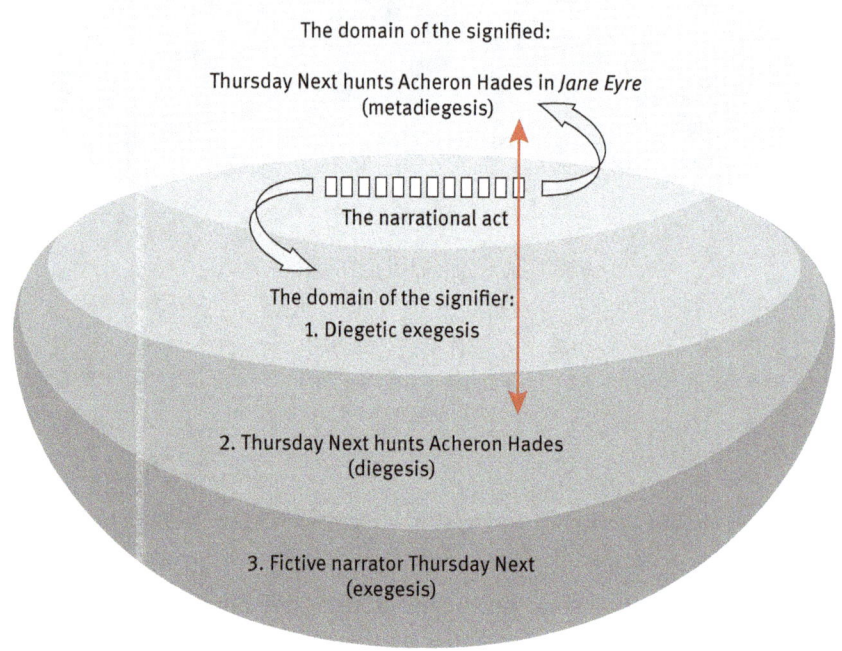

Figure 14: A Model of a Metaleptic Transgression in Jasper Fforde's *The Eyre Affair* II

Figure 14 visualizes the metaleptic logic of the presentation of the novel's final fight between Thursday Next and Acheron Hades in the metadiegesis of '*Jane Eyre*' (which, thanks to the madwoman in the attic, Thursday manages to win). This presentation presupposes a tripartite subdivision of the domain of the signifier (the white rectangles again represent the physical object directly accessible for readers of the novel). The narrational act creates/cues the construction of what could be called 'the fight for *Jane Eyre*' – the domain of the signified of this act is the metadiegesis whose genesis can be interpreted according to the contextual information of the preceding narration and according to pragmatic rules. For the fictive narrator (exegesis) tells of the storyworld (diegesis) in which she literally enters the storyworld (metadiegesis) of the novel *Jane Eyre* (which is created by the production of 'diegetic signs' which, as a fictional narrative, imply the fictive production context of a diegetic exegesis). Yet, a construction of such a hierarchical structure of narrational acts representing narrational acts cannot be inferred from the passage in isolation. The passage in question simply presents a fight involving four people on the roof of a burning house (which, in a different context, would not be metaleptic at all).

The concept of diegetic levels, this model suggests, is nothing more (and nothing less) than a geometrical construction of the spatiotemporal dimensions of narrative understanding – the domain of the signifier and the domain of the signified. It is a precondition of the logic of metaleptic narration that represented narrational acts cue the same construction of dimensions. The model presented above does not purport to offer some essential and unchanging form of the narrative device but represents possible metaleptic relations between the worlds that emerge in narrative understanding. In narratological accounts of metalepsis, such relations are visualized with the help of the Chinese boxes models of diegetic levels and arrows. Wagner's model (2002, 244) or Klimek's (2010, 70) modification of Wagner's model can be taken as typical examples of this (even though the boxes are no longer contained within each other).[56] What distinguishes the model above is the visualization of the sequence of semiotic signs that engenders a dichotomy of relatedness, a dynamic act that results in a static relation. What the model above has in common with other models is that all graphic presentations suggest an ahistorical structure (and possible set of structural relations) that informs each act of understanding. Yet what all of these boxes and arrows present is nothing but an abstraction from the enormous complexity and endless variation of the hermeneutic situations in which narrative is understood as metaleptic. It is, simply put, the attempt to visualize what all metalepses have in common. Despite obvious merits, such an endeavour cannot supply the metaleptic form once and for all. As the various visualizations already suggest, each attempt to offer such an abstraction is one interpretative visual simplification of 'metalepsis.' As such, the elements of the model above (domains of the signified/signifier, act of narration) cannot be prior to or more fundamental than the historical act of understanding in which they emerge. Yet the reduction of complexity this model offers can be a useful heuristic in attempts to structure readings of metaleptic narratives.

This model is based on the insight that the establishment of the domains of the signifier/signified relies not only on representational logic and semantic aspects, but also on pragmatic competence and contextual information. An analysis of certain pragmatic dimensions of narrational acts may offer a heuristic that explains when and why readers assume that metaleptic games imply the 'real' world. Narratological discussions have rarely specified under what circumstances (if at all) metalepsis can imply or violate the 'boundary' between

---

[56] Other examples can be found in Ryan (2006), Meister (2005) and Limoges (2008, 2011).

fiction and the 'real' world. Some critics have broadened the scope of metalepsis, applying the concept to the act of narration that marks the boundary between fiction-internal stratifications and the extratextual world in which the narrative is read (or heard, seen, etc.). Debra Malina, for instance, has characterized the boundary that separates "the text that seems to be contained within the covers of a novel and the discursive world outside these covers" (2002, 9) as a boundary that may be affected by metaleptic transgression:

> [M]etalepsis in fictional texts bears a *mimetic* relation to subject-construction processes in our own world, and that, thanks in part to the parallel operation of boundary violation in both worlds, which are, from the constructionist perspective, equally discursive, it may be made to reach through the final frontier, the boundary between fictional text and extratextual reader, to effect *our* construction as subjects [...]. (2002, 9)

According to Malina, the metaleptic transgression may not only violate the boundaries between extradiegetic, diegetic, and hypodiegetic "universes" (ibid., 4), but can also effect "a more radical dissolution of the boundary between the diegetic reader and her extratextual counterpart" (ibid., 64). In the context of her deconstructive approach to the narratological category, Malina does not offer a static delineation of what that boundary consists in, but emphasizes the dynamic process in which "the extratextual reader engaged in reading the text [...] undergoes the kind of destabilizing experience that effectively deconstructs the boundaries of narrative (and the notion of extratextuality itself)" (ibid., 136). Thus, according to Malina, the process of constructing and deconstructing textual worlds (each of which "seems to be contained within the covers of a novel" [ibid., 9]) is, in the last analysis, not fundamentally different from the construction of "the discursive world outside these covers" (ibid.). Here, Malina's approach moves beyond Genette's (1972), as she explicitly incorporates the 'discursive world' in which we read fiction into the hierarchy of diegetic levels (cf. Malina 2002, 1–11). However, Malina never attempts to delineate explicitly and precisely the boundary that separates (or boundaries that separate) these 'textual' and 'discursive worlds' – this boundary is merely *implicit* in her discussion as the dividing line necessitated by the construction of the various discursive textual (and 'real') worlds that are logically distinct from each other.

I would like to offer a first pragmatic rule at this point that applies to all narratives: Fiction and non-fiction may (indirectly) shape how we make sense of the world, may even influence or guide behaviour, yet they cannot *literally* shape the world in which narratives are understood. In Umberto Eco's *The Name of the Rose* (1983), it is poison that kills and not the metaleptic intervention of an act of narrative representation.⁵⁷ Thus, the *literal* transgression that crosses the boundary between the narrative act of representation (mirrored by an act of understanding) that is situated in the 'real' world and the (fictive) entities it creates is the prerequisite of fictional acts of narrative representation. In the 'real' world, diegetic entities can only be *implied* in the form of a playful suspension of disbelief that is typical for fiction. Cosplay may suggest otherwise, but we cannot be literally visited by that which we represent in narratives. This distinction becomes obvious when one considers the moment when *The War of the Worlds* was aired as an episode of the American radio drama anthology series "Mercury Theatre on the Air" on October 30, 1938: Many people understood this as a non-fictional account and were convinced that an actual Martian invasion was taking place. Yet, as a representation, while the narrative act of *The War of the Worlds* could generate panic, it could not generate Martians (neither could a non-fictional account – people would be visited by Martians that were there before and independently of the narrative act that 'creates' a simulation of the invasion).

Even though I basically agree with Malina, there are nevertheless pragmatic conventions that distinguish the act of fictive narrative representation from 'discursive constructions of reality.' While each act of narrative representation is external to the *representation* of the events it describes, the relationships established between fictional and non-fictional narrative acts and their represented entities seem to differ – readers and viewers of narrative fiction do not usually assume that the world in which they live is populated by entities created by fictive acts of narration: the narrative act that creates fictional narrative is a *performative* act. As such, it cannot magically create the physical appearance beyond the signification. The concept of performativity is here derived from John Austin (1962) and John R. Searle (1969) and is used to mean that fictional narratives in their description of states of affairs *create* what is described. Originally, Austin distinguishes constative utterances, which describe a state of affairs and refer to what already exists, and performative utterances, which perform the act to which they refer (as in 'I promise,' 'I order' or, in the case of a marriage ceremony, 'I do'). Literary discourse offers a strange oscillation be-

---

57 In her discussion of metaleptic effects on "so called reality" (2004, 209) Marie-Laure Ryan approaches the question from a similar angle (though she does not mention Umberto Eco and offers a renegade version of the same idea): "A story can represent the murder of a fictional reader by the protagonist of a fictional novel, but the only way for a real-world author to kill the actual reader would be by non-literary means, for instance, by sprinkling anthrax between the pages of the book. In other words, the actual base of the narrative stack, the world of ground zero, remains protected from metaleptic phenomena" (ibid.).

tween both kinds of utterance. On the one hand, to use *War and Peace* as an example, it refers to that which already exists (for instance, the historical Napoleon); on the other hand, it *creates* the fictional *homologue* of Napoleon and his 'world.' This distinction may possibly prove helpful, if one wants to avoid the extreme of a concept of metalepsis that includes practically all fictional writing (for which Genette argued in 2004). Literary discourse (like any discourse) can of course refer to recognizable concepts, states of affairs, human beings, etc. that already (and literally) exist (such as, for instance a recognizable 'world' of nineteenth-century Russia).[58] If one concludes that nineteenth-century Russia has metaleptically entered *War and Peace*, then this is, I would maintain, a confusion of the constative with the performative. Even though understanding *War and Peace* relies on diverse cognitive schemata, historical knowledge, etc. (and thus on states of affairs which already exist), the narrative is at the same time a *performative* act *creating* the diegesis, the fictional world of *War and Peace*. Even though that diegesis 'contains' recognizable elements that already exist in the extratextual world, this does not allow the conclusion that these elements have metaleptically entered the diegesis of *War and Peace*. The pragmatic rule that governs such decisions (I assume practically no readers will be baffled by metaleptic transgressions in *War and Peace*) could be that fiction is understood as being 'only represented': "Regardless of origin, all thematic entities become fictive by appearing in a fictional world" (Schmid 2010, 30).

Fictional narrative can refer to nineteenth-century Russia very much as any other constative utterance: meaningful and true, if it conforms to the facts of the matter (thus, a historical novel can be historically accurate or inaccurate). That does not mean, however, that the facts of the matter are *literally* 'contained' within the diegetic universe of, say *War and Peace*. Since fictional narrative at the same time *creates* a narrative world (which is triggered by semiotic signs, drawings, images, etc.), the fictive homologues of historical persons (or the facts of whatever non-fictive matter) are usually regarded as the result of a performative act and not the metaleptic appearance of the extratextual in the domain of the signified. In this domain, a fictional homologue of 'Napoleon' has the same ontological status as any narrative's fictive elements – the creation of semiotic signs: neither the diegetic 'Napoleon' nor the diegetic Natasha Rostova can visit any flesh-and-blood reader for a cup of tea. This is, I maintain, what

---

[58] Paradoxically, as Jacques Derrida (1977) and especially Judith Butler (1990, 1993) have argued, performativity relies on iterable or repeatable elements in order to be recognizable. At the same time, it may also be argued (as Judith Butler has repeatedly done in the context of gendered identities) that non-fiction is in a similar manner performative.

induces readers (or viewers, etc.) to construct a metaleptic violation: the violation of the *performative* function of acts of narration. If Thursday Next from *The Eyre Affair* drinks tea with metadiegetic 'Napoleon' and Natasha Rostova from the fictional homologue of *War and Peace* in the diegesis of an upcoming novel, then this is a denial of the categorical ontological distinction instigated by the *performative* act of *fictive* narration (naturally, this is impossible for extratextual readers – we could only drink tea with someone acting 'Napoleon' and 'Natasha Rostova' in the mode of a playful suspension of disbelief). Yet there can be any number of constative utterances in a fictional narrative without triggering metalepses, because readers approach fiction with the pragmatic rule that *qua* representation, the represented is ontologically distinct from the world of the narration or representation (the domain of the signifier) – even if the non-fictional 'reality' and a narrative fiction resemble each other in many ways. Unless, it may be added, as the example of Laurence Sterne's sermon[59] may remind us, the 'reality' which is involved in the potential metaleptic transgression consists of semiotic signs, an act of narration. As such, extratextual and diegetic signs can only be distinguished by the contexts in which they appear.

I would argue that the notion of performativity can provide a helpful distinction between two functions of narrative acts and an explanation as to why, generally, readers do not experience 'Napoleon' in *War and Peace* as a transgression of narrative logic. The model offered above can furthermore foster and

---

[59] In Chapter 4.2.2., I offer an extensive analysis of ontological status of the famous sermon 'Abuses of Conscience' in chapter II/xvii of *Tristram Shandy*. It had been preached by the historical author Laurence Sterne in 1750 in York before it appeared (as the fictional homologue of that sermon) on the diegetic level of *Tristram Shandy*, where its author is the fictive character Yorick, and where that sermon is read aloud by Trim and commented on by Slop, Walter and uncle Toby. I assume that for most readers this sermon belongs to the world inhabited by the fictive characters in the diegesis and can be viewed as a diegetic act of narration. However, the sermon can at the same time be interpreted as an ontological anomaly distinct from the world of the embedding diegesis since it 'belongs' to the extratextual world of the author Laurence Sterne. What becomes evident in this example is that the 'shifting frontier of the narrating' (cf. Genette 1980, 236) is inevitably anchored in a context, a world in which it is embedded.

When Laurence Sterne's sermons were published in two volumes in 1760, the first title page read *The Sermons of Mr Yorick* and the second title page read *Sermons by Laurence Sterne, A.M. Prebendary of York, and Vicar of Sutton on the Forest, and of Stillington near York*. Somewhat expectedly, this commercial strategy with a metaleptic twist proved effective, despite the outrage it caused (cf. Ross 2001, 245): The words originally written by Laurence Sterne have attained a fictive creator (Yorick) who publishes in the 'real' world (a newspaper article of 1760 refers to Sterne as "the rev. Laurence Sterne, editor of Yorick's sermons" [qtd. in Ross 2001, 226–227]) and in the fictive diegesis of Tristram Shandy.

structure the analysis of certain pragmatic dimensions of the 'boundary' of diegetic universes and can explain when and why readers assume that metaleptic games imply the world in which they read. It seems that the 'real' world can only be metaleptically involved in the mode of a playful suspension of disbelief, or if the entity from the 'real' world implied in the metaleptic transgression is solely considered as a set of signs from a semiotic system. Metalepsis violates the pragmatic rules that define how narrational acts 'represent' and/or evoke the domain of the signifier as well as the (fictive) context of their production; only the violation of the 'boundary' that 'consists' in the semiotic signs that create, connect and separate diegetic levels, is metaleptic.

Consequently, as maintained in the preceding chapter, I do not consider horizontal transgressions or transmigrations as metaleptic (instead I consider them as cases of transfictionality). I would, however, like to briefly consider the notion of 'horizontal metalepses' again and present an argument that this widening of the scope entails a loss of precision and heuristic value. Werner Wolf offers a transmedial definition, designed as part of a "conceptual and terminological framework for interdisciplinary comparisons and descriptions" (2009b, 7), which is applicable to phenomena in diverse media such as film, theatre, the pictorial arts and music:

> Metalepsis presupposes the existence of at least two different 'worlds' or (onto)logical levels, at least one of which must be inside the representation or be the representation itself. It is helpful to postulate 'levels' or 'worlds' as a minimal condition in order to be able to accommodate metaleptic phenomena that do not only involve the classical case of a transgression between the 'vertically stacked' levels of the representation and the represented within a representational work but also the following phenomena: a – seeming – transgression between a work and the world of the author or recipient outside it, transgressions between parallel or 'horizontal' subworlds within a work. (Ibid., 51–52)

In this inclusive definition of metalepsis, Wolf, in agreement with Malina, incorporates possible violations of the boundary that separates the world of historical authors and readers or recipients from the represented 'world(s)' of the work of art. However, it is striking that he does not attempt to delineate the *relations* between the worlds that are transgressed. The implication is seemingly that each 'world' is per se ontologically distinct from all others. This is similar in Jeff Thoss' conceptualization of metaleptic prototypes that are "[based] upon the idea that this device essentially consists of violating a storyworld's autonomy" (Thoss 2011, 190). "It is precisely this self-contained nature of the storyworld that metalepsis throws into turmoil by violating the line that separates the inside from the outside of a particular world, and it does so in a way that is perceived to be paradoxical (in the sense of contrary to received opinion)" (ibid., 192).

Alber and Bell take this conceptualization of metalepsis to its logical conclusion: If transmigrations between horizontal 'worlds' within one work are metaleptic, and if metalepsis violates "a storyworld's autonomy" (Thoss 2011, 160), why should the concept of metalepsis not include horizontal transmigrations that "represent cases of [...] 'transfictionality'" (Alber and Bell 2012, 168)? In other words, on what basis can an entity be unequivocally allocated to a world? It is uncontentious that the constructions of such 'worlds' are part of the conceptual framework with which narrative phenomena are interpreted; they emerge as the spatiotemporal framework of the events in novels or, say, movies (as, for instance, the 'worlds' of Winnetou and Robin Hood respectively). Whether the existents of those 'worlds,' whose construction was originally instigated by previous narratives involving Winnetou and Robin Hood, can share one diegesis with or without a metaleptic transgression, according to the criteria outlined above, depends on how basic conceptual frameworks operate in the understanding of a text.

Sonja Klimek maintains that 'horizontal metalepses' as developed by Wagner (2002) are a kind of "intertextual game" (cf. Klimek 2009, 171–17?) and that, consequently, the meeting of Winnetou and Robin Hood is simply the "quoting" (ibid., 171) of a character "already famous in world literature" (ibid.). In 'horizontal metalepses,' which are, according to Klimek, not metalepses in Genette's sense but "metalepsis-like phenomena" (ibid.), the transgression must be conceptualized as a movement between two 'worlds' which (in the narrative in question) belong to one diegetic level and are thus distinct and incompatible, not because of the representational logic of hierarchically organized acts of narration, but because of the unstable category of what might be termed the 'closed' narrative 'world' from which they originate.

I agree with Klimek's argument for a more restrictive use of metalepsis, because the existing definitions of a 'horizontal' type invite questions that challenge the heuristic value of the category: Can one narrative 'world' extend over various dieges which are narrated by different narrators/authors? Is there, consequently, a transgression, if characters from two previous fictional narratives, two fictive narrative worlds, populate one 'present' narrative world? Is there a new (third) narrative world? Or have the two worlds been contaminated by each other in a move across the narrative acts that created them? I would argue that the attempt to answer such questions relies on the construction of the representational logic of – and the pragmatic rules that apply to – the acts of narrative representation involved. An interesting case in point would be the argument presented in the second book of *Don Quixote*, in which the case is made that other narratives which claim to portray the adventures of Don Quixote and Sancho Pansa are fraudulent. Yet, *Don Quixote*'s narrative form, its episodic structure (which relates the work to the Spanish Picaresque novel) invites the writing of a sequel, a 'continuation' of the narrative world it has created. Definitions of horizontal metalepses entail that such sequels (and not the fact that they are mentioned in the diegesis of *Don Quixote*)[60] have a metaleptic quality, too. Another interesting example is the narrative world of *Pamela* (*Pamela, or Virtue Rewarded* [1740]) and *Shamela* (*An Apology for the Life of Mrs Shamela Andrews* [1741]). Here, two diegetic 'worlds' created by two different epistolary novels by two different authors (Richardson and Fielding) arguably present one and the same narrative world. If Fielding 'rewrites' the diegesis Richardson invented in *Pamela*, then does the inclusion of characters out of Richardson's novel make his narrative metaleptic?

The conclusion which suggests itself when metalepsis is conceptualized along these lines is that fiction is generally metaleptic (cf. Genette 2004). Yet as the philosopher Nelson Goodman reminds us, "worldmaking as we know it always starts from worlds already on hand; the making is a remaking" (1978, 6). As maintained above, all narrational acts 'refer' to states of affairs from other (narrative) 'worlds' with constative utterances. No single diegetic world, it can easily be argued, comes from nothing, but each one is built from elements familiar from other 'worlds.' However, at the same time, narration is a performative act that creates its referent. If a narrative contains Winnetou and Robin Hood, it could be argued that it does not follow that this is a metaleptic transgression of narrative logic. Both characters evoke different contexts (and different continents for that matter), but a story in which one visits the other (let's say by means of a time machine) may be bad and have little tellability – yet it is not,

---

[60] Notable exceptions are Bareis (2008) and Thoss (2015), whose definition of horizontal metalepsis includes the criterion that the autonomy of a storyworld is only metaleptically violated if horizontal movements are *highlighted* by the narrative in question ("[A] narrative needs to specify that one of its entities originates from a different fictional world before this entity's presence in the narrative can be qualified as metaleptic" [Thoss 2015, 13]). This criterion is not without problems. On the one hand, when horizontal transgressions are explicitly mentioned in narratives, such narratives usually display metaleptic potential that violates the hierarchical structure of narrative. A good example for this can be found in Thoss' discussion of *Stay Tuned* in which he acknowledges that the metaleptic presence of Helen and Roy Knable (*Stay Tuned* serves as an example of horizontal metalepsis) in various TV shows is "still the presence of primary-world entities in secondary worlds" (2015, 26–27). Moreover, the question remains what kind of 'narrative specification' turns cases of transfictionality into metalepsis.

I would argue, necessarily constructed as paradoxical. The prerequisites of horizontal metalepsis seem to imply a violation of the pragmatic rules that govern the construction of the domains of the signifier/signified. It would be hard to find a non-metaleptic text that does not incorporate some element that could be constructed as belonging to another (narrative) 'world.' I maintain, then, that 'worldmaking' does not invariably entail metalepses.

The model proposed above visualizes a less broad definition of metalepsis. Metalepsis presupposes the violation of the logic of the narrational act or acts that create and connect the worlds which are involved in the transgression. Metalepsis, in other words, consists in a violation of the pragmatic rules that govern the construction of the hierarchical relation(s) of the worlds instigated and connected by narrational acts. As such, metaleptic transgressions result in a paradoxical violation of representational logic (even if this paradox can become generically conventional). This does not apply to horizontal metalepsis since, as Sonja Klimek has convincingly argued, the notion implies that "metalepsis would no longer be a paradoxical phenomenon in the strict sense of defying formal logic (that is, the logic of representation)" (2011, 26). What comes into view in the consideration of the act of narrative representation is, on the one hand, the complexity of the hermeneutic situation in which the text, the conceptual frameworks of the reader, and pragmatic rules (as well as the traditions of reading) equally contribute to the metaleptic transgression. On the other hand, it becomes evident that the hermeneutic situations that generate metaleptic transgressions become hopelessly byzantine, if metalepsis is taken to deny the autonomy of any narrative worlds. Metalepsis does not deny the distinctness of *any* two (or more) narrative worlds but the distinction between the narrative 'worlds' that are hierarchically and logically connected by signification. Perhaps it is preferable to employ the metaphor of the boundary slightly differently and use it for the combination of signs produced by narrational acts: As each sign links the material entity (signifier) and a mental concept (signified), the combination of signs produced by narrational acts link (what can be inferred as) the material dimension(s) of production and the narratives evoked – and functions, metaphorically speaking, as a 'boundary' between those domains.

2.2.3 A Transmedial Definition of Metalepsis

The transmediality of metalepsis is undisputed today. The narratological concept of metalepsis has not only been applied to phenomena in a wide variety of media, but has also been theoretically expanded to account for certain kinds of transgressive features in, to name but a few genres, drama (Landfester 1997, Fludernik 2003b, Genette 2004, Klimek 2009/2010), lyric poetry (Wolf 2005), pop lyrics (Ben-Merre 2011), film (Genette 2004, Limoges 2008, Klimek 2009, Thoss 2011a, Sarkhosh 2011, Thoss 2015) and TV series (Morsch 2012), animation film (Limoges 2011), comics (Wolf 2005, Kukkonen 2011a), picture-books (Klimek 2010), hypertext fiction (Alber and Bell 2012) and videogames (Harpold 2008, Bell 2016), or even the hologram performance of the virtual pop band 'Gorillaz' (Hofer 2011). More often than not, Werner Wolf's (2005, 2009b) transgeneric and transmedial account is quoted and used as a theoretical framework for discussions of metaleptic phenomena across media:

> [T]he prototypical case of metalepsis can be defined as a salient phenomenon occurring exclusively in representations, namely as a usually non-accidental and paradoxical transgression of the border between levels or (sub)worlds that are ontologically (in particular concerning the opposition between reality vs. fiction) or logically differentiated (logically in a wide, not only formal sense), including, e.g., temporal or spatial differences).[61] (Wolf, 2009b, 50)

Two things are remarkable about this wide and inclusive definition. Firstly, it does not restrict metaleptic phenomena to narrative and thus implies that all representations can employ metaleptic transgressions. Secondly, it avoids a precise delineation of the relation between the 'worlds' involved in the transgressions. Since Wolf wants to include horizontal metalepsis, he does not connect metalepsis to the representational logic of acts of representation. Yet, as I have argued in the preceding sub-chapter, there are good reasons to posit a denial of the spatiotemporal logic of the act of (narrative) representation as a prerequisite of metalepsis. Following Genette (1972), I argue for a narrower definition of metalepsis and propose the denial of the hierarchical relation between the world represented and the world of the representation as a necessary condition in that definition (following Wolf's insight that metalepsis is a possibility only in representational media).

The application of the narratological category outside the realm of literary texts (which Wolf advocated and predicted in 2005) has become commonplace. One of the reasons for the success of the transdisciplinary 'export' of metalepsis

---

[61] This builds on Werner Wolf's earlier definition which defines metalepsis as "a usually intentional paradoxical transgression of, or confusion between, (onto)logically distinct (sub)worlds and/or levels that exist, or are referred to, within representations of possible worlds" (2005, 91).

lies in the structural similarity of all representations. The crucial distinction between metalepses in verbal narratives and in other media relies on the fact that different media offer different semiotic systems for acts of representation. In films, comics, videogames or theatre performances, different non-verbal semiotic modes interact to guide the process of constructing the represented 'worlds.' For example, the worlds of Mel Brooks' *Robin Hood: Men in Tights* (1993), Will Eisner's comic book character 'The Spirit' (who made his first appearance in American newspapers on June 2, 1940), the first person shooter video game series *Call of Duty*, the painting *The Master of the Revels* (1926) by René Magritte and Sarah Kane's *Cleansed* (which premiered at the Royal Court in April 1998) rely on verbal as well as non-verbal (auditory, visual, locomotive and proxemic, etc.) signs. I maintain that the construction of (narrative) worlds evoked by different semiotic systems in various media is fundamentally similar, insofar as they reflect human sense-making capabilities. Film, comic, videogame and drama (etc.) all rely on the representational logic and spatiotemporal make-up of lived human experience that separates the worlds of the representation and the represented. Irrespective of the semiotic systems employed, acts of representation are created/approached with the assumption that the following structural relations are instigated by the combination of signs in which a given representation consists:

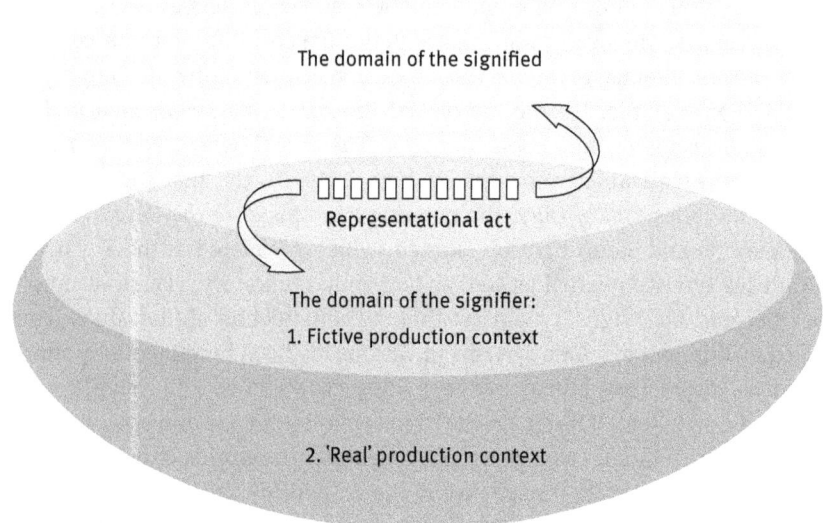

Figure 15: Representational Acts Cue the Construction of the Domains of the Signifier/Signified

Figure 15 visualizes how the combinations of signs that are the result of representational acts cue the construction of the domain of the signified and the domain of the signifier (recipients situate the production and/or reception of the signs they receive). The subdivision of the domain of the signifier is optional: the construction of a fictive production context is a *possibility* of fictional representations. It should also be added that the context of the reception of the signs (the world in which the representation is understood) is not visualized here as it either correlates with the 'real' production context or 'replaces' the contexts of production. The domain of the signified could also be further subdivided, as it can contain representations (which, in turn, can contain further representations). What this figure visualizes is what I take to be the fundamental prerequisite for metalepsis (which is denied in the transgression): every representation presupposes the distinction between representation and that which is represented. Such a distinction implies, of course, that someone (*in* the world in which the representation is located) intentionally represents something (which is situated *in* the world that is represented), which, in turn, is understood by someone in the world in which that representation is received (which may or may not be distinct from the world in which the representation is created). This distinction is, in other words, indebted in large part to the contextual assumptions of the creators and recipients of representations. This does not amount to the claim that recipients of, say, movies or paintings construct a detailed domain of the signifier all the time (one can view a movie or painting without such an awareness). However, metaleptic representations highlight the assumption that all intentionally produced combinations of signs are situated in a domain that is categorically distinct from the domain of the signified, an assumption that is the prerequisite of metalepsis. In most fictional representations, the domains of the signifier/signified can be easily correlated with Genette's distinctions between extradiegesis, diegesis, meta- or hypodiegesis (etc.) and the extratextual world.[62] This, I argue, is transmedially valid.

I want to briefly return to the claim that Figure 15 shows that the signs used in an act of representation imply their intentional creation. When something is considered as a representation (and not as arbitrary resemblance), this necessitates the construction of the context of their production. In this sense, understanding representation is distinct from understanding resemblance. The recipient's construction of a production context in the 'real' (the extranarrative or extrarepresentational) world needs to be differentiated from the construction of the *fictive* extradiegesis/exegesis in a novel or the *fictive* production context in a movie like Mel Brooks' *Robin Hood: Men in Tights* (1993). Not all narratives/representations necessitate the construction of a fictive production context – yet all media potentially allow the evocation of an exegesis or fictive con-

---

62 In the context of film studies, this correlation has been challenged. There is, for instance, the long history of theoretical discussion following Chatman's (1990) proposal that film narration necessitates a 'cinematic narrator,' "the composite of a large and complex variety of communicating devices" (Chatman 1990, 134). In the wake of David Bordwell's influential *Narration in the Fiction Film* (1985), it has been argued against Chatman that film narration has no sender, and, as Bordwell claims, no extradiegesis (cf. Bordwell 1985, 62). Consequently, there is no 'world' in which such a sender and the act of representation are situated. For two recent surveys of that ongoing discussion, see Kuhn (2011, 75–80) and Schmidt (2009). I maintain that signification is inevitably situated and that most accounts of film narration and their varying terminologies imply the following: there is a world in which the 'image-maker,' the 'intrinsic narrator,' the 'camera eye,' the 'primary narrative agency,' the film narrator,' or the 'filmic composition device' operate. Even though the one-to-one correlation between a novelistic and filmic extradiegesis (or exegesis) may prove at times difficult, I argue that the recipients situate the signs they see (and hear etc.) – and that the situatedness of the signs (the domain of the signifier) may be fictive (exegesis) or 'real' (extratextual or extrarepresentational). Corroborating this, Kuhn's own visualization of narrative levels in the communication model of narrative film is structurally similar to the communication model of verbal narrative and locates the visual and verbal narrative instances of film narration in the extradiegesis (cf. 2011, 82–87).

text of sign production. An example of how such a fictive production context (exegesis) can be involved in a potential metalepsis is the scene in which the diegetic Robin Hood (from Mel Brooks' movie) takes a look at the script after losing an archery contest ("I lost. I lost? I am not supposed to lose. Let me see the script."). The script determines that he gets another shot, which is acknowledged by various diegetic characters (who pull out copies of the script and read the passage in question). One way of reading this is that this knowledge (of a script that 'narrates' and thus determines diegetic existence) is an instance of epistemological metalepsis and that the script (as an element from the fictive production context of the movie) has metaleptically entered the diegesis of the movie. The metaleptic joke relies on the fact that the diegetic characters do *not* 'step out of their role' and emerge as 'actors' who could just reshoot the scene (Robin's opponents sadly acknowledge that he gets another shot and attempt to murder him before he is able to shoot his arrow).

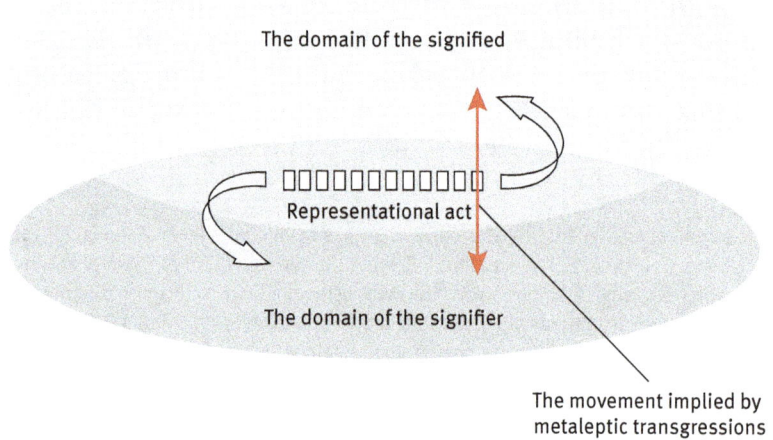

Figure 16: A Transmedial Model of Metalepsis

I propose this transmedial model of metalepsis as a visualization of the following transmedial definition of metalepsis:

> Metalepsis occurs when and if a recipient of a (narrative) representation feels that the logic of acts of (narrative) representation is violated or negated in such a way that the 'natural' spatial, temporal and hierarchical relationships between the domain(s) of the signifier and the domain(s) of the signified no longer apply.[63]

The example from Mel Brooks' *Robin Hood: Men in Tights* shows how the domain of the signifier can be further subdivided into fictive and 'real' contexts of production – or even into various fictive and/or 'real' contexts of production. The signs of the representation can consist of more than one semiotic system created in one or more contexts of production. The verbal, auditory and visual signs in a given movie, for example, can imply different contexts of production.[64] As communication models of narrative fiction demonstrate, signs from one semiotic system can also imply various contexts of production. Potentially, the domain of the signifier can be further subdivided in (fictive or 'real') collaborative acts of representation. This simple model offers the possibility to visualize metaleptic transgressions in various media – independent of the semiotic system employed and irrespective of the question of whether a given representation counts as narrative or not. Moreover, it can visualize how acts of (narrative) representation in their entirety cue recipients to structure and subdivide the domains of the signifier and signified.

It should be added that acts of representation can consist of one sign (in the pictorial arts) and may still have, in borderline cases, limited metaleptic potential. Corroborating this, Werner Wolf claims that metalepsis also describes transgressions "between a representation and a non-representational sub-level

---

[63] This definition of metalepsis is indebted to Roy Sommer, who, in a conversation in the summer of 2013, argued that metalepsis "occurs when and if a recipient of a narrative feels that laws of probability are violated or negated by the use of specific strategies in such a way, that the 'natural' hierarchical relationships between characters and mediating entities no longer apply."

[64] Voice-over narration, if non-diegetic, may complement the diegetic scenes and imply a different context of production. This applies not only to the 'real' world (because the voice-over is *per definitionem* not recorded simultaneously while shooting the images), but also to a potentially fictive origin of voice and the relation of that voice to the diegesis. Terence Malick's *The Thin Red Line* (1998) may serve as an interesting example. When the philosophical voice-over narration does not belong to a character who comments on diegetic events, it seems to be completely dematerialized and/or cannot be situated in a 'conventional' context of production: "Oh my soul," the dead character Witt seems to say from beyond the grave, "let me be in you now. Look out through my eyes. Look out at the things you made. All things shining."

(e.g. a hypothetical abstract painting one of whose abstract forms 'leaps out' of the frame and becomes alive on the diegetic level of a film" (2009b, 52). The very words that describe the movement from the non-representational to the representational 'level' ('leap out of the frame') suggest that the notion of two distinct spatiotemporal frames of reference basically remains intact in such borderline cases. Or, rather, these words show how abstract art demonstrates how we usually make sense of the world. Notably, Wolf also argues elsewhere that metalepsis "exclusively occurs – or seems to occur – within representations and thus representational media" (ibid., 51). This, I argue, is the scope of the metaleptic model: it describes the 'vertical' breach of the boundary between the 'world' of the represented and the 'world' of the representation.

This moves beyond Genette's initial account in two decisive ways: Firstly, metalepsis is a transmedial phenomenon not restricted to narrative but to representational media, and secondly, metaleptic transgressions may *imply* the 'real' world.[65] The domain of the signifier can be further subdivided – the signs of Mel Brooks' movie *Robin Hood* can be situated in the fictive exegesis *and* the 'real' world in which that exegesis is created. The script which the diegetic Robin Hood uses in the scene briefly mentioned above can be understood as the exegetic script that says he gets another shot or the 'real' script that says he takes a look at the script which says he gets another shot. This scene may have limited metaleptic potential, but it demonstrates how representational signs can be situated in the domain of the signifier.

In an engaging example of metalepsis to be found in a computer game mentioned by Harpold (2008), the choice of the player's avatar has serious consequences. In the erotic adult computer adventure *Virtual Valerie* (1990) designed by Mike Saenz, Valerie eventually asks the avatar whether he (the avatar is of course male) wants to get down to business. Responding by clicking the 'Yes' button will immediately transport avatar and Valerie to a bedroom and set off the spectacle of crudely animated sex.

---

[65] Sonja Klimek has offered a transmedial definition of metalepsis as "strictly fiction-internal vertical transgressions of different levels of representation (i.e., fictitious [sub-]worlds), [...] violating the 'sacred' frontier between the world of the creator (where the act of representation takes place) and the world that is represented (i.e., is created in the case of fictional artefacts)" (2009, 171). Klimek restricts metalepsis to kinds of transgression that are closer to Genette (1972) and acknowledge the hierarchical relation instigated by 'acts of representation.' Metaleptic phenomena cross the boundary between the worlds of the represented (told) and the representation (telling). However, there seems to be little merit in the categorical denial that this may (at least potentially) involve the 'real' world.

More than this possibly tempting opportunity hangs on your choice: if you reject Valerie's invitation and click on the "No" or "Huh?" buttons, *your computer will reboot*. No advance warning is given: the game was written in Macromedia Director, and your misplaced mouse click simply invokes Director's rarely-used "Restart" command. In 1990, there was good reason to avoid it, as the Mac OS had limited support for multitasking and no memory protection; any application – including the operating system – open at the time you made the wrong choice was at risk of being damaged by Valerie's sudden exit. "The forced reboots," Saenz explains, "were my method of punishing the player for 'trespasses.' I tried to imagine how Valerie might slap the player's face, and a reboot was the closest approximation I could come up with" [...]. It is to my knowledge the only showstopper of its kind in modern computer gaming. (Harpold 2008, 98)

Whether this reboot is understood as a slap in the face the person playing the game (in the real world) receives from the diegetic Valerie or not (one could, of course, also conceptualize the boundary between real world and diegesis as intact), this example shows that, potentially, the real world may be playfully involved in metaleptic transgressions.[66] As an intentional set-up, there seems to be some metaleptic potential if the choices of the avatar damage the software of the computer on which the game is played. At the very least, it is highly debatable whether such possibilities can be ruled out once and for all for the myriad of

---

66 There are examples in a variety of media that corroborate this. It has been argued that in the final scene in Charlie Chaplin's *The Great Dictator* (1940), the barber in the ghetto (played by Chaplin) gradually metamorphoses into the actor in a 'progressive' metalepsis (cf. Schaeffer 2005, 327). The visual and auditive elements of the speech can either be conceptualized as a metamorphosis from diegetic barber to extradiegetic or even extratextual actor or writer. As Dahlberg has implied, such a metamorphosis could penetrate the real world: "For instance it might at first seem to be a merging of extra-diegesis and diegesis where the scriptwriter and film director is represented in his own work. However, the film metalepsis does not consist of an overstepping of the separation of narrator and narrated, but of that between actor (Chaplin) and character (barber)." This is one example which highlights how the 'real' world can be metaleptically approached by certain narratives (or representations). Such an approach relies on the ability of recipients to establish hierarchically related contexts: whereas the actor Charlie Chaplin belongs to the world of the representation (domain of the signifier), the character played by Chaplin belongs to the world of the represented (domain of the signified). Exploring how conventional forms of digital interaction in digital fiction can become metaleptic, Alice Bell offers examples in her recent article "Interactional Metalepsis and Unnatural Narratology" (2016) that seem to be structurally similar. One of the interactional metalepses she analyzes, for instance, "relies on the reader's interaction with the text via hardware – specifically the webcam – and it places the reader visually within the storyworld" (ibid., 304). I would argue that the realization of the metaleptic potential of such "a metaleptic insertion" (ibid., 305) is connected to the ability to understand the image of the reader (taken by the webcam) as part of the domain of the signified (as part of the storyworld) or as part of the domain of the signifier (the world in which that narrative is read and in which the picture was taken).

hermeneutic situations in which (potentially) metaleptic artefacts are understood. As the example of Laurence Sterne's sermon demonstrates (cf. Chapter 2.2.2.), the situatedness of acts of representation can be ambiguous. As such, extratextual (or extrarepresentational), exegetic or diegetic signs (etc.) can only be distinguished by the contexts in which they appear. I do not categorically exclude the 'real' world; I simply define metalepsis as the transgression between the domain of the signifier (the world of the representation/telling) and the domain of the signified (the world of the represented/told).

What also comes into view in a transdisciplinary approach is that metalepses have distinct medial characteristics: different media offer different metaleptic possibilities. Harpold's assumption that metalepsis must have "a medial basis" (2008, 100) acknowledges that. If, for instance, the example above is interpreted as a metaleptic transgression, then the rules that apply to a diegetic world in a computer game can extend "to the material conditions of play" (ibid.) in distinct ways that are impossible in other media. The possibility that choices in the diegetic 'world' of a game affect the very software (and potentially the hardware) that runs the game is, to my knowledge, a unique characteristic of computer games (albeit one that is for obvious reasons rarely explored). Computer games also offer various ways in which 'recipients' can shape the narrative of the game they play with their avatars – yet even though this offers new metaleptic possibilities, such interactions do not necessarily violate the boundary between the domains of the signifier/signified. Another example of unique medial possibilities for metalepsis can be found in Roberta Hofer's (2011) insightful article "Metalepsis in Live Performance: Holographic Projections of the Cartoon Band 'Gorillaz' as a Means of Metalepsis," which convincingly shows how the technical possibilities of holography and projection can metaleptically imply the 'real' world of the recipient in ways that are impossible in other media. The holographic projection can imply the metaleptic meeting of the domain of the signified (the cartoon band 'Gorillaz') and the domain of the signifier (in this case, the world in which the signs are received). As Hofer argues, these are not only "possible examples of metalepsis, but also a colourful bouquet of different stages along the spectrum of fiction and reality" (2011, 242). However, even if one considers this as a special type of immersive illusion (and not metalepsis), I would argue that borderline cases such as this demonstrate the heuristic value of the model proposed above: this is an instance of metalepsis if recipients assume that the act of representation transports entities from the domain of the signified into the domain of the signifier.

With further technical advancement, the future will present holographic projections that, from the perspective of recipients, are indistinguishable from their surroundings. Virtual Reality could take this metaleptic game further and not only introduce entities from the domain of the signified into the domain of the signifier, but replace the domain of the signifier by the domain of the signified altogether. The metaleptic potential of (future) possibilities of different media is far from exhausted:

> If VR [virtual reality] were perfect (and it could be someday), if a computer could create images of objects and feed into our brains sensory stimuli similar to those occasioned by the real object, there would be no way to distinguish the two versions, and the simulated would become the real. But the day when technology becomes sophisticated enough to make us perceive images as the real thing, its "victims" will have no knowledge of the metaleptic takeover. (Ryan 2006, 229)

Medial representations will predictably become more metaleptic as technical sophistication increasingly allows for the 'simulated to become real.'

2.2.4 Metaleptic Types

Twenty-five years after Genette's "original conception of narrative metalepsis [had] hinted at a typology without actually proposing one" (Pier 2009, 197), William Nelles (1997, 154) suggested a distinction into two basic types of narrative metalepsis and differentiated what he termed the "unmarked case" of metalepsis from those cases that were distinctly marked. The 'unmarked case,' in which neither a narrator moves into the 'embedded narrative' nor a character to the embedding level of the narrator, consists in "a temporary sharing of a common level" (ibid.).[67] This 'temporary sharing' in which the transgression is only *implicit* is, Nelles maintains, distinct from the 'marked case' in which there is a clearly discernible literal 'movement' of one of the dramatis personae (narrator, narratee, or character) into a neighbouring level. What William Nelles termed the 'unmarked case' has seemingly become common ground in modern narratological typologies of metalepsis. The notion of 'rhetorical metalepsis' (Marie-Laure Ryan and later Monika Fludernik), 'minimal metalepsis' (John Pier 2009, 192) and 'pseudo-performative Erzählakte' (Bernd Häsner 2005, 20)[68], all basi-

---

[67] Nelles' example for the 'unmarked case' is the example from Balzac that Genette briefly discusses as metaleptic (cf. 1997, 154).
[68] Bernd Häsner argues for a narrowing of the field of metaleptic transgressions and restricts the use of the term 'metalepsis' to exclusively describe phenomena which Nelles termed 'the unmarked case': "Der Begriff der Metalepse soll [...] also, anders als bei Genette, einem spezifischen Typus von Transgressionen vorbehalten bleiben – [...] pseudo-performativen Narrati-

cally reiterate what Nelles has termed the 'unmarked case.' However, since Nelles' *Frameworks* were, it seems, not widely read, it was Ryan's account that popularized the idea and supplied new terms for both types of transgression: the term 'rhetorical metalepsis' is now widely used and the 'marked case' is most often termed 'ontological metalepsis.'

I propose the following structure tree of metaleptic types. This is partly a summary of Nelles' (1997), Fludernik's (2003b), Klimek's (2010) and Ryan's (2006) typologies, yet it also introduces a new systematization of preceding types and offers new distinctions and terms. The new terms I propose are 'figurative metalepsis' (as a category that subsumes epistemological and rhetorical metalepses), along with a new opposition between 'immersive' and 'recursive' types (which are both literal transgressions of the logic of the act of representation):

---

onsakten, die [...] über die Simultaneisierung von erzählendem *discours* und der über diesen *discours* konstituierten *histoire* paradoxe und logische und semantische Effekte hervorbringen." (2005, 21)

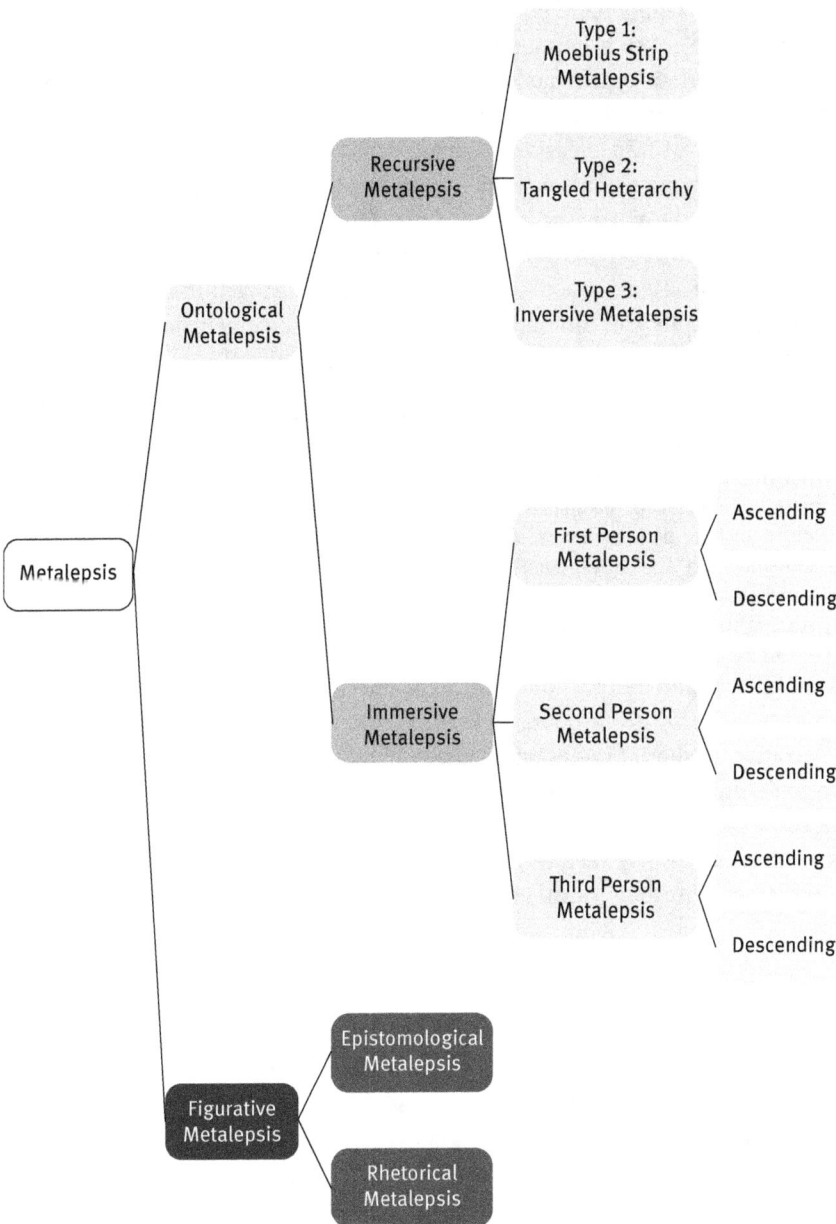

Figure 17: A Typology of Metaleptic Transgressions

This proposal of metaleptic types comes with a *caveat*: the application of this typology is subject to a hermeneutic situation in which there can be no pure forms of the various types that transcend the particular act of understanding in which they come into being. Figurative metalepses often imply an ontological and thus physical transgression, whereas ontological metalepses often rely on figurative language or on semantic possibilities that are by no means without alternatives in the particular hermeneutic situation in which they come into being. This distinction into types structures and systematizes the metaleptic potential of narrative – a potential which has to be realized in the event of understanding metalepsis. Similarly, Fludernik lucidly comments on the problematic nature of a binary logic that supports such distinctions:

> The distinction between 'real' and 'metaphorical' metalepsis, between an actual crossing of *ontological* boundaries and a merely imaginative transcendence of narrative levels, is a fine one. Not only is this true from a Derridean perspective clearly suggests that a metaphoric component of metalepsis will inevitably involve metalepsis in the intractabilities of distinguishing between the 'proper' and the 'metaphoric' use of the term 'ontological crossing.' [sic]. The critical impasse that is here seen to rear its head is additionally aggravated by the insight that the ontology of narratological levels exists only in the mind of readers and critics. (2003b, 396)

I would like to add that this ontology exists not only in the mind of recipients of narrative, but also in traditions of reading, the potential semantic possibilities of narrative, authorial intention, or the conventionalized practice of interpretative communities. Consequently, in view of what John Pier terms "the fluid transitions between these [i.e. Fludernik's] types" (2009, 192), such a descriptive framework can best be seen as presenting *interpretative possibilities* – which are always open to further questions.

2.2.4.1 Figurative Metalepsis

I propose the term 'figurative metalepsis' for those transgressions that are either 'imaginary' or limited to the denial of certain properties of diegetic universes (or to 'minimal' transgressions of those properties). It is a transgression in the figurative sense when the transgression between the domains of the signifier and the signified is *implied* or *suggested* – thus realizing only limited metaleptic potential. The transgression is neither complete (there is no narrative entity that moves 'physically' and *illicitly* from one diegetic universe to another), nor does it deny the logic of the act of narrative representation in a fundamental manner. Epistemological and rhetorical metalepsis are both figurative in this sense.

2.2.4.1.1 Figurative Metalepsis I: Epistemological Metalepsis

According to William Nelles (1997, 152–157), epistemological metalepsis is a subtype of the 'marked case,' which can be further subdivided into the dichotomy of epistemological (verbal) metalepsis and ontological (modal) metalepsis. The first kind (epistemological metalepsis) consists in a character's knowledge of the world of the narration, whereas the latter kind (ontological metalepsis) consists in a physical transgression of the boundary between the embedding and the embedded. It should be noted here that 'epistemological metalepses' can only refer to narrative agents that are narrated – a narrator knows *per definitionem* about the 'world' of his or her narration. It is maybe for this reason that the notion of epistemological metalepsis is conspicuously absent from most accounts of metalepsis, one of the few exceptions being Werner Wolf (cf. 2009b, 52–53). Wolf places epistemological metalepsis between the ontological and rhetorical kinds and defines it as that transgression which consists in "an 'impossible' knowledge fictional characters appear to have of their being mere characters" (ibid.):

> As for epistemological metalepsis, which may be regarded as a form between ontological and rhetorical metalepsis, its metareferential potential can be qualified as correspondingly intermediate, for on the one hand the transgression remains on this side of an actualized impossibility, but on the other hand the transgression is more than an (in part) conventionalized rhetorical device and, particularly when it is a speech act of represented characters, borders on ontological metalepsis. (Ibid., 54)

I agree with Wolf that epistemological metalepsis remains on "this side of an actualized impossibility." There is no literal physical transgression of the act of narrative representation, but 'only' a character's display of knowledge of superordinate diegetic universes in a paradoxical violation of representational logic. While this type often has more radical metaleptic potential than rhetorical metalepsis and is frequently the precursor of more radical transgressions (the example of the comic book superhero Deadpool who acknowledges or guesses at the presence of his readers [an example of epistemological metalepsis] is followed by more radical ontological transgressions, cf. Chapter 5), it does not violate the spatial, temporal or semantic parameters of diegetic levels, but only their hierarchical relations. With the help of the scalar model introduced in Chapter 2.2.1., epistemological metalepsis could be visualized in the following manner (the dot shows to what extent the diegetic properties are denied in the metaleptic transgression):

86 — Framing the Structure of Narrative Metalepsis

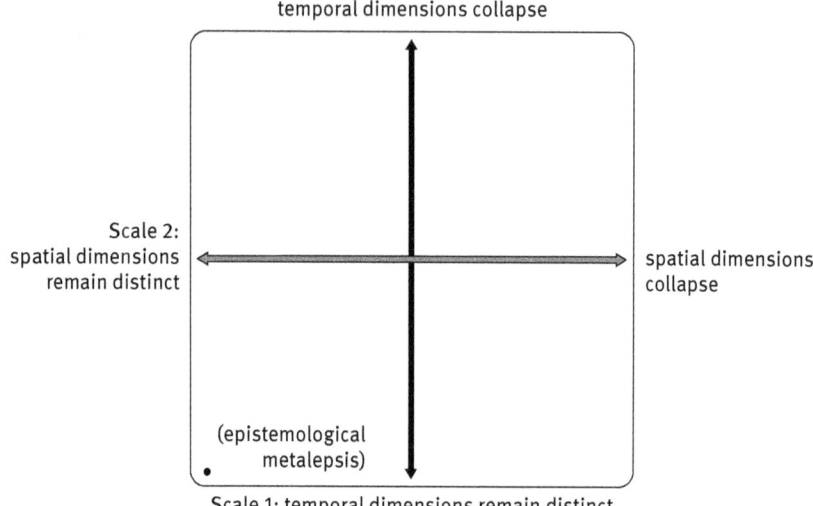

Figure 18: The Temporal and Spatial Dimensions of the Diegetic Levels in Epistemological Metalepsis

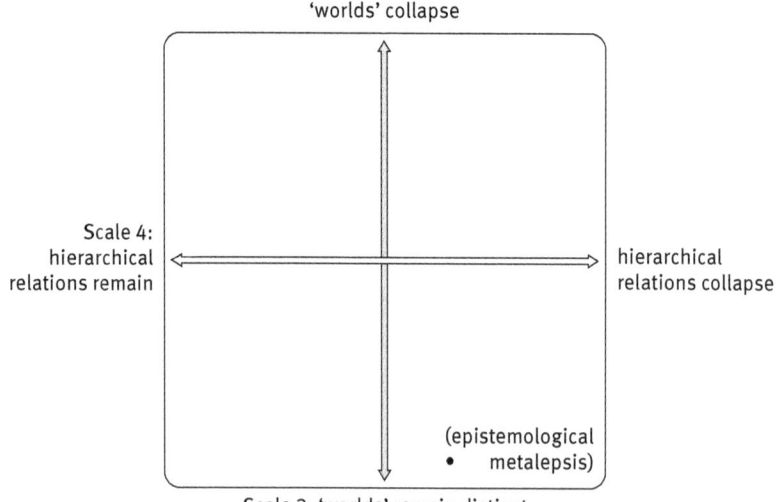

Figure 19: The 'Worlds' and Hierarchical Relations of the Diegetic Levels in Epistemological Metalepsis

What is denied about the properties of diegetic levels is not the spatiotemporal bifurcation instigated by acts of narrative representation but the hierarchical relation of the diegetic levels. Knowledge of the status as narrated entity is the prerogative of the creator of the narration – if represented entities display such knowledge, hierarchical relations between diegetic levels are denied. This, in turn, *implies* a more radical transgression (such as the ability to see or hear the domain of the signifier), which is, however, not realized in epistemological metalepsis.

Marie-Laure Ryan discusses an interesting example of epistemological metalepsis from the gameworld of *Super Mario Sunshine* (2002) in *Avatars of Story* (cf. 2006, 224–225). In this game, multifunction water cannon (F.L.U.D.D., Flash Liquidizer Ultra Dousing Device) with a water tank, two handles, and various nozzles allows Mario to clean dirty buildings, to hover and to spray water at enemies (among other things). When Mario first encounters F.L.U.D.D. on the ground of the Airstrip of the island "Isle Delfino," it introduces itself to Mario and then offers the player instructions with the help of a short video that demonstrates how to use and change the nozzles, etc. (it tells the player which buttons to push on the controller). Thus, the F.L.U.D.D. displays some 'knowledge' of being part of a GameCube game played by human beings with the help of a controller. Players do not have to pause the game to learn to operate the F.L.U.D.D. – this example of epistemological metalepsis does not negate the logic of diegetic universes but, as "an immersion-preserving device that integrates real-world discourse – the instructions of the game – into the real world" (Ryan 2006, 224), it only violates the hierarchical relation between the domain of the signified (diegesis) and the domain of the signifier (in this case, the extrafictional context in which the game is played).

2.2.4.1.2 Figurative Metalepsis II: Rhetorical Metalepsis

Marie-Laure Ryan has maintained that two basic categories can be distinguished in the usage of the term metalepsis: "(1) the rhetorical type, described by Gérard Genette, and (2) the ontological type, described by Brian McHale in conjunction with postmodern narrative" (2004, 441).[69] A classic example[70] of

---

[69] It should be noted that Genette's definition includes all the cases of rhetorical and ontological metalepses Ryan supplies. Ryan is aware of the fact that her distinction is a subdivision of Genette's model of metalepsis: "Genette also described cases that I regard as ontological [...], but he does not distinguish the two types" (2006, 247).

what Ryan would consider the first type can be found in *Tristram Shandy*'s chapter III/xxx, in which the narrator Tristram Shandy leaves Walter "upon the bed for half an hour" and uncle Toby "in his old fringed chair sitting beside him" in order to explain something else, thus highlighting the fictional character of his diegesis while playing with the double temporality of narrating time (*Erzählzeit*) and story time (*erzählte Zeit*). Ryan defines such transgressions in the following manner:

> Rhetorical metalepsis opens a small window that allows a quick glance across levels, but the window closes after a few sentences, and the operation ends up reasserting the existence of boundaries. This temporary breach of illusion does not threaten the basic structure of the narrative universe. In the rhetorical brand of metalepsis, the author may speak *about* her characters, presenting them as creations of her imagination rather than as autonomous human beings, but she doesn't speak *to* them, because they belong to another level of reality. (Ryan 2006, 207)

Thus, rhetorical metalepsis outlined by Ryan is a subtype of the narratological category developed by Genette and must be distinguished from the classical rhetorical trope. Fludernik builds her analysis of rhetorical metalepsis on what was at the time an unpublished paper Ryan gave at a conference[71] in November 2002 (cf. Fludernik 2003b, 397) and argues that 'rhetorical metalepsis' or 'discourse metalepsis' (Fludernik's terminological suggestion) is a frequently employed device that can be traced back to Sidney's *Old Arcadia* (cf. ibid., 387). Fludernik's analysis precisely delineates how rhetorical metalepsis defies representational logic in a synchronization of the narrating time and story time she refers to as "projected simultaneity" (ibid.). Among the examples Fludernik supplies is the following quote from *Tristram Shandy*:

> My mother, you must know,——but I have a fifty things more necessary to let you know first,—I have a hundred difficulties which I have promised to clear up, and a thousand distresses and domestic misadventures crowding in upon me thick and three-fold, one upon the neck of another,——[...] I have left my father lying across his bed, and my uncle Toby

---

70 Ryan cites a moment in Diderot's *Jacques le fataliste*, which is one of the examples supplied by Genette, as the paradigm of rhetorical metalepsis (cf. Ryan 2006, 206; Genette 1980, 234).

71 Fludernik (2003) makes reference to an – in 2003 still – unpublished draft of Ryan's article "Logique culturelle de la métalepse, ou la métalepse dans tous ses états," which – just like Genette's monograph *Métalepse* – grew out of the occasion of the international conference "La métalepse, aujourd'hui" (cf. Pier/Schaeffer 2005, 9) and which was published three years later in the collection of essays *Métalepses: Entorses au pacte de la representation* (2005) edited by John Pier and Jean-Marie Schaeffer. An earlier English version of this article was published under the title "Metaleptic Machines" in the journal *Semiotica* in 2004.

in his old fringed chair, sitting beside him, and promised I would go back to them in half an hour, and five and thirty minutes are lapsed already. (III.xxxviii)

The transgression of diegetic levels in this case consists in the fact "that the projected simultaneity metaphorically moves the narrator into the realm of the fictional world" (Fludernik 2003b, 387). It is the narrator who exclusively acknowledges (the creation of) this "projected simultaneity" of worlds that are logically and temporally distinct in conventional storytelling. In this case, the simultaneity could possibly be extended to include the implicit description of the narrative situation, which would be a third element – story, discourse and meta-discourse are all equally present tense – as the narrator seemingly inhabits different diegetic levels and records his failure to disentangle himself from the 'impossible' narrative situation he has created.

Following Nelles, Ryan and Fludernik, I define the rhetorical type of the narratological category as the 'temporary breach' in which the boundary is *implicitly* crossed by a narrator (or a similar entity in a fictive production context) who seemingly shares the diegesis of his fictional characters as if he had stepped onto the stage of a play. The distinguishing characteristic of rhetorical metalepsis is that the transgressive move is 'one sided,' insofar as the narrator 'joins' the diegesis, interrupting or commenting on the action without any physical or verbal interaction with the storyworld (characters do not acknowledge the narrator's or narratee's existence).[72] Less metaphorically, rhetorical metalepsis subjects the narrational act and that which is narrated to a single temporality. In other words, rhetorical metalepsis consists in the pretension of telling as if the telling were contemporaneous with the told. Ontological metalepses, on the other hand, involve reciprocal communication across diegetic levels, or a transgression of the boundary that is in a certain sense 'complete.' With the help of the scalar model of the denial of the diegetic prerequisites, rhetorical metalepses can be visualized in the following manner:

---

[72] Monika Fludernik has pointed out that Genette has compared this type of metalepsis to a metaphoric Gygean ring – "a figure that Genette borrows from Théophile Gautier – that allows narrator and narratee to be present but invisible on the scene" (2003b, 383).

90 — Framing the Structure of Narrative Metalepsis

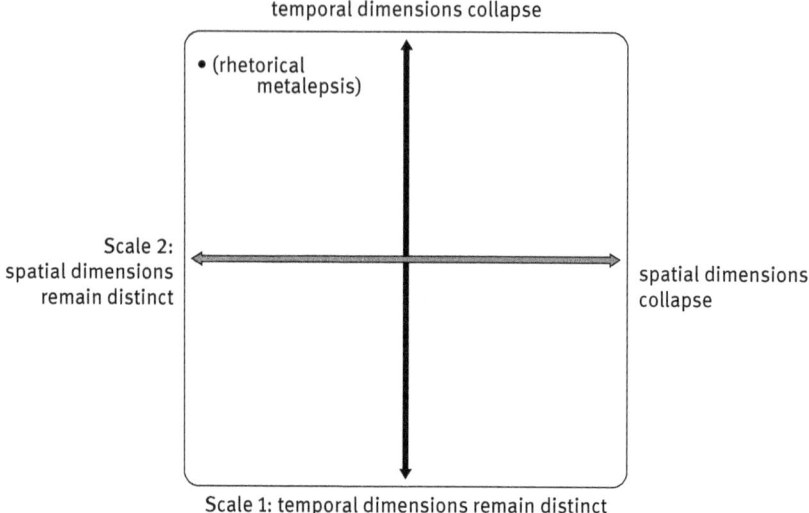

Figure 20: The Temporal and Spatial Dimensions of the Diegetic Levels in Rhetorical Metalepsis

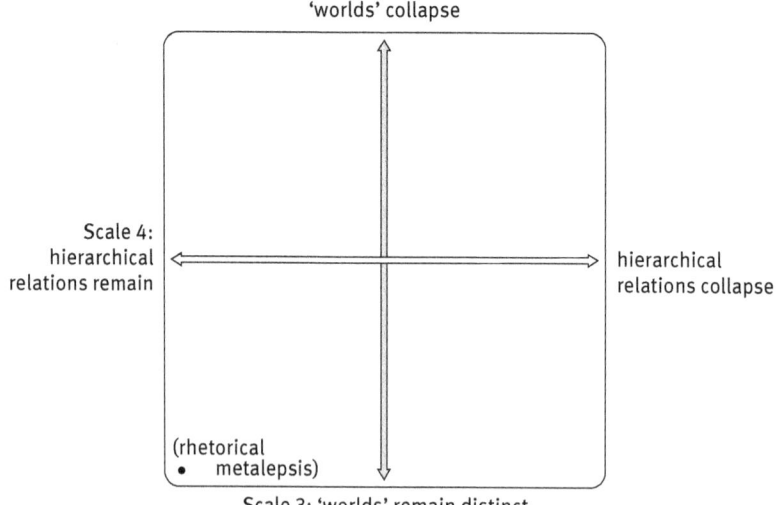

Figure 21: The 'Worlds' and Hierarchical Relations of the Diegetic Levels in Rhetorical Metalepsis

Neither the holistically structured networks of meaning and relatedness (Scale 3), which coincide with the diegetic levels, nor the hierarchical relations between the diegetic universes (Scale 4) are negated by rhetorical metalepsis. Yet this "temporary sharing of a common level" (Nelles 1997, 154) may in some instances involve or imply the spatial dimensions of the domain of the signified as well. I consider the following example in which the heterodiegetic narrator of Henry Fielding's *Tom Jones* (1749) addresses the reader in Chapter IV of Book I as an example of rhetorical metalepsis: "Reader, take care. I have unadvisedly led thee to the top of as high a hill as Mr Allworthy's, and how to get thee down without breaking thy neck, I do not well know. However, let us e'en venture to slide down together; for Miss Bridget rings her bell, and Mr Allworthy is summoned to breakfast, where I must attend, and, if you please, shall be glad of your company."[73] I would argue that this is still very much an implied transgression (even though transitions between rhetorical and ontological metalepses are fluid), as the narrator pretends to guide the reader invisibly through the physical surroundings which his narration creates – and can be visualized thus:

---

[73] A shorter version of this quote is used by Bernd Häsner as his first example of metaleptic transgressions (cf. 2005, 1).

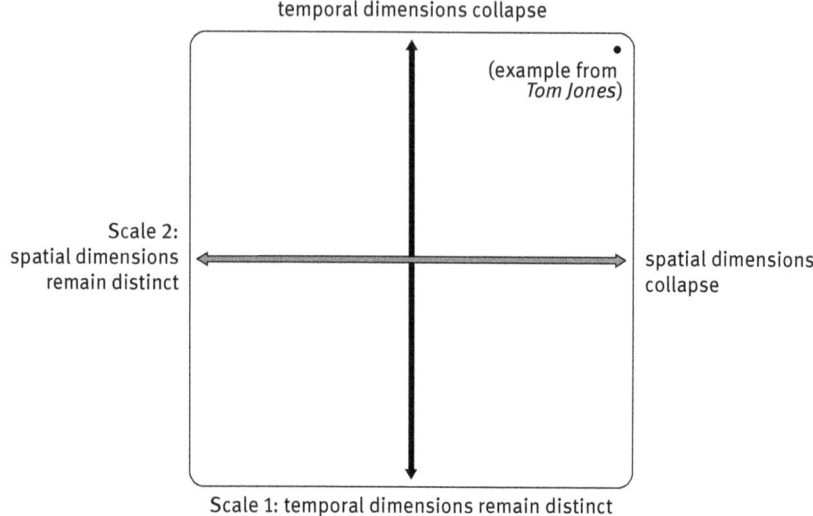

Figure 22: The Temporal and Spatial Dimensions of the Diegetic Levels in Rhetorical Metalepsis (Example from Book I, Chapter IV from Henry Fielding's Tom Jones)

Apart from this 'projected simultaneity' and 'projected shared space,' the world of the extradiegetic readers and the world of Tom Jones do not interact physically, but remain distinct (no character acknowledges the narrator's existence). Thus – and this is characteristic of all rhetorical metalepses – the worlds (i.e. holistically structured networks of meaning and relatedness) that coincide with the diegetic levels and their hierarchical relation remain undisturbed: the world of the telling and the world of the told remain separate, apart from the *projection* of a shared space and a shared time.

As outlined above, Ryan's model of metalepsis additionally discriminates the qualitative characteristics of two kinds of boundaries (illocutionary and ontological) that can be metaleptically crossed, a distinction that serves as the (formal) foundation of rhetorical and ontological metalepses respectively. This contrasts sharply with Genette, who in his initial (1972) definition delineates the type of boundary that can be violated by metalepsis as one that is generated by the narrative act of each narrator (whether extra- or intradiegetic), rather than being qualitatively modified by the status (fictional or non-fictional) of the story. Here, in the example from *Tom Jones*, the heterodiegetic narrative act explicitly creates the fictive world of Tom Jones, Allworthy and Sophia. According to Ryan, rhetorical metalepses negate only 'illocutionary' boundaries – in this example, however, (what could be classified as) a rhetorical metalepsis negates the boundary Ryan terms 'ontological.' Thus, the distinction between 'illocutionary' and 'ontological' boundaries (if it can be made) does not always coincide with the type of transgression Ryan assigns to those boundaries.

Rhetorical metalepsis is often considered less transgressive than ontological metalepsis, "since as a mere discursive effect, and one that is highly conventionalized at that, this device does not seriously impair the logic of a representation" (Wolf 2009b, 53). Yet not all rhetorical metalepses are without radical effects. In the example cited above in Chapter III/xxxviii of *Tristram Shandy*, the very *act* of narration that creates the 'world' of Tristram's father and marks its 'boundary,' places the world of narrative mediation (the world in which Tristram narrates) on the same temporal plane. Subjected to one temporality, the narrated world meets the world in which that narrative world is told. The temporal deixis, which simultaneously refers to the worlds in which and of which the narrator tells, collapses the distinction between the diegetic and the extradiegetic level, insofar as the diegetic and extradiegetic relations of temporality are arrayed relative to *one* frame of reference. As the reader is confronted in this manner with the problem of multiple duration in the narrative situation, he or she becomes aware of the conventional assumptions guiding the hermeneutic dialogue with narrative texts. Usually, Genette argues, "the fictive narrating [...] is considered to have no duration; or, more exactly, everything takes place as if the question of its duration had no relevance"[74] (1980, 222). The duration of Tristram's narration is often highly and humorously relevant. One potential effect of rhetorical metalepsis is thus a foregrounding of hermeneutic assumptions that shape the basic make-up of a given narrative situation.

2.2.4.2 'The Marked Case': Ontological Metalepsis

Ontological metalepsis is characterized by Ryan as an "interpenetration, or mutual contamination" (2006, 207) of diegetic universes. Werner Wolf has defined ontological metalepsis as "the paradoxical, yet seemingly actual, physical transgression of a logical or ontological border between two levels/worlds by a character or object" (2009b, 53). I follow these accounts with the addition, in line with the model of metaleptic transgression proposed above, that the violation of pragmatic rules (which govern the construction of the hierarchical relation(s) of the worlds instigated and connected by narrational acts) is a *necessary*

---

[74] Gérard Genette cites *Tristram Shandy* as one of the very few exceptions to this general rule (cf. 1980, 222).

condition in a definition of metalepsis – metalepsis violates the representational logic of the signs that create, connect and separate diegetic levels. Ontological metalepsis thus designates the narrative phenomenon which, in paradoxical violation of representational logic, triggers the construction of a narrator, existent, event or utterance that 'literally' moves across this very 'boundary,' or fundamentally negates the relation of the domains of signifier/signified instigated by the signs.

2.2.4.2.1 Immersive Metalepsis

Immersive metalepsis designates the narrative phenomenon which triggers the construction of a narrator, existent, event or utterance that 'literally' moves from the domain of the signified to the domain of the signifier (or vice versa) in a negation of the logic of the act of narrative representation. The notion of immersion is here not used to evoke the 'willing suspension of disbelief' of narrative addressees, but to express the fact that ontological metalepses *literally* place narrative entities in a diegetic universe to which they do not 'belong.' In Woody Allen's short story "The Kugelmass Episode" (1980), the diegetic character Kugelmass is in this sense immersed (literally placed) in the metadiegetic storyworld of a fictional novel and can walk in that world, talk to its characters and even sleep with that novel's heroine (and permanently ends up in the 'metadiegesis' of a vocabulary book). 'Immersion' here thus refers to the direct experience of a state of affairs from the perspective of the narrative entity that 'performs' or 'suffers' the metaleptic movement, an experience that many realist narratives seek to emulate but can never actually create: the unmediated experience of diegetic universes inaccessible to representational logic. In contrast to figurative metalepsis, the transgression is 'complete' and sometimes permanent, as in the "The Kugelmass Episode" by Woody Allen.

Fludernik has influentially distinguished the Genettian account of metalepsis into four types that integrate Ryan's differentiation between rhetorical and ontological metalepses. According to her, four kinds of transgressive acts can (following Genette) be distinguished:

> Type 1 (Virgil has Dido die): "authorial" metalepsis
> Type 2 (narrator moves into story with narratee): ontological metalepsis 1: narratorial metalepsis
> Type 3 (narratee/protagonist exchange): ontological metalepsis 2: lectorial metalepsis
> Type 4 (while-formula): rhetorical metalepsis or discourse metalepsis
> (Fludernik 2003b, 389)

While most narratologists follow the distinction between rhetorical metalepsis and ontological metalepsis, the distinction between narratorial and lectorial metalepsis has not been taken up again. In what follows, I propose a distinction between three kinds of immersive transgression that draw on Fludernik's distinction between narratorial and lectorial metalepses. Moreover, type 1 in the typology is a highly problematical case that I consider to have very limited metaleptic potential, and which is, therefore, not considered here as a distinct kind of metalepsis. According to Fludernik, 'authorial metalepsis' is paradigmatically captured by the narrator in *Jacques le fataliste*: "What would prevent *me from getting the Master married and making him a cuckold*?" (Diderot, qtd. in Genette 1980, 234). This can be interpreted as a violation of the conventional pretence that what the discourse is relating is the literal truth (and consequently not attributable to the narrator). Fludernik asserts that "the transgression of narrative levels [in authorial metalepsis] occurs in a distancing from the truth-related narrative illusion" (2003b, 384). Yet neither Fludernik nor Genette (who originally supplied the quote in *Narrative Discourse*) specify how exactly such "distancing" might involve various diegetic levels and their transgression. The fact that in such cases "the story becomes a function of narratorial discourse, [and] its separate existence (and truth) are denied" (ibid., 388) hardly constitutes a violation of the logic of diegetic levels. This is rather a metafictional comment that lays bare, from the perspective of the narrator, the fictional narrative situation. This is connected to the narrative paradox that consists in the relationship of tension between the story recounted by an act of narration and the act of narration that generates the story (cf. Abbott 2005, 535).[75]

1. First Person and Third Person Metalepsis (Narratorial Metalepsis)

Fludernik cites Woody Allen's "The Kugelmass Episode" as an example of the kind of transgression she terms 'narratorial' (cf. 2003b, 384): "The second type of metalepsis that Genette proposes consists in the literal move of the narrator to a lower narrative level of embedded storyworld, or of a character to a lower (intra)diegetic level" (ibid.). Fludernik's account is firmly situated in the literary tradition of Genette's *Narrative Discourse*. Loosely following this definition of a

---

[75] Genette first dubbed this particular quote narrative metalepsis and characterized it as an "intrusion" of the extradiegetic narrator into the diegesis (cf. 1980, 234). This seems to imply that any story that lays bare its fictionality is metaleptic (and is thus a first version of Genette's later argument [2004] that all fiction is metaleptic). Yet I would argue that it makes more sense to distinguish metaleptic fictions from non-metaleptic fictions. Even if a narrator or character makes up a story, that story is still in a certain sense inaccessible: the narrator can change the events in the fictional storyworld but cannot be physically present in it as a character without a metaleptic violation.

metaleptic type, I would like to offer terms that are transmedially applicable and to distinguish the implied positions of characters and narrators: first person metalepsis and third person metalepsis separate the position from which the metaleptic 'immersion' is presented. If (character-)narrators mediate the immersive metaleptic transgression they undergo or perform, then this represents an instance of first person metalepsis. A filmic equivalent is the subjective shot that shows the immersion of the metaleptic experience from the perspective of the diegetic characters who metaleptically travel to a different diegetic level. An example for this are the diegetic characters in *Being John Malkovich* (1999), who travel the portal into Malkovich's mind and whose experience is presented with subjective shots. The character Craig is able to control Malkovich and 'narrate' his diegetic existence (which, once controlled by a diegetic character, could be argued to have attained a metadiegetic status). In first person metalepsis, the metaleptic transgression is mediated by (or presented from the position of) the one who transgresses the boundary between the domains of the signifier/signified: An example of first person metalepsis is the following excerpt from *The Eyre Affair* (2001) – here, the autodiegetic narrator Thursday Next relates her first metaleptic visit to *Jane Eyre*, which takes place while a Japanese tourist is reading excerpts of the novel:

> I closed my eyes and a thin chill suddenly filled the air around me. The tourist's voice was clear now, as though speaking in the open air, and when I opened my eyes the museum had gone. In its place was a country lane of another place entirely. It was a fine winter's evening and the sun was just dipping below the horizon. [...] As I looked about I could see that I was not alone. Barely ten feet away a young woman, dressed in a cloak and bonnet, was sitting on a stile watching the moon that had just risen behind us. (2001, 66)

This is an instance of immersive first-person metalepsis ('metaleptic immersion from the inside') in which the metaleptic 'immersion' is presented from the position of the character-narrator who crosses the boundary.

In the very same novel, the narrator Thursday Next recounts the arrival of Mr Briggs, a character from the metadiegetic *Jane Eyre*, at the diegetic wedding ceremony of Landen, the man she loves:

> 'The marriage cannot go on: I declare the existence of an impediment!'
> One hundred and fifty heads turned to see who the speaker was. [...] I stared at Landen, who looked confused at the turn of events. Was he married already? I couldn't believe it. I looked back at the speaker and my heart missed a beat. It was Mr Briggs, the solicitor I had last seen in the church at Thornfield! [...]
> 'What is the nature of this impediment? Perhaps it may be got over – explained away?'
> 'Hardly,' was the answer. 'I have called it insuperable and I speak advisedly. It consists simply of a previous marriage.' (Ibid., 352–353)

Here, Thursday Next narrates how Mr. Briggs (John Eyre's attorney in *Jane Eyre*) prevents Daisy's bigamous (and diegetic) marriage to Landen, a metaleptic mirroring of the events in the metadiegetic storyworld of *Jane Eyre* (where Mr. Briggs prevents Jane's bigamous marriage to Rochester). This is an instance of third person metalepsis ('metaleptic immersion from the outside'). Immersive third-person metalepsis designates those metalepses in which the entities (characters, objects and other existents) which transgress the boundary between the domains of the signifier/signified are presented from a vantage point that is distinct from the entity in question (and, in line with the grammatical category, does not address that entity). The individual or object metaleptically immersed is neither addressee of the act of (narrative) representation nor the creator of the representation.

All immersive metalepses imply a 'movement' that has a certain direction: both first- and third-person metalepses may move 'upwards' (ascending metalepsis) or 'downwards' (descending metalepsis) in the hierarchy of diegetic universes.[76] While Thursday Next moves from the diegesis into the metadiegesis in the first example (an instance of what I propose to call descending first-person metalepsis), she narrates Mr. Briggs' movement from the metadiegesis into the diegesis in the second example (an instance of ascending third-person metalepsis). The often quoted example of "The Kugelmass Episode" presents ascending and descending third-person metalepses: Kugelmass' literal descent into the metadiegetic storyworld of *Madame Bovary* is mirrored by Madame Bovary's week in the diegesis originally inhabited by Kugelmass (an instance of ascending third person metalepsis).

2. Second Person Metalepsis (Lectorial Metalepsis)

Lectorial or second person metalepsis designates those transgressions in which a protagonist (in second-person fiction) or the narratee, addressed by narrative *you*, moves from one diegetic level to another. This metaleptic type is instigated by the consequences and implications of the direct address of narratees or viewers. Such metalepses can attain additional complexity from one of the effects narrative *you* can produce – which has been described by David Herman as "ontological hesitation" (2002, 338): Narrative *you* "can induce hesitation be-

---

[76] William Nelles (1997, 152–157) first offered this distinction when he argued that the 'marked case' of metalepsis (ontological metalepsis) can be subdivided in the following manner: the transgression can result in a movement from the embedding narrative to the embedded ("intrametalepsis") or from the embedded narrative to the embedding ("extrametalepsis"). Debra Malina has basically reiterated that distinction with the terms "inward" and "outward" metalepses (cf. 2002, 46–50). More recently, Alber and Bell (2012, 172–173) have done the same with the terms 'descending' and 'ascending' metalepses.

tween reference to entities, situations, and events internal to the storyworld and events external to the storyworld" (ibid.). This hesitation is often induced by the ambiguous reference of narrative *you* that creates metaleptic potential. The notion of second person metalepsis is indebted to Fludernik's account of lectorial metalepsis:

> Genette's third type of metalepsis implicates the narratee on the story level or the protagonist as narratee on a superior (discourse) level. For instance, in Michel de Pure's seventeenth-century novel *La Pretieuse ou le mystere des ruelles*, [...] an embedded narrative contains characters who are also the narratees listening to the narration of this embedded tale [...]. This implication of the narratee on the story level or the raising of a character from an embedded tale onto the superior (usually extradiegetic) plane correlates with two strategies commonly employed in second-person fiction. Either the addressee, first conceived of as extradiegetic, turns out to be a character (as in Italo Calvino's *If on a Winter's Night a Traveller*), or the second-person narrative operates by address to a story-internal recipient who then turns out to have some existential link with the extradiegetic story level as well. (Fludernik 2003b, 385)

Simplifying matters, I propose to confine the term second person (or lectorial) metalepsis to those transgressions in which the individual or being *addressed* moves across the boundary between the domains of the signified and the domain of the signifier. The 'ontological hesitation' potentially induced by the use of narrative *you* often suggests more than one context in which the 'you' being addressed is located (or, perhaps more accurately, in which reader, listeners or viewers locate the addressed entity/being; a constructive effort which may imply the 'real' world). A particularly pertinent example of what I propose to call second-person metalepsis has been analyzed by Jeff Thoss (2011b, 2015) and Karin Kukkonen (2011a). Issue 19 of the comic book *Animal Man* by Grant Morrison (1988–1990) contains the hero's peyote trip which induces Animal Man's ability to return the reader's gaze and look at those who are reading the comic book. A reader or readers are the addressee of the diegetic character's words and the bearer of the look:

Figure 23: Morrison 2003, no pagination

This is, in more than one way, a borderline case. Karin Kukkonen considers it a rhetorical metalepsis (cf. 2011a, 223) in which the diegetic character does not physically leave the storyworld. However, I would argue that this splash page offers more radical readings as well. If the panel conventionally opens a window into the storyworld of a comic book, this particular 'window' has radically changed, as Animal Man stands in the same spatiotemporal domain as his 'readers.' Since there are other instances in this comic book where Animal Man meets his fictive creator 'Grant Morrison' in the world in which the comic book is created (cf. Thoss 2011b, 195–200 and Thoss 2015, 161–175), this page could be read as the metaleptic collapse of extradiegesis (fictive context of production) and diegesis. And since the combination of deictic reference and image (and that image's context) in a sense *create* its metaleptic referent, this could be interpreted as an instance of immersive (descending) second person metalepsis –

in which fictive readers have entered the domain of the signified (the storyworld of Animal Man).

Yet – and this is typical for second-person metalepses (or, more precisely, passages with such potential) – there are other possibilities of meaning. The aforementioned example could be seen not only as rhetorical (the signs imply a figurative transgression, but the diegetic universes remain distinct), epistemological (Animal Man knows that he is narrated but cannot literally see his readers), or ontological. It could also be seen as not constituting a metaleptic transgression at all (Animal Man imagines he can see readers, but he is hallucinating). Moreover, as an immersive metalepsis, it could be seen as first-person metalepsis (Animal Man narrates his own immersion in the world in which he is created), second-person (Animal Man addresses the being that has moved from one diegetic universe to another), or third-person (the fictive creator 'Grant Morrison' creates an act of representation that presents Animal Man's immersion in the extradiegesis). Most importantly, if it is considered a second-person metalepsis, this instance offers 'real' readers in the extrafictional world the possibility to construct themselves as the ones who are addressed by the diegetic character Animal Man. Even though such a metaleptic implication of the 'real' world has distinct limitations (Animal Man cannot be touched), this is the radical game that potential second-person metalepses often imply or suggest.

2.2.4.2.2 Recursive Metalepsis

Not all fundamental negations of the relation of the domains of signifier and signified are the result of the immersion of single entities or beings that travel across the 'boundary' separating these domains. I propose the term 'recursive metalepsis' for those transgressions that reiterate the higher-order and/or lower-order domains in a violation of (representational) logic, or make the distinction between higher-order and lower-order domains impossible – i.e. transgressions of the relation between domains (signifying or signified) that deny the representational logic of acts of (narrative) representation. The prerequisite for the *literal* transgressive recursion is the iterative relation of stories within stories (or representations within representations). Recursive metalepses resemble Hofstadter's 'strange loops' and 'tangled hierarchies,' which "[occur] when what you presume are clear hierarchical levels take you by surprise and fold back in a hierarchy violating-way" (Hofstadter 1979, 391).[77] Following Klimek's (2010, 2011) outline of what she terms complex forms of metalepsis, which she further distinguishes into 'Moebius strip stories' and 'tangled heterarchies' (cf. 2011, 33–37), I differentiate three types of recursive metalepsis: the two offered by Klimek, as well as a third that I propose to term 'inversive metalepsis.'

Moebius strip stories are metaleptic because they imply a particular 'strange loop,' where the storyworld is created by an act of narrative representation situated within the storyworld it generates.[78] André Gide's *The Counterfeiters* (1925) contains a novel within a novel, a metadiegesis called '*The Counterfeiters*' (written by the diegetic character Édouard). This metadiegetic novel suggests that the diegetic exegesis (which is in this case identical with the diegesis) is the world in which the act of narrative representation that creates the diegesis is situated – thus, the world of the told constitutes the world of the telling (and vice versa):

---

[77] Brian McHale was the first to analyse metalepsis as a 'strange loop' or 'tangled hierarchy' in his *Postmodernist Fiction* (1987). Among others, Werner Wolf (1993) and Marie-Laure Ryan (2006) followed suit. However, in contrast to McHale, neither Wolf nor Ryan equate metalepsis and 'strange loops.'

[78] Sonja Klimek's account is indebted to Werner Wolf (cf. Klimek 2011, 33 and Wolf 1993, 361), who was the first to consider Moebius strip stories as complex metalepses.

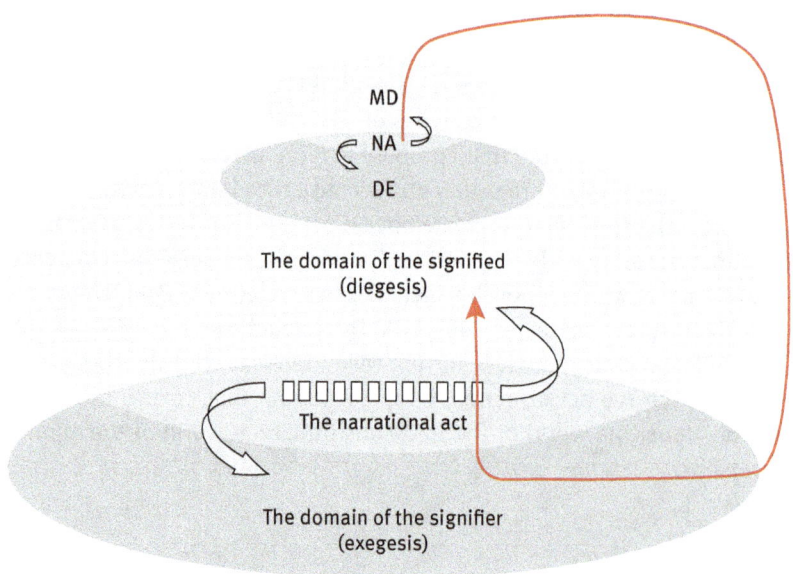

Figure 24: Recursive Metalepsis I: Moebius Strip Metalepsis

Figure 24 offers a possible visualization of Moebius strip metalepsis. 'DE' stands for diegetic exegesis, 'NA' for the diegetic narrational act, and 'MD' for metadiegesis. Herman argues in his short analysis of Gide's *The Counterfeiters* that "one of the characters writes a novel, that is, as it turns out, the narrative of *The Counterfeiters* itself. Here the text enables interpreters to world the story as one that contains Gide's own novel – thereby unworlding, at another level (and in a most M. C. Escher-like fashion), this very narrative" (2013, 155). Herman calls this "the limit case of metalepsis" (ibid.) and argues that, in examples such as this, metalepsis and *mise en abyme* overlap. He quotes the definition from Prince, who defines *mise en abyme* as "a textual part reduplicating, reflecting, or mirroring (one or more than one aspect of) the textual whole" (Prince 2003, 53). It should be added that the metaleptic potential of Moebius strip metalepsis relies on the suggestion that the narrative creates an 'M. C. Escher-like' circularity – a mere reflection or mirroring of the events of the higher-order narrative universe will presumably not induce interpreters to construct a transgression of the narrative logic of acts of narration (the play within a play in *Hamlet*, I would argue, has no metaleptic potential). Only the *literal* recursion (or, with less metaleptic potential, the suggestion of a literal recursion) makes a narrative passage an example of Moebius strip metalepsis. Reading Gide's novel as a metaleptic narrative thus presupposes the 'impossible' implications that the diegesis (the world in which Édouard writes) is created by the narrative act of representation that is situated in the diegesis and that the metadiegesis constitutes the diegesis in which it comes into being. In other words, the diegesis creates the metadiegesis, the metadiegesis creates the diegesis.[79]

The metaleptic phenomenon Klimek terms 'tangled heterarchy' is, while related to Moebius strip metalepsis, more complex and more radical, as it

> completely destroys the hierarchical relationships between the different levels of story and storytelling within fictional texts. I use the term "tangled heterarchy" for situations in which a single diegetic level becomes at the same time the result of a higher, representing level and the reason for representation of this higher level. McHale (1987: 120) took the term "heterarchy" from information science, where it is used to indicate "a multi-level structure in which there is no single 'highest level.' (2011, 34)

In contrast to Moebius strip, the tangled heterarchy does not suggest the infinite recursion of two mirrors that are exactly parallel with each other, but denies the notion of a hierarchy in more complex fashion. Tangled heterarchies do not recursively duplicate the higher or lower-order diegetic level or universe *in toto*. The *literal* recursion of tangled heterarchies involves the combination of *parts* of diegetic universes (and their characteristics) that hierarchically belong to higher-order and lower-order domains in a diegetic universe that can no longer be assigned a place in a hierarchy. In other words, 'tangled heterarchy' is used for acts of representation that create domains that are at the same time both higher-order and lower-order.

Klimek's example (cf. 2011, 35–37) shows that this is easier to illustrate than define: *The Land of Laughs* (1980) by Jonathan Carroll displays the metaleptic structure of a tangled heterarchy. The homodiegetic narrator Thomas Abbey narrates the fantastic occurrences in a town called Galen, the hometown of the diegetic Marshall France, a famous writer of fantasy fiction (among the books France wrote is '*The Land of Laughs*,' a potential Moebius strip metalepsis). Thomas Abbey visits Galen to write the biography of France, who is dead. This can be described as a basic structural set-up in which the worlds of the telling (Abbey's visit to Galen) and the told (the biography, the metadiegetic novels written by France) are unambiguously distinct. However, this is where *The Land of Laughs* supplies many metaleptic twists. First of all, Galen is filled with char-

---

[79] There are some indications in the novel, however, that this is not the case, such as, for instance, the fact that Édouard chooses not to include the death of Boris in his novel, or occasional hints that the novel will never be written.

acters that have metaleptically ascended from the metadiegetic novels by France (instances of immersive third person metalepses). Secondly, as France's daughter tells Thomas Abbey, France wrote that, after his death, his biographer would come to recreate him (just as his characters, he would be able to metaleptically enter diegetic Galen from his biography). Thirdly, Thomas Abbey's biography, the novel implies, recreates the diegetic Marshall France. This can be visualized in the following manner:

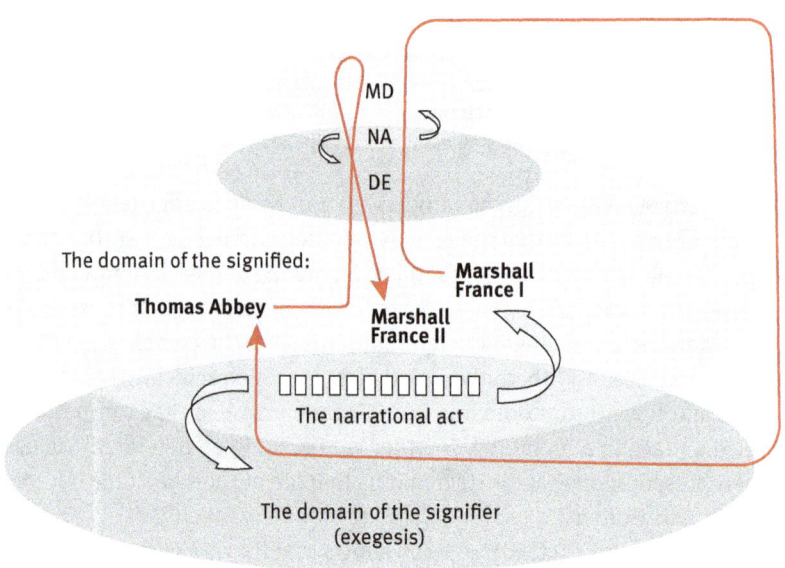

Figure 25: Recursive Metalepsis II: A Tangled Heterarchy in Jonathan Carroll's *The Land of Laughs*

The homodiegetic narrator Thomas Abbey narrates how the diegetic Thomas Abbey writes the metadiegetic biography of the dead author Marshall France in Galen. When this biography reaches the point where the metadiegetic France arrives in Galen, the novel suggests, France arrives in diegetic Galen as well (an instance of immersive third-person metalepsis). After his arrival in Galen, France writes fantasy novels which create what they purport to represent (diegetic Galen is filled with metadiegetic characters). Before his death, he writes of his biographer, who writes a biography that recreates/resurrects Marshall France. France's act of narrative representation creates Abbey, whose act of narrative representation creates France. Accordingly, Abbey's homodiegetic narrative act can be seen as the metadiegetic narrative act (within a metadiegetic story written by France) that creates the meta-metadiegesis of the storyworld that creates the diegetic France (consequently, the exegesis implied by Abbey's narrative act becomes a diegetic exegesis). Yet at the same time, France's act of narration is dependent upon the lower-order narrative that recreates him – higher-order and lower-order diegetic levels have metaleptically merged. In this structure, each level is the higher-order *and* lower-order level of the preceding (higher-order) level. Tangled hierarchies designate the narrative structures that contain self-similar objects in terms of hierarchical relation: they consist of diegetic universes that are exactly similar to a part of themselves, in the sense that they are hierarchically superior and dependent at the same time. Tangled hierarchies contain oscillating hierarchies that have no single highest-order diegetic level.

I propose the term 'inversive metalepsis' for those rare transgressions in which the hierarchical relation of two diegetic universes that are connected by an act of narrative representation is unambiguously reversed. The metaleptic configuration of the short story "Tlön, Uqbar, Orbis Tertius" by Jorge Luis Borges (1964 [1962]) consists in an exchange of the metadiegesis and the 'world' of the diegesis/exegesis (and thus in an inversion of their original hierarchical relation) – but not in a mutual contamination of levels:

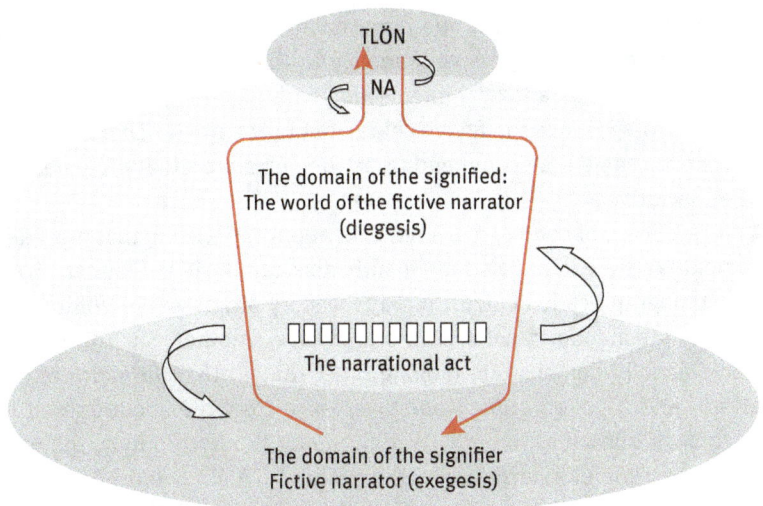

Figure 26: Recursive Metalepsis III: Inversive Metalepsis in J. L. Borges' "Tlön, Uqbar, Orbis Tertius"

A secret society invents the world of Tlön, an invention that ultimately replaces the diegetic reality of the short story: "The contact and habit of Tlön have disintegrated this world. Enchanted by its rigour, humanity forgets over and again that it is the rigour of chess masters, not of angels. [...] English and French and mere Spanish will disappear from the globe. The world will be Tlön" (Borges 1964 [1962], 18). This prediction of the narrator implies that the 'reality' in which the homodiegetic narrator narrates (exegesis) and of which the narrator tells (diegesis) is ultimately and fundamentally replaced by the metadiegetic invention of a world called 'Tlön.' The narrator's translation of Browne's *Urn Burial* with which the short story ends relegates the 'reality' in which he narrates to the position of a diegetic fiction in the exegesis that constitutes 'Tlön.'

It should be added that I do not claim that the three types outlined above exhaust all possibilities of recursive metalepsis. As the following example demonstrates, the potential for literal (and thus metaleptic) recursion can be found in many borderline cases. I have argued above that the following sentence by the narrator in *Jacques le fataliste* has little or no metaleptic potential (despite the fact that Genette quotes this as an example of metalepsis): "What would prevent me from *getting the Master married* and *making him a cuckold*?" (Diderot, qtd. in Genette 1980, 234). Fludernik considers this an instance of what she terms 'authorial metalepsis' in which "the story becomes a function of narratorial discourse, [and] its separate existence (and truth) are denied" (Fludernik 2003b, 388). I have argued above, however, that such a denial does not involve the transgression of the representational logic of acts of narration. There is, however, a transgressive tendency in this and similar examples that seems to be due to a paradoxical intersection with metaleptic recursion. For the narrator who foregrounds the fictive character of his story (as Diderot's narrator above) is at the same time commenting on the narrative situation generated by his or her narrative act.

A narrator can, of course, make remarks about the writing that precedes the metafictional comment, as Tristram Shandy does famously in Chapter VI/xl – in which he typographically depicts the way the story progresses in Volumes I–V – without any metaleptic transfer from one level to another. Such metafictional comments usually demonstrate (among other things) that the narrator cannot be narrator and narrated *at the same time*, since "to write about oneself is implicitly to posit oneself as 'other'" (Waugh 1994, 135). Accordingly, the narrator referred to by Diderot's narrator (by the pronoun "me") could be analysed as belonging to the diegetic level as the 'other' posited by the narrator's self-observation. Whenever a narrator fictionalizes his or her own narration, he or she may be argued to be the extradiegetic narrating instance generating the fictionalized narrative act, and thus distinct from the narrator of that fictionalized act, which belongs to the diegetic level.[80]

But the narrator addressed (by the pronoun "me") by the narratorial comment above is in a certain sense identical with the narrator whose narrative act generates the sentence, insofar as that comment's diegetic narrative act could be interpreted as coinciding with the 'now' of the extradiegetic narrative act ('what would prevent me *right now*?'). Since there is no temporal hiatus between the (implicitly) self-reflexive narrative comment and the narration to which it refers, this sentence could be interpreted as commenting on itself ('I am writing fiction *right now*'), without positing its narrative situation as 'other.' In such moments, the reader encounters a narrative situation that enacts the impossibility of what could be termed the self-reflexive paradox:

> Observation and description presupposes a *difference* between the observer/describer and his or her object; but *self*-description intentionally negates this difference [...] From beginning to end self-description [...] is concerned with this problem, which can be apprehended only as paradoxical (and hence as demanding concealment).[81]

The transgression of diegetic levels in such instances as in Diderot's above could be attributed to the attempt to negate this difference. As the narrator – at least implicitly – comments on the narration in the very moment it comes into being, he is simultaneously the observer and the observed, and hence belongs to two distinct diegetic levels. Since this is a logical impossibility, the metaleptic tendency is a matter of degree and can only be approximated by the following formula: the closer the narrated narration is to the narration with regard to time, the more metaleptic the narrative situation becomes. Thus, the limited transgressive potential in Fludernik's (and Genette's) example of authorial metalepsis is not due to the diminution or devaluation of the story told but to the fact that narrator and narrative act seem to have left the extradiegetic level – *and* to have remained on that level at the same time.

---

80 Alternatively, this structure could be moved one level in the direction of the extratextual author. As the narratorial discourse – at least implicitly – comments on itself, it has logically left the extradiegesis and must be located at a vantage point from which self-observation is possible (a place that could be termed extra-extradiegesis).
81 "Beobachten und Beschreiben setzt eine *Differenz* voraus zwischen dem Beobachter/Beschreiber und seinem Gegenstand; aber die Absicht der *Selbst*beschreibung negiert genau diese Differenz [...] Von Anfang bis Ende hat die Selbstbeschreibung [...] es mit diesem nur als Paradoxie beobachtbaren (und daher zu verdeckenden) Problem zu tun." (Luhmann 1995, 487–488; translated by Joseph Swann).

The key to the metaleptically recursive potential of such passages is the impossible simultaneity of levels that according to representational logic have to be kept apart by a temporal hiatus. Such borderline cases show, on the one hand, that recursive metalepsis is a potential that derives from the iterative relation of stories within stories (or representations within representations). Since acts of representation are situated, and since the situatedness of a single act of representation can be manifold, the context of the production of the signs can be ambiguous. On the other hand, borderline cases may demonstrate that metaleptic types have points of intersection, as a single entity (a narrator) may suggest a domain (the extradiegesis in which the act of narration is situated), and a reference to a domain may suggest a single entity. In the short story "Tlön, Uqbar, Orbis Tertius" by Borges, the first metaleptic occurrence is the mysterious appearance of an object from Tlön, which is made of a material that originally does not exist in the world in which the narrator narrates. In isolation, this is an instance of immersive metalepsis that foreshadows the fundamental exchange of the domains of the signifier/signified which I propose to term 'recursive metalepsis.' While the term 'immersive metalepsis' describes those transgressions in which an existent from the domain of the signified literally becomes part of the domain of the signifier or vice versa, 'recursive metalepsis' refers to violations of the 'boundary' between the domains of the signifier/signified that exchange the domains involved – or fundamentally deny their hierarchical and logical relation. As the mysterious object from Tlön may exemplify, one kind of metalepsis may suggest the other.

2.2.5 Metaleptic Effects

The preceding sections have presented the attempt to trace metaleptic form and supply models of metaleptic narrative structure. This sub-chapter, in contrast, considers some of the potential effects metaleptic narrative structure can elicit. Such an endeavour rests on the assumption that the formal properties of narrative can be distinguished and meaningfully correlated with potential functions. Roy Sommer's (2000) often quoted differentiation between the various aspects of what is understood by functional properties of narrative is based on the recognition of the multitude of meanings covered by the term 'function.' He distinguishes the 'intended effect' of the author, the text's 'potential functions,' and the 'historical effect,' which refers to the readings of historical recipients in different contexts. Sommer's consideration of the retrospective ascription of functions to narrative that is part of literary history is decidedly hermeneutic.

He argues that such an endeavour is characterized by the attempt to correlate the 'intended effect,' the 'potential functions' of narrative strategies and 'historical effects' with the interests and the hermeneutic assumptions of the critic. Thus, the potential functions (*Funktionspotentiale*) of narrative techniques are, on the one hand, inextricably linked to the content that they structure, and, on the other, to the hypotheses that 'realize' them.[82] Accordingly, narratives do not *have* functions independent of a necessarily historical hermeneutic situation; attempting to create coherent readings, readers assign meaning to narrative (strategies) and form hypotheses concerning their functions based on their conceptual prerequisites. This sub-chapter is guided by the assumption that narratives neither have a metaleptic *function* nor a metaleptic *form* independent of the necessarily historical situation in which they come into being.

As the scalar model of metalepsis proposed above (Chapter 2.2.2) demonstrates, the negation of diegetic prerequisites that characterizes a narrative as metaleptic depends on a complex ascription of *meaning*. Thus, the classification of metaleptic form cannot be based on as wide understanding of 'form' as the non-representational properties of a text. Metaleptic form is always 'beholden to meaning.'[83] David Herman's article "Toward a Formal Description of Narrative Metalepsis" (1997) offers the attempt to distinguish the following two "dimensions" (133) along which metalepsis can be characterized: "The first dimension centers on the formal profile of metaleptic narration, particularly the formal features attaching to distinct yet interactive diegetic levels; the second dimension centers on the semantic or world-creating (and -destroying) functions performed by metaleptic technique in narrative contexts" (ibid.). Nevertheless, I argue that the very basis of metaleptic form is the "world-creating (and -destroying) functions performed by metaleptic technique in narrative contexts" (ibid.). There can be no diegetic levels (to which formal features could be attributed) independent of 'semantic' or 'world-creating functions.'[84] Alternative-

---

82 According to Roy Sommer, *potential functions* constitute "eine vom Text her begründbare Annahme über die möglichen Effekte der narrativen Strategien, die den nacherzählbaren Inhalt eines literarischen Textes strukturieren und organisieren und damit für den Sinn entscheidend sind" (2000, 328).
83 This formulation is indebted to Newmeyer (2000), who raises the question whether "form is so beholden to meaning, discourse, and processing that it is wrong-headed to specify the distribution of the formal elements of language by means of an independent set of rules or principles" (10) within linguistics.
84 Recently, Herman has supplied a similar argument in his introduction to *The Emergence of Mind* (2011). He argues that what he calls "the entanglement of the 'what' and 'how' aspects of mind representation" (ibid., 32) makes it impossible to restrict narratological analysis of narra-

ly, seen from the opposite angle, metaleptic form is so beholden to meaning that the formal aspects of metalepsis are always already functional – that is, if one equates 'semantic' with 'functional.'

As the preceding sections have demonstrated, there are good reasons to equate what Herman calls 'semantic functions' with metaleptic 'form.'[85] The functions of that 'form' are the result of a further ascription of meaning. In other words, it is possible to ascribe certain effects to the narrative device once it has been identified (that is, interpreted as metalepsis). But neither the identification of the narrative device metalepsis nor a reading of its possible effects can do without what Herman calls "narrative contexts" (1997, 133). It is not coincidental that Herman feels compelled to concede that the formal features in his investigation, which he characterizes as "lexical ambiguation and as register-shifting and -mixing, are perhaps neither necessary nor sufficient conditions for metalepsis […]" (1997, 135). Metalepsis, I would conclude in agreement with Herman, can neither be exclusively described nor established by the formalist terms he suggests. In other words, the construction of a narrating instance, a (fictive) communicative situation and the worlds in which and of which a narrator tells, as well as any metaleptic movement between those worlds, are necessarily established by the interpretation of the *semantic* aspects of a text. Thus, a formal description of metalepsis fails to take into account that how metalepsis works is always superimposed on what metalepsis means. Rather than dealing with the arduous problems generated by a correlation of semantic aspects and functionality, it is preferable to conceptualize metalepsis as a narrative device whose formal properties cannot ultimately be distinguished from its semantic aspects in the hermeneutic dialogue in which it comes into being.[86]

---

tive representations of mind to 'matters of technique' as these necessarily encompass 'matters of theme' (cf. ibid., especially notes 2 and 8).

85 Narratological definitions of metaleptic transgressions and analyses of their effects can be taken to substantiate the claim that metaleptic form is beholden to meaning. A particularly pertinent example of this is supplied by Kukkonen's (2011b) proposition of what constitutes the basic function of metalepsis: "[T]he basic function of metalepsis remains a crossing of the border between the fictional world and (a representation of) the real world" (6). Since this reads like a reiteration of Genette's definition of metalepsis (if one equates those worlds with the domains of the signifier/signified), this comes strangely close to the (decidedly hermeneutic) statement that the 'basic function' of metalepsis is its form.

86 A serious hermeneutic lesson one might draw from the fact that the identification of metalepsis relies on an ascription of meaning and that metaleptic effects rely, again, on a further ascription of meaning, and that such ascriptions of meaning are based on fundamental parameters of human understanding and rely on a complex hermeneutic situation, is that the metaleptic dynamic potentially offers complexities of meaning that contradict the model. What

From a hermeneutic perspective, fundamental sense-making capabilities and their particular historical characteristics come into focus in every discussion of potential effects usually ascribed to metalepsis. In the double ascription of (paradoxical) meaning on which metaleptic effects rely, basic parameters of human understanding become visible. Understanding metalepsis entails the awareness that the representational logic with which we distinguish represented and representation has been violated. Such awareness is necessary, at least to a certain degree, to account for the 'transgressive' nature of metalepsis. Metalepses would *not* be a narrative possibility if the representational logic of everyday life was not an influential conceptual part of the understanding of narrative; if, in other words, representation and represented were (ontologically) indistinguishable in the first place. It is an interesting question whether a metaleptic 'text' which *permanently* collapses the world of the telling and the world of the told is a logical possibility. Understanding even anti-narratives, such as Robbe-Grillet's *La Jalousie* (1957) or Christine Brooke-Rose's *Thru* (1975), with its ambiguous and "excessive narrative structure" (Malina 2002, 89), unfolds into a process in which distinct 'worlds' emerge, albeit temporarily. To my knowledge, the novel without a diegesis has yet to be written.

If there is such a thing, this may constitute the narrative device's most basic function. The foregrounding of the extratextual reader's concepts is certainly a fundamental interpretative possibility and a fundamental part of understanding the metaleptic dynamic. Structurally, metaleptic transgressions deny the very basis on which they rely: a hierarchical conception of (diegetic) levels whose boundaries constitute the sacrosanct threshold between the world of the represented and the world of the representation. The *hermeneutic effect* of metalepses is connected to the fact that in understanding metaleptic transgressions readers (possibly) become aware of the (transgressed) representational logic on which the conception of narrative (understanding) usually relies: (narrative) representations communicate what is *not* present itself. This is the basic condition de-

---

follows from this is the insight that most metaleptic texts, rather than offering clear-cut cases of the phenomenon (and clearly delimitable effects), have a metaleptic potential that needs to be realized by a reader or viewer. The metaleptic form does not consist in an ahistorical essentialist structure independent of the situation in which it is understood. Thus, even before there can be any consideration of metaleptic effects, the metaleptic potential of a given text has to be realized in the complex and potentially interminable hermeneutic situation in which it arises. The semantic instabilities (who speaks to whom, what are the spatiotemporal conditions of the narrated/narration, etc.) of potentially metaleptic passages demonstrate that the metaleptic form must be extricated from unstable meanings which no Chinese box model can stabilize once and for all.

nied in metaleptic transgressions. Conventionally, the represented is ontologically distinct from the representation, either because it is fictional or because the non-fictional represented belongs to a spatiotemporal locus distinct from the world of the representation.[87] When this spatiotemporal duplicity (or multiplicity) is denied, the result is fundamental disorientation. Understanding metalepsis thus involves understanding oneself: what concepts, what epistemological prerequisites enable narrative understanding? Werner Wolf has discussed similar 'epistemological reflections' as a possible metaleptic effect:

> Generally, as metalepsis typically operates across the boundary between 'reality' and 'fiction,' it can serve as a *trigger to reflections* on this boundary or – as in the postmodernist use of the device – it can also undermine it under the auspices of a deconstructionist belief in 'pan-fictionality.' All this could be regarded – if the employment of metalepsis stems from a serious and not merely ludic or sensational motivation – as a contribution to yet another function mentioned by Ryan, namely *exploring (or acknowledging) the limits of human knowledge and concepts* [...]. Such epistemological reflections are, however, only a special case of another general effect of metalepsis, namely that it *activates the recipient*. [...] [S]ome activity will always be elicited in the recipients by the paradoxical nature of metalepsis: for the 'madness' of this device will inevitably make them look for a 'method in't' and will thereby refer them to some of the abovementioned functions or to still other functions, for the list given here does not purport to be complete. (2005, 103)

Leaving aside the question whether a complete list of metaleptic effects[88] would have a decidedly Shandean quality, Wolf's impressive (if incomplete) list is precisely that: it supplies 'methods' with which the metaleptic 'madness' can be turned into something which 'makes' sense. Each effect is an attempt to supply metalepsis with the closure of a coherent reading. Even though 'activation' is an unfortunate term, since it suggests that narrative understanding is automatic until that understanding is triggered by the metaleptic transgression, this is

---

[87] Even in non-fictional simultaneous narration (for instance, the live broadcast) there is a minimal temporal distance between seeing and speaking.

[88] Wolf lists and discusses the ludic effect, the sensational function, comic valorization, the effect of enhancing the attractiveness of the 'product,' the (covert) celebration of the author and/or imagination, metalepsis as a marker of fictionality (in the sense of invention), the anti-illusionist effect and the meta-fictional or meta-aesthetic effect (cf. 2005, 101–104). He draws on the article "Logique culturelle de la métalepse, ou la métalepse dans tous ses états" (2005) by Marie-Laure Ryan which was at the time forthcoming. Alber and Bell offer the following list of effects: "(1) Metalepsis as a Form of Escapism (2) Metalepsis as an Exercise of Control (3) Metalepsis as Highlighting the Power and Potential Danger of Fiction (4) Metalepsis as Mutual Understanding (5) Metalepsis as a Challenge to the Creator – A Loss of Control over the Creation" (2012, 176).

very close to what I would call the device's *hermeneutic effect*. Yet the metaleptic transgression is not only 'mad' in the sense that a certain key, a certain concept, or a certain motivation is needed to supply a particular reading of the device's paradoxicality with coherence. Metalepsis not only offers the paradoxical impossibility of denying its own prerequisites, but also denies the very spatiotemporal make-up of our understanding, of how we make sense of the world. It is this denial that destabilizes readings, proliferates meanings, and prolongs the dynamic instigated by such transgressions. Thus, the device's hermeneutic effect, which lays bare the concepts that make metalepsis possible in the first place, can be conceptualized as the gnomonic shadow haunting all attempts to make sense of metalepsis. This is why no list of metaleptic effects can ever be complete.

This hypothesis can, of course, easily be questioned by the commonness of metaleptic phenomena in today's cultural artefacts. The ubiquity of playful transgressions of narrative logic in fantasy literature certainly does not 'trigger reflections on the boundary between reality and fiction' (cf. Wolf 2005, 103) in each single case, but rather belongs to a compendium of strategies that is very much taken for granted and which can further imaginative immersion in the storyworld. A short (and by no means conclusive) survey of effects typically ascribed to metaleptic transgressions can be used to demonstrate that metalepses characteristically (and necessarily) yield such oscillating interpretative possibilities. Nevertheless, this does not amount to the contention that there are no common functions or typical effects, but rather that metalepses cannot be *reduced* to essential metaleptic effects that are valid beyond the complex hermeneutic situations in which they come into being.

First of all, there is, as Genette has it, the "effect of strangeness that is either comical [...] or fantastic" (1980, 235). There is something strange and laughable about metaleptic transgressions. Yet what precisely is funny? The humorous side of metalepsis is rarely ever commented on, possibly because it is notoriously difficult to define the comic, which is usually analyzed according to the *superiority*, *relief*, and *incongruity* theories of humour. Each of these theories could be taken as a starting point for a discussion of the humorous effects of metaleptic transgressions. Usually cited as a proponent of the latter of the three, Immanuel Kant, for instance, in the Critique of Judgment, defines humour and laughter as a response to incongruity: "Something absurd (something in which, therefore, the understanding can of itself find no delight) must be present in whatever is to raise a hearty convulsive laugh. Laughter is an affect arising from a strained expectation being suddenly reduced to nothing" (2007 [first German ed. 1790], 161). This definition correlates the humorous object with the response evoked. Along these lines it could be argued that a metaleptic effect is the particular response evoked by a narrative device which is absurd (as it includes ambiguity, logical impossibility, and possibly irrelevance) in such a way that 'understanding can find no satisfaction.' The incongruity between the expectations of readers or viewers and the object that transforms the strained expectations of narrative into nothing leads to an affection in the moment of comic relief.

This leads once again to the question in what ways expectations of readers, viewers, and listeners are changed by the (post)modern proliferation of the phenomenon. Can the absurd be transformed into something else by continued use? Has the continued use of metalepses subverted the expectations that are, according to the incongruity theory, the necessary condition for humour? More simply, have metaleptic transgressions become tedious? Or has the ubiquity of metaleptic phenomena become inadvertently comic? According to Henri Bergson's famous essay "Laughter" (1980 [first French ed. 1900], 84), the comic is something "mechanical encrusted upon the living." The employment of metalepsis in comic books, fantasy literature, movies, video games and advertisements, etc. has indeed lost its sense of novelty and intellectual artifice. We have come to expect metalepses as part of the games our fictive 'representations' self-referentially play. So the argument could be made that metalepsis is something "mechanical encrusted upon the living," where the incongruity between human intelligence and the habitual or maybe even mechanical repetition of metaleptic games leads to (inadvertent) humour. In another sense (and on another level), narratological analyses (of metalepses) possibly supply a mechanics of their own which may be incongruous with the living art of narrative. Perhaps a fitting (albeit somewhat mechanical) conclusion to a discussion of metalepses and humour is that a more detailed account of the humorous effects and potentials of metalepsis remains a lacuna of narrative theory – a conclusion that is carefully questioned by suggesting that we may be forced to relegate humour to an untheorizable limbo.

A more substantial (and, if possible, more serious) take on humorous metaleptic effects could follow the definition of humour offered by John Morreall in *Comic Relief: a Comprehensive Philosophy of Humor* (2009):

> The central idea [...] is that in humor we experience a sudden change of mental state – a cognitive shift, I call it – that would be disturbing under normal conditions, that is, if we took it seriously. Disengaged from ordinary concerns, however, we take it playfully and enjoy it. Humans, along with the apes that have learned a language, are the only animals who can do this. (xii)

Non-fictive metaleptic phenomena would surely be terrifying. If the relation of what happened yesterday collapsed the distinction between past and present and made the past present or the present past, or, possibly worse, if the telling of horrors created that horror's reality (and, eventually, someone would just have to tell a story like *The Hills Have Eyes* or *Hostel*), metalepses would have to be taken seriously indeed. The humorous disengagement with which such possibilities can be thought, watched or read is due to the fact that metalepses do *not* touch our ordinary concerns. The 'cognitive shift' induced by the transgression of diegetic levels (as that which was thought to belong to the world of the told is suddenly part of the world of the telling or vice versa) is not disturbing because it belongs to a realm of play, clearly disengaged from the world in which the metalepsis is understood. The moment metalepsis not only implies but literally and physically 'contaminates' the world in which we understand, we may argue that madness has replaced the comic. Should this 'effect' exist, and the condition called 'clinical vampirism' possibly suggests it does, this may be termed *metaleptic madness*.

The humorous potential of metalepses, however, is presumably the result of an unengaged and unconcerned reader, listener or viewer who experiences (the incongruity of) a 'sudden change of mental state.' This is corroborated by all the examples of metaleptic transgression discussed by Marie-Laure Ryan in *Avatars of Story*, in which

> the so-called reality that becomes affected by the events of a higher level is not the world in which the actual reader and author are located, but the first level of the fictional tower. A story can represent the murder of a fictional reader by the protagonist of a fictional novel, but the only way for a real-world author to kill the actual reader would be by non-literary means, for instance by sprinkling anthrax between the pages of the book. In other words, the actual base of the narrative stack, the world of ground zero, remains protected from metaleptic phenomena. (2006, 209)

Werner Wolf has argued in contradistinction to Ryan that metaleptic transgressions can include possible violations of the boundary that separates the world of historical authors and readers or recipients from the representational world(s) of the work of art. One metaleptic effect is thus that the device undermines this distinction "under the auspices of a deconstructionist belief in 'pan-fictionality'" (2005, 103). As mentioned above, this is indebted to Malina's *Breaking the Frame,* in which she develops the argument that metaleptic subject construction within fiction mirrors non-fictional processes of subject construction. She claims that the metaleptic dynamic "mirrors the process by which our sometimes violent narrative framings, deframings, and reframings of our world, ourselves and others make us what we, for all practical purposes, *are*" (2002, 3;

emphasis in the original). Thus, metalepsis can be seen as a device that is humorously 'disengaged from ordinary concerns,' while at the same time mirroring and influencing our most fundamental ways of identity formation. Or, more radically, and contrary to Ryan's assessment above, one possible effect of metaleptic transgressions is the denial of the epistemological conditions with which we distinguish fiction and non-fiction, especially their respective and equally discursive 'worlds.'

Among other things, it is indicative of today's critical climate that within most narratological accounts of metaleptic effects the attribution of meaning to the metaleptic dynamic has a decidedly postmodernist slant – a slant that is at the same time guardedly questioned. I have argued that, typically, for each metaleptic effect, there is an interpretative counterpart or companion piece. This is particularly evident in the common argument that metalepses cut across the imaginative immersion/anti-illusionist divide. In the introduction to the Volume *Metalepsis in Popular Culture* (2011), Karin Kukkonen reiterates the narratological consensus in a typical manner. First she quotes well-known discussions of the device's "strong anti-illusionist effect" (Wolf 2005, 103) that destroys the immersive quality of the fictional world whose boundaries have been metaleptically questioned: "Metalepsis seems to be essentially anti-illusionist because it destroys the coherence of the fictional world by transgressing its boundary. Contributing to the persuasive power of this assumption is certainly the perceived rise of metalepsis (and other means of metareference) in the disruptive and deconstructive narratives of postmodernism" (Kukkonen 2011b, 10). Then, she carefully questions this and presents the argument that the "intentionally engineered effects" of metalepses in popular culture can be located in "[t]he dichotomy between immersion in the fictional world and the anti-illusionist rupture of immersion" (ibid., 12). Kukkonen's prime example of what one could call the *immersive effects* of metalepsis is Klimek's analysis of metalepses in fantasy literature in the same volume (cf. 2011b, 22–40). Accordingly, she concludes that "the narrative function of metalepses is often tied to a genre" (Kukkonen 2011b, 12).

In contrast to that, Fludernik implies that it is not the genre but rather the historical development of a *type* of metaleptic transgression that enables the conclusion that metalepses "tend to enhance the realistic illusion of storyworld representation, aiding the narratee's (as well as the reader's) imaginative immersion into the story rather than foregrounding the metafictional and transgressive (nonrealistic) properties of such an imaginative stepping into the storyworld" (2003b, 383). This, Fludernik argues, is one of the effects of rhetorical metalepses. Typical examples of this can be found in Henry Fielding's *Tom*

Jones (1749), in which the "projected simultaneity" (ibid., 387) of authorial narrator, narratee addressed and the diegetic universe can be understood as a (metaphorical) move into the fictional diegesis: "The reader will be pleased, I believe, to return with me to Sophia. She passed the night, after we saw her last, in no very agreeable manner" (Book 4, Chapter 12).[89] If one understands this as an instance of (metaphorical) immersion into the storyworld, then this could be termed a strange kind of metaleptic realism. It is as if narrator and narratee were literally present in one place and time in the storyworld and that the omniscient narrator needed to tell the narratee what had happened during the time of that presence in other places in the diegesis. What is seemingly the synchronization of extradiegetic and diegetic time suggests a metaleptically collapsed narrative situation in which time passes in the diegesis elsewhere, while the narrator is relating what is happening. In other words, the narrator has to tell 'afterwards' what he can no longer metaleptically show.[90] This seems to be a characteristic that is often attributed to rhetorical metalepses: if the worlds (the holistically structured networks of meaning and relatedness) that coincide with the diegetic levels and their hierarchical relation remain undisturbed – that is, if the world of the telling and the world of the told remain separate alongside the *projection* of a shared space and a shared time, then the *implied* transgression has only a limited (or no) disruptive effect. Rhetorical metalepses can foster a heightened immersion because the denial of the logic of acts of representation is figurative rather than literal. The disruptive effects of a literal denial of this logic by ontological metalepses may often challenge or overwrite the immersion-enhancing potential of metalepsis.

A similar and related set of (opposing) effects can be found in a discussion of the narrative device's connection to the illusion of unmediated experience. Mediation, some metalepses suggest, collapses in the experience of another

---

[89] Monika Fludernik supplies a similar instance of what can be conceptualized as an instance of rhetorical metalepsis in Fielding's *Tom Jones*: "As we have now brought Sophia into safe hands, the reader will, I apprehend, be contented to *deposit her there awhile, and to look a little after other personages*, and particularly poor Jones, whom we have left long enough to do penance for his past offences" (Fludernik 2003b, 390; *Tom Jones*, ending of book 11).
[90] Curiously, this strange blend of 'impossibilities' is characteristic of a kind of writing that made Fielding the father of the English realist novel – which complements the fact that it displays its own artifice in a metafictional manner. Thus, the metaleptic 'showing' of diegetic events is a narrative strategy that made Fielding, in Byron's famous words, "the prose Homer of human nature" (1875, 247). Even though it is debatable whether rhetorical metalepses have a function in Fielding's novels that is essentially 'realistic,' they can at least potentially foster imaginative immersion into the diegetic universe (Cf. e.g. Scott Robertson 2010, 222–225).

experientiality – an experientiality that no longer belongs to a spatiotemporal frame distinct from its mediation. For the extradiegetic reader in that often quoted story by Julio Cortázar, the diegetic experience of being killed has seemingly no longer the status of a *mediated* experience but has taken on an extradiegetic 'reality.' Since the reader of that novel is presumably killed by a character in that novel, this is no longer an immersive experience by proxy (cf. Gavins 2007, 4); it is the very same experience. There is, of course, a hermeneutic tradition that addresses the question whether it is possible not only to understand (in the sense of an analytical construction of meaning) but to *fully* experience the lived experience of another. Schleiermacher's Romantic hermeneutics relies on the term 'divination,' which refers to the hypothetical reconstruction, or, rather, re*creation* of the creative act of the author; thus apprehending the inner space of the author, the inner origin of a work's composition. Ultimately, according to Schleiermacher's famous formulation, the aim of the one who understands is 'to understand a text better than its author' (cf. 1977, 112):

> For Schleiermacher, objective interpretation has a psychological, divinatory component [...]: so the goal of interpretation is to inhabit – inhabit immediately, without mediation, as in a moment of psychic identity – the self-understanding, the inner space of the one who writes. [...] This is what motivates hermeneutics, the study of history, and indeed all human sciences; perhaps it is the motivation of thinking itself, in the sense that what calls for thinking is always the thinking of another and not just the disembodied problem or transcendental question. (Bruns 1992, 160)

Some metalepses potentially enact this goal of Romantic hermeneutics – in those instances when what was at a mediated distance, beyond the boundary that separates diegetic levels, is suddenly experienced without mediation, as in Cortázar's famous example mentioned above. This, however, seems to apply only to the fiction-internal narrative personalia. For fiction-external readers and/or viewers (etc.), the decidedly metaleptic phenomenon in which the mediated experientiality of another is experienced as unmediated experience is the unattainable goal of all representations that strive for aesthetic illusion. In the context of new media studies, Jay David Bolter and Richard Grusin have discussed the imperative to erase the traces of media technologies and render the medium as completely transparent under the label 'immediacy,' which they define as the logic that "dictates that the medium itself should disappear and leave us in the presence of the thing represented" (1999, 11).[91] Even though a

---

[91] Today, the apotheosis of media technologies that enable the most 'immediate' interaction with a 3D virtual reality may be the room-sized Cave Automatic Virtual Environment (the acro-

substantial segment of the new media strives for 'transparent immediacy,' the impossible simultaneity of two perspectives involved if one knows or experiences the other as one knows or experiences oneself is only granted to fictional characters like those who travel the secret portal into John Malkovich's brain in *Being John Malkovich* (1999). This is the impossibility that (this particular account of) the Romantic version of the hermeneutic endeavour strives for:

> to know or to experience from the inside out – experience in the sense of appropriating or possessing as our own (the way we know, or think we know, or possess, or think we possess, ourselves). What we desire is the reality of the other; and this is, of course, just what we cannot know, not too say possess. (Bruns 1992, 167)

Metalepses potentially enact this desire for the reality of the other. Each metaleptic transgression approaches unmediated knowing or experiencing, as some narrator or character, some narrative entity comes closer to knowing 'from the inside out.' Of course, and this is typical of the interpretative possibilities metalepses offer, such knowing 'from the inside out' is an impossibility which at the same time highlights the mediated character of such a (fictional) experience.

When Catherine professes to be Heathcliff in Emily Brontë's *Wuthering Heights* (1847), there is a metaleptic potential if this sentence is taken to refer to a diegetic level created by Catherine's literal narration: "Nelly, I *am* Heathcliff! – He's always, always in my mind – not as a pleasure, any more than I am always a pleasure to myself – but as my own being" (1992 [1847], 120), says Catherine-says-Nelly-writes Lockwood. If we do believe that despite all the demonic possessions that seem to haunt Catherine and Heathcliff, they both are (initially and fundamentally) distinct human beings, not essentially different from all other characters in the novel and read this as the meta-metadiegesis constructed by Catherine, we can conclude that this meta-metadiegetic construction of Heathcliff metaleptically spills into the metadiegesis. In other words, experiencing Heathcliff 'from the inside out – in the sense of appropriating or possessing

---

nym CAVE of course suggests Plato's famous allegory and questions the distinction between the intelligible and the changing world of material objects; what the CAVE shows is in a certain sense always the same), the aim of which is certainly to create the completely immersive experience. However, as Alice Bell and Astrid Ensslin have pointed out, the CAVE can be conceptualized as serving the same function as second person narration: "[W]hat is experienced by players as highly individualized and immediate immersion in a virtual game world is based on textual mechanisms directed quasi-apostrophically at a general audience of gamers who are allowed to traverse the game world freely – within the boundaries dictated by the code" (2011, 313). The presence of the medium is constituted by (the awareness) of precisely such boundaries.

as her own,' is the result of a metaleptic subject construction. In this sense, the demonic possession is metaleptically *created* by Catherine's metadiegetic narration. 'I am Heathcliff,' can in this manner be read as the metaleptic enactment of "the infinite desire to surrender to, and lose oneself in, the existence of others" (Dilthey 1976, 215). This, of course, raises yet again the question of the threshold between fiction and non-fiction and, particularly the distinction between fictional and non-fictional understanding of the self and others.

For most metaleptic effects one could develop a scalar model that attempts to trace some of the interpretative possibilities offered. The effects of (un)mediatedness that emerge in the dynamic process of understanding metaleptic texts can be thought of as a continuum linking the most extreme forms of unmediated experience (the madness that annihilates the self; for truly becoming the other amounts to the annihilation of the self) with the foregrounding of the mediated nature of metaleptic experience. The one end of the scale is predominantly an extradiegetic or diegetic phenomenon, the other (mainly) extratextual. Metaleptic madness may be argued to obtain the moment the boundary is dissolved that separates the world in which this book is read from something that is – necessarily – mediated: metaleptic madness is the unmediated experience of mediated experientiality. The metaleptic dynamic thus plays with possibilities of human understanding and, ultimately, its inescapable limitations.

This leads us back to what I have termed the hermeneutic effect of metalepses. The oscillating interpretative possibilities outlined above foreground the hermeneutic situations in which they come into being: Wolf's impressive list of metaleptic effects (which draws on Ryan) implies a wide variety of concepts of literature, research interests and hermeneutic assumptions. That is why a list of metaleptic effects can always be expanded and provided with varying foci. One of the most basic assumptions that links all these effects is that metalepsis is an intentional narrative device that has genuine (literary) merit. All the functions I have discussed and added at least agree with the first part of that assumption and some form a cut set with effects described by Wolf, Ryan and others: *humorous effect(s), hermeneutic effect(s), effects of (un)mediatedness, metaleptic realism* and *metaleptic madness* are, as ascriptions of meaning, all embedded in a myriad of narrative contexts and the unimaginably complex process of interpretation.

3 Breaking the Frame: Metalepsis as Hermeneutic Experience

3.1 Narratology and Hermeneutics

> Be certain that conceptual thoughts and fleeting memories are not strictly identifiable,
> But insubstantial in their motion, like the breezes of the atmosphere.
> Look at your own mind to see whether it is like that or not!
> — *Padmasaṃbhava, and Terton Karma Lingpa, The Tibetan Book of the Dead*

Chapter 3 considers the phenomenon designated 'metalepsis' as hermeneutic experience. This approach, in opposition to the structuralist analysis of the preceding chapter, is twofold. Firstly Chapter 3.1 considers metalepsis as part of a *narratological* framework of categories, and seeks to establish what it means to engage in narratological practice. It reflects, in other words, the hermeneutic conditions under which the understanding of narrative designated 'narratological' becomes possible – it reflects the hermeneutics of narratology. Moreover, it emphasizes how this hermeneutics is questioned by the insights offered by the category of metalepsis and aims to show how a consideration of ontological hermeneutics can become relevant for analyses of metalepsis. Chapter 3.2 considers metalepsis as a *phenomenon*, insofar as it demonstrates how the frameworks with which narrative is approached are subjected to an aporetic movement in the event of understanding metalepsis.

Among narratological categories metalepsis holds a unique position: metalepsis is the 'narrative structure' which *per definitionem* denies its own prerequisites – it is the conception of a narrative phenomenon that denies the very basis of how narratology conceptualizes narrative. The denial of certain properties of diegetic universes triggers complex readerly ascriptions of meaning which are invariably characterized by an element of negativity: the notion of the 'diegesis,' one of the most fundamental narratological concepts, implies that the world of the narrating and the world of the narrated are categorically distinct; in metaleptic narratives, the world of the narrating and the world of the narrated are in some respects 'merged.' Both propositions (diegetic levels are distinct/diegetic levels are not distinct), while they are necessary constituents of an analysis of metalepsis, contradict one another. In the complex metaleptic dynamic which ensues, meanings proliferate as spatiotemporal dimensions (temporarily) collapse. The preceding chapter conceptualizes metalepsis as a possibility of narrative that can be modelled by a structuralist category. Thus,

Chapter 2 can be characterized as belonging to 'formal narratology' (in the sense of Sommer 2012, cf. 153), which has its roots in a structuralist tradition. Chapter 3 acknowledges the hermeneutic implications of the fact that metalepsis at the same time relies on *and* resists structural analysis.

The following hermeneutic consideration of narratology acknowledges the complexity and limitation of human understanding. I agree with John Pier's assessment that metalepsis can serve as "a threshold lying in wait within structuralist narratology, later to contribute to a new take on the theory of narrative" (2011, 268) – not only in the sense that metalepsis as a narratological category models (and presupposes) certain structures that emerge in the experience of narratives, but also in the sense that the experience of metalepsis has hermeneutic repercussions that throw light on the conditions and limitations of a narratological analysis.

Chapter 3.1.1 argues that narratological analyses of metalepsis presuppose the drawing of the boundaries of narratology, and poses the question: What are the proceedings that literary scholars term 'narratology'? After an analysis of typical characteristics of contemporary outlines of narratology, I propose to draw the boundaries of narratology from a hermeneutic perspective. This is based on the insight that the analysis of metaleptic narratives presupposes the simple telos that narratives can be metaleptically configured; a configuration that emerges as the unity of the experience of certain narratives. Such an analysis is, in other words, based on and directed towards what is common to certain experiences. Accordingly, one way to draw the boundaries of narratology is to maintain that it is the practice that conceives of the experience of understanding narrative *teleologically* – that is, narratology is structured towards and outlines the *unity* of experiencing narratives from an analytical distance.

Striving for "a better understanding of what stories are and how they work" (Herman 2009), post- and neoclassical approaches to narratology have in the past decade offered a growing number of explanatory paradigms that acknowledge the limitations of structuralist analyses. Chapter 3.1.2 argues that narratological practice and its explanatory paradigms still tend to be informed by a hermeneutics of 'distanciation' that strives for the methodological distance of the understanding subject. From this distance the object of narrative is seen in terms of a methodological reflection that allows the description of matters seemingly untouched by just such an understanding subjectivity. If we think of the narratological paradigm as the structure established from an analytical distance, then ontological hermeneutics offers the reintegration of that structure into an act of understanding that belongs ontologically to what it understands; the hermeneutics of 'belonging.' While the explanatory paradigm of, say, cognitive narratology considers the experience of understanding narrative in terms of knowledge, ontological hermeneutics embeds (narratological) knowledge in a complex experiential process that does not posit the understood as an 'other.' Following Gadamer and Ricœur, this chapter argues that it is this dialectic between the hermeneutics of distanciation and the hermeneutics of belonging that characterizes narratology today: post- and neoclassical approaches to narratology still rely on a hermeneutics that (temporarily) situates itself analytically outside of what it belongs to ontologically.

Even though 'a more or less complex model of the object narrative' may be an essential part of the hermeneutic encounter in which metalepses come into being, the narratological analysis of metaleptic narration does not simply consist in the unproblematic identification and description of the properties of an object. As metalepsis foregrounds what the one who understands supplies in the act of understanding, the 'object' merges into the oscillating dialogue between recipient, narrative, and traditions of reading. Thus, metaleptic transgressions are neither some deep-structure logic which precedes – and may become manifest in – the structural analysis of narrative, nor a place of stable meanings that transcend the hermeneutic situation in which they come into being. Chapter 3.1.3 shows how this hermeneutic insight can become relevant for analyses of metalepsis. Understanding metalepsis inevitably involves an element of negativity which throws into relief fundamental conditions of narrative sense-making. Drawing on Gadamer's account of the negativity that characterizes human understanding, the *experience* of metalepsis can be framed as 'impossible narration.' The *Tibetan Book of the Dead* acknowledges that a human perspective cannot conceptually transcend such an experience; metalepsis is a concept that denies the stability which narratological practice seemingly engenders: "Be certain that conceptual thoughts and fleeting memories are not strictly identifiable" (Padmasaṃbhava and Lingpa 2005, 44).

3.1.1 Drawing the Boundaries of Narratology: The Practice that Conceives of the Experience of Narrative Teleologically

> How should we explain to someone what a game is? I imagine that we should describe games to him, and we might add: "This and similar things are called 'games.'" And do we know any more about it ourselves? Is it only other people whom we cannot tell exactly what a game is? But this is not ignorance. We do not know the boundaries because none have been drawn.
>
> — Ludwig Wittgenstein, Philosophical Investigations, aph. 69.

How should we explain to someone what narratology is? What are the proceedings that literary scholars term 'narratology'? The question is deceptively simple. The language use of narratologists implies that all narratological analyses have at least one thing in common (how else would they all deserve the label 'narratological'?). Yet, in the age of myriad approaches which claim to transcend classical structuralist narratology, what could possibly constitute such common ground? What indeed do feminist, cognitive, contextualist, deconstructive etc. narratologies have in common? If Ansgar Nünning feels compelled to concede that there is no consensus "either about the main aims and objectives of narratology or about the extension of its research domain" (2009, 52), can we then conclude, with Wittgenstein, that 'we do not know the boundaries because none have been (successfully) drawn'? The notion that a word has very vague meanings at best and is dependent on each situation in which it is used – i.e. a particular practice that ties it to a particular definition – can perhaps elucidate why the drawing of narratology's boundaries has proved exceedingly difficult. One possible conclusion is that there simply is no practice common to all proceedings called 'narratology': unless a certain practice ties 'narratology' to a certain definition, it may be argued that 'no boundaries have been drawn.'

Yet there exists a growing number of attempts to draw the boundaries of what has alternatively been described as "a theory of narrative" (Prince 1995, 110), a "school of thought" (Fludernik 2000, 83), a "heuristic tool" (Kindt and Müller 2003, 211) or, more recently, "a humanities discipline dedicated to the study of the logic, principles, and practices of narrative representation" (Meister 2009, 329). Two intricately related characteristics are particularly pertinent for such delineations of contemporary narratology. On the one hand, structuralist narratology is regularly presented as the model case that is no longer the model case – the structuralist 'other' of a discipline that has superseded its 'classical'[92] roots. On the other hand, in the attempt to move beyond a rich structuralist heritage, narratologists have become, as H. Porter Abbott puts it, "scholar pirates who plunder for their purposes troves of hypotheses, bright ideas, and yes, rigorous scientific work" (2006, 714). In other words, narratologists adopt an eclectic approach to make up for what are considered the limitations of classical narratology – which is replaced or augmented by methodologies and approaches from other disciplines (such as cognitive science), or, as many contextual narratologies demonstrate, enriched by considerations of the contexts and historicity of narrative forms.

These two characteristics of contemporary delineations of narratology are offered as a vantage point from which the proceedings called 'narratology' can be approached from a hermeneutic perspective; they constitute the drawing of the boundaries of narratology, which, one could argue with Wittgenstein, relies on the attempt to say 'this, and similar things, are called narratology.' Thus taking into account the 'things that are called narratology,' this chapter presents an analysis of the (dis)continuities between narratology's structuralist heritage and postclassical approaches and proposes the drawing of the boundaries of narratology in a new manner: narratology is the practice that conceives of the experience of narrative teleologically – the *telos* of narratologically informed analyses is the (assumption of) unity in historically contingent experiences of narrative(s). This, I argue, is a delineation of the proceedings that literary scholars term 'narratology'; a delineation that encompasses structuralist narratology as well as postclassical narratologies.

Structuralist narratology is the model case that is no longer the model case. This is the first of two characteristics which are particularly pertinent for any attempt to draw the boundaries of contemporary narratology. Versions of this argument rely on a particular version of structuralism that brackets the hermeneutic considerations of its major proponents, say, Todorov, Barthes and Ge-

---

[92] The distinction between a 'structuralist' and a 'postclassical phase' of narratology in its historical development was made (and the categories so named) by Herman in 1999. This distinction has become influential for what Matías Martínez terms the "usual master narrative" that "tells the story of modern narratology in three steps [...]: First there were the protonarratological beginnings of Russian Formalism in the 1910s and 1920s. Then French Structuralism produced in the 1960s to 1970s systematic accounts of narrative structures, either in form of universal generative narrative grammars or as 'low structuralism' providing equally universal tools for textual analysis. Finally, this classical phase of narratology has been expanded or modified towards postclassical narratologies which take the specificities of cultural, political and cognitive contexts into account" (2012, 134).

nette.⁹³ What I consider the model case of structuralist narratology in the twenty-first century is supplied by the objective of restrictive theorists such as Gerald Prince, who endeavour to "trace explicitly the definitional boundaries of narrative (to specify what all and only narratives have in common)" (Prince 2005, 374). Such an objective, in keeping with the traditional view of narratology as "the science of narrative" (Prince 2003, 1), implies that interpretation does not belong to the realm of narratology. Narratology understood in this restrictive manner is concerned with the analysis of *all* narratives according to scientific standards with the aim of establishing the general characteristics of narrative *per se* instead of arriving at and offering interpretations of single texts: "[N]arratology has proven to be an important participant in the assault against viewing literary studies as devoted above all to the interpretation of texts" (Prince 1995, 130). Thus, narratology is often seen in opposition to hermeneutics – a theory of (the formal properties of the scientific object) narrative which is distinct from (the theory of) interpretation. The drawing of such boundaries naturally relies on particular hermeneutic (and epistemological) assumptions. Implicit assumptions of this view are that the object studied (narrative) is a distinct entity whose (formal) properties exist independently of the observer and that the general characteristics of narrative are independent of the contexts in which they are encountered and, by extension, the content they transmit. What such an approach brackets, for instance, is the question how formal properties (the characteristics of narrative *per se*) are related to the scientific standard that supplies a consistent methodological frame in which they emerge.

Restrictive theorists such as Gerard Prince or, in Germany, Hans-Harald Müller and Tom Kindt, do not express general consensus – rather, the boundaries they draw offer a foil against which postclassical narratology is often defined. Accounts of narratology in the twenty-first century typically argue that a structuralist approach to narrative (Genette's categories are often considered the epitome of this approach) can no longer exclusively supply the boundaries of narratology. Two recent accounts of postclassical narratologies, such as the introductions to the volumes *Postclassical Narratology* (2010, edited by Jan Al-

---

93 Structuralist critics have often demonstrated an awareness of the hermeneutic dimensions of structuralist accounts of narrative. Tzvetan Todorov's outline of 'the structural approach to literature' in his "Structural Analysis of Narrative" distinguishes the 'description' of the internal literary features of single works from the 'structural analysis' of the abstract structure of which such features are "possible realizations" (1969, 2024): "It must immediately be added that, in practice, structural analysis will also refer to real works […]. In practice, it is always a question of going continually back and forth, from abstract literary properties to individual works and vice versa. Poetics and description are in fact two complementary activities" (2025).

ber and Monika Fludernik) or *Current Trends in Narratology* (2011, edited by Greta Olsen), define the heterogeneous field of postclassical narratology *via negativa*. Olsen maintains that "'post' narratologies depart from the classical emphasis on prose literary texts and its disavowal of contextual and ideological issues that often characterized classical narratological theory" (2011, 3); Alber and Fludernik assert that 'postclassical narratology' can be described as a "radical frame-transcending or frameshattering handling of the classical paradigm" (2010, 4). Strikingly, the latter definition of postclassical narratologies resembles the metaleptic movement (which is here seemingly the source domain), inasmuch as it violates the structuralist paradigm on which it relies. Metalepsis, one of the categories of the classical paradigm, relies on the negation of the binaries that constitute the prerequisites of the negation. The metaleptic transgression is made visible with the heuristic of (binary) structural relations within narrative. This, and similar things, Alber and Fludernik seem to argue, fall under the heading of postclassical narratological practice: the model case of a structuralist category that relies on *and* denies its structuralist prerequisites.

There is a certain irony in the fact that postclassical narratology can seemingly only be defined against the foil of its classical precursor. But the precursor, by contrast, underscores the characteristics of a paradigm shift that moves narratology beyond binary thinking – while the contrast itself establishes a new binarism. Alber and Fludernik have presented a similar argument in their evaluation of Ansgar Nünning's 2003 survey article ("Narratology or Narratologies? Taking Stock of Recent Developments, Critique and Modest Proposals for Future Usages of the Term"): "Paradoxically, Nünning's rhetorical strategy of establishing open, non-taxonomic postclassical narratologies actually involves the dualism of a before and after and therefore relies on a structural binarism of the very kind that it is trying to transcend" (2010, 6). No doubt, the very notion of a narratology which transcends its structuralist paradigm rests on a structural binarism. Yet how does postclassical narratology deal with narratological categories that are indebted to structuralist narratology? This question leads to the second characteristic of outlines of contemporary narratology that I want to discuss.

Postclassical narratologies integrate the narrative forms established by structuralist narratology into various contexts (considering their inevitable historicity) or approach them from a decidedly eclectic perspective. Even though most narratologists have dismissed the 'boundaries' drawn by structuralist narratology in theory, they still in practice employ Genettian categories as a "heuristic for interpretation" (Kindt and Müller 2003, 208) – and embed or augment these categories within different frameworks such as, for instance, cognitivism. Roy Sommer (2007) argues that this position – the view that "narratological analysis can only supply points of reference for stimulating, structuring and problematizing interpretations" (Kindt and Müller 2003, 208) – is the "sine qua non of all applied, thematic or 'hyphenated' narratologies (which [...] constantly refer to, discuss and apply the categories developed by Gérard Genette [...])" (Sommer 2007, 64). The conceptual framework of such approaches seems to be based on the notion that structural features of narrative can either in some sense 'represent,' or be correlated with, ideas, thoughts, or concepts. In other words, these approaches imply that structural features are, to say the very least, always embedded in the process of meaning-creation that necessarily moves beyond the 'object' of narrative structure: "Over the past twenty years, narratologists have paid increasing attention to the historicity and contextuality of modes of narrative representation as well as to its pragmatic function across various media, while research into narrative universals has been extended to cover narrative's cognitive and epistemological functions" (Meister 2009, 330).

Two conclusions can be drawn from this: on the one hand, contextualist narratologies demonstrate that it is impossible for any formal analysis of a text to bracket all traces of a context. Yet at the same time, since they continually employ Genette's categories, they also demonstrate that they rely on the notion of narrative forms that themselves rely on structural relations.[94] Ansgar Nünning seems to substantiate that view when he argues that the distinction between classical narratology and the "contextualist dimensions of contemporary 'postclassical' narratological scholarship" (Darby 2001, 423) is a dichotomy fraught with problems:

---

94 This becomes evident when one considers how postclassical narratologies offer to transcend the structural binarisms of classical narratology: Herman's answer is that "scholarship along these lines draws a fuzzy rather than a binarized distinction between narrative poetics and narrative criticism, using but not limiting itself to the tools of structuralist narratology" (Herman 2004, 575). Yet despite a predilection for 'fuzzy sets' and 'scalar properties' (cf. Ryan 2006, 7–10), the 'new or postclassical narratologies' (labels coined by Herman 1997, 1999), or if one prefers, the heterogeneous fields of 'postclassical narratology' (cf. Alber and Fludernik 2010) have all – narratologists never seem to grow tired of insisting – retained a strong element of the objectifying tendencies of an originally scientific approach. They rely on the notion of a formal narrative poetics distinct from interpretive possibilities – no matter how fuzzy the line drawn between them, no matter how often this distinction is negated. Even a deconstructivist narratology exemplifies binary thinking insofar as the "self-deconstructive aspects of narrative" (Malina 2002, 138) undermine the illusion of essence (cf. ibid.) – that is, its structuralist other.

> They [such dichotomies] present us, surely, with a set of false choices: between text and context, between form and content as well as form and context, between formalism and contextualism, between bottom-up analysis and top-down synthesis, and between 'neutral' description and 'ideological' evaluation. The problem with such binarisms is [...] the failure of such rigid distinctions to do justice to the aims and complexities of textual analysis, interpretation, and cultural history. (Nünning 2009, 52)

Yet what follows from the insight that the distinction between form and context is a 'false choice'? One answer to this question is supplied by the work of feminist narratologists such as Susan Lanser or Robyn Warhol. Feminist narratology is based on the premise that narrative form is "(a kind of) content and, as such, socially meaningful" (Lanser 2010, 186), and that this form therefore mirrors "complex and changing conventions that are themselves produced in and by the relations of power that implicate writer, reader, and text" (Lanser 1992, 5). The logical conclusion of the position that structuralist narratology is the model case whose binaries have been superseded may be the idea that form is always already content and there is no content independent of form. This is the description of a narratological practice that cannot be subsumed under the understanding that narratology denotes and analyzes the formalist *how* as distinct from the interpretive *why*. According to the boundaries drawn by feminist narratology, the complexities of narratological analyses cannot be reduced to fit into clear binarisms that distinguish structuralism and hermeneutics, theory of narrative and theory of interpretation, or form and content. Such a practice (the practice of 'contextualist' and 'interdisciplinary' narratologies) undermines the distinction between a structural 'object' of narrative and the interpretive practice of literary scholars. Contextual dimensions, this narratological practice seems to imply, determine not only each approach to a text, they determine the text itself. Following Nünning's insight, it could then be argued that narratology need not – and indeed should not – situate itself on either side of the formalism/contextualism divide.

Roy Sommer corroborates this in his account of what he terms "existing attempts at mapping the field" (2012, 143) of narratology, on which he builds his own attempt to draw new boundaries in the field(s) of classical and postclassical narratologies. It is interesting that his account not only introduces 'formal narratologies' as a subgenre of postclassical narratology, but also highlights the pervasiveness of structuralism: "Structural analysis is neither a (merely temporal) predecessor of, nor a theoretical alternative to postclassical narratology; it is an integral part (though no longer exclusively representative) of contemporary narrative theory" (ibid., 151). This is mirrored by his structural analysis of postclassical narratology, which he distinguishes with the help of a structure tree into formal and contextual narratologies, which, in turn, are distinguished into synchronic and diachronic approaches and corpus-based and process-oriented approaches (cf. ibid., 153). Yet this structure tree is accompanied by what could be termed a hermeneutic caveat: Sommer considers formal narratologies as "a dynamic theory that is still developing" (ibid., 153) and not as the static heuristic "of structuralist orthodoxy" (ibid., 154). Moreover, he argues that the state of the art of narratology consists in "intensified interaction between classical and postclassical approaches" (ibid., 154).

This is a version of the second typical characteristic of recent attempts to draw narratology's boundaries: narratology is an eclectic approach that replaces or augments what are considered the limitations of structuralist narratology by creating interdisciplinary methodologies on the one hand and/or by contextualizing narrative poetics on the other. If the narrative poetics of "structuralist orthodoxy" (Sommer 2012, 154) are continually questioned by new approaches and embedded in dynamic contexts, then the drawing of the boundaries of contemporary narratology is seemingly connected to the hermeneutic understanding of structural description. The dynamic nature of understanding is, it could be argued, reflected by a dynamic development of eclectic approaches (the insight that structuralist narratology from Todorov to Ricœur is an eclectic discipline to begin with yet again highlights the continuities between narratology's structuralist heritage and postclassical approaches). I would argue that the history of the narratological classification of narratology is decidedly hermeneutic, as it continually attempts to redraw its boundaries in the attempt to understand what a narratological practice denotes.

Interestingly, the relationship between (structuralist) narratology and (philosophical) hermeneutics has rarely been considered. It is indicative of this neglect that neither the many excellent survey articles which trace the historical development of narratology (cf., for instance, Fludernik 2005 and Herman 2005a) nor the synchronic descriptions of the many postclassical narratologies (cf. Herman 1999; Nünning 2003, 2009; or Alber and Fludernik 2010) mention hermeneutics. The article "Narrative Theory and/or/as Theory of Interpretation" (Kindt and Müller 2003) simply argues that hermeneutics and narratology are and should be two distinct operations: "the concepts of narrative theory should be 'neutral' with regard to the theory of interpretation, so that their use remains independent of the choice of a concrete interpretive approach" (213).

In her recent study *Ethos and Narrative Interpretation* (2014), Liesbeth Korthals Altes contradicts this and argues that narratology "cannot and should not avoid interpretation. It involves interpretation in two distinct ways: as a task for which it develops heuristic tools, and as an object of study" (50). This insight is Korthals Altes' starting point of a rare consideration of the hermeneutic dimensions of narratology. Mapping recent developments within narratology "according to the role of interpretation (ibid., 95), she maintains that there are a

> variety of objectives cultivated by narratologists, which lead to quite different kinds of investigation and validation procedures. These various understandings of narratology can be set out on a scale, with on the one side (cognitive) science and ideals of scientific rigor and, on the other, the practice of interpretation. Somewhere in between there is the place for what I call narratology as metahermeneutics. (Ibid., xi)

Korthals Altes' conception of what she terms "a metahermeneutic narratology" (ibid., 96) describes a particular kind of investigation that she claims is typical for narratologists (located between a theory of narrative and interpretation [cf. ibid., 95–99]). It is an investigation that focuses "on reconstructing interpretive processes and conventions" (ibid., 96), an investigation that makes *interpretation* the object of study. Establishing how hermeneutic questions (can) become relevant for a narratological analysis of ethos attributions, this is precisely what *Ethos and Narrative Interpretation* convincingly provides – which is particularly insightful when it comes to an exploration of a diversity of interpretations.

Yet the prefix 'meta' in 'metahermeneutic' is, I would venture to add, an unlucky and misleading choice. In my reading of her book, *metahermeneutic* denotes the analysis of "interpretive pathways" (ibid., 255) that can be intersubjectively shared (cf. ibid., 48), connected to certain triggers or clues and, at least potentially, empirically validated (cf. ibid., 249). Such an undertaking does not need the prefix 'meta.' And it is certainly very much unlike the endeavor of philosophical hermeneutics which I connect with Heidegger and Gadamer. Even though she uses the term at one point interchangeably with philosophical hermeneutics ("Hermeneutics refers not just to individual, subjective practices of interpreting and evaluating texts, or artifacts more generally. Philosophical hermeneutics, or metahermeneutics, always also strives to gain insight into the processes and conditions of how people interpret" [ibid., 37]), and even though the hermeneutic reflections proposed by Korthals Altes are drawn from a wide (and impressive) variety of sources, her metahermeneutics is fundamentally interested in interpretation "as an object of study" (ibid., 50). Korthals Altes' approach thus focuses on the similarities between hermeneutics and other (scientific) approaches to narrative that make interpretation accessible as an *object*.

The Finnish narratologist Bo Petterson offers another attempt to 'merge' hermeneutics and narratology in the book article "Narratology and Hermeneutics: Forging the Missing Link" (2009). Arguing that "even though some attempts have been made to combine an interpretive angle with narrative-theoretical concerns, narratology and hermeneutics are still a long way apart" (2009, 13), Petterson delineates a tripartite account that advocates the following combination of narratology and hermeneutics: "Classical narratology offers the textual tools, post-classical narratology the contextual and cognitive tools, and a hermeneutics based on contextual intention reference provides an account that is able to deal with narratology's interpretive features and approximate interpretive validity" (2009, 21–22). Rejecting Gadamer and Ricœur, Petterson arrives at an unconvincing combination of approaches, as he attempts to harmonize the text (the object of classical narratology) with cognitive processes and contextual parameters that embed this text (more or less the objective of postclassical narratology), while at the same time attempting to achieve interpretive validity with the help of a hermeneutic approach based on nineteenth-century hermeneutics. However, this uneasy combination is largely irrelevant for his exemplary analysis of Kate Chopin's *The Awakening* (1899), which is mainly concerned with the contexts and readings established by a number of critics who have analyzed Chopin's masterpiece (cf. Petterson 2009, 22–31). Strangely enough, Petterson's analysis does not employ the tools of postclassical narratology at all and mentions the 'textual tools' of structuralist narratology only once or twice. Commenting on focalization in Chopin's *œuvre*, Petterson implies that a text has an ahistorical structure independent of the hermeneutic situation in which this structure comes into being. Thus he correlates what he terms the 'formal aspects' of narrative (in this case the distribution of focalization in terms of gender) with a particular reading (Chopin is not a feminist author) – without ever questioning the hermeneutical situation that establishes from which spatiotemporal and/or conceptual position the narrated events are perceived (cf. ibid., 22–23).[95]

Thus, despite the outline of a tripartite narratological-hermeneutic approach, Petterson's analysis confirms what Tom Kindt has specified as narratology's scope: "From a conceptual perspective, narratology is an object-theory; it is in other words, a more or less complex model of the object narrative, narration, or the like" (Kindt 2009, 38). Tom Kindt's controversial attempt to draw narratology's boundaries is restrictive and excludes some of the proceedings

---

95 I would argue that a hermeneutic approach would highlight the provisional nature of such structures. Ever since Mieke Bal (1985) suggested that a 'narrator-focalizer' can 'perceive' the narrated events outside the diegesis, narratological discussions of focalization have demonstrated that the 'loci' from which we look into the house of fiction are not exclusively a matter of a narrative's ahistorical structure.

which may be termed 'narratological analysis.' A genuine narratological-hermeneutic approach that opposes this assessment and that could be situated at the opposite end of the scale is offered by Ricœur's analysis of narrative structures. In his article "Narrative Time" (1981a [1980], 165), he takes "temporality to be that structure of existence that reaches language in narrativity and narrativity to be the language structure that has temporality as its ultimate referent." Drawing on Heidegger, Ricœur argues that an existential analysis of time is reciprocal to narrative structures. Thus, from a conceptual perspective, this is not an object-theory – it is a hermeneutic consideration of temporality that does not pose narrative as an *object* in the world but analyses it as a fundamental way of *being* in the world. Ricœur, Kindt would have to conclude, is not concerned with narratology. In contrast to this, I want to offer a delineation of narratology that describes both Ricœur's and Kindt's narratological practice.[96]

Even though it is impossible to draw the boundaries of narratology once and for all, I propose drawing those boundaries in a less restrictive manner, namely that narratology conceives of the experience of understanding narrative *teleologically* – i.e. that narratology is structured towards and outlines the *unity* of experiencing narratives (usually without claiming to supply an ultimate telos towards which *all* narratives are directed, or narrative's ultimate form). This unity is the telos of narratology: narratology is always concerned with "narrative qua narrative" (Prince 1990, 10) – and not with the singularities of contingent observations. In other words, narratology is teleological without its telos being situated beyond the endeavour to find a *unity* in contingent historical attempts to make sense of narrative(s).

What I call 'the unity of experiencing narrative' is indebted to Hans-Georg Gadamer, who traces the Aristotelian account of universality in experience in the chapter 'The Concept of Experience and the Nature of Hermeneutic Experience' ("Der Begriff der Erfahrung und das Wesen der hermeneutischen Erfahrung") of *Truth and Method*:

> Only when the universality found in experience has been attained can we look for the reason and hence begin a scientific inquiry. We ask again: what kind of universality is this? It is obviously concerned with the undifferentiated commonality of many single observations. It is because we retain these that we can make certain predictions. (2013, 359)

---

[96] Since every attempt to draw the boundaries of narratology is dependent on and belongs to a particular hermeneutic situation, a certain practice, or as Wittgenstein would have it, a form of life, one possible (counter-) conclusion is that such boundaries necessarily remain unstable and cannot offer transhistorical meanings (that unify diverse hermeneutic situations, etc.).

Aristotle, Gadamer argues, conceives of experience in terms of knowledge. Following this line of thought, I would argue that Aristotle offers an experiential basis for (narratological) knowledge that cuts right across the distinctions between form and content, text and context or even a "methodological distinction between hermeneutic and heuristic functions" (Meister 2009, 341). Narratological analyses have as their telos the unity that generates (or is generated by) "the undifferentiated commonality [das ununterschiedene Gemeinsame] of many single observations" (Gadamer, 2013, 359). What defines all narratological analyses, Genette's categories and Ricœur's mimesis I–III, I maintain, is similar to what Gadamer sees as the retained commonality of an accretion of observations:

> Aristotle has a very fine image for the logic of this procedure. He compares the many observations someone makes to a fleeing army. They too hurry away – i.e., they do not stand fast. But if in this general flight an observation is confirmed by its being experienced repeatedly, then it does stand fast. [...] The image is important for us because it illustrates the crucial element in the nature of experience. (Ibid., 360)

Gadamer argues that this metaphor, despite its shortcomings, illustrates "the birth of experience as an event over which no one has control" (ibid.). It reflects the openness that characterizes the contingent situatedness of experience. Yet, and this may contradict Gadamer's account of the generation of knowledge, this metaphor implies that before the general flight, the army was already an army. What shows itself as the commonality of experience was, the metaphor implies, logically and temporally prior:

> Aristotle here presupposes that what persists in the flight of observations and emerges as a universal is, in fact, something common to them: for him the universality of the concept is ontologically prior. What concerns Aristotle about experience is merely how it contributes to the formation of concepts. (Ibid., 361)

What concerns narratologists about experiencing narrative is oriented towards the *telos*, the unity, the commonality. While such a unity is often conceived of as ontologically prior in narratological analyses, this is not a distinctive characteristic of all narratologies. The notion of narratological categories as a "heuristic for interpretation" (Kindt and Müller 2003, 208) entails the insight that the model that serves as a heuristic has certain limitations. A heuristic may aid discoveries ('heuristic' is etymologically connected to 'discovery'), it may enable a new understanding, but, I would argue, it does not supply an ultimate *telos* or the form of narrative that is, in the above sense, ontologically prior. Yet, and this is the structure of all narratological analyses, a heuristic is teleological in the sense that it is based on what is common to certain experiences – "conceiving of experience in terms of knowledge and result" (Weinsheimer 1985, 202). This applies to Genette's categories, as well as to postclassical approaches. Even when narratologists are concerned with the process of understanding or the ideology of narrative form, their approach is oriented towards the telos of what is common in historical experiences of narrative(s).[97]

David Herman may serve as an example for the fact that proponents of postclassical narratology consider narrative teleologically in this sense. Herman has proposed the regrounding of narratology in a "new explanatory paradigm" (Herman 2003, 304) which consists in "a triangulation of three major profiles under which narrative can be viewed: as a semiotic structure, as a cognitive resource, and as an artefact both shaping and shaped by social conditions and processes" (ibid., 328). Thus, Herman proposes that narratology should become an "integrated, cross-disciplinary approach" (ibid., 303) making use of concepts and methods from other fields, especially those of cognitive science. These concepts and methodological procedures in turn are to be applied with the aim of continually developing and improving the explanatory paradigm of the forms and functions of texts and practice of readers. Ultimately, the scientific goal of this approach is to render the experience of reading explicable (and predictable) with a dimension of historicity supplied by the sociolinguistic environment of the reader. In 2010, Herman, in a similar manner, triangulates "storytelling practices, communicative media, and the mind" (139) and reconsiders the beginning of the 'cognitive revolution' in literary studies:

> In this groundbreaking, agenda-setting contribution to the field, Turner draws on ideas from cognitive linguistics to triangulate literary scholarship with the study of language and of mind. Working against the grain of what he characterizes as default assumptions in the humanities in general and literary studies in particular, Turner suggests that practitioners should shift from producing ever more sophisticated readings of individual works, to developing an account of the basic and general principles underlying the process of reading itself. Cognitive linguistics, Turner argues, affords invaluable tools when it comes to this reprioritizing of reading over readings. At issue is a reassessment that places systematicity over nuance; common, everyday cognitive abilities over ostensibly unique or special capacities bound up with literary expression; and unconscious sense-making operations over what falls within the (narrow) domain of conscious awareness. (2010, 137–138)

---

[97] Diachronic narratology, concerned with the evolution of narrative forms and functions, presupposes a framework that is teleological in the same way. A historical perspective that records change relies on what is common in historical experiences of narrative(s) – how else could that change be recorded?

Here, cognitive narratology offers a new 'systematicity' of *reading*; that is, an account of the general principles underlying each historical event of understanding narrative. The theoretical triangulation draws the boundaries of narratology, allowing "a more coordinated effort to accomplish what remains the overarching goal of narrative inquiry: coming to a better understanding of what stories are and how they work" (ibid., 159). The overarching goal of narrative inquiry is thus still for the most part indebted to the logic of experiencing narrative in terms of knowledge and result ('the basic and general principles underlying the process of experiencing narrative').

3.1.2 A Hermeneutic Perspective on Narratological Practice: The Hermeneutics of Distanciation and the Hermeneutics of Belonging

Drawing the boundaries of narratology from a hermeneutic perspective, I have argued in the preceding section that a narratological analysis projects the telos of the unity of narrative experiences onto the semiotic object it sets out to describe. Narratological categories in this manner presuppose what could be termed 'distanciation,' a hermeneutic term which Merold Westphal understands as "methodological reflection in service of the objectivity available to an unconditioned subject" (2011, 43). Without analytical distance, the objectification that specifies and describes what narratives have in common is impossible. Thus, in loose analogy with Merold Westphal's argument in his book article "The dialectic of Belonging and Distanciation in Gadamer and Ricœur" (2011), the hermeneutic assumptions of the narratological enterprise can for the most part be characterized as 'distanciation,' where the (scientific) object of narrative is seen in terms of a methodological reflection allowing the description of elements untouched by the contingency of (the historical event of) an understanding subjectivity. This underlying hermeneutic framework allows, even for postclassical narratological analyses, the priority of "systematicity over nuance" (Herman 2010, 137).

The hermeneutics of belonging, on the other hand, is determined by "the notion of the interpreter as belonging to a world, a horizon of meaning and expectation that functions as the a priori condition of the possibility of experience as interpretation" (Westphal 2011, 48). Accordingly, the interpreter belongs not only to history (traditions, conceptual frameworks, life-worlds, etc.) but also to the narrative that is the supposed object of understanding. Thus, from the perspective of philosophical hermeneutics, understanding narrative is a process to which one ontologically belongs; a belonging that narratological categories can never transcend. Following Ricœur and Gadamer, this section will attempt to trace the dialectic between the hermeneutics of distanciation and the hermeneutics of belonging which characterizes narratological practice (a practice that is teleological without any telos beyond the endeavour to find the unity in contingent historical attempts to make sense of narrative); for both post- and neoclassical approaches to narratology rely on a hermeneutics that (temporarily) situates itself analytically outside of what it belongs to ontologically.

According to Westphal, one version of a hermeneutics of distanciation is provided by Dilthey in his essay "The Rise of Hermeneutics" (cf. Westphal 2011, 53–54). In this essay, after stating his goals as 'objectivity' and 'universal validity,' Dilthey outlines how such goals are to be achieved: "[R]ule-guided understanding of fixed and relatively permanent objectifications of life is what we call exegesis of interpretation" (1976, 235). In this manner, Dilthey attempts to supply a basis for the objectification which moves the act of understanding beyond historical relativity. Since Dilthey is convinced that there is a basic coherence between the subject and object of history, the objective and reflective distance is not *imposed* on history but is rather part of the structure of historical life. Joel C. Weinsheimer argues that Dilthey's "appeal to the notion of structure" implies "that historical experience can be understood in terms of itself and not by reference to some extrinsic standard" (1985, 152):

> Dilthey looks finally to historical method for the ground of truth – not to historical experience, not to the finite, conditioned experience of men who by reason of that finitude are permanently in need of history in order to understand themselves and the truth. Insofar as one sees human finitude as an obstacle to the truth, one will already have missed it, for the truth is: men are historical, conditioned, finite. Method is the attempt to deny that truth, and also the truth about truth which it implies – namely, that truth arises precisely in finite, historical experience. (Ibid., 154–155)

Leaving aside the question of whether Weinsheimer's critique of Dilthey (which reiterates Gadamer's critique of Dilthey in *Truth and Method*) is entirely just, he rightly points out that, for Dilthey, the lived experience of the one who understands history supplies an accurate model of the historical experience of others: "The first condition for the possibility of historical knowledge lies in the fact that I myself am a historical being, that he who investigates history is the same as he who makes history" (Dilthey 1976, 278). It is in this sense that no *extrinsic* standard is needed to understand historical experience. The 'rules' of historical method, then, include a reflective (and thus distanced) attitude towards what is understood as history. In this manner, historical knowledge is not concerned with a finite historical experience but with life, because "[l]ife itself gives rise to objectivity, certainty, and fixity in Dilthey's view" (Weinsheimer 1985, 156). Life gives rise to certainty when 'structures' emerge which are independent of the historical act that creates them (as, for instance, in language, which in a certain sense can be viewed as a 'fixity' that transcends the utterance; as, for instance in narratological categories, which in a certain sense can be viewed as a 'fixity' that transcends the individual story). Westphal claims that Dilthey's rules are "the method of distanciation by means of which objective and universally valid knowledge of historically relative cultures will be obtained. Cultures may be tradition-relative, but scientific knowledge need not be" (2011, 54). Narratology and narratological practice still tend to be informed by a hermeneutics of distanciation, a hermeneutics that strives for the methodological *distance* of the understanding subject, a distance which allows the structural 'fixity' that eludes contingent historical experience. It is this distance that enables scholars to conceptualize a teleological structure. Such a distance is assumed by analyses of, say, the culture-relativity of narrative. In order to demonstrate such relativity, the narratological frameworks need to be 'fixed' (and not culture-relative) in order to create the possibility of gauging that relativity.

A hermeneutic account of narratological knowledge that is indebted to ontological hermeneutics can locate (the generation of) this knowledge in hermeneutic experience; an experience which emerges in a hermeneutic situation (including, in the case of written narratives, writer, reader, text, traditions of writing and reading, etc.) and which recognizes its inescapable historical situatedness. The *experience* of what narratological concepts designate can never consist in a static result that supplies the state of affairs of what we term narrative once and for all. In *Truth and Method*, Gadamer offers a conception of experience characterized by a hermeneutics of belonging. In other words, as Weinsheimer points out, Gadamer contradicts our habitual conception of "experience conceived teleologically" (Weinsheimer 1985, 202):

> Normally we would say that the end of experience is knowledge, and certainly Gadamer concurs that the experience of history leads to historical knowledge. But in his consideration of hermeneutic experience he is concerned to reverse the normal line of thought – that is, he conceives of knowledge in terms of experience and process rather than conceiving of experience in terms of knowledge and result. (Ibid.)

Gadamer, then, characterizes a conception of understanding that does not *cancel* the possibility of knowledge but embeds it in a complex experiential process that does not posit the understood as an 'other,' as the ahistorical object of an understanding subject. Narratology, on the other hand, is structured teleologically and conceives of experience "in terms of knowledge and result" (ibid.): the experience of narrative leads to narratological knowledge. As Genette has famously demonstrated in *Narrative Discourse* (1972), to give one example, reading narrative yields categories (which, in turn, structure reading narrative). From a hermeneutic perspective, such narratological 'knowledge' (and its teleological structure) can be analyzed in terms of experience and process, an analysis which highlights and challenges the preconditions of narratological knowledge as contingent and historical. In other words, the narratological category does not offer a locus where the (understanding of) description of narrative comes to an end, and a classical narratological approach cannot supply a methodology that transcends the hermeneutic situations in which recipients of narrative find themselves. While the narratological category offers a teleological model reductive of complexity, a hermeneutic consideration of the event of understanding in which such models emerge 'models' the complexity – a complexity that challenges the human structuring of what Nietzsche calls 'the continuum that stands before us.' And this continuum is not itself teleological: it is that whose structuring *creates* a telos.

Narratology today characteristically identifies the limits (or historicality) of structuralist narratology while bracketing the limitations of narratological analyses informed by, say, cognitive science. Each (new) model of narrative (as a cognitive process, a social phenomenon, a semiotic structure, etc.), however, relies on the hermeneutics of distanciation (making a model entails the notion of an object of which the model is a model); the sum of all narratological analyses demonstrates that such a model engenders a process which confronts narratology with the limits of narratological analyses – of their models, epistemological foundations and hermeneutic assumptions. Analyses of metalepses might serve as the perfect example for this. I have argued above that the 'problem' of metalepsis consists in the complex dynamic that unfolds when the fundamental spatiotemporal (and, in the case of narrative, generic) make-up of human understanding is denied, and that the varying narratological accounts of metalepses reflect the unimaginable complexity and inescapable historicity of this dynamic. The hermeneutics of distanciation attempts to transcend the belonging characteristic of each attempt to understand metalepses. We belong to tradition, we belong to the text – the teleological projection of a unity in the experience of narrative is one example for this. What all analyses of metalepses taken together bring to the foreground is what Gadamer focuses on: "My real concern," Gadamer insists in the foreword to the second edition of *Truth and Method*, "was and is philosophic: not what we do or what we ought to do, but what happens to us over and above our wanting and doing" (2013, xxvi). Because something happens "over and above our wanting and doing" when we understand metaleptic transgressions, Werner Wolf feels compelled to concede that "metalepsis does not (yet) have a generally accepted definition" (2009b, 50–51). A hermeneutics of belonging can bring into focus what happens in the event of understanding metalepsis.

Following Gadamer's *Truth and Method*, the (restrictive) narratological enterprise can be framed as the approach that brackets the situatedness, historicality and finitude of understanding which inescapably encounters narrative as resistant to objectivization. It should be stressed at this point that Gadamerian hermeneutics strives to avoid all dualistic implications. In what Gadamer calls 'hermeneutic experience,' narrative, the other, or the work of art cannot be encountered as the object in a clear subject/object dichotomy. The question for Gadamer is thus not whether

> the meaning of a text is determined by the author or by the reader (Gadamer doesn't really make use of anything like an analytic concept of meaning); rather, the two positions taken together describe the movement of understanding itself, where understanding does not stop with the determination of meanings but is an ongoing critical reflection in which we see ourselves and what matters to us in the light of the text, even as we see the text in the light of ourselves and our interest. (Bruns 1992, 11)

The narrative in question is always already constituted by the hermeneutic situation in which it is understood. There is no valid principle *beyond* the event of understanding (such an event can of course include the application of narratological categories/methodological distanciation). It is this that ultimately grounds and determines the properties of the understood object or the unbiased position of the understanding subject.[98]

---

[98] How, then, can one ground understanding narrative if there is no recourse to an outside standard which precedes the "unimaginable complexity of interpretation" (Nordlund 2002, 326) and against which the properties of narrative can be (conclusively and objectively) measured and validated? This does not amount to the contention that every interpretation and every methodological approach is equally tenable and valid. Each approach or interpretation can still be subjected to what might be referred to as the *pragmatic* success or failure of interpretation and explanation – which itself relies on the pragmatic conception and coherence of "criteria that must be fulfilled if in a given context one is able to speak about truth in an unambiguous and meaningful manner" (Kockelmans 1991, 237). The conditions of 'successful' interpretation and explanation follow logically from the perspective of the interpreter, a perspective which is necessarily "seen from some limited context of meaning" (Kockelmans 1991, 238). Gadamer corroborates this when he insists in his postscript to the third edition of *Wahrheit und Methode* that "die immanente Geltung der kritischen Methodik der Wissenschaften" is uncontentious despite ontological hermeneutics. Günter Abel argues within the context of his interpretationist approach for a *Wahrheitsbegriff* that does not contradict Gadamerian

Against this background, understanding narrative can best be described as a (hermeneutic) dialogue whose movement questions or even transcends the clear distinctions that are presupposed by the analytical distance of a teleological approach. If, for instance, there is – as cognitive narratology claims – a "physical process of reading [which] is situated at the interface between narrative text and narrative understanding" (Jahn 2005, 68) and which connects the text and the conceptual representation this triggers, then the notion of such a process involving schemata or frames grapples with the fact that this process can only be observed *indirectly*. This old epistemological problem has been rephrased by Fauconnier as the following quandary in *Mental Spaces: Aspects of Meaning Construction in Natural Language* (1994):

> When language, mind, and culture are the object of scientific study, the investigator is no longer a mere spectator. He or she is one of the actors, part of the phenomenon under study: The thinking and talking that need to be demystified are also the thinking and talking used to carry out the demystification. The investigation that will reveal backstage secrets is also part of the main show, and clearly we are on intellectually perilous ground. (xvii)

When metalepsis is the object of scientific study, language, mind and culture emerge as the loci of metalepsis in which the metaleptic dynamic can be carried out as the hermeneutic encounter which is always already that which it preliminarily poses as object: an encounter that seemingly consists in the interplay of author/creator, narrative, recipient and the social, historical and linguistic practices that are narrative's prerequisite. Yet this need not be conceived as 'intellectually perilous ground.' It is rather the hermeneutic ground of understanding that is potentially thrown into relief by the metaleptic dynamic.

This take on narrative understanding (instigated by a hermeneutic consideration of metalepsis) reiterates elements of Gadamer's "central analogy between the process of understanding and the dialogue" (Holub 2005, 271) – an analogy that establishes a dialogical paradigm in the context of tradition that Robert C. Holub calls a 'model':

> According to this model, when we encounter a text we enter into an open conversation with a past in which [...] the questioning and answering, leads to understanding. Applica-

---

hermeneutics: "[D]ie Wahrheitsfrage wird zu einer Frage der gültigen Kohärenz innerhalb des Interpretations-Horizonts und der Interpretations-Praxis. Dies gilt zunächst für das Verhältnis von Sätzen zu anderen und bereits für wahr gehaltenen Sätzen innerhalb des umfassenderen [...] Interpretationen-Hintergrunds" (1995, 186).

tion[99], then, can be described as mediation between the then of the text and the now of the reader, as a conversation between the 'thou' of the past and the 'I' of the present. (Holub 2005, 271)

In his essay "Temporal Distance and Death in History," Paul Ricœur considers "Gadamer's notion of the transmission of tradition" (2002, 250) in a similar manner:

> In *Truth and Method*, this notion expresses at the same time the efficiency of the mediations that turn temporal distance from an empty space into a field of energy. Gadamer uses the superb phrase *Wirkungsgeschichte*, or the history of effect, which adds a positive aspect to what would otherwise be a simple crossing of temporal distance. In the end, it is all about reopening the past onto the future, more precisely onto the future of that past. (Ibid.)

Every encounter with narrative is, as a dialogical 'reopening of the past onto the future,' prejudiced by the linguistic constitution of understanding. It is the medium of language that fuses the fundamental elements of hermeneutic experience in what Gadamer terms 'effective history' (*Wirkungsgeschichte*), to whose 'existence' (*Dasein*, [cf. Gadamer XIX]) belong both that which is understood and understanding. Joel C. Weinsheimer points out the interconnectedness of Gadamer's conception of *Wirkungsgeschichte*, which is "the reality of history in that it is the history of realization" (1985, 181). In this manner Gadamer grounds understanding "not through identifying one element as its 'source,' nor through relating understanding to something apart from it, but precisely through exhibiting its own interconnected and dynamic structure" (Malpas 2002, 212). The banal proposition that narrative, recipient and author/creator (in their respec-

---

[99] The term 'application' (*Anwenden*) is used by Gadamer for an activity of consciousness that accompanies every interpretation. In a conversation with Carsten Dutt, Gadamer retraces what he means by application: "In unserem Jahrhundert hat dann Heidegger im Anschluß an Dilthey den entscheidenden Denkschritt getan, und im Anschluß daran habe ich selber unter Einschränkung der Geltungsweite des wissenschaftlichen Methodenbegriffs gezeigt, daß in allem Verstehen als drittes Vollzugsmoment Sich-selbst-Verstehen liegt, – eine Art Anwendung, die man im Pietismus die *subtilitas applicandi* nannte. Nicht nur das Verstehen und Auslegen, sondern auch das Anwenden, das Sich-selbst-Verstehen, ist Teil des hermeneutischen Vorgangs. Ich gebe gerne zu, daß der zufällige, sich geschichtlich anbietende Begriff der Applikation künstlich und irreführend ist. Aber ich habe nicht damit gerechnet, daß man meinen könnte, daß man Verstehen auf etwas anderes anwende. Nein, – ich meine, man soll es auf sich selbst anwenden" (Gadamer, qtd. in Dutt 1995, 10).

tive historical situatedness), the prejudices[100] of the interpreter, and the tradition in which the interpreter encounters the text, each presuppose all other elements of the "interconnected and dynamic structure" (ibid.) of narrative understanding has important consequences. Ultimately, validity and meaning can only be grounded in the hermeneutic dialogue that unites all these elements, a dialogue that can never reach transhistorical conclusiveness but only coherence within the historically situated elements it consists of – a dialogue which, consequently, is always open to further questions.[101]

Striving for "a better understanding of what stories are and how they work" (Herman 2010, 159), postclassical narratology attempts to employ various methodological approaches to better understand what is still implicitly considered the *object* of enquiry. Yet, as these varying approaches and their historical development taken together demonstrate, there is neither a single object of inquiry nor a common analytical procedure that substantiates the hermeneutics of distanciation employed (or at least implied) by narratological analyses. This hermeneutics inevitably encounters the limits of human understanding:

> It is not always the case that what happens in understanding is that one understands something in the sense of grasping or solving it. What happens, what happens also or instead is that one *always* confronts the limits – in Gadamer's language, the finitude or historicality, the situatedness – of understanding itself. (Bruns 1992, 180)

The acknowledgement of the situatedness of narratological analyses is the beginning of the hermeneutics of belonging.

I argue that understanding metalepsis oscillates between the telos of what is common in (the experience of) certain narratives and the ontological belonging which denies the basis of a teleological approach – a dialectic that has

---

100 By prejudices, Gadamer means the necessary (and neutral) pre-judgement on the basis of which understanding becomes possible, the "fore-structure of understanding" (Warnke 2002, 316) which is shaped by what is handed down in tradition, "the historical experiences and traditions of interpretation which we inherit" (ibid.).
101 Gadamer's hermeneutics has been criticized (for example, by E. D. Hirsch) precisely because it supposedly makes a valid standard for interpretation impossible. Yet, as maintained above, while the dialogical model of understanding is connected to "the idea of context relativity" (Kertscher 2002, 150), which is related by Jens Kertscher to Wittgenstein's philosophy of language (cf. ibid. 150–154), this does not mean that all interpretations are equally valid. Thus, while what Hirsch would in all likelihood consider a valid standard for interpretation is indeed contradicted by *Truth and Method*: questions of truth and validity are not done away with once and for all – they are, as Kertscher observes, still part of "the practice of language, of describing and embedding utterances in their specific contexts" (ibid. 153).

shaped the history of narratology. It is this tension between the hermeneutics of distanciation and the hermeneutics of belonging that arguably characterizes narratology today – not in the sense that narratologists dialogically engage with philosophical hermeneutics but in the sense that narratological analyses always grapple with the problems that the hermeneutics of distanciation entails. Postclassical narratology draws on a rich heritage which relies on the establishment of analytical distance to the object 'narrative,' as well as on challenges to the results of such analyses.

What is the relationship between the hermeneutics of distanciation and the hermeneutics of belonging? It is no coincidence that Ricœur's hermeneutics relies on the distinction between structure and event. While every event belongs ontologically to a concrete (historical) hermeneutic situation, structure is an intrinsic formal or logical condition that makes any event intelligible. Ricœur draws on Heidegger's and Gadamer's ontological hermeneutics (of belonging) as well as on structuralist accounts of language (which rely for the most part on a hermeneutics of distanciation). Gerald Bruns has argued that this distinction enables Ricœur to think about language "in terms of signs or in terms of saying; that is, we can think of what words mean in relation to other words in any linguistic or semiotic system or of what they mean when they are used in actual speech, say, in sentences" (1992, 235). As mentioned above, this dialectic relies on Ricœur's well-known distinction between structure and event, the notion of language as a system (to which meaning is entirely internal) and the contingent historical event that does not allow the distanciation which is the prerequisite of the notion of the structural object of the text. Not surprisingly, Ricœur claims that the "distanciation in which [Gadamer's] hermeneutics tends to see a sort of ontological fall from grace appears as a positive component of being for the text; it characteristically belongs to interpretation, not as its contrary but as its condition" (1981b [first French ed. 1973], 91). Of course, Ricœur does not claim that we can emancipate ourselves from our historicality or transcend the hermeneutic situation to which each event of understanding belongs ("the critique of ideology, supported by a specific interest, never breaks its link to the basis of belonging" [Ricœur 1991, 269]). Yet he does not rule out the possibility of a hermeneutics that temporarily situates itself analytically outside of what it belongs to ontologically (cf. Bruns 1993, 235–238). Inga Römer argues in a similar manner that Ricœur's hermeneutics consists in an open dialectic that includes distanciation and belonging, *distanciation* and *appartenance*:

> *Distanciation* is itself a moment of *appartenance*, not its opposite, let alone its inversion. It is the aspect that allows the critique of ideology, the analysis of language – and with it the analysis of signs, symbols, texts and actions characteristic of Anglo-American language

philosophy – to be understood not as the perversion of something primordial but as the deepening of an underlying open dialectic between those two elements. [...] Ricœur [sees] this dialectic, devoid of all synthesis or resolution, as the fundamental ongoing interplay of all these components in a process of understanding that is transparent to itself. *Distanciation* belongs essentially to *appartenance*.[102]

This is, in part, a criticism of Gadamer. For Gadamer, the methodology of the hermeneutics of distanciation is always already steeped in tradition, in *wirkungsgeschichtliches Bewusstsein*, in the hermeneutics of belonging. Thus, when Ricœur claimed in the French journal *Esprit* in 1963 that "it will never be possible to do hermeneutics without structuralism" (cf. 622; this is a loose translation offered by Alison Scott-Baumann in 2009, cf. 22), he meant that belonging is not in any sense prior to, or more fundamental than distanciation.

The approach of Chapter 2 of this book is based on a hermeneutics of distanciation. The present chapter is indebted to the insight that an analysis of the metaleptic dynamic begins with the outline of a structural relation and its denial: it offers another focus, arguing with Gadamer that 'it will never be possible to do structuralism without hermeneutics.' Metalepses, enacting the dialectic between distanciation and belonging, characteristically offer the insight that distanciation is embedded in a hermeneutic situation in which the recipient ontologically belongs to what is understood: a narratological analysis is made possible by an interpreter who belongs to a history, (narratological) tradition, *Wirkungsgeschichte*, etc., that make interpretation possible; moreover, according to Gadamer, as a reader, the interpreter "belongs to the text he is reading" (2013, 340). The text makes a claim on the one who attempts to understand it. Within this dialogical encounter, Gadamer argues, there is ultimately no analytical distance that enables methodological objectivism. But it should be noted that, while it is certainly the case that "[d]istanciation does not get much respect in Gadamer's hermeneutics, which is overwhelmingly devoted to belonging" (Westphal 2011, 53), Gadamer carefully considers its possibility:

---

102 "Die *distanciation* ist als Moment der *appartenance* selbst und nicht als ihr Gegenstück oder gar ihre Verfremdung zu verstehen. Die *distanciation* in der *appartenance* erlaubt es, Ideologiekritik, Sprachanalyse und damit die angelsächsische Sprachphilosophie, die Analyse von Zeichen, Symbolen, Texten und Handlungen nicht als Verfremdung einer Ursprünglichkeit, sondern als eine Vertiefung der grundlegenden offenen Dialektik von *appartenance* und *distanciation* zu verstehen. [...] Ricœur [sieht] eine grundlegendste offene Dialektik, d. h. eine Dialektik ohne aufhebende Synthese, darin, dass all diese Komponenten immer schon ineinander spielen und einen Prozess der Vertiefung des Verstehens und Sichverstehens bewirken. Die *distanciation* gehört schon selbst zur *appartenance*" (2010, 246–247; translated by Joseph Swann).

> [*Truth and Method*] tries to develop [...] a conception of knowledge and of truth that corresponds to the whole of our hermeneutic experience. Just as in the experience of art, we are concerned with truths that go essentially beyond the range of methodical knowledge, so the same thing is true of the whole of the human sciences: in them our historical tradition in all its forms is certainly made the *object* of investigation, but at the same time *truth comes to speech in it*. Fundamentally, the experience of historical tradition reaches far beyond those aspects of it that can be objectively investigated. (2013, xxii)

Distanciation is, of course, possible but it is incompatible with what Gadamer calls "a conception of truth that corresponds to the whole of our hermeneutic experience" (ibid.). 'Belonging,' in Gadamer's sense, becomes evident when one considers narrative as a dynamic, as hermeneutic experience rather than the (static) object of investigation. The truth that 'comes to speech' in metaleptic narratives demonstrates that understanding narrative 'reaches far beyond those aspects that can be objectively investigated.' Inextricably linked to the supposed 'object' of study, the history of narrative theory (as well as the history of narratological analyses of metalepses) demonstrates what Gadamer terms 'belonging.' For Gadamer, too, "there is a legitimate place for distanciation, but it is *aufgehoben* in a historical belonging that it cannot and need not escape" (Westphal 2011, 58). Thus, following Westphal's conception of Hegelian *Aufhebung*, I would maintain that the distanciation implied and presupposed by the category of metalepsis is, on the one hand, 'denied autonomy and primacy' and, on the other, is a 'subordinate moment' in an ontological belonging which narrative understanding cannot and need not escape (cf. Westphal 2011, 57–59).[103] This, it could be said following Gadamer, is 'not what narrative theorists do or ought to do, but what happens over and above wanting and doing' – and it is precisely what 'happens over and above our wanting and doing' that comes to prominence in the event of understanding metalepsis.

3.1.3 The Negativity of Hermeneutic Experience

What follows from these hermeneutic insights for narratologically informed readings of metalepsis? And how can this challenge or change the shape of

---

[103] It seems debatable whether Gadamer's and Ricœur's respective positions are strictly speaking incompatible. Rather, they place different emphases on relationship between structure and event. Even though Westphal argues that "Gadamer and Ricœur, together, expose the dialectic of belonging and distanciation" (43), Gadamer undermines this dialectic, inasmuch as he grounds 'distanciation' in the 'belonging' that inevitably characterizes human understanding.

narratological analyses? I have argued above (Chapter 3.1.1) that the boundaries of narratology are drawn by a necessarily historical narratological practice. If, in other words, the form of narrative and the textual structure(s) of narratology are determined by historical acts of 'drawing boundaries,' it follows from this that the histories of narratological theory and practice imply changing paradigms, epistemological frameworks, varying sets of rules, etc. I have suggested that one way to draw the boundaries of narratology is the designation of a practice that conceives of the experience of narrative teleologically (the *telos* being the assumption that the unity in historically contingent experiences of narrative can be modelled). Twentieth-century hermeneutics not only offers a way to conceptualize the integration of that telos in the hermeneutic situation in which it emerges (even though a single analysis may bracket the historicity of its approach, a history of narratological analyses reveals the dialectic between the hermeneutics of distanciation and the hermeneutics of belonging). It also offers an analysis of the negativity generated by (narratological) processes of understanding narrative. Such an analysis describes (textual) structures as a provisional moment in the process of understanding – based, as I have argued above (Chapter 3.1.2), on the knowledge of 'what all narratives have in common' and which cannot be located in the isolated object narrative).

It is my contention that in reading metalepses one potentially encounters what Gadamer has termed the 'negativity of hermeneutic experience,' the *experience* of a self-reflexive, dynamic, dialogical structure that results in an oscillating openness. This openness can, in turn, be correlated with the unstable 'ontological status' of metaleptic entities and identities, as well as with the unstable conceptual frameworks on which narratological analyses invariably rely. In what follows, the attempt will be made to outline the extent to which analyses of metaleptic transgression can profit from Gadamer's treatment of what he terms the 'historically effected consciousness' (*wirkungsgeschichtliches Bewusstsein*) – essentially a philosophy of hermeneutic experience expounded in the chapter 'The Concept of Experience and the Nature of Hermeneutic Experience' ("Der Begriff der Erfahrung und das Wesen der hermeneutischen Erfahrung") of *Truth and Method*.

In two respects Gadamer's insight that every (necessarily historical) act of understanding is subject to the principle of 'effective history' (*Wirkungsgeschichte*) – a principle which describes the prerequisites that temporally and logically precede consciousness as determining understanding – is indebted to Hegel's notion of 'experience.' On the one hand, the Hegelian concept of experience, developed in the *Phänomenologie des Geistes* (1832) has an element of (curiously productive) negativity, which Gadamer conceives as the decisive characteristic of the hermeneutic experience:

> Gadamer understands this dialectical character of experience as a 'scepticism in action' where the experiencing consciousness gives *voice* to an otherness in experience as it (the otherness) confronts the experiencing consciousness about its initially fixed determination of the actuality of its experience. (Risser 1997, 88)

According to Gadamer, the *negativity* of the hermeneutic experience, or experience proper, takes place in a dialectical *movement*, which, in contrast to Hegel, neither transcends itself nor reaches the level of absolute knowledge: "The dialectics of experience achieves its end not in a [moment of] completed knowledge but in that opening out to experience that is the (liberating) fruit of experience itself."[104] Experience in this sense is always experience of human finitude ("Erfahrung der menschlichen Endlichkeit" [Gadamer 1999a, 363]) and can consequently not be converted into conclusive knowledge, cannot simply arrive at a new conception of a supposedly valid object of knowledge. Experience leads to *openness*, to further experience, an openness which results from the insight into the limits of human existence ("Einsicht in die Grenzen des Menschseins" [Gadamer 1999a, 363]); and human existence, as a matter of principle, has to undergo experience as something that always involves negativity. Hermeneutic experience, it may therefore be argued, consists in the insight into this process and, as such, is the result of a disappointment which anticipates an endless succession of further disappointments:

> Thus the historical nature of man essentially implies a fundamental negativity that emerges in the relation between experience and insight. Insight is more than the knowledge of this or that situation. It always involves an escape from something that had deceived us and held us captive. Thus insight always involves an element of self-knowledge and constitutes a necessary side of what we called experience in the proper sense. (Gadamer 2013, 350)

Therefore, the 'openness' of the hermeneutic experience also describes the changing self of the one who experiences and who, as the one who is experienced, is 'radically undogmatic' This is the second element of Hegel's *Erfahrungsbegriff* on which Gadamer draws: that experience always implies change to the experiencing self. Experience, Gadamer writes (following Hegel),

---

[104] "Die Dialektik der Erfahrung hat ihre eigene Vollendung nicht in einem abschließenden Wissen, sondern in jener Offenheit für Erfahrung, die durch die Erfahrung selbst freigespielt wird" (Gadamer 1999a, 361; translated by Joseph Swann).

is the "reversal that consciousness undergoes when it recognizes itself in what is alien and different" (2013, 349). The closely interwoven nature of understanding and effective history leads to an openness that moves beyond understanding subject and understood object. According to Gadamer, this openness – in which 'the new object' of understanding, on the one hand, admittedly 'contains the truth about the old object' (cf. ibid., 360) – always already entails, on the other hand, a relatedness to new experience ("The truth of experience always implies an orientation toward new experience" [Gadamer 2013, 350]). *In Hermeneutics Ancient and Modern (1992),* Bruns characterized this openness as

> a sort of emancipation or releasement. […] A releasement, say, from some prior certainty or ground, some vocabulary or framework or settled self-understanding; or say that the hermeneutical experience always entails an 'epistemological crisis' that calls for the reinterpretation of our situation, or ourselves, a critical dismantling of what had been decided. (184)

This is what Gadamer's insight into experience in general or experience as a whole ("Erfahrung im ganzen" [Gadamer 1999a, 361]) demands of the specific situation in which the literary text is understood – a situation always already woven into 'effective history.' The negativity of hermeneutic experience is not the negativity of an object that can be analyzed from a safe distance. Metalepsis potentially demonstrates that the negativity encountered is our negativity, is what happens to us 'over and above our wanting and doing.' Understanding metalepsis foregrounds the epistemological, logical and mimetic 'impossibilities' that are conventionally bracketed in narrative comprehension. As interpreters, we *belong* to the negativity of metaleptic transgressions. To reveal the prejudiced nature of one's understanding, to expose the prejudices that enable understanding in the first place, allows the awareness of the provisional nature of the prerequisites of historical interpretation. To see then how one's own prejudices (in the sense of conceptual frameworks) become questionable in the act of interpretation is *application* in the Gadamerian sense:

> A truly historical [act of] understanding must take account of one's own historicality. Only then will it – rather than pursuing the phantom of an ongoing historical research object – recognize in its object the Other of the Own and hence come to know the one as it does the other. The true historical object is not an object: it is the unity of this One-and-Other, a re-

lation which constitutes the reality of history just as it does the reality of historical understanding.[105]

Narratological analyses typically bracket this. In other words, even postclassical narratologies seemingly consider the experience of understanding narrative as something that resembles the 'phantom of a historical object,' i.e. the object of progressive research. The narratological objective of restrictive theorists such as Gerald Prince, in keeping with the traditional structuralist view of narratology as "the science of narrative" (Prince 2003, 11), is akin to Aristotelian thought which conceptualizes the unity of experience as the telos which precedes experience (Gadamer refers to this in *Truth and Method*). Following the scientific logic of induction, the attempt is made to render the experience of understanding (at least partially) as the objectifiable, and hence repeatable telos. This orientation towards the universality of the concept (or principle), which always knows the result of understanding in advance (that is, prior to experience, or caused by the ahistorical *object* of 'experience') is – in its reliance on a hermeneutics of distanciation – incompatible with hermeneutic experience in Gadamer's sense:

> If we thus regard experience in terms of its result, we have ignored the fact that experience is a process. In fact, this process is essentially negative. It cannot be described simply as the unbroken generation of typical universals. Rather, this generation takes place as false generalizations are continually refuted by experience and what was regarded as typical is shown not to be so. (2013, 347)

It is precisely this process of experience in which the typical becomes untypical that is instigated by metaleptic transgression. Metalepsis introduces this negativity into the narratological grid of diegetic levels, and understanding metalepsis introduces it into every hermeneutic situation in which it is understood. This is indeed 'typical' of metalepses. This does not mean that metaleptic narratives cannot be considered in terms simply of knowledge and result; but this can only be done if the process of experience and the negativity it entails are bracketed. If that process itself becomes the focus of attention, understanding metalepsis

---

[105]"Ein wirklich historisches Verstehen muß die eigene Geschichtlichkeit mitdenken. Nur dann wird es nicht dem Phantom eines historischen Objektes nachjagen, das Gegenstand fortschreitender Forschung ist, sondern wird in dem Objekt das Andere des Eigenen und damit das Eine wie das Andere erkennen lernen. Der wahre historische Gegenstand ist kein Gegenstand, sondern die Einheit dieses Einen und Anderen, ein Verhältnis, in dem die Wirklichkeit der Geschichte ebenso wie die Wirklichkeit des geschichtlichen Verstehens besteht" (Gadamer 1999b, 64–65; translated by Joseph Swann).

can be considered as hermeneutic *experience* – unstable, manifold and self-referential, forcing the concepts that temporally and logically precede it into a dialogical openness that resists all attempts at objectification and 'finalization.'

An important hermeneutic insight can be drawn from this discussion. The various nuances of meaning, as well as the contradictions, which emerge in narratological discussions of metalepsis reveal that the experience of negativity ultimately cannot be bracketed. Such nuances of meaning and such contradictions belong ineradicably to what could be termed the *Wirkungsgeschichte* of metalepsis. Striving for coherence within the elements of the hermeneutic situation cannot yield an "unbroken generation of typical universals" (Gadamer 2013, 347) that transcend the historicity of their generation. Yet such an analysis of the hermeneutics of narratology is not concerned with 'what narratologists ought to do': this chapter does not argue that structuralism or model-making should be given up. As such, teleological model-making and its reliance on the hermeneutics of distanciation is a necessary component of the event of understanding. Yet an awareness of what is involved in the event of understanding may help in an outline of the scope of narratological categories and enrich the following interpretations of instances of metaleptic transgression.[106]

---

[106] It is an interesting question whether philosophical or ontological hermeneutics should lead to a distinguished kind of literary criticism. Gadamer has often been criticized for an apparent discontinuity between his literary analyses and ontological hermeneutics: Gadamer "seems to be able to admit historicity only on an abstract theoretical level. When he himself analyzes texts – whether it is a poem by Rainer Maria Rilke or a novel by Karl Immermann – the potentially radical notion of being-in-the-world produces a philosophical criticism akin to the most ahistorical, New Critical readings" (Holub 2005, 272). But Holub's expectation that ontological hermeneutics should lead to a kind of literary criticism that exclusively addresses ontological-existential questions may be misguided. Gadamerian hermeneutics, it could equally be argued, does not in any strict sense contradict New Critical readings but offers an analysis of the conditions and possibilities, as well as human limitations, by which such readings are shaped.

3.2 The Metaleptic Transgression: 'Impossible Narration'

> ... damn! ... things are really getting screwed up here! If you guys keep circulating like that, freely, and without any warning, from present to past, back and forth, up and down, to and fro, without any respect for the logic of this recitation, and without even asking for my permission, it's really going to make a mess of this already shaky situation!
> — Raymond Federman, Take It or Leave It

This section of Chapter 3 attempts to show how the analysis of metalepsis can profit from the insight that (the event of) understanding metalepses potentially enacts what Gadamer terms 'hermeneutic experience.' How can the claim be substantiated that "what happens to us over and above our wanting and doing" (Gadamer 2013, xxvi) becomes prominent in that (heuristic) event? Or to put it differently: that the event of understanding metalepsis entails the negativity of hermeneutic experience, and that the frameworks with which narrative is approached are subjected to an aporetic movement in the event of understanding. This is connected to the question how the hermeneutic consideration of narratology in the preceding sections of this chapter bears on the analysis of metaleptic narratives.

The definition of metalepsis contains an element of negativity. 'Impossibly,' metalepses *per definitionem* deny their conceptual prerequisites; they rely on and at the same time deny the "shifting but sacred frontier between two worlds, the world in which one tells, the world of which one tells" (Genette 1980, 236). This definition introduces a vicious circularity which has often been compared to logical paradoxes in mathematics (cf. for instance, Hofstadter 1979, McHale 1987, Meister 2005, Ryan 2006, Pier 2009, and Klimek 2010): metalepses have accordingly been classified as self-referential and paradoxical – the 'impossible narration' which resembles the 'strange loops' and 'tangled hierarchies' which occur, according to Hofstadter, "when what you presume are clear hierarchical levels take you by surprise and fold back in a hierarchy-violating way" (Hofstadter 1979, 391).[107] This section argues that the 'tangled hierarchies' of metalepses constitute aporetic configurations; in a sense, understanding metalepsis is the enactment of the structural relation that collapses itself – a 'movement' that is closely related to the notion of *aporia*:

---

[107] Brian McHale was the first to analyze metalepsis as a 'strange loop' or tangled hierarchy' in his *Postmodernist Fiction* (1987). Among others, Werner Wolf (1993) and Marie-Laure Ryan (2006) have followed suit.

> Aporia comes from the Greek *aporos*, which means 'without passage' or 'without issue.' An aporia is something which is impracticable. A route which is impracticable is one that cannot be traversed, it is an uncrossable path. Without passage, not treadable. For the Eleatic Zeno, who, it is generally recognized, was the first to use the term consistently, aporia implied the suspension (*epokhe*) of judgement. At the point where the path of thinking stopped, judgement was suspended. This definition of aporia was inherited by the presocratic sophists who called an aporia two contradictory sayings of equal value. The suspension of judgement was a mode of perplexity before the inability to ground either saying. (Beardsworth 1996, 32)

Metalepsis implies sayings that are impossible to 'ground.' Breaking its frame, the metaleptic dynamic is antithetical to the logic of narrative representation on which it relies. Neither thesis (e.g. the boundary between [extra-]diegetic levels or universes cannot be literally crossed or denied) nor antithesis (e.g. the boundary between [extra-]diegetic levels or universes can be literally crossed or denied) can supply the phenomenon's trajectory. Nor does metalepsis consist in a synthesis of conflicting forces transcending the dialectic instigated by negativity. It is impossible to 'stop' the dynamic and describe its definite shape once and for all. The aporetic 'impossibility' of metalepsis induces 'a mode of perplexity' precisely because the dynamic as a whole moves through and oscillates between the logical and hierarchical order of two distinct spatiotemporal positions and their disorderly and illogical conflation/negation. In the following, I argue from a hermeneutic perspective that this element of negativity potentially throws into relief fundamental conditions (and limitations) of narrative sensemaking.

Many narratologists emphasize the 'impossible' nature of metaleptic narration. Werner Wolf maintains that the "paradoxical 'impossibility' of metaleptic transgressions seems to lay bare the fictionality of the work in which they occur and thus implies a metastatement on its medial nature as an artefact" (2009, 50). For Wolf, the emphasis is on a logical 'impossibility' opposing or denying the logic that governs non-fictional writing; an 'impossibility,' in other words, that contrasts with the possibilities of, say, historical representation, and marks the writing as fictional. This is connected to the contention that metalepsis is typical of a certain kind of experimental narrative of the twentieth and twenty-first centuries which highlight and/or create certain epistemological problems. In contrast to this, I contend that the metaleptic dynamic (at least potentially) lays bare the 'impossibilities' of fictional as well as non-fictional narration *in general*. I employ the concept of 'impossible narration'[108] not only to refer to the aporetic configuration of metalepsis (a 'movement' impossible to ground), but also to highlight that metalepses have the capacity to foreground the 'impossibilities' that emerge, albeit mostly unnoticed or bracketed, in very conventional attempts to understand narrative. Hence the 'impossibility' of metalepsis cannot exhaustively be described as the playful violation of representational logic and/or generic codes, because the metaleptic dynamic questions the very foundations of narration – which are inevitably connected to human epistemological conditions and hermeneutic capabilities. Discussing the Formalist approach to the 'literariness' of literary texts, Tony Bennett has presented a similar argument concerning the effects of defamiliarization, effects which Formalists considered a defining characteristic of literature:

> [T]he 'reality' which literary works are said to defamiliarize is not some presumed raw, conceptually unprocessed, 'out there' reality but 'reality' as mediated through the categories of some other form of cognition. Literature characteristically works on and subverts those linguistic, perceptual and cognitive forms which conventionally condition our access to 'reality' and which, in their taken-for-grantedness, present the particular 'reality' they construct as *reality* itself. Literature thus effects a two-fold shift of perceptions. For what it makes appear strange is not merely the 'reality' which has been distanced from habitual modes of representation but also those habitual modes of representation themselves. Literature offers not only a new insight into 'reality' but also reveals the formal operations whereby what is commonly taken for 'reality' is constructed. (Bennett 1979, 44)

---

108 The notion of 'impossible narration' has been employed by Brian Richardson in the context of what he, Jan Alber, Stefan Iversen and Henrik Skov Nielsen have termed 'unnatural narratology' (cf. Richardson et al. 2010). Unnatural narratology, the study of unnatural narratives, investigates "anti-mimetic texts that violate the parameters of traditional realism [...] or move beyond the conventions of natural narrative, i.e., forms of spontaneous oral storytelling" (Richardson et al. 2010, 115). In *Unnatural Voices* (2006), Brian Richardson introduces the category of 'impossible narration' into an extension of Stanzel's narrative circle and situates it alongside first person, second person, third person and multiperson narrative. He defines 'impossible narration' as "metaleptic texts that contain discourse that cannot possibly be spoken or written by the purported narrators and may involve the kind of ontological frame-breaking typical of postmodern worlds" (Richardson 2006, 76). This cannot occur in nonfictional discourse (cf. ibid.).

It makes perfect sense to use 'impossible narration' as a designation for metaleptic narration or "impossibly conflated acts of narration" (ibid., 78) such as Christine Brooke-Rose's *Thru* (1975), Beckett's *The Unnamable* (1953 [first English ed. 1958]) and, another example supplied by Richardson, the later novels of Robbe-Grillet. The notion of 'impossibility' employed by Richardson is explicitly positioned opposite the 'possibilities' of traditional realism or oral storytelling. The premise of this chapter is that metalepsis highlights the 'impossibilities' that cut across this opposition.

It is the latter shift in perception that is of interest here. The foundations highlighted and questioned by metalepsis are the forms of knowledge and perception which "conventionally condition our access to 'reality'"; these (linguistic, perceptual and cognitive) forms, which 'support' fictional narrative and the narrative construction of 'reality' alike, become visible if 'reality' is represented unconventionally and, as in the case of metalepsis, 'impossibly.' Metalepsis is, in this sense, not only part of a tradition that 'defamiliarizes' familiar ways of making sense. The metaleptic defamiliarization, I would argue, potentially uncovers aporetic configurations that come into being in human mediations of 'reality.'

In other words, a detailed analysis of the element of negativity that is part of the metaleptic dynamic potentially highlights and reflects the fact that the representational logic of 'habitual modes of representation' involves aporia and 'paradoxical impossibilities' which are indebted to human limitations (of knowledge). Metalepsis negates the emerging structure of distinct spatiotemporal positions that is the prerequisite of all narrative understanding; it creates *and* denies the 'presence' of what it represents; it playfully engages with the self-referential potential of narrative (and the paradoxes implied in the notion of self-reference); and it lays bare the temporal multiplicity concealed in the conventional, if mostly implicit, notion of the "atemporal space of the narrative as text" (Genette 1980, 223). Or to put it yet another way, it connects the aporetic structure of narrative with the 'here and now' that is part of the hermeneutic situation in which the metaleptic dynamic emerges.

The postmodern discussion of the relationship between historical writing and fictional narrative might serve as an illustration of how aporetic 'structures' of narrative are embedded in, or rather how they open up into the hermeneutic situation in which they emerge. In the wake of Hayden White's influential *The Content of Form: Narrative Discourse and Historical Representation* (1987), many critics have argued that historical writing is not only structurally similar to literary texts, but also (and this not necessarily in agreement with White) fictional in the sense of 'constructed' (*fictio*), if not in the sense of 'made up' (*fictum*). Such positions are indebted to poststructuralist accounts of narrative (theory) which argue that narrative operates within the self-enclosed system of language (cf. for instance, Marie-Laure Ryan 1997, O'Neill 1994, Gibson 1996). Since it is impossible to gauge the exact relation between 'world' and language, between represented and representation, the counter-argument can be made that narrative is and is not referentially void – narrative allows the conclusion, in other words, that the narrated 'world' (whether conceptualized as an external referent or not) is mysteriously present and non-existent at the same time.[109]

I maintain that such aporias amount, in Gadamerian terms, to 'the experience of human finitude' ("Erfahrung der menschlichen Endlichkeit" [Gadamer 1999a, 363]). Understanding narrative thus potentially involves the recognition that what is posed as an object is always already the subject position from which it is encountered. In this manner, 'impossible narration' may be seen from a hermeneutic perspective as radically evading the safe distance from the understanding subject that is the prerequisite of what we call objectivity. Metalepsis is not an aporetic object watched from a safe distance. The fact that we cannot transcend our hermeneutic encounter with any (narrative) representation and its historically contingent reception can lead to the realization that narrative *conventionally* transcends human limitations 'impossibly,' preliminarily, by proxy. An example of this is the (logically impossible) perspective of an omniscient and omnipresent narrator in fictional narration, or of the voices that belong to two distinct hierarchical narrative levels that merge in free indirect discourse.[110] Thus, the (metaleptic) strategy of narrating 'impossibly' not only forces the reader to become aware of (some of the) the conditions, conventionalities, and possibilities of narrative representation that traditionally direct the reader's expectations, but also potentially brings the experience of human finitude into play.

In Raymond Federman's *Take It or Leave It* (1976), the protagonist claims that he has been deserted by his narrator ("the second-hand teller"; Chapter XVII, no pagination) and finds that the audience (presumably extradiegetic narratees) have sent a delegate to his very own space and time. In Chapter XVIII, the protagonist complains: "If you guys keep circulating like that, freely, [...] it's really going to make a mess of this already shaky situation" (Federman 1976, no pagination). Metalepsis, connected to human aporia and liminality, the

---

[109] Ryan for instance claims that "fictional texts," in contrast to non-fiction, "do not share their reference world with other texts" (1997, 167). A more radical implication of poststructuralist thought is that representations cannot share a 'reference world' – there is nothing beyond the text (or created by the text) that stabilizes its semantic possibilities, as it can, from a Derridean perspective, only ever refer to signification. For a detailed analysis of O'Neill's (1994) postmodern narratology and Gibson's (1996) deconstructive (or deconstructed) narratology, and a discussion of their aporetic implications, see Sandra Heinen (2002).

[110] This of course presupposes that free indirect discourse is conceptualized as consisting of a narrator's and a character's language, a position which has been under attack since Banfield's (1982) claim that such representations of subjectivity are 'narratorless.' For a survey of debates, see Brian McHale (2009).

present section of this chapter argues, does *not* consist in the denial of the impeccable representational logic of narrative, but rather 'makes a mess of an already shaky situation.'

Each of the following four sections relates how a specific (structuralist, literary, philosophical) framework with which narrative is approached is subjected to an aporetic 'movement' in the event of understanding metalepsis. Chapter 3.2.1 deals with the questionable nature of the structural prerequisites of metalepsis that emerges in the practice of coherently establishing the concept of diegetic 'levels' or 'universes.' Each of these constitutes a distinct "narrative reality" (O'Neill 1994, 60), which representational logic requires to be hierarchically ordered and separated by a temporal hiatus. Chapter 3.2.2 claims that Gadamer's retrieval of Aristotelian mimesis has a metaleptic quality and argues that the metaleptic dynamic enacts *and* disrupts mimesis, as it foregrounds the aporetic presence of the represented. Chapter 3.2.3 offers a brief analysis of the aporia(s) of realism and investigates the extent to which metaleptic structures mark the place where, impossibly, world and language, represented and representation, meet. In a further section (3.2.4.), it will be argued that metalepsis lays bare the self-referential structure of narrative (and literary texts) insofar as the narrative situation becomes visible as 'communicated communication' in the transgression of the boundary that separates the worlds in which and of which a narrator tells; that is to say, this section, traces the hermeneutic experience of understanding metalepsis.

3.2.1 'Impossible Narration' I: Aporia and Paradox in the Establishment of Diegetic Levels

Genette's classification of diegetic levels seemingly originates in the view that narrative is basically a recounting (cf. Prince 2003, 58), and that what is recounted (whether an event, existent or another act of recounting) is logically prior to its narration: "any event a narrative recounts is at a diegetic level immediately higher than the level at which the narrating act producing this narrative is placed" (Genette 1980, 228). Slomith Rimmon-Kenan, in her definition of diegetic levels, turns this whole structure upside down, claiming that "narration is always at a higher narrative level than the story it narrates" (Rimmon-Kenan 1983, 92). The question which stratum in the diegetic relay has priority over the others is here consequent upon the conception that narrative is in principle a constructive act and that the precedence of narration over story is the precedence of that act over the story it generates.

Dealing with the triad *histoire*, *récit* and *narration* in *Narrative Discourse Revisited* (1988), Genette specifies that the question which comes first in the temporal and logical sequence of story and narration depends on the narrative's "real or fictive genesis" (14), the real or fictive narrative situation in whose context the narrative comes into being:

> In a nonfictional (for example, historical) narrative, the actual order is obviously *story* (the completed events), *narrating* (the narrative act of the historian), *and narrative* (the product of that act, potentially or virtually capable of surviving it in the form of a written text, a recording, or a human memory). [...] In fiction, the real narrative situation is pretended to – and this pretence, or *simulation* (which is perhaps the best translation of the Greek *mimésis*), is precisely what defines the work of fiction. But the true order is instead something like narrating < story/narrative, with the narrative act initiating (inventing) *both* the story and its narrative, which are then completely indissociable. But has a pure fiction ever existed? And a pure nonfiction? (Genette 1988, 14–15; emphasis in the original)

The answer to these rhetorical questions is of course negative in both cases. Since it is impossible to (formally) establish to what degree a narrative is fictional, that is, to what degree – if at all – a story and its narrative are engendered by the act of narration, this binary opposition cannot ultimately solve the problem; it transfers the establishment of the actual order of Genette's triad (in other words, the temporal and logical sequence of the elements of narrative) back to the realm of (literary) interpretation, and thus back to a perspective shaped by a complex and unique hermeneutic situation. A novel such as Mark Z. Danielewski's *House of Leaves* (2000) plays with this opposition as its remediations make it impossible to establish whether, in Genette's words, 'the real narrative situation is pretended to' or not. The novel continually suggests that the complex interplay between diegetic levels is *both* indebted to the logic that the story told is temporally and logically prior to the telling (and may become metaleptically present in the telling) *and* indebted to the logic that the haunted house tale is a fabrication and thus logically and temporally subsequent to the telling (cf. Hanebeck 2011).

There are many metaleptic transgressions that subvert the paradigm of 'nonfictional narrative.' Federman's *Take It or Leave It* (1976) questions the temporal and logical sequentiality of narrative representations, a fact that induces the protagonist to complain about the narratee who, as a metaleptic presence, shares the protagonist's diegetic space and time:

> And furthermore the more I think about it the more I am convinced there is something illegal about your presence here in the middle of my story, some twenty years too soon. How the hell did you manage to pass from the level of the present to the level of the past? From outside to inside this very personal recitation? Doesn't make sense! Normally such

transfers are not permitted. They go against the logic of traditional narrative techniques! (Federman 1976, Chapter XVII, no pagination)

The metaleptic potential of this passage playfully engages with "the logic of traditional narrative techniques" which can be correlated with what Genette terms "the real narrative situation." The complaint that the movement from 'outside to inside the recitation' is illicit, implies a knowledge of the 'rule' that the event is conventionally prior to its telling. Yet such a metaleptic movement not only relies on the logic it denies, it also demonstrates that the fictive world 'recounted' is constituted by the recounting. "In the beginning was the word," the opening of the Gospel of John, paradigmatically captures this sense of primacy of the word that creates the world of which it tells. Yet fictional narrational acts, even though they create the world of which they tell, are an imitative practice as well: every fictive event is in a certain sense an emulation of other (fictive) events, every fictive discursive practice an emulation of other discursive practices. Each fiction refers to something that is logically and temporally antecedent, such as (generic) traditions of reading and writing, human experientiality, etc. The passage from *Take It Or Leave It* foregrounds the fact that fiction is an 'impure' recounting that shapes the past which it purports to represent – a past of 'passing' events and existents – and, contrary to convention, also narrates 'from the level of the present to the level of the past.' Federman acknowledges the logic of the primacy of the word, as well as the logic of the primacy of the 'world' – an aporia which leaves us unable "to ground either saying" (Beardsworth 1996, 32).

Abbott has critically assessed this relationship of tension between the story that is recounted by an act of narration and the act of narration that generates the story. Abbott traces this insight into the paradoxical relationship between event and recounted event back to Jonathan Culler's landmark essay "Story and Discourse in the Analysis of Narrative" (1981) and argues that although "the sense of precedence of the event (true or false, fictional or nonfictional) is a *defining feature of narrative*" (Abbott 2005, 535), narrative is also governed by the "opposite and irreconcilable" (ibid., 535) logic "by which event is a product of discursive forces rather than a given reported by discourse" (Culler 1981, 175). Each of these principles excludes the other, yet each principle is part of the understanding of narrative. 'Impossibly,' both principles are the valid inference from the narrative situations outlined in *Narrative Discourse Revisited*. 'Has a pure fiction ever existed?' Narrative, of course, is never entirely 'pure.'

This aporia is enacted by the tendency of "the normal and canonical system of fiction (the one challenged by *Tristram Shandy, Jacques le fataliste,* and a number of modern narratives)" (Genette 1988, 15) to conventionally imitate what is usually construed as nonfiction in the above sense. The vast majority of eighteenth-century novels can be cited as evidence of that convention: Often disguised as histories, they employ techniques designed to convince readers that what they are reading is historically attested, such as the fictional editor who vouches for the novel's authenticity. In this manner, Defoe managed to convince his contemporary readers that the events in *Robinson Crusoe* (1917) had actually taken place (cf. Mayer 1997, 197). Ian Watt has famously connected this tendency in the early English novel with what he terms "formal realism [...]: the premise, or primary convention, that the novel is a full and authentic report of human experience" (1967, 32). This premise, which Defoe and Richardson "accepted very literally" (ibid.), is, according to Watt, "implicit in the novel form in general" (ibid.).

Unlike Defoe and Richardson, Laurence Sterne foregrounds this aporia: in the hands of Laurence Sterne and his narrator Tristram Shandy, the 'novel form' is playfully and metaleptically dramatized as the 'full and authentic' recounting of a prior experience – yet at the same time negates the validity of this undertaking by constantly reminding the reader of the fictional narrative situation that generates and thus precedes the narrated events: on the one hand, Tristram is the "historiographer" (I.xiv) who looks into the historical document of his mother's marriage settlement to authenticate his story (cf. I.xiv); on the other hand, he is able to change the events in the diegesis because he feels compelled to do so by a dialogue with a "hypercritick" (cf. II.viii) in which he is admonished for an unlikely occurrence of events. Tristram's final contribution to the dialogue suggests that he is changing the events that had been criticized: "If I am thus pressed—I then put an end to the whole objection and controversy about it all at once,---by acquainting him [the hypercritick], that *Obadiah* had not got above threescore yards from the stable-yard before he met with Dr. *Slop*" (II.viii). Here, Tristram Shandy shows how he transfers events "from the level of the present to the level of the past" (Federman 1976, Chapter XVII, no pagination). The potentially metaleptic influence of (extradiegetic) narratees on the events of the diegesis counterbalances the premise that the events are logically and temporally antecedent to their recounting. It is one of many singular characteristics of *Tristram Shandy* that this narrative paradox is explicitly and metaleptically spelled out in the narrator's comments and dialogues.

How do narratological accounts of diegetic levels mirror this aporia? Herman has maintained that the story/discourse distinction that engenders this paradox "should be viewed as a more or less valuable heuristic device" (Herman 2002, 215) rather than a rigid imperative and that "setting up an impermeable ontological barrier between the domain of the narrating and the domain of the narrated [...] could [...] vitiate the phenomenology of reading" (ibid.). The metaleptic solution to the paradox enacted by *Tristram Shandy* (of a story recounted by an act of narration which generates the story) thus relies on the permeability of the boundary that separates the domains of the narrated and the narrating. Reading narrative, Herman implies, has a strong metaleptic potential. Moreover, the tentative character of these suggestions and the fact that they are obviously to be gauged by resorting to "the phenomenology of reading," of how the *récit* appears to the reader, (metaleptically) questions Genette's triad of narrative levels in a specific way. For the implicit perspective of Genette's triad of narrative levels is that of the author whose act of narration can either generate non-fiction (as a historian) or fiction, the simulation that invents "*both* the story and its narrative" (cf. Genette 1988, 14–15; emphasis in the original). Herman's (metaleptic) questioning of "an impermeable ontological barrier between the domain of the narrating and the domain of the narrated" can be attributed to the (additional) logic that establishes the structure of narrative from the point of view of the recipient. From the point of view of the reader (listener, spectator, etc.), it is not the narrative act but the (re)constructive effort of the *act of reading* (listening, watching, etc.) that establishes the narrative situation. Even though the narrative act can emerge in a narrative situation established in this manner as the *logical* cause of the story, this cause is nevertheless nothing more than an abstraction and thus (paradoxically) generated by the act of reading which it logically precedes.

The contingent character of the vantage point from which the narrative situation and its constituent parts are established (a vantage point from which a narratological analysis of the narrative situation must proceed) typically generates epistemological problems. Marie-Laure Ryan's definition of 'story' attempts to sidestep such problems by defining 'story' in a way that is neither indebted to the logic that sees narrative as a representation or a recounting of events and existents nor as the material sign which engenders the events and existents it purports to represent:

> So what is story if it is not a type of thing found in the world as existents and events are, nor a textual representation of this type of thing (as discourse is)? Story, like narrative discourse, is a representation, but unlike discourse it is not a representation encoded in material signs. Story is a mental image, a cognitive construct that concerns certain types of entities and relations between these entities. (Ryan 2006, 7)

This analysis raises familiar epistemological problems: representation here seems to be used in a sense that asserts the independent existence of certain abstract entities and their relations, namely, some kind of noumenal existents and events which can then become cognitive and linguistic representations in what indeed could be termed the "narratological imaginary" (Gibson 1996, 216). The charges of Platonism and essentialism have been levelled against narratological analyses more than once.[111] Any model that distinguishes story from discourse – the chronological series of events from the manner in which these events are arranged by the act of narration or text – seemingly entails a contestable commitment to the notion of "some abstract story which subtends all the possible discursive manifestations of a given narrative" (Herman 2002, 214). In the case of Ryan's model above, story has become an ephemeral 'cognitive construct' in a recipient's (or possibly the author's) mind and is similar to discourse, insofar as both represent and correspond to things "found in the world." Thus, her model displays a quandary that is structurally similar to the narrative paradox outlined above, namely the commitment to the notion of a pre-linguistic experience of the world which has to be distinguished from the narrative that represents that world linguistically (discourse) and cognitively (story). Yet, it could always be asked, where is the story (and that which it represents), if it is not realized by narrative discourse? The notion of a cognitive construct that can be encoded in material signs creates a structure of layers or levels that resembles diegetic levels. There is the sense in which one part of this structure is generated by the other, whether the cognitive construct by the material signs or the material signs by the cognitive construct; whether the world by the word or the word by the world; whether the cognitive construct 'story' by noumenal existents and events or vice versa. The paradox remains – 'impossibly,' narrative creates that which is prior to narrative.

One possible conclusion is that the establishment of categorical distinctions between various narrative and diegetic levels (and the establishment of their hierarchical order) is a notoriously problematic enterprise made exceedingly difficult by what Herman describes as the "nonformalizable, and anti-totalizing forces and effects of narrative" (Herman 1999, 28). Many critics with a poststructuralist or deconstructionist bent have highlighted the epistemological problems, paradoxes and aporias that emerge in the (structural) analysis of narrative. Denying the possibility of stable meanings and highlighting the notion of

---

[111] See, for instance, Smith (1981) and Gibson (1996). Gerald Prince counters that charge by claiming that "few if any narratologists believe that stories exist prior to and independently of discourse and text (to say, for example, that two different narratives – one in English and one in French – tell the same story in no way implies that the latter [...] can exist by itself)" (1995, 126). It is striking that this approximates a version of the narrative paradox outlined in this chapter.

text as a dynamic process, poststructuralist critiques of narratology emphasise what O'Neill has termed the "ludic, metonymic, and paradoxical relationship of the levels of narration" (1994, 108). Malina, in the attempt to arrive at a deconstructive narratology, maintains in a similar vein that the "self-deconstructive aspects of narrative" (2002, 138), of which metalepsis is one, undermine "narratives' illusions of bounded, essential selves and worlds" (ibid.).

Such criticism demonstrates that narratology cannot once and for all deliver the structures of all narratives at all times. In *Towards a Postmodern Theory of Narrative* (1996), Andrew Gibson sardonically concludes that "[n]arrative [...] does not require us to stratify it. Rather, it is itself a form of resistance to our stratifying procedures. It ceaselessly denies or obscures the clear distinctions that it fleetingly appears to encourage. It allows hierarchical structures to emerge only as phantom shapes which can never prove adequate to the phenomena they seek to formulate" (234). Gibson's dismissal of narrative and diegetic levels has a decidedly metaleptic ring to it: narrative phenomena resist narratological stratification. Yet this conclusion, I would argue, offers only one part of the aporetic character of (a structural analysis of) narrative representation, insofar as it attempts to ground one of two contradictory yet equally *valid* sayings.[112] It presents the (metaleptic) denial of narrative structures as inherent in narrative, yet it does not consider that 'the distinctions that narrative fleetingly appears to encourage' are not only the prerequisites of a metaleptic denial of narrative structures, but also of his own critique. Vis-à-vis structuralism, his conclusion dismisses the concept of narrative and diegetic levels in an ahistorical and universalist manner, yet fails, for instance, to account for the many ways in which a narrative obliges recipients to construct boundaries equivalent to the 'phantom shape of hierarchical structures.'

The metaleptic narration of Laurence Sterne's narrator Tristram Shandy not only questions hierarchical structures, but also demonstrates that those 'phantom shapes' are not easy to dismiss. In chapter xx of Volume VI, the narrator, having informed the reader that the setting will be changed, attempts to vanish with the setting that is to be left behind:

> We are now going to enter upon a new scene of events.——
> —Leave we then the breeches in the taylor's hands, with my father standing over him with his cane, reading him as he sat at work a lecture upon the *latus clavus*, and pointing to the precise part of the waistband, where he was determined to have it sewed on.—— [...]

---

[112] Didier Coste and John Pier implicitly corroborate this claim when they argue that Gibson, in his critique of 'narratological geometrics,' "makes ample use of the very terminology and concepts he denounces" (2009, 301–302).

> Leave we *Slop* likewise to the full profits of all my dishonours.—— [...] And last of all,—because hardest of all——
> Let us leave, if possible, *myself*:———But 'tis impossible,—I must go along with you to the end of the work.

The narrator Tristram Shandy and his narrational act cannot be exchanged or left behind in the same way as (the setting of) the storyworld (the world 'in which the narrated events occur') and its characters can be left behind. Since the following Volumes (VII, VIII, and IX) focus on Toby's amours with widow Wadman and Tristram's (the narrating adult's) journey through France, in which he is followed by death, Tristram Shandy is indeed left behind – as a young boy, as the developing character and as the central subject of his own autobiography. But for the reader, it is impossible to leave Tristram Shandy behind – as the narrator who fictionalizes his own narrative act of producing *écriture* – without leaving behind the whole work. Here, the reader encounters distinct ontological realms: the distinction between the world in which Tristram Shandy's narrating act is situated and the world produced by that act cannot be done away with, since each logically presupposes the other. In Genettian terms, Tristram's attempt to metaleptically treat the extradiegesis as an item of setting that can be 'removed' (the literary companion piece to Gibson's postmodern theory of narrative) not only fails, but actually foregrounds the 'phantom shape' of the extradiegesis. "Narrative [...] does not require us to stratify it," Gibson argues (1996, 234) – the narrative *Tristram Shandy*, despite the fact that it violates conventional stratifications, 'requires us to stratify it' after all. While (Tristram's) narration goes on, readers are unable "to ground either saying" (Beardsworth 1996, 32).

Yet how can this stratification be described? The passage above raises many questions concerning the structure of diegetic levels in *Tristram Shandy*'s narrative situation that cannot be answered simply by referring to the common distinction between the extradiegetic act of narration that engenders the primary narrative which constitutes the diegesis.[113] In fictionalizing this *narration*, this act of narration arguably usurps the level of the story realm and becomes die-

---

[113] According to Gérard Genette's application of his descriptive vocabulary, Tristram Shandy would simply be intradiegetic as a character and extradiegetic as the homodiegetic narrator (cf. 1988, 130–134). The addressees corresponding to these levels would be the intradiegetic narratee (for instance, uncle Toby listening to a sermon read by Trim) and the extradiegetic narratee. This is problematic insofar as Genette maintains that the extradiegetic narratee "merges totally with [the] implied reader" (ibid., 131), a highly controversial narrative agent incompatible with the fictive narratees addressed by the extradiegetic narrator Tristram Shandy.

getic, while another extradiegetic narrative act necessarily persists (and the diegesis becomes metadiegetic). Here, the narrator encounters himself in the mirror image of his narration and humorously acknowledges the necessity of an extradiegetic frame. In other words, the pragmatic rule that narrational acts cue the construction of the domains of the signifier and signified is foregrounded by a playful attempt to create an 'impossible' narration that cuts across this distinction. The narration of this narration (as well as the narration of the reception of this narration)[114] potentially proliferates the structural relations presupposed and created by narrational acts.

The logical necessity involved in this is analogous to the situation Tristram Shandy (the narrator) evokes in the context of one of his many metanarrative digressions on how to write well: "Every man chuses to be present at the shaving of his own beard (though there is no rule without an exception) and unavoidably sits overagainst himself the whole time it is doing, in case he has a hand in it—" (IX.xiii). In the passage quoted above in which the autodiegetic narrator Tristram Shandy attempts to leave himself behind, he finds himself sitting 'overagainst himself' in a similar manner. What comes into focus here is that poststructuralist criticism cannot do away with diegetic levels once and for all; narratives cue the construction of the domains of the signifier and the signified. Metalepsis may teach us that narrated worlds and their hierarchical relations 'impossibly,' aporetically *remain* – and that if the metaleptic denial of narrated worlds (and worlds of narration) is 'complete,' narration ceases.

3.2.2 'Impossible Narration' II: The Mimetic Presence of the Represented

At some point, almost all narratological discussions of metalepsis conceptualize the phenomenon as the disruptive counterpart to mimetic illusion; in this man-

---

[114] Who renders the famous 'drawing room conversations' between the narrator Tristram Shandy and some of his readers or listeners? This question is related to the question who is directly addressed by Tristram – one, or more than one, of the fictive narratees that seemingly populate the same diegetic level as the narrator? Throughout the novel, Tristram Shandy continually refers to his addressees with deictic references that present the narrative situation as changeable and even ambiguous. Does the narrative situation change with each new fictional narratee, addressed, for instance, as 'Madam,' 'Sir,' 'your reverences' or 'lads'? Some of those addressed apparently have physical access to the world in which Tristram narrates, because they can not only be reproached for their reading (and listening) habits, they talk back, and even sit on and – if understood literally – wear the fool's cap of the narrator (cf. Chapter VII/xxvi).

ner, metaleptic texts are often characterized as 'unnatural' (Richardson 2006) – the "anti-mimetic texts that violate the parameters of traditional realism" (Richardson et al. 2010). In a similar manner, John Pier has recently designated the "intrusion of the world of the narrated by the world of the narrating, or vice versa" as "anti-mimesis" in his afterword to the essay collection *Metalepsis in Popular Culture* (2011, 268). The 'anti-mimesis' of metalepses, it is sometimes argued, not only destroys the immersive quality of the metaleptic text but also demonstrates that fictional narrative is by nature (at least potentially) metaleptic. Such accounts seemingly employ the term 'mimesis' to designate "the faithful reproduction of what we take to be reality" (McHale 2009, 438) and can be brought into accord with the notion that narrative understanding cognitively relies on frames and schemata of 'real-world experience' which Fludernik terms 'narrative mimesis.'[115]

However, Aristotle's concept of *mimesis* developed in the *Poetics* (335 BCE) goes beyond such conceptions – conceptions which are related to eighteenth-century classicist aesthetics where art is regarded as the imitation of nature. A discussion of the prerequisites of metalepsis can profit from a more differentiated presentation of mimesis and thereby move beyond the obvious and sensible assumption that metalepses have "a strong anti-illusionist effect" (Wolf 2005, 103). First, this chapter offers an analysis of Hans-Georg Gadamer's retrieval of Aristotelian mimesis, which moves beyond the understanding of mimesis as 'the faithful reproduction of what we take to be reality,' and argues that what Gadamer terms "the original mimetic relation" (1986b, 128) has a curiously metaleptic quality. Mimetic behaviour creates the *presence* of the represented despite the ontological distance between the representation and what is represented. In true hermeneutic fashion, Gadamer's interpretation of mimesis relies on the act of identification that recognizes something as 'that which it is': a recognition that completes the "transformation into structure" (*Verwandlung ins Gebilde*, cf. Gadamer 2013, 110), elevating the mimetic to a kind of ideality. In a second step, I will briefly trace the intricate relationship between Gadamerian mimesis and metalepsis, and argue that the metaleptic dynamic enacts and disrupts the 'original mimetic relation' as the diegetic telling which mimetically 'shows.' I have argued in Chapter 2.2.4 that what I would like to call the *herme-*

---

[115] For Fludernik, narrative mimesis "evokes a world, whether that world is identical to the interlocutors' shared environment, to a historical reality or to an invented fictional fantasy. And in so far as all reading is interpreting along the lines of a represented world, it necessarily relies on the parameters and frames of real-world experience and their underlying cognitive understandings" (Fludernik 1996, 37).

neutic effect of metalepses is connected to the fact that in understanding metaleptic transgressions readers (possibly) become aware of the (transgressed) representational logic on which the conception of narrative understanding conventionally relies. This logic entails that narrative representations communicate something that is not present itself. Metalepsis, I conclude, foregrounds the aporetic presence of the represented as – and inasmuch as – it enacts and disrupts 'mimesis.'

The epistemological problems inherent in the notion of mimesis as 'the faithful reproduction of what we take to be reality' can be traced back to Plato's well-known discussion of *mimesis* in Book X of *The Republic* (380 BCE), where 'mimesis' is understood as the emulation of appearances, and seen as essentially lacking in comparison with what it emulates. Painting, music, poetry – any human activity which is connected to the making of images – is understood by Plato as an imitation of the original creation of the Divine Demiurge. And since only that original act is true, all subsequent copies are just *copies* of the *appearance* of that original act's result. Here, in Plato's derogatory view of the visual artist or poet, the elements of mimesis emerge in their unstable relationship. There is an original (that which is presented), a presentation (by a poet or actor) and, at least by implication, an act of recognition which evaluates the ontological distance between the two. According to Plato, mimetic acts rely on an element of creativity[116], which on the one hand fails to be original (being a mere echo of the original act of the Divine Demiurge) and on the other hand fails to be the faithful copy of some pre-existing material.[117] Thus, the elements of mimesis

---

[116] The element of creativity plays a central role in Gunter Gebauer and Christoph Wulf's *Mimesis* (1995). Among other things, this influential study attempts to rehabilitate mimesis with the help of Goodman's theory of worldmaking and to characterize it as a *creative* construction which is dependent upon "the practical mimesis of daily life," without which "literary mimesis would bear no reference to the world" (Gebauer and Wulf 1995, 23). However, the common claim that it was Aristotle who "made mimesis creative" (Willbergh 2006, 52) fails to acknowledge the fact that this element of creativity is condemned and declared illusory by Plato's analogy with the creative act of the Divine Demiurge.

[117] It is striking that Plato's account of mimetic behaviour has a decidedly postmodern slant: it proclaims a crisis of representation and insurmountable epistemological problems for the work of art that is lowered to the position of a mere copy that can never fully represent non-discursive reality. Steven Shankman has argued that "Plato in fact shares some of the concerns of 'postmodern' theory and that Plato anticipated [...] many of the kinds of criticisms made by later thinkers, including some of today's literary theorists" (1994, 4). Following Plato, it may be argued along these lines that creativity condemns the work of art to a state of simulation which is always somehow inadequate and cannot represent what exists beyond it. Thus, Platonic

are destabilized by the creativity which makes the representation *unlike* what it presents. Narrative representation, according to Plato, is thus the failure to 'faithfully reproduce what we take to be the reality' beyond the representation.

Precisely this element of creativity is emphasized in the Aristotelian account of *mimesis* developed in the *Poetics*, which 'elevates' Platonic *mimesis* to the level of the universal possibilities of being:

> At the centre of painting and poetry lies mimesis; but it does not imply the mere copying of the externalities of nature and the portrayal of individual features. Art and poetry aim much more at "beautifying" and "improving" individual features, at a *universalization*. Mimesis is thus copying and changing in one. (Gebauer and Wulf 1995, 54)

Aristotelian mimesis not only refers to *imitatio*, but also to the universal 'truths' that the work of art may uncover: in this manner, Aristotle arrives at his famous dictum that poetry as the *imitatio* of the universal is superior to the factual representation of events in historical writing. What unites Aristotelian and Platonic mimesis, however, is the instability of the conflicting movements of imitation and creation. Whereas Plato emphasizes the insurmountable difference that emerges in all attempts to create similarity between representation and its object, between the original act of the Divine Demiurge and its human copy, Aristotle finds a more profound similarity in difference. The central paradox of mimesis in Aristotle's *Poetics* is that "the poet is an 'imitator' by virtue of being a maker" (Else 1957, 106), that, in other words, the poet's originality is the emulation of an original (the universal possibilities of being).

Gadamer's retrieval of Aristotelian mimesis conceptualizes the work of art as an event of being (*Seinsvorgang der Darstellung*) in which the elements of the hermeneutic situation in which the work of art is understood are no longer characterized by the ontological distance between presented and representation. The actual being of the work, Gadamer writes, "belongs to the world to which it represents itself" (Gadamer 2013, 115), to the world in which an act of recognition confirms and bears witness to the fact that mimetic behaviour makes something present. The central enigma that lies at the heart of Gadamerian mimesis is thus the *presence* which manifests itself in mimetic behaviour despite the ontological distance between the representation and what it represents; a presence that metaleptically transcends the hierarchies established by this ontological distance.

---

mimesis, prefiguring the simulacra which 'later thinkers' thought of as 'copies without originals,' stands in diametrical opposition to conventional conceptions of mimesis today.

Long before Plato's and Aristotle's accounts of mimesis, the Greek term described the acts performed by a priest in Dionysian cult (cf. Tatarkiewicz 1980, 266–274). 'Ritualistic mimesis' designates the incarnation or impersonation that *presents* the divine rather than imitates its echoes.[118] Gadamer argues in "Poetry and Mimesis" (1972) that Aristotle's concept of mimesis is still closely related to the notion of mimetic representation as part of the cultic event:

> We can still see quite clearly in Aristotle that mimetic representation is part of a cultic event [...].The act in which something is recognized here is not an act of distinction, but of identification. However ineliminable it may be, and however we may emphasize it, the distance between the image and the original has something inappropriate about it as far as the real ontological meaning of mimesis is concerned. [...] The *paradigma* (to which, according to Plato, every representation is related as an image, and which it necessarily falls short of) is not present as such (for *paradigma* means 'what is shown alongside'). No one points to it as something that stands alongside the presentation. (1986a [first German ed. 1972], 120)

What Gadamer terms 'mimetic representation' is, then, an imitation which does not point to something that stands alongside it. Mimesis is realized by an act of recognition that anchors the recognized presence to the world in which it is understood. "It is a matter neither of there and then, nor of here and now, but it is encountered as the very self-same" (ibid.). 'As the very self-same,' the ontological meaning of mimesis metaleptically transcends the spatiotemporal dimensions of representation. Strikingly, Gadamer's first example of the mimetic is the behaviour of children. In *Truth and Method* he writes that children who dress up "intend a representation of such a kind that only what is represented exists. [...] We are supposed to recognize what it 'is'" (2013, 113). Along these lines it could be argued that the child who dresses up as Spiderman intends the *presence* of 'Spiderman' and does not want to create a copy that points beyond itself to an 'original' by virtue of its resemblance (needless to add, the child who dresses up as Spiderman is my own example, not Gadamer's). The metaleptic quality of such recognition is not concerned with (or rather transcends) the

---

[118] An echo of ritualistic mimesis may be found in the hymn-like evocation and address of (semi-)gods in ancient Greek Literature. Irene de Jong argues that such apostrophes can function as a "form of ancient metalepsis" (2009, 97) that differs from 'modern' metalepsis: "it is neither 'anti-illusionistic' not 'comical' but, on the contrary, adds to the authenticity of the story and the admiration for the semi-divine heroes" (ibid.). Metaleptic apostrophes (such as the invocations of Muses) thus *present* the divinity that they, from a modern perspective, purport to *represent*. Presumably, from the perspective of contemporary recipients of ancient Greek narratives, it was a common assumption that the divine cuts across the distinctions of human storytelling and representation.

distinction between representation and represented, telling and told. This is not to say that we cannot concern ourselves with that ontological distinction (between representation and represented). We can – but that, according to Gadamer, is a secondary phenomenon:

> The original mimetic relation is not an imitation in which we strive to approach an original by copying it as nearly as possible. On the contrary, it is a kind of showing. [...] When we show something, we do not intend a relation between the one who shows and the thing shown. Showing points away from itself. We cannot show anything to the person who looks at the act of showing itself, like the dog that looks at the pointed hand. On the contrary, showing something means that the one to whom something is shown sees it correctly for himself. It is in this sense that imitation is a showing. For imitation enables us to see more than so-called reality. What is shown is, so to speak, elicited from the flux of manifold reality. Only what is shown is intended and nothing else. As intended, it is held in view, and thus elevated to a kind of ideality. (1986b, 128)

Yet what is it precisely that manifests itself as present in mimetic behaviour? What is the kind of ideality elicited from the flux of manifold reality? The example of children who dress up already suggests that the recognized presence is in a certain sense distinct from the materiality of the showing. The original mimetic relation is realized by the recognition of 'Spiderman,' but not by acknowledging the particular act of showing, the artful costume, the relation between the showing and what we take to be the original.[119] "Where something is recognized, it has liberated itself from the uniqueness and contingency of the circumstances in which it was encountered," Gadamer writes in "Poetry and Mimesis" (1986a [first German ed. 1972], 120). This does not mean, however, that mimesis is related to something beyond the representation. It is *in* the event of being (*Seinsvorgang der Darstellung*) that this ideality emerges (while everything else is bracketed).

The liberation from the uniqueness and contingency of circumstance on which mimesis relies is understood by Gadamer as a "transformation into structure" (*Verwandlung ins Gebilde*, cf. Gadamer 2013, 110). This notion is indebted to his analysis of the concept of play. It has been claimed that Gadamer's originality "in elaborating the hermeneutics of the artwork lies primarily in his mobilizing the concept of play as a way of thinking the essence of art" (Sallis 2007, 49–50). In *Truth and Method*, Gadamer argues that the player experiences the

---

[119] I can tell my daughter that, as Spiderman, she should not be wearing green socks – but that is not the response she intended when she dressed up as Spiderman. She does not want to be recognized as a mediation/representation of an original Spiderman to which her appearance can be compared: she wants to be recognized *as* Spiderman.

game "as a reality that surpasses him" (2013, 109). This reality is the self-presentation of play that creates what Gadamer calls a meaningful whole (*Sinnganzes*):

> I call this change, in which human play comes to its true consummation in being art, *transformation into structure*. Only through this change does play achieve ideality, so that it can be intended and understood as play. Only now does it emerge as detached from the representing activity of the players and consist in the pure appearance (Erscheinung) of what they are playing. As such, the play – even the unforeseen elements of improvisation – is in principle repeatable and hence permanent. It has the character of a work, of an *ergon* and not only of *energeia*. In this sense I call it a structure (Gebilde). (Gadamer 2013, 110; emphasis in the original).

The concept of transformation characterizes the 'superior mode of being' of the structure (*Gebilde*), which is the pure appearance of play. From this perspective, 'reality' is defined by Gadamer as "what is untransformed" (ibid. 112), where "lines of meaning scatter in the void" (ibid.). In contrast to that, a structure (*Gebilde*) constitutes a "closed circle of meaning" (ibid.). Such a structure emerges in the event of being that is play and art. Gadamer never thinks of the structure as distinct from the event of being: a structure is such insofar as "it presents itself as a meaningful whole. It does not exist in itself, nor is it encountered in a mediation accidental to it; rather, it acquires its proper being in being mediated" (ibid. 117).

According to Aristotle, it is, of course, the formation of a *mythos*, the (narrative) structuring of events that is decisive, as it is thus that the poet transforms the action (*praxis*) into a unified and dramatic unfolding of a plot. Daniel Tate argues that this 'poetic unity' is appropriated by Gadamer as 'transformation into structure' (*Verwandlung ins Gebilde*). Tate describes the paradoxical nature of this structure (*Gebilde*) in the following manner:

> Transforming the action it 'imitates' into a meaningful whole, the plot thereby elevates the imitated action into the ideal being proper to it as a form, an *eidos*. [...] Organizing events into a coherent, ordered and unified structure, the *mythos* elevates the *praxis* such that it is no longer something accidental and singular but now something necessary and universal. This means that the action imitated in the plot is *both* the action itself as the unique, never to be repeated occurrence *and* the permanent and repeatable imitation. So while the imitation refers to the singular and transitory action it imitates, the imitation elevates the action, transforming it into an ideal structure, a *Gebilde* that renders the imitated action essentially repeatable and hence permanent. (Tate 2008, 191)

But narrative metalepsis at the same time enacts the original mimetic relation and disrupts the creation of a *Gebilde*. At least by implication, metaleptic *presence* 'belongs to the world to which it represents itself.' As mentioned in the previous chapter, one of the classic narratological examples of metalepsis is

"The Kugelmass Episode" (1980), a short story by Woody Allen in which the protagonist Kugelmass is transported by means of his psychiatrist's machine into Flaubert's novel *Madame Bovary*, where he begins an affair with Emma. Emma is in this case the heroine of the fictional *homologue* of *Madame Bovary* and belongs to the metadiegetic level of Woody Allen's story. Here, Allen's diegetic character Kugelmass encounters the 'imitation' as a literal presence – in other words, from the perspective of Kugelmass, the metadiegesis has become unmediated (diegetic) experience. Subsequently, readers of the fictional homologue of *Madame Bovary* belonging to the diegesis of "The Kugelmass Episode" encounter Emma making love to Kugelmass. From the perspective of diegetic characters, Kugelmass has become metadiegetic fiction.

On the one hand, via analogy, metaleptic transgressions demonstrate how the being of the work 'belongs to the world to which it represents itself,' how the recognized *presence* of the work of art literally and physically belongs to the world in which it is understood. On the other hand, such a transgression of representational logic forces the reader to acknowledge the distance of the various levels or worlds involved in representations.

Another potentially metaleptic passage that fosters and at the same time destroys the 'transformation into structure' can be found in Laurence Sterne's *Tristram Shandy*:

> Let love therefore be what it will,—my uncle *Toby* fell into it.——And possibly, gentle reader, with such a temptation—so wouldst thou: For never did thy eyes behold, or thy concupiscence covet any thing in this world, more concupiscible than widow *Wadman*.

This is the last paragraph of Chapter xxxvii in Volume VI of *Tristram Shandy*. The following chapter VI/xxxviii supplies the following instruction:

> To conceive this right,—call for pen and ink—here's paper ready to your hand.——Sit down, Sir, paint her to your own mind——as like your mistress as you can——as unlike your wife as your conscience will let you—'tis all one to me——please but your own fancy in it.

The 'paper ready to the reader's hand' can be constructed as the blank page that immediately follows this quotation. Here, extratextual readers (or, possibly, the extradiegetic narratee) are asked to create mimetic presence by representing what has been diegetically told. Here, the story told acquires "its proper being in being mediated" (Gadamer 2013, 117), that is, in the (potential) drawing of readers. Here, indeed, the metaleptic dynamic seems to involve the diegetic telling that mimetically shows – that, in particular, (in Gadamer's sense) mimetically shows how we understand narrative. Thus this passage humorously enacts the creation of the original mimetic relation; for the (potential) drawing can be correlated with an act of recognition that anchors the recognized presence to the world in which it is understood. In this manner, the event of being in which the 'ideality' of widow Wadman emerges is foregrounded. However, this playful engagement with mimetic presence is at the same time (if not ultimately) anti-mimetic: the differentiation between presentation and presented is highlighted by the very metaleptic act that denies it. By foregrounding the contingent nature on which the creation of *Gebilde* relies, Laurence Sterne's novel is no longer recognizable as such. Readers are forced to forego mimesis and deal with the secondary phenomenon of thinking the ontological distance between representation and represented.

That this secondary phenomenon can be as rewarding as Gadamerian mimesis (the original mimetic relation) is demonstrated on the page following the blank one, where the dialogue between what could be conceptualized as narrator and fictional extradiegetic narratee evaluates the possible result of the effort: "——Was ever anything in Nature so sweet!—so exquisite!—Then, dear Sir, how could my uncle *Toby* resist it?" (VI.xxxix) If the extratextual reader has drawn his wife or widow Wadman, then this passage inverts the original mimetic relation, as it is the extradiegetic narratee who recognizes the mimetic presence of widow Wadman (created by the extratextual reader). Such an inversion that metaleptically implies the world of flesh-and-blood readers inevitably forces readers to 'look at the act of showing itself.' Here, the metaleptic dynamic lays bare that 'showing points away from itself' by (implicitly) pointing to the showing, thus disrupting the meaningful whole of the *Gebilde*, a disruption which returns it into the untransformed reality where 'lines of meaning scatter in the void.'[120]

I have argued that the 'original mimetic relation' is metaleptic and that metalepsis potentially enacts the original mimetic relation. However, the metaleptic dynamic at the same time presents an anti-mimetic movement. Even though some narrative phenomena, in a certain sense, metaleptically *show* what is recognized without "a relation between the one who shows and the thing shown" (Gadamer 1986b, 128), the very metaleptic act of showing *points to* the ontological distance which the 'original mimetic relation' intends to bracket. Thus, from the perspective of Kugelmass, Emma emerges in 'the event of being' as a kind of (unmediated) ideality: for Kugelmass, Emma is no longer the 'original' evoked in and by the discourse, she is no longer "what stands alongside

---

[120] It is an interesting thought that the playful character of this exercise may provide a meaningful whole again.

the presentation" (Gadamer 1986a [first German ed. 1972], 120). For readers of "The Kugelmass Episode," however, the manufacture of sense that creates a *Gebilde* out of manifold reality is foregrounded, and in this manner made 'impossible.'

3.2.3 'Impossible Narration' III: Realist Aporias

This section examines the extent to which the 'impossibility' of the metaleptic dynamic mirrors the aporia(s) of realism – the basic dilemma of which has come up time and again (relatively unchanged) throughout the history of philosophy's 'realism debate': namely that, without an independent epistemic vantage point, we are forced to concede that 'the world' and our representations and knowledge of the world remain inseparable and unstable. This quandary can of course be easily connected to Genette's equation of diegetic levels and 'worlds,' as well as to a realist conception of narrative, for this seemingly depends on the notion that representations of human experience epistemically rely on real-world knowledge (cf. Fludernik 1996, 38). Fludernik's concept of 'realism' and 'narrative mimesis' can be related to Barthes' *effet de réel* (1968) and to Wolf's 'aesthetic illusion' (1993, 2009a). What links 'aesthetic illusion' and *effet de réel* with concepts such as 'narrative mimesis' and 'realism' as outlined by Fludernik is the underlying assumption that certain narratives induce a mental state that is in essence a simulation of real-life experience: "Aesthetic illusion always has a quasi-experiential quality about it" (Wolf 2009a, 145). According to Wolf, this experiential quality is modelled on the real-life experience of 'live now and tell later,' which serves as the (cognitive) model of the reception process of many 'illusionist' (cf. ibid.) novels, or, more generally (and transgenerically), 'illusionist works': The hub of this is the basic "analogy between real-life experience and the experience provided by illusionist works" (ibid., 157).

Aesthetic illusion, realism, *effet de réel* are all connected to what has been called the realist position in art: the assumption that the set of signs and the (experience of) things in the world they represent non-problematically *correspond*. For narrative, such correspondence is usually (and yet again paradoxically) conceptualized with the aid of notions such as transparency, verisimilitude, or, from the perspective of cognitive linguistics, with iconicity (cf. Ronen 2005, 488). Metalepsis denies the relation of correspondence between sets of signs and the (experience of) things in the world they (purport to) represent and establishes an aporetic relation of identity and non-identity between the 'levels' or 'worlds' which frame either of the two (that is, the set of signs, on the one hand, and the 'things in the world,' on the other). Metalepsis not only questions the ontological status of represented entities but also what David Lewis (1978) has famously described as the truth value status (of the sequence of propositions) of fictional narrative, thus highlighting a quandary which haunts all discussions of realism: what links the beliefs and the states of affairs they supposedly represent (if these states of affairs are independent of the beliefs)?

Thus, narrative fiction is in a sense always related to the underlying epistemological problem of realism in modern philosophy that deals with the ontological status of the represented entities. This realism debate is so diverse and intricate that it is beyond the scope of this chapter to offer an overview of the entire range of positions; however, a discussion of metalepsis and the notion of diegetic levels or diegetic universes can profit from the insight that "[r]*ealism says nothing semantic at all* beyond [...] making the negative point that our semantic capacities do *not* constitute the world"[121] (Devitt 1991, 39). Thus, realism in this sense claims that the represented entity *exists* (e.g. the moon and its properties, such as being roughly spherical, have existence) and exists *independently* of linguistic practice, schemata, etc.; that is, the represented entity exists independently of the models projected onto it.

Accordingly, challenges to what is usually referred to as 'generic realism' in modern philosophy are for the most part directed at either the 'existence dimension' or the 'independence dimension.' Classically, the challenge to both aspects of realism took the form of *idealism*, the view that all objects of cognition are mental phenomena. George Berkeley famously claimed in *A Treatise Concerning the Principles of Human Knowledge* (1957 [1710]) that the moons of Jupiter (as well as tables, chairs, cats, etc.) subsist in the mind:

> Some truths are so near and obvious to the mind that a man need only open his eyes to see them. Such I take this important one to be, namely, that all the choir of heaven and furniture of the earth, in a word, all those bodies which compose the mighty frame of the world, do not have any substance without a mind – that their being (esse) is to be perceived or known. (Part I, § 6)

Berkeley's claim that 'to be is to be perceived' does, however, not amount to the claim that finite minds create what they perceive. It amounts to the claim that, as Hilary Putnam puts it, "*[n]othing can be similar to a sensation or image except another sensation or image*" (1981, 59; emphasis in the original). Berkeley's im-

---

[121] This is, of course, an objection to semantic realism. In short, semantic realism claims that sentences relate to entities that render each of the sentences determinately true or false (independently of our capacity to *know* that this is the case).

materialism rather acknowledges the aporetic structure of a noumenal and material thing-in-itself that shapes our mental representation of it. Even though idealism is no longer en vogue in contemporary philosophy, the more recent and sophisticated ways of opposing realism still challenge existence and/or independence dimensions in a similar manner. Wright has summarized one central twentieth-century challenge to realism (developed by the analytical philosopher Michael Dummett) in the introduction to his book *Realism, Meaning & Truth* (1987):

> How are we supposed to be able to *form* any understanding of what it is for a particular statement to be true if the kind of state of affairs it would take to make it true is conceived, *ex hypothesi*, as something beyond our experience, something which we cannot confirm and which is insulated from any distinctive impact on our consciousness? (13; emphasis in the original)

The curious impasse reached at this point is not only restricted to the question of whether the truth value of a proposition can be known, but haunts all discussions of realism. How can the ontological status of the represented entity be determined if it is 'beyond our experience'? In connection to narrative, it could thus be asked whether there is a human experience beyond or independent of the linguistic signs which constitute any given narrative. The epistemological problem here is twofold. On the one hand, if, according to a realist conception of narrative representation, the semantic capacities of writers and readers do *not* constitute the 'world' of the story, what is it that can be correlated with those semantic capacities? In other words, the assumption that there is indeed a represented entity which can be distinguished from the representation (true or untrue, historical fact or fictional cognitive construct), entails the problem of an evidence-transcendent ephemeral represented. How can we talk about or tell of something we cannot access with language? On the other hand, if the semantic capacity *does* constitute the story, if there is no experience or 'world' external to and independent of our language, the strange consequence is that readers experience a shared solipsism.

However, most of the novels written in the eighteenth, nineteenth, and twentieth centuries *conventionally* deny these epistemological problems. As such, the genre is intricately related to the conception that what narrative relates 'exists' independently of the telling. This conception, in turn, is closely related to mimetic representation in the Platonic sense of an 'as if,' a simulacrum that is modelled on something that exists independently of the flawed copy. Similarly, the Aristotelian conception of mimesis offers the view that mimetic representations can be modelled on a realist paradigm, in the sense that an *imitatio* can generally uncover 'ontological possibilities,' and are accordingly not referentially void. Thus, narrative is conventionally based on the notion that the represented entities *exist* and exist *independently* of linguistic practice, no matter whether they are modelled on a Platonic idea, Aristotelian ontological possibilities, or some notion of human experientiality. This seemingly applies to non-fictional and fictional narrative alike. Most readers read *Tom Jones* as if Tom Jones exists/existed independently of the telling; in other words, from the perspective of the reader, the textual universes in the fictive narrative situation are understood with the conceptual schemata and linguistic practice of a realist worldview, and thus induce the "quasi-experiential quality" (Wolf 2009a, 145) of aesthetic illusion.

Even though "invented entities and actions are the common stuff of fiction, and for this reason the idea of the non-referential status of the portrayed universe is part of our standard understanding of fictional narrative" (Schaeffer 2009, 105–106), this understanding is intricately related to a realist paradigm. Despite the fact that no reader assumes that the elves in J. R. R. Tolkien's *The Lord of the Rings* (1954/1955) have, to use the terminology Schaeffer applies, 'referential status,' the understanding of such narratives involves the 'quasi-experiential quality' of realism, as the universe portrayed becomes 'real' in the 'willing suspension of disbelief.' The (emotional) responses that narratives such as *The Lord of the Rings* elicit suggest that they are conventionally understood 'as if' they had referential status (as if the entities represented existed).

Undoubtedly, from the perspective of the reader, any attempt to understand narrative to some degree 'relies cognitively and epistemically on real-world knowledge' (cf. Fludernik 1996, 38). From a cognitivist perspective, all mental representations (of fictive diegetic universes as well as nonfictive discourse worlds) must be conceptualized as essentially *analogue*. Just as discourse-worlds and text-worlds (both of which are mental representations) are habitually created during real-world experiences, so the understanding of postmodern narratives involves the creation of mental models of diegetic 'universes' which are not fundamentally different from the construction of real-world mental representations. Such diegetic universes may be referentially void in the strict sense, but as constructions they have the same ontological status as representations of the elusive 'reality.'

Even though the diegesis of Angela Carter's *The Infernal Desire Machines of Doctor Hoffman* (1972) negates physical and logical laws, this diegesis is still in every sense of the word a 'world' (or, possibly, a 'multiplicity of worlds') – a temporal and spatial continuum in which agents act. One may argue that Carter's narrative creates fictional universes which are fundamentally anti-realist insofar as they depend on what could be termed 'libidinal idealism': the diegesis of *The Infernal Desire Machines of Doctor Hoffman* is a place in which desire (metaleptically) creates reality. In this sense, the novel seems to argue that for the beings who, in Carter's words, "emanated from the dark country where desire is objectified and lives" (2011 [1972], 134) "*[n]othing can be similar to a sensation or image except another sensation or image*" (Putnam 1981, 59). Read as an allegory for the narrative process in which the distinct narrative worlds of conventional storytelling emerge, Carter's metaleptic beings implicitly acknowledge the aporetic structure of a noumenal and material thing-in-itself that shapes and determines our mental representation of it. In other words, if the emanations from the infernal desire machines cannot be distinguished from the diegetic 'real world,' then the aporetic epistemology is highlighted with which we distinguish the imaginary from the real.

This aporia can perhaps be better described with Lorenz B. Puntel's (and Alan White's) analysis of two errors that emerge in the 'realism/anti-realism debate':

> The first reason or error is the failure to problematize the putatively clear notions of dependence on, and independence from, mind and/or language. Virtually all parties in the debate understand the relevant mind and language to be *our* language or *our* minds. If this is presupposed, a radical aporia is unavoidable: because *our* minds and *our* language are contingent, they are from the outset factors that are too negligible to serve as absolute with respect to the determination (i.e., here, the existence and the structuring) of the world or universe, which, after all, was around long before there were human minds or human languages. But if, from their inadequacy as such decisive factors, one concludes that the world or universe must be absolutely independent of language and thus of structuring, what results appears to be unintelligible: a non-structured, utterly unarticulated and inarticulable, hence un-understood and ununderstandable 'world.' This is the metaphysical realist's aporia.
>
> Anti-realists are confronted by an aporia that is, in a certain respect, precisely the opposite of that of the metaphysical realists: if they make *our* minds and/or languages the unconditional factor and thus measure for an intelligible world, then they can no longer coherently maintain the existence of what both ordinary language (in an intuitive and imprecise manner) and particularly the language of physics [...] term the 'real world' or 'the real universe, in all of its dimensions.' (2008, 375)

Metalepsis potentially presents us with this dilemma – either we forego the 'real world' or we forego the 'real world' as something that can be understood. Metalepsis highlights the aporias of realism insofar as it demonstrates that what we 'term the real world in an intuitive and imprecise manner' literally depends on (the world of) the telling – that is, our very capacities which purport to represent the 'real world.' In *The Infernal Desire Machines of Doctor Hoffman*, the narrator

Desiderio questions the independence from his own mind of his desired, Dr. Hoffman's daughter Albertina: "I did not know then that she travelled with me for she was inextricably mingled with my idea of her and her substance was so flexible she could have worn a left glove on her right hand – if she had wanted to, that is" (2011, 166). Here, the potentially metaleptic Albertina can be interpreted as the enactment of Desiderio's structuring of the unintelligible and marks the place where, impossibly, world and language, the incomprehensible world and the structuring of the mind, the constituent parts of an aporetic structure meet: "'Don't you see it's quite out of the question, at the moment?' [Albertina] said. 'You have never made love to me because, all the time you have known me, I've been maintained in my various appearances only by the power of your desire" (ibid. 243). Unable to forego 'the real world' as something that exists independently of himself, Desiderio eventually kills Albertina, whom he calls "my Platonic other, my necessary extinction, my dream made flesh" (ibid. 257). Killing Albertina amounts to the attempt to distinguish dream and flesh; the attempt to leave the realm where desire, our minds and languages are 'the unconditional factor and thus measure for an intelligible world.' After Albertina's death, Desiderio returns to the 'real' world and the representational logic of diegetic levels is reinstated: the world he lives in is no longer metaleptically questioned by beings that emanate from language, mind, or desire.

In agreement with Genette, I have argued that diegetic levels are conventionally understood analogously to what Fludernik terms 'real-world experience' (that is, as diegetic *universes*): this entails that a diegetic level is conventionally understood (a) as if it *existed* (existence can only be thought of in terms of a world), and (b) as if it existed *independently* of linguistic practice and conceptual schemes. Especially the myriad of (post-) modern narratives that address the epistemological problems of a realist conception of representation demonstrate by *via negativa* how narrative is usually and conventionally processed. Very much like the diegetic universes of *The Infernal Desire Machines of Dr. Hofman* and, say, of *Alphabetical Africa*[122], the 'impossible narration' of me-

---

[122] *Alphabetical Africa* (1974) by Walter Abish, which is famous for its unusual formal constraints, demonstrates this. As is well known, the first chapter of *Alphabetical Africa* is composed exclusively with words that begin with the letter 'a,' the second chapter with words beginning with either 'a' or 'b,' the third with either 'a,' 'b' or 'c' and so on. Each chapter adds a letter until the 26th chapter makes use of words beginning with any letter – at which point the process reverses. An example from Chapter 1 demonstrates how difficult it is to understand these arbitrary sentences as having referential status: "Ages ago an archaeologist, Albert, alias Arthur, ably attended an archaic African armchair affair at Antibes, attracting attention as an archeologist and atheist" (1974, 1). As the novel progresses, however, it becomes more and

taleptic transgressions presupposes and at the same time questions this realist paradigm. All metaleptic transgressions presuppose the assumption that diegetic 'universes' (the 'referent' of the linguistic signs) exist independently of linguistic signs: exist, in other words, as spatiotemporally distinct from the spatiotemporal dimensions in which the linguistic signs succeed one another (whether in an act of creation or re-creation/understanding). The denial of these assumptions marks the beginning of the metaleptic dynamic. In this manner, metalepses deny the schemata which agree with 'generic realism.' The denial of either of the conditions (that the world that is told does not exist, or that it does not exist independently of its telling) immediately marks narrative as 'unnatural' – as an 'anti-mimetic' text that violates "the parameters of traditional realism" (Richardson et al. 2010, 115). Because the schemata of 'generic realism' are so ingrained, because the world-as-accessible-to-us is intuitively (and conventionally) conceptualized in terms of independence from the structuring process of language, the aporias of realism are hidden in a dichotomy that considers represented entities either as artifice (fiction) or 'reality' (fact). Metalepsis highlights the 'impossibility' that lies hidden in realist narratives, an impossibility that mirrors the aporias of philosophical realism: We cannot understand narrative without the construction of a 'world' that is distinct from the telling – ultimately, this schema cannot be avoided, not even when reading *Alphabetical Africa* – yet we have no access to this 'world' apart from the telling. This aporia can be described as the impossibility to form a stable understanding of what it is that we experience in understanding narrative. Following Wright, it could be argued that we experience what is told as something that collapses in the telling; something 'beyond our experience, something which we cannot confirm and which is insulated from any distinctive impact on our consciousness.'

---

more difficult to understand without a 'realist' conception of diegetic levels – which entails the notion, it could be argued, that the diegesis exists independently of the extradiegesis, that the represented entities exist independently of the telling. Yet this gradual build-up of a narrative 'world' which exists independently of the discourse and the act of understanding, is metaleptically threatened. For as the process reverses, as the chapters 'lose' more and more letters (and hence possibilities), the diegesis collapses into the 'world' *in which* we understand.

3.2.4 'Impossible Narration' IV: Metaization and the Self-Reflexive Paradox

Metalepsis is often described as an at least potentially self-referential or self-reflexive[123] phenomenon (cf. Wolf 2009b, 50–55). On the one hand, it may be argued that this phenomenon implies a reference to aspects of the medial condition that make metaleptic transgression possible, and thus foregrounds the make-up of the medium and/or its status as fictional. Thus, Werner Wolf describes ontological metalepsis as an implicit metareference that "may be conceived of as implying an ontological comment on the entirety of the representation in question, namely 'this is fiction'" (2009b, 53). On the other hand, metalepsis may be conceived as highlighting the cognitive and/or theoretical frames in and through which it is understood, which is what Hans Krah implies when he describes metalepsis as the 'fundamental operation for the construction of self-reference'[124]. The fact that all discussions of metaleptic transgression and its potential effects have at least touched upon self-reflexivity and dealt with what John Pier calls the "metatextual status of metalepsis" (2009, 190) is without doubt connected to the long tradition of monographs on metafiction[125] within literary studies.

---

[123] In the tradition of German literary studies, there have been many attempts to arrive at a terminology offering concepts and descriptive criteria that adequately represent the variety of self-reflexive phenomena found in various genre and media of different epochs (as opposed to the tradition of describing self-reflexive literary phenomena as distinguishing characteristics of so-called postmodern literature). Among suggestions for a generic term of this kind are *Autoreflexivität* (Hempfer 1982), *Selbstreflexion* (Scheffel 1997), and *Potenzierung* (Fricke 2003). Janine Hauthal, Julijana Nadj, Ansgar Nünning and Henning Peters offer a more extensive list and an interesting discussion of this tradition (cf. Hauthal 2007). The increasing speed with which new terminologies are developed – especially in relation to what some critics call the current 'metareferential turn' (cf. Wolf 2009b, 11) – seems to imply that metareferential (or, more generally self-referential) phenomena have significantly increased in literary texts and other media at some point in the second half of the twentieth century. It is an interesting question whether and to what degree this 'turn' consists in an increase in a distinct kind of phenomenon and how intimately the 'turn' is connected to changing paradigms underlying analyses of Western culture and the contemporary focus on 'meta-levels.'

[124] "Grundlegende Operation für den Aufbau eines selbstreferentiellen Bezuges stellt [...] sicher die Metalepse dar, wie Genette [...] den Bruch von eigentlich zu unterscheidenden Ebenen und das Ineinandergreifen dieser Ebenen benannt hat" (Krah 2005, 6).

[125] The term 'metafiction' was independently coined by William H. Gass (1970) and Robert Scholes (1970) (cf. Werner Wolf 2009b, 3). From the mid-1970s onwards, metafiction (the capacity of fictional texts to reflect on their own mediality and assumptions) has either been discussed as a distinguishing characteristic of postmodern narrative (cf. for instance, Hutcheon 1980) or as a phenomenon that has distinguished the novel as a genre throughout its long

Birgit Neumann and Ansgar Nünning have maintained that the term 'metafiction' in literary studies describes "the capacity of fiction to reflect on its own status as fiction and thus refers to all self-reflexive utterances which thematize the fictionality (in the sense of imaginary reference and/or constructedness) of narrative" (2009, 204). The neat formula that metafiction is fiction about fiction is, of course, indebted to Hutcheon's influential study *Narcissistic Narrative: The Metafictional Paradox* (1980). However, the term metafiction has been and still is so widely used that it is not only employed to describe all narrative techniques that question or undermine the aesthetic illusion of narrative texts, but also forms of metanarration that are not necessarily anti-illusionistic[126]. Attempting to avoid such connotations, Werner Wolf's elegant delineation of 'metaization' (the most recent of many terms used in literary studies to refer to self-reflexive phenomena, first employed by Hempfer [1982, 130]) defines such phenomena as "the movement from a first cognitive or communicative level to a higher one on which the first-level thoughts and utterances, and above all the means and media used for such utterances, self-reflexively become objects of reflection and communication in their own right" (2009b, 3).

What all the phenomena thus described have in common is that they logically presuppose what the philosopher Rudolf Carnap described as 'object language' and 'metalanguage': "The language which is the object of study is called the *object language*. [...] The language we use in speaking about the object language is called the *metalanguage*" (1958, 78). The basic insight that all self-reflexive phenomena rely on an 'interpreting system' that consists of *meta-* and *object*-language has a long tradition in logic and the philosophy of language. It has thus often been claimed that Russell's paradox (or Russell's antinomy) is the result of the confusion of these two (logically) distinct languages; that, in other words, paradoxes and tautologies emerge if object language and metalanguage are confused. The implication (or, rather, foundation) of this view is that self-referring statements are for logical or semantic reasons *illegitimate* (cf.

---

history (cf. for instance, Alter 1975). Werner Wolf (1993), on the other hand, focuses on the formal variety of metafiction and offers a detailed typology of forms and effects. Among the most influential studies are Booth (1952), Alter (1975), Scholes (1979), Hutcheon (1980), Hempfer (1982), Waugh (1984), Imhof (1986), Wolf (1993), Currie (ed.) (1995), Scheffel (1997), Nünning (1995, 2001, 2004), and more recently, Fludernik (2003a), Huber/Middeke/Zapf (2005) and Greber (2006).

126 For accounts (and typologies) of metanarration (contrasted with metafiction), see Fludernik 2003a, Nünning 2004, and Neumann & Nünning 2009.

Whewell 1987, 31–32). Russell's solution to the paradox initially consisted in the introduction of hierarchical levels into set theory.[127]

A hierarchy of distinct logical levels is, of course, the hallmark of structuralist accounts of narrative, which underlie many accounts of self-reflexive phenomena in literary studies. On the one hand, 'metaization' thus reiterates the logical distinction between the two distinct kinds of 'languages' which are presupposed by all self-reflexive phenomena. On the other, it incorporates this logical distinction within a narratological model of communication. The paradoxes and tautologies which emerge when the difference between object language and metalanguage in analytical philosophy is denied are similar to metaleptic (and other) phenomena which transgress and thus question the difference between diegetic and/or narrative levels. It is precisely such a hierarchy of levels, however, that metaleptic transgressions and their self-referential potential deny (in violation, one could say, of the scope of application of a narrator's sentences). In doing so, metalepses 'impossibly' violate the logic that separates object language and metalanguage. It is not surprising, then, that a self-reflexive (and even metaleptic)[128] potential has been ascribed to narrative in general; the metaleptic dynamic demonstrates that narrative is always in danger of the paradoxical collapse of object and metalanguage, of diegetic and extradiegetic levels, of embedded narrative and embedding narrative.

Yet 'the metaization of metalepsis' is more than a violation of the scope of a narrator's sentences: in what follows, I maintain that metalepsis lays bare the

---

127 Originally, the position that all self-referring statements are meaningless was advanced by Bertrand Russell as a consequence of his theory of types (cf. Russell 1903, 1908 [especially pages 523–528]). The theory of types was developed in order to get rid of the self-referential paradoxes which prevented Russell's, and – according to Russell's paradox – also Frege's attempts to formalize the foundations of mathematics. Russell divided propositional functions (such as sentences) into a hierarchy of 'types' with the help of which the specification of each function's domain (its applicability) should be defined. Only after specifying the propositional function's scope of application (to which 'types' can the function be assigned?), can the propositional function (sentence) be defined. The hierarchy of 'types' to which entities can be assigned consists of various 'levels.' One level 'contains' sentences about individuals. The next level consists of sentences about sets of individuals. And the level after that comprises the sentences about sets of sets of individuals, and so on. This hierarchy of levels allows for the specification of the propositional function's scope of application (for instance, a sentence's scope of application). Only if all objects for which a given predicate holds belong to the same 'type' or level in the hierarchy, so the argument goes, can self-referential paradoxes (such as Russell's paradox) be avoided.

128 Genette claimed in 2004 that all fictional narratives are 'woven through with metalepses' (cf. Genette 2004, 131).

'doubling of communication systems' which, according to Schmid (2005, 2010), is distinctive of fictional narratives. Wolf Schmid argues that the 'narrated world' (*erzählte Welt*) in fictional narratives is, in a certain sense, analogical to the 'entities' of narrator, addressee and narrative act (cf. 2005, 41), even though it is the fictional narrator who 'designs' (*entwerfen*) the narrated world. According to Wolf Schmid, this is due to the fact that the 'narrated world' and the communication system which includes narrator, addressee and narrative act are in turn presented by the historical author and thus constitute the 'presented world' (*dargestellte Welt*) as 'fictive entities' (*fiktive Einheiten*). According to this model of fictional narration, the act of communication that creates the 'narrated world' (narrated by the narrator) is thus always already part of the 'presented world' (narrated by the historical author); this act of narration and its communication system (narrator, addressee, narrative act) are mediated by a second communication system (historical author and [potential] readers) that not only presents but also mirrors the system it presents in what Schmid terms a 'doubling of communication systems':

> The *narrated world* is the world created by the narrator. The *represented world* created by the author is not limited to the narrated world. The represented world includes the narrator, his or her addressee and the narration itself. The narrator, the listener or reader whom the narrator assumes and the act of narration are represented in the fictional world and are fictive entities. Therefore a narrative work does just narrate [sic], but represents an act of narration. The art of narrative is structurally characterized by the doubling of the communication system: the *narrator's communication* in which the narrated world is created is part of the fictive represented world, which is the object of the real *author's communication*.[129] (Schmid 2010, 32–33)

Following Schmid, Michael Scheffel has maintained that the cultural practice of literary narration and its characteristic "Dopplungsstruktur" (2007, 158) can be conceptualized as the "Metaisierung des Erzählens" (ibid.), the 'metaization of narration' (cf. Scheffel 2007, 155–159).[130]

---

129 "Die *erzählte Welt* ist jene, die vom Erzähler entworfen wird. Die vom Autor *dargestellte Welt* erschöpft sich freilich nicht in der erzählten Welt. In die dargestellte Welt gehen auch der Erzähler, sein Adressat und das Erzählen selbst ein. Der Erzähler, der von ihm vorausgesetzte Leser oder Hörer und der Erzählakt sind im fiktionalen Werk dargestellte und folglich fiktive Einheiten. Somit wird im Erzählwerk nicht einfach erzählt, sondern ein Erzählakt dargestellt. Die Erzählkunst ist strukturell durch die Doppelung des Kommunikationssystems charakterisiert: Die Erzählkommunikation, in der die erzählte Welt entworfen wird, ist Teil der fiktiven dargestellten Welt, die das Objekt der realen Autorkommunikation ist" (Schmid 2005, 41).
130 The claim that fictional narration is principally a form of metaization because the structure of such narration at least implies 'the movement from a first communicative level to a higher

Leaving aside discussions of whether a model is tenable that presumes that all sentences of a narrative text are enunciated by a narrator[131], Michael Scheffel argues that, at least for literary narration, metaization is a structural phenomenon. That the *structure* of all literary narration is at least potentially self-reflexive (since it constitutes communicated communication), is the starting point for Scheffel from which he develops a typology that allows the classification of various forms of self-reflexive narration (1997, 2007) – one of the most extreme forms of literary self-reference being, according to Scheffel, metalepsis (cf. 2007, 168). Yet how exactly is metalepsis as a form of self-reference connected to the 'doubling of communication systems? One possible answer is supplied by Linda Hutcheon, who claims that what she terms the 'reflexivity'[132] of narrative offers a 'mimesis of process':

> Reflexivity is obviously a structural issue for narrative, as many have shown [...]; but it also results in a hermeneutic paradox for readers who are forced to acknowledge the artifice of what they are reading, while at the same time becoming active co-creators of the meaning of the work. Indeed, reflexive narratives make overt demands for intellectual and affective engagement comparable in scope and intensity to any other in life [...]. Reflexivity offers, in fact, a kind of mimesis of process; it is process made visible. (2005, 495)

This hermeneutic paradox is precisely what metaleptic narratives enact when they are "conceived of as implying an ontological comment on the entirety of the representation in question, namely 'this is fiction'" (Wolf 2009b, 53). Metalepsis potentially lays bare the reflexivity, the self-referential structure of narrative (and literary texts) insofar as the narrative situation becomes visible as 'communicated communication' in the transgression of the boundary that separates the worlds in which, and of which, a narrator tells. The reader is forced to acknowledge the 'artifice' of embedded narrative as foregrounded by the collapse of diegetic worlds. In this 'collapse,' the constructions (or 'co-creations')

---

one on which the first level utterances self-reflexively become objects of reflection' is connected to the tradition in literary studies that postulates self-reflexivity as one of the characteristics of poetic language. Umberto Eco, Roman Jakobson and Jan Mukařovský, for instance, have all claimed that poetic language is *necessarily* self-referential. For a critique of the view that literary or poetic language is fundamentally self-referential, see Scheffel (1997, 11–23).

131 Influential studies that claim that certain sentences cannot be said to be the enunciation of a narrator are, for instance, Benveniste (1966), Hamburger (1977 [1957]), Banfield (1982), or, more recently D. A. Miller (2003).

132 According to Hutcheon, 'reflexivity' is a more general term for metafiction and refers to texts which make the storytelling part of the story told, a foregrounding of the conventions of storytelling (cf. Hutcheon 2005, 494).

with which readers establish narrative situations are exposed as prerequisites for the understanding of a culturally constructed *artefact* that emerges in the hermeneutic situation – more precisely, as the reception of the 'communicated communication' that allows the metaleptic movement in the first place. In other words, as metaleptic narratives create *and* deny the world(s) of which (or in which) a narrator tells, they enact the self-referential structure of narrative. 'Impossibly' and paradoxically, the metaleptic movement is always already twofold; its operation relies on the reader's 'co-creation' of an aesthetic illusion whose basis is foregrounded as the 'doubling of communication systems' characteristic of literary narrative. The self-referential circularity of metalepsis potentially highlights this doubling as the anti-illusionistic basis of illusion. As this basis is denied and as the process of mimesis is brought into focus, understanding the metaleptic dynamic can indeed be described as 'the mimesis of process.'

Yet this "hermeneutic paradox" (Hutcheon 2005, 495) of an anti-illusionist aesthetic illusion, which lays bare 'the doubling of communication systems' is not the only sense in which metalepsis involves paradox. Hutcheon's 'hermeneutic paradox' relies on an unproblematic relation between the cognitive or communicative levels that constitute the basis of 'reflexivity.' If a text delivers a "first interpretative commentary" (Hutcheon 2005, 494) on itself, what is presupposed is precisely the movement of metaization "from a first cognitive or communicative level to a higher one on which the first-level thoughts and utterances, and, above all, the means and media used for such utterances, self-reflexively become objects of reflection and communication in their own right" (Wolf 2009b, 3). The text that comments on itself has already been distinguished into a hierarchy of (communicative) levels.

It has been argued above that the conflation of what can be seen as (the analogues of) 'object language' and 'metalanguage' is an 'impossibility' with which metaleptic transgressions playfully engage. In the metaleptic transgression this distinction is seemingly blurred. The 'impossible' collapse of diegetic 'worlds' is accompanied by an implicit meta-metalanguage which questions the possibility of establishing object language and metalanguage in the first place. Chapter xxviii of Volume VII of Sterne's *Tristram Shandy* potentially serves as an example of a 'conflation' which at least potentially collapses what can be seen as analogical to 'object language' and 'metalanguage':

> ––Now this is the puzzled skein of all––for in this last chapter, as far at least as it help'd me through *Auxerre*, I have been getting forwards in two different journeys together, and with the same dash of the pen—for I have got entirely out of Auxerre in this journey which I am writing now, and I am got halfway out of Auxerre in that which I shall write hereaf-

ter——There is but a certain degree of perfection in every thing; and by pushing at something beyond that, I have brought myself into such a situation, as no traveller ever stood before me; for I am this moment walking across the market-place of Auxerre with my father and my uncle Toby, in our way back to dinner——and I am this moment also entering Lyons with my post-chaise broke into a thousand pieces—and I am moreover this moment in a handsome pavilion built by Pringello, upon the banks of the Garonne, which Mons. Sligniac has lent me, and where I now sit rhapsodizing all these affairs.
——Let me collect myself, and pursue my journey. (VII.xxviii)

The narrator's deictic reference 'this moment' refers to two diegetic events in Auxerre and Lyons (both a long time apart) as well as to the pavilion on the Garonne which is the (extradiegetic) scene of the act of narration. Thus, the final sentence of the paragraph in question ("Let me collect myself, and pursue my journey") could be taken to refer to any of the three perspectives, or to all of them simultaneously. Here, the distinction between the 'object language' (the diegetic events in Auxerre and Lyon) and what is in a sense the 'metalanguage' (which self-reflexively refers to the extradiegetic event of the *narration* of these diegetic events as problematic) arguably collapses. The sentence 'Let me collect myself, and pursue my journey' can thus be read (a) as a metaphorical comment on the extradiegetic act of narration as well as (b) the diegetic voice of the narrated Tristram Shandy (for instance in Auxerre) who – impossibly – intends to narrate his story himself; or (c) the metaleptic simultaneity of a voice that is diegetic and extradiegetic at the same time. Without Genettian terminology, one could say that the sentence in question oscillates between object language and metalanguage: a playful and deliberate subversion of the either/or logic of the conventional (eighteenth-century) literary text. Moreover, this passage demonstrates that in the 'doubling of communication systems' of narrative, which theoretically allows an endless array of further embedded communication systems, metalanguage and object language become strangely alike.

The questioning or negation of the text-internal communicative levels naturally has implications for the (cognitive) reception of such a text. On the one hand, this can be read as an implicit self-reflexive or metareferential comment on the narrative's fictionality. On the other, this 'comment' questions the logical and foundational structure of reflexivity, the notion of reflexivity as a "turning back on oneself, a form of self-awareness" (Lawson 1985, 9). Thus, this instance of metalepsis suggests and enacts what could be termed the impossibility of self-reflexivity, of genuine self-awareness, which has a long tradition in Western philosophy. Hume claimed that, since the self can never be directly apprehended, it is nothing besides a non-substantial 'bundle' of 'particular perceptions':

> For my part, when I enter most intimately into what I call *myself*, I always stumble upon some particular perception or other, of heat or cold, light or shade, love or hatred, pain or pleasure. I never can catch *myself* at any time without a perception, and can never observe anything but the perception. When my perceptions are remov'd for any time, as by sound sleep; so long am I insensible of *myself*, and may truly be said not to exist. (1978 [1739–1740], 252)

The insight that subject and object can never coincide in an act of understanding has induced Hume to suppose that there is no 'substantial' self beyond the 'objects' of perception. Even though Immanuel Kant followed Hume on this epistemological problem (introspection does allow the intuition of mental states but does not reveal the self that possesses them) in the *Critique of Pure Reason* (1781), he did not draw the radical conclusion that there is *no* noumenal self: "[I]n attaching 'I' to our thoughts, we designate the subject only transcendentally [...] without noting in it any quality whatsoever – in fact, without knowing anything of it either directly or by inference" (1996 [first German ed. 1781], 392). The strange solution of the early Kant seems to lie in the proposition that self-awareness is not connected to knowledge of any properties. This anticipates some of the key issues of the (largely self-contained) discussion of self-awareness within analytical philosophy: the seminal papers by Hector-Neri Castañeda (1966), Sidney Shoemaker (1968), John Perry (1979) and Gareth Evans (1982) have established the following peculiarities that awareness of self (as opposed to awareness of other things) entails:

> 1. In certain kinds of awareness of self, first-person indexicals (I, me, my, mine) cannot be analyzed out in favor of anything else, in particular anything descriptionlike,
> and that,
> 2. In such cases, awareness of self is via what Shoemaker calls self-reference without identification. One can be aware of something as oneself without identifying it (or anything) as oneself via properties that one has ascribed to the thing. (Brook 2001, 9)

According to analytical philosophy, this is the strange and unstable ground of self-awareness: this using of 'I' to refer to the subject of thoughts that seem to belong to an entity or perspective (which is 'mine') without noting any quality in myself, the peculiar possibility of reference to oneself *as* oneself without any other identification, is what Shoemaker calls 'self-reference without identification.'

Implicitly, the metaleptic transgression quoted above (*Tristram Shandy*, Chapter xxviii in Volume VII) shows the elusiveness of the noumenal 'I' which is the centre of the narrative worlds represented (in first person narration). This vanishing 'self' is the vanishing point of each understanding (to which many metalepses can be related as the effect of that subject's self-reflexive multiplication of 'itself'). In each act of understanding the noumenal self posits an other, the object of perception or cognition. In looking at itself, the self is always already the phenomenal *object* that is not identical with the 'vanishing' subject: the moment this 'I' sees itself, the qualities seen can no longer be *knowledge* of the noumenal 'I,' but rather refer to a phenomenal *object* (to which we can successfully attribute the very qualities that turn it into the object of the vanishing self). Since each subject necessarily sees 'itself' as an object, the 'I' that sees and the 'I' that is seen can never coincide and can never reach a state of identity.

In the passage from *Tristram Shandy* quoted above, this is mirrored by the diegetic worlds which 'contain' the multiple selves that are Tristram's 'objects' in a necessary unfolding of hierarchies. The moment the extradiegetic narrator narrates his narrating, his act of narration becomes extra-extradiegetic (or his narrated act of narration becomes diegetic). The metaleptic violation of this hierarchy, then, simply *highlights* the self-referential paradox: in referring to and describing himself, the narrator Tristram Shandy multiplies his diegetic levels, i.e. the levels required by representational logic. Genuine self-reference is pronounced impossible in Sterne's metaleptic example above, which playfully 'demonstrates' that the vanishing self is the unstable centre that proves elusive (from the point of view of the narrator). What was formerly the extradiegetic subject is turned into the diegetic (or extradiegetic) object, created by an extradiegetic (or extra-extradiegetic) act of enunciation by a fictional subject. The infinite regression that haunts such a model was famously expounded by Samuel Coleridge in the 13th chapter of his *Biographia Literaria*:

> It may however be shown, and has in part already been shown earlier, that even when the Objective is assumed as the first, we yet can never pass beyond the principle of self-consciousness. Should we attempt it, we must be driven back from ground to ground, each of which would cease to be a Ground the moment we pressed on it. We must be whirl'd down the gulf of an infinite series. But this would make our reason baffle the end and purpose of all reason, namely, unity and system. Or we must break off the series arbitrarily, and affirm an absolute something that is in and of itself at once cause and effect (causa sui), subject and object, or rather the absolute identity of both. (1983 [1817], 285)

The self-reflexive potential of the metalepsis cited above has fundamental philosophical implications, as it not only highlights the unstable ground of self-awareness (demonstrating that 'we must break off the series arbitrarily' at some point) but also playfully offers the 'identity of both,' the identity of subject and object. In the example above, some of Tristram Shandy's sentences can be understood as the simultaneous enunciation of narrator and narrated. This metaleptic speech act 'impossibly' creates the identity of subject and object, or, more precisely, a (fictional) locus where the teller and the told are in a certain sense identical.[133]

Metaleptic transgressions potentially perform the 'impossible': they demonstrate that narrative is always in danger of the paradoxical collapse of object language and metalanguage (of embedded narrative and embedding narrative), while questioning the validity of that very distinction. They foreground the *Dopplungsstruktur* of literary narrative and thereby enact the 'metaization of narration,' the process of mimesis made visible as 'the mimesis of process' – a process that creates *and* undermines the aesthetic illusion. They show that the vanishing self is the unstable and elusive centre of narrative (at least for homodiegetic narration) and offer the 'impossible' identity of subject and object. Fundamentally, they perform the aporias of metaization and playfully engage with the impossibility of genuine self-reference. "Let me collect myself and pursue my journey": the metaleptic existent "is driven back from ground to ground, each of which would cease to be a ground the moment we pressed on it" (Coleridge, ibid.).

---

[133] This is connected to the question of the extent to which metalepsis involves what Winfried Nöth calls "performative metareference" (2009, 111); how far, in other words, the metaleptic transgression is *performatively* self-referential and/or metareferential (cf. ibid. 104–108). Drawing on Austin and Searle, Nöth defines performative speech acts as those "in which the act of speaking does not only have a referent, as all words have, but in which it has a referent which only comes to existence by the utterance of the very words to which it refers" (ibid. 111). The metaleptic speech act comes into existence by the utterance of the words to which it refers. Just as the performative verb to *resign* performs that to which it refers, so do metaleptic sentences – in a certain sense – perform the crossing of the boundary that separates diegetic levels. Thus when Corporal Trim resumes relating the story of the young Beguine to Uncle Toby at the beginning of Chapter VIII/xxii of *Tristram Shandy* ("I had escaped, continued the corporal, all that time from falling in love, and had gone on to the end of the chapter, had it not been predestined otherwise"), it is precisely the diegetic character's reference to a chapter that performs the metalepsis, as it does not refer to something that already exists (if one does not interpret the chapter as a part of the story which Trim relates). William Nelles terms the exhibition of such knowledge (knowledge of the world in which the narrator narrates his story) verbal or epistemological metalepsis (cf. Nelles 1997, 152–57).

4 The 'Model' Case: 'Impossible Narration' and Metaleptic Transgressions in Laurence Sterne's *Tristram Shandy* (1759–1767)

4.1 "Any One Is Welcome to Take My Pen, and Go on with the Story for Me That Will": Tristram Shandy's 'Impossible Narration'

> The Life and Opinions of Tristram Shandy [...] affects (and not unsuccessfully) to please, by a contempt of all the rules observed in other writings, and therefore cannot justly have its merit measured by them.
>
> —Extract from an unsigned notice in the *Royal Female Magazine* (February 1760)

Wayne Booth remarked that "in a sense *Tristram Shandy* is an elaborate evasion of the promise given in the title" (1952, 169). This comment highlights the fact that any attempt to read and understand Laurence Sterne's novel is governed by numerous conventions, expectations and conditions that arise within the hermeneutic situation in which it is understood. One convention that guides the expectations of readers is paratextual information. Thus, many readers will share (and will at the time have shared) Booth's assumption that the novel's title is indeed a "promise," and expect an autodiegetic narrator who tells the story of his life in agreement with conventions established by writers such as Daniel Defoe, Tobias Smollett, Samuel Richardson, Charlotte Lennox or Sarah and Henry Fielding in what was in the eighteenth-century the relatively young genre of the novel. An unsigned notice published in the *Royal Female Magazine* early in 1760, one of the earliest reviews of *Tristram Shandy,* acknowledges the existence of generic conventions by a reference to "the rules observed in other writings" (qtd. in Howes 1958, 53) – 'rules' that govern and apply to the eighteenth-century novel and, by extension, possibly also the tradition in which *Tristram Shandy* places itself.[134] Since *Tristram Shandy* displays contempt of these

---

[134] A list of (literary) models belonging to that tradition usually includes Swift, Montaigne, Robert Burton, and Ephraim Chambers' *Cyclopedia: or, an Universal Dictionary of Arts and Sciences* (1738), "from which [Laurence Sterne] derived most of his learned references" (Richetti 1999, 271). Allusions to Cervantes (cf. Sterne Chapter I.xii) and evidence that the *Third Book* of *Gargantua and Pantagruel* was a main source for Sterne's 'thieving scholarship' (cf.

rules and "cannot justly have its merit measured by them" (ibid.), the notice implies, it is a *model* of its own. What then, it may be asked, is the nature of Sterne's 'model'? What is the nature of that, in Booth's words, "elaborate evasion"?

The Life and Opinions of Tristram Shandy, Gentleman is a 'model' case in more than one sense. It is, first of all, to my knowledge the narrative which displays most metalepses (or most metaleptic potential) of all narratives in the eighteenth and nineteenth centuries.[135] Even most twentieth-century narratives seem unable to match the ingenuity with which Sterne investigates the metaleptic potential of narrative. This indeed makes *Tristram Shandy* a 'model' case in more than one sense. One of the first, and possibly one of the most consistent attempts to narrate metaleptically, the novel, at least potentially, lays bare the 'impossibilities' of narration – the very model that questions our models of sense-making. I have argued above (in Chapter 3.2) that metalepsis is part of a tradition that 'defamiliarizes' familiar ways of making sense and that 'metaleptic defamiliarization' potentially uncovers aporetic configurations that emerge in human mediations of 'reality.' In a similar manner, the novel has often been discussed from the vantage point of the Formalist approach to 'literariness.' It is, in Shklovsky's sense (cf. "Art as Technique," first published in 1917), a 'model' of defamiliarization. Discussing the Formalist approach to the 'literariness' of literary texts, Bennett (1979) argues that "[l]iterature thus effects a two-fold shift of perceptions. For what it makes appear strange is not merely the 'reality' which has been distanced from habitual modes of representation but also those habitual modes of representation themselves" (44). It may be no exaggeration to produce the quip that *Tristram Shandy* established metalepsis as a 'habitual

---

Laudando 1996, 157) indicate that the tradition in which *Tristram Shandy* places itself also includes Rabelais and the Spanish picaresque novel.

135 This assessment can probably be expanded to include all narratives written before the twentieth century. This also applies, I would argue, to the seventeenth-century narrative *Don Quixote*. I agree, for the most part, with Brian D. Patrick who argues that "much of what has been written on metalepsis and *Don Quixote* is plagued by conceptual imprecision and many overstated claims. This is the case for Cervantes scholars working within a Genettian framework and for narrative theorists who use *Don Quixote* to illustrate their ideas. Both parties tend to see cases of narrative transgression and paradox where none actually exists. For Cervantes scholars, this has meant extending Genette's definition of metalepsis to cover cases with no real narrative transgression. Theorists of metalepsis, on the other hand, have tended to misread *Don Quixote* in ways that bring the text in line with their narratological categories" (2008, 116). I would argue that *Don Quixote* offers little metaleptic potential, and certainly offered Sterne no model of metaleptic narration.

mode of representation' – the very mode of representation that characterizes modes of representation as 'habitual.'

Metalepsis in Laurence Sterne's *Tristram Shandy* is no isolated phenomenon: it is part of a general strategy to narrate 'impossibly,' a strategy that not only violates narrative conventions but also potentially uncovers aporetic configurations that come into being in (fictional) mediations of 'reality.' In the following, a brief narratological outline of this strategy will be offered, which not only supplies a field of reference for metalepses in *Tristram Shandy*, but also explores how the elements of the repertoire of novelistic narrative techniques employed by Tristram metaleptically challenge each other. Part of the hermeneutic experience of reading *Tristram Shandy* is the encounter with elements that deny the assumptions and conceptual frameworks which guide one's attempt to make sense of the tradition from Rabelais to Sterne, and from Sterne to the present day. Tristram's 'impossible' narration investigates the limits of narrative tradition, the limits of understanding narrative, and the limits of the 'novel form.'[136]

One way to start an investigation of *Tristram Shandy*'s relationship with the 'novel form' is a close look at Fielding's *The History of Tom Jones*. It is typical of the emerging genre of the eighteenth-century novel that the paratext formulaically refers to the work in question ('novel' is the genre's later name) as an authentic 'Life,' 'History,' or 'Adventure.' In *Tom Jones*, the heterodiegetic narrator presents himself as the writer of a 'history,' a writer who appears in the opening chapters of each book and who comments on the characters, their actions, or on the narrative situation. In the conventional attempt to justify himself and his

---

[136] Robert Alter has claimed that Sterne "parodies all the principal models of novel writing available to him" (1987, 93), including *Don Quixote*. However, I would argue that parody in Laurence Sterne's novel is directed primarily at the major exponents of the eighteenth-century novel and the narrative strategies they employ. Sterne's relationship with Cervantes and Rabelais seems to be rather one of emulation, since both works are repeatedly presented as models worthy of imitation by the narrator Tristram Shandy. Alter offers the following exposition of what he sees as the parody of *Don Quixote*: "'Cervantick' realism, Sterne perceived, operates by a repeated juxtaposition of soaring fantasy with [...] coarse-grained actuality, the quixotic principle colliding with the sanchesque. *Tristram Shandy* comically and philosophically expands this central strategy of *Don Quixote* by making it the ubiquitous pattern of every man's relation to every other and to the world of physical existence" (ibid.). This is an interesting insight, but it is questionable whether it can be characterised as parody. It is the present author's contention that even though *Don Quixote* was no doubt an important model for Laurence Sterne (to which he refers time and again in his novels and letters), it is evident that Cervantes is neither satirized nor parodied by Tristram Shandy. However, to treat such a dispute extensively is beyond the scope of this study.

method in Chapter I of Book II, the narrator compares his work to other 'histories' and claims that he has invented a new form of writing. As the raconteur who intends to recount at large "[w]hen an extraordinary scene presents itself" (Fielding II.i) and to sum up uneventful years in a few sentences, Fielding's narrator frees himself from the constraints of the 'historian' who must avoid a "chasm in [his] history" (ibid.). In *Tom Jones*, the narrator chooses to relate only what is "worthy of [the reader's] notice" (II.i) in the storyworld to which he seemingly has unlimited access. It is the general consensus that one of Fielding's innovations was the introduction of the authorial narrative situation into the eighteenth-century novel.[137] This releases the narrator from the need to justify how he obtained the information he or she relates – unlike the homodiegetic narrators of Defoe or the letter writers (and their editor) of Richardson, who seek to convince the reader that their writing is the authentic report of human experience (cf. Watt 1967, 32). Accordingly, Fielding claims that he cannot be judged according to the rules of other 'histories':

> [F]or as I am, in reality, the founder of a new province of writing, so I am at liberty to make what laws I please therein. And these laws, my readers, whom I consider as my subjects, are bound to believe in and to obey; with which that they may readily and cheerfully comply, I do hereby assure them, that I shall principally regard their ease and advantage in all such institutions. (II.i)

While the narrator, Tristram Shandy, playfully evokes the narrative position(s)[138] of Fielding's narrator, he at the same time self-referentially uncovers the inherent inconsistencies and impossibilities of those strategies; for Tristram, too, depicts himself as "the founder of a new province of writing"[139] in which he refuses to confine himself to "any man's rules that ever lived" (Sterne I.iv). Since such a narrator is, to a large degree, responsible for the laws that govern his writing, he is in a position to break those laws. In contrast to Fielding's narrator, Tristram Shandy not only disregards the rules of other 'histories' but his own as well. The comical oscillation between incompatible narrative positions is the frequent result of the refusal to confine himself to the rules that follow logically from his own narrative perspective. On the one hand, Tristram Shandy

---

137 Vera and Ansgar Nünning have emphasized that the new type of novel Fielding created is the first instance of what Stanzel referred to as the authorial narrative situation in England (cf. Nünning 1998, 142).
138 Narrative position here simply refers to the "perceptual or conceptual position in terms of which the narrated situations and events are presented" (Prince 2003, 75), and is thus a logical consequence and defining characteristic of the narrative situation.
139 Cf. Chapter I/xxii, in which Tristram claims that his "work is of a species by itself."

is a truly omniscient narrator who knows everything about his story. He can minutely portray a thought floating in Dr. Slop's mind (III.ix) or the exact posture of Trim reading the Sermon (II.xvii). On the other hand, as the homo- and autodiegetic narrator, he has only limited access to the storyworld and finds Toby's "apologetical oration" (VI.xxxii) among the papers of his father. From this limited perspective, the dialogues and monologues of the characters Uncle Toby, Trim, Slop or Yorick are an 'impossibility.' These dialogues and monologues are repeated word for word although they occurred before Tristram's birth (which Nelles, following Beth Newman, has aptly described as "an extended ventriloquism" [1997, 122]). In this manner, the very diegetic 'document' that guarantees the authenticity of Toby's oration undermines the authenticity of all diegetic speech acts rendered from a position of omniscience. This 'impossible' perspectivity has (limited) metaleptic implications. On the one hand, Tristram (as the omniscient narrator) occupies a perceptual position that situates him outside the diegetic world. On the other hand, Tristram (as an autodiegetic narrator) is subjected to the conditions of the diegesis. The narrator Tristram is always in (potentially metaleptic) danger of succumbing to the logic of the diegetic world of which he tells or of ascending to a hierarchically superior position from which the diegesis can be completely controlled. In other words, the oscillating possibilities of extradiegetic narration employed by Tristram Shandy metaleptically challenge each other.

For the most part, Tristram's narration displays the characteristics of the authorial narrative situation – or rather, an idiosyncratic version of authorial narration that imposes curious restrictions upon itself. Whereas Fielding's narrator is very much in control of his storyworld, his narration and the reader, Tristram continually claims to have no control over the narrative act, the story he tells or his readers: "——But this is neither here nor there—why do I mention it?——Ask my pen,—it governs me,—I govern not it" (VI.vi). Here, Tristram jokingly claims to be governed by "his pen," which may refer to the tradition in which he writes, the materiality of the writing process, or the automatism with which that process unfolds. What is decisive is the lack of control and agency, and it is this that is so humorously conveyed. The text, pen, process of writing (and narrative positions so engendered), the tradition in which one stands, and (here lies some metaleptic potential) the *diegesis* itself cannot be held at bay, cannot be kept at a safe distance from which the narrator may exert control. The narrator is indeed 'neither truly here nor there,' but is always both here *and* there, reconciling what logically cannot be reconciled.

Yet the position of authority and control proper to Fielding's narrator is at the same time humorously enacted by Tristram. Threatening the reader with a lengthy rendition of a siege by Rapin in Chapter VII/v, he begins the following chapter thus: "—But courage! gentle reader!—I scorn it—'tis enough to have thee in my power" (VII.vi). Here, he jokingly adopts a position of authority extending to the world of the reader like that of Fielding's narrator, who refers to his readers as his "subjects." It is this position of authority that enables the narrator Tristram to act on his impulses in a parody of Richardson's 'writing to the moment': "A sudden impulse comes across me—drop the curtain, *Shandy*—I drop it—Strike a line here across the paper, *Tristram*—I strike it—and hey for a new chapter!" (IV.x).[140] Here, the narrator's position is thoroughly *unlike* a metaphoric Gygean ring that allows narrator and narratee to be present but invisible in the storyworld—the narrator becomes visible as the story vanishes from sight. Authority thus understood, it would seem, is the authority of the narrating instance that creates and holds sway over the story. At this moment, the autodiegetic narrator seems to have severed his ontological connection with the diegesis and become the heterodiegetic creator of fiction. The (limited) metaleptic potential here relies on this 'movement' from inhabiting to creating a storyworld.[141] Such a 'movement' destabilizes the boundary between the domain of the signified and the domain of the signifier.

Tristram's authority is 'neither truly here nor there' and remains in a relationship of tension with his continued claims to be neither in control of the world *of which* nor of the world *in which* he tells. The mock helplessness induced by the 'inability' to control the telling of his life and the contradictory implication that this life is fictive (from the perspective of the narrator Tristram – which, at least in a certain sense, would imply that he is very much in control of the story) cannot be subsumed under a consistent narrative position. Hamilton Beck offers the formula that "if Fielding's narrator can be said to be omniscient and omnipotent within the confines of the novel, Sterne's narrator is omniscient and impotent" (1987, 44). However, such formulae negate the perspectival and conceptual alternations Tristram playfully presents. 'Impossibly,' Sterne's narrator is omnipotent *and* impotent, omniscient *and* ignorant.

---

140 Similarly, Alter has argued that "Walter Shandy's advancing foot, hovering over the first step from the landing for the whole length of a chapter in which Sterne reflects upon chapters (4, 10–12), is surely [...] a comic blow-up of Richardsonian narrative pace" (1987, 97).
141 In Genette's terminology, this can be described as the 'impossibility' to reconcile the homodiegetic narrator Tristram (who belongs to the diegetic world of which he narrates) with the heterodiegetic narrator Tristram who *creates* the diegetic and fictive world with his extradiegetic narrative act. The narrator cannot be located at any logically consistent conceptual/perceptual position.

Moreover, such self-reflexive comments of the highly visible narrator ("—drop the curtain, *Shandy*" [IV.x]) not only emphasize the fictive nature of his story, but also present *the narrator* Tristram Shandy as a *character* in the fictionalization of the narrative act – a recursive structure with a metaleptic ring to it. The seemingly arbitrary manner in which the 'dramatized' narrator acts is part of an overall strategy that repeatedly subordinates the rules of representational logic and the conventions of storytelling to his idiosyncratic will. In Chapter IV/x, after acting on his impulse to "strike a line" (IV.x), Tristram defends his impulses as the organizing principle of his narration in what could be argued to be a mockery of the conventional attempts at justification common in the eighteenth-century novel:

> The duce of any other rule have I to govern myself by in this affair—and if I had one—as I do all things out of rule—I would twist it and tear it to pieces, and throw it into the fire when I had done—Am I warm? I am, and the cause demands it—a pretty story! Is a man to follow rules—or rules to follow him?
> Now this, you must know, being my chapter upon chapters, which I promised to write before I went to sleep, I thought it meet to ease my conscience entirely before I lay'd down, by telling the world all I knew about the matter at once. (IV.x)

Since rules are to follow him, Tristram is in a position to fictionalize his work's genesis, revealing the circumstances and idiosyncrasies that shape his narrative act, and hence, too, the story dependent upon that act. Such a fictionalization of the narrative act undermines the authority of the narrator and 'lays bare'[142] the constructedness of Tristram's 'omniscience' and the fact that an omniscient narrative stance (such as Fielding's) ultimately has its source in the limited and subjective perspective of a human being. The 'impossible' amalgamation of an omniscient narrator and a continuously self-reflexive and idiosyncratic narrator who displays his human limitations not only highlights the unavoidable perspectivity of all narration, but also implies a metaleptic movement that locates the omniscient narrator within the diegesis he creates. As the omniscient narrator, he is not subject to perceptual or conceptual restrictions; as the autodiegetic narrator, Tristram Shandy is bound by the way in which the very concept of telling one's life depends on the limited human perspective of the life told.

The 'irreconcilable' narrative positions *Tristram Shandy* combines inform the book's 'irreconcilable' narrative situations. Even though he repeatedly insinuates that it is his narration, his idiosyncratic narrative authority, that gen-

---

[142] Famously, it was Viktor Shklovsky who first maintained that Sterne's "typical method is to proceed by 'laying bare' the literary device" (1968 [first Russian ed. 1921], 66).

erates the (fictive) story, Tristram Shandy presents his narrative as an act of recounting that potentially overstretches his abilities: "I feel the difficulties of the descriptions I'm going to give—and feel the want of my powers" (IX.xxiv). This prolepsis is a typical example of Tristram's 'impossible' narration. Although he from time to time jokingly praises his fictive writing ("I set no small store by myself upon this very account, that my reader has never yet been able to guess at any thing" [I.xxv]), he still voices doubts as to whether his abilities will enable him to successfully render the "choicest morsel" (IX.xxiv) of the story he is narrating. In this manner, he often looks ahead to a future rendering of a past event and comments on the 'necessities'[143] imposed upon his discourse by the storyworld. Paradoxically, the domain of the signified is presented as prior to and independent of the domain of the signifier, a presentation itself 'created' by signification. Despite the fact that there is no outside standard against which the accuracy[144] of his (fictional) narrative situation can be gauged, Tristram claims that the storyworld 'demands' more accurate mediation. The oscillation between non-metaleptic conventions (an abstract and independent story is 'represented' by fictional narration) is a potentially metaleptic technique connecting the (changing) narrative positions and situations with epistemological quandaries.

Thus, for instance, the lack of agreement in his narratorial stance might be attributed to an epistemological problem resulting from omniscience within the confines of the storyworld. If one knows everything about (or can bring about anything in) the storyworld, how is one to choose among the myriad of causes and effects of the events one relates? How does one single anything out? Tristram demonstrates that, while an omniscient narrator might know all, it is impossible for him to narrate all. His professed attempt to narrate in such a man-

---

[143] For instance, in the example of rhetorical metalepsis in Chapter III/xxxviii (quoted above in the section on figurative metalepses), the narrator interrupts himself thus: "—but I have a fifty things more necessary to let you know first [...]." The question as to what necessity can be involved in Tristram's narrative situation is, of course, humorous. Here the breathless feel both supplies and mocks the logic of conventional narrative. Again, since Tristram ignores many conventional requirements of narrative writing, and since his 'necessities' do not logically follow from a consistent narrative situation, they must, it seems, derive from his idiosyncratic character.

[144] Moreover, Tristram argues time and again that there is no acceptable outside standard against which the *quality* of his writing can be gauged. Two examples among many are Chapter IX/xvii, in which he once again dismisses the judgements of his readers, and the early Chapter I/iv, in which he maintains that he will neither confine himself to *Horace's* nor "to any man's rules that ever lived."

ner that "nothing which has touched me will be thought trifling in its nature, or tedious in its telling" (I.vi) and his design to "come at the first springs of the events I tell" (I.xxi), inevitably fails. Instead, he demonstrates the elusive nature of the life he attempts to depict, the infinite regression that opens up at each attempt to characterize the chain of causes and effects in which each event consists. Interrupting his narration in mid-sentence, Tristram describes this dilemma in the often quoted excerpt from Chapter IV/xiii:

> I will not finish that sentence till I have made an observation upon the strange state of affairs between the reader and myself, just as things stand at present—an observation never applicable before to any one biographical writer since the creation of the world, but to myself—and I believe will never hold good to any other, until its final destruction [...].

This paragraph introduces the subject of the problematic nature of novelistic time – the time of the storyworld, the time it takes for the narrator to narrate *and* the time the reader needs for reading are all temporally (and, potentially, metaleptically) referred to by "at present" and are all included in "the strange state of affairs" Tristram proceeds to illustrate:

> I am this month one whole year older than I was this time twelve-month; and having got, as you perceive, almost into the middle of my fourth volume—and no farther than to my first day's life—'tis demonstrative that I have three hundred and sixty-four days more life to write just now, than when I first set out; so that instead of advancing, as a common writer, in my work with what I have been doing at it—on the contrary, I am just thrown so many volumes back—was every day of my life to be as busy a day as this—And why not?—and the transactions and opinions of it to take up as much description—And for what reason should they be cut short? As at this rate I should just live 364 times faster than I should write—It must follow, an' please your worships, that the more I write, the more I shall have to write—and consequently, the more your worships read, the more your worships will have to read.
> Will this be good for your worships eyes?

John Traugott has called *Tristram Shandy* a "resolutely nonlogical work" (1954, 126). And, indeed, this idiosyncratic attempt to narrate nothing but his whole life seems to be akin to the *Tristrapaedia* and its "doomed and heroically absurd battle against time" (Ricks 1997, xxiii). Both defy the laws of logic and baffle in a way which resembles Zeno's paradox[145] of the race between Achilles and the tortoise. Achilles, the fastest runner in Greece, has a race with the slowest ani-

---

[145] The paradox usually referred to in this manner is actually only the most famous of Zeno's many paradoxes. The version supplied in this chapter relies on the third chapter of *The Paradoxes of Zeno* (1996) by J.A. Faris.

mal, the tortoise. The tortoise gets a head start and walks (for instance) ten feet. To catch the tortoise Achilles first needs to run to the tortoise's position ten feet away. But when he reaches the point ten feet away the tortoise is further on. When he reaches that point in turn the tortoise has moved on again. To catch the tortoise Achilles has to traverse an infinity of such points in a finite time. Because this is impossible, Achilles will never overtake the tortoise. This conclusion has of course met with opposition: "It is true that [the tortoise] is not overtaken while it holds a lead, but still it is overtaken, if it be allowed that a finite line can be traversed to the end" (Aristotle, qtd. in Faris 1996, 26).

Accordingly, it does not logically follow that the "transactions and opinions" recounted 'take up a certain amount of description' (cf. IV.xiii). There is no fixed temporal reciprocity between the domain of the signifier and the domain of the signified that the narrator (or any other narrative agent) must follow. The temporal reciprocity between the world of the telling and the world of the told, *Tristram Shandy* implies, is a metaleptic projection which is the result of the habitual employment of narrative techniques. Tristram Shandy can alternate summary, scene and descriptive pause in the same way as Fielding's narrator, and 'progress' in his narration – a feat of which he shows himself capable as the author of an extremely condensed rendition of the story of Amanda and Amundus given in Chapter VII/xxxi. Compared with the narrative speed with which he relates his own life (as in Chapters IV/xi and IV/xii – it takes one chapter for each of the first two steps Walter Shandy and Uncle Toby take on their way downstairs), there is an antithetically rapid progression in Tristram's humorous account of the thwarted lovers whose supposed tomb he visits in Lyon. In Chapter VII/xxxi he relates their whole life in less than one page of writing:

> A story [...] of two fond lovers, separated from each other by cruel parents, and by still more cruel destiny——
> Amandus——He
> Amanda——She—
> each ignorant of the other's course,
> He——east
> She——west
> Amandus taken captive by the Turks, and carried to the emperor of Morocco's court, where the princess of Morocco falling in love with him, keeps him twenty years in prison, for the love of Amanda——
> She—(Amanda) all the time wandering barefoot, and with dishevelled hair, o'er rocks and mountains enquiring for Amandus——Amandus! Amandus!—making every hill and valley to echo back his name——[...] till,——[...] chance unexpected bringing them at the same moment of the night, though by different ways, to the gate of Lyons their native city, and each in well known accents calling out aloud,

> Is Amandus ⎫
> Is my Amanda ⎭ still alive?
>
> they fly into each other's arms, and both drop down dead for joy. (VII.xxxi)

Despite the alternation of summary and scene, the minimal story of Amanda and Amundus approaches maximal narrative speed, culminating in the diagrammatic representation of simultaneously voiced last words.[146] The narrative speed of the account of Tristram's life is diametrically opposed to this humorous shorthand of a story. When he relates his own life, the narrator mostly alternates between descriptive pauses (in which there is some stretch of text but no time 'passes' in the diegesis), descriptive passages (which relate minute details[147] over various pages), and scenes (where discourse time and story time are usually taken to be approximately congruent). In almost all of these alternations, the narrating time (*Erzählzeit*) takes more time than the story time (*erzählte Zeit*). Since Tristram – as the writer of an autobiography – is so circumstantial that his narration takes longer than what he narrates, and since the *Erzählzeit* (as part of Tristram's life) will become *erzählte Zeit* in a later chapter of his book, he is not only unable to proceed beyond his fifth year, but also unable to 'progress' in his narration. The logic of this resembles the 'infinity' of finite points between the tortoise and Achilles. Yet, as the Amanda/Amundus story demonstrates, a whole life can be told in less than a page and Achilles can outrun a tortoise. A life (whether conceptualized as preceding or dependent upon the narrative act) can be reduced in storytelling to a structured and finite representation. In fact, and this is foregrounded by Sterne's novel, each story told is necessarily a reduction or selection of the 'infinity' of moments that constitute its events. The refusal to reduce and structure the diegetic events from a position of authority supplies the diegesis with a metaleptic sense of irreducible 'reality.'

Tristram Shandy highlights the fact that the general selectivity of narrative discourse is arbitrary and conventional – even though most (if not all) eighteenth-century narrators maintain or imply that a meaningful configuration is established by choosing and concentrating on *significant* episodes. The assumption that some of the "transactions and opinions" (IV/xiii) are more significant than others is denied by Tristram: "And for what reason should they be cut

---

[146] Incidentally, this seems to be another 'impossibility.' How does one read the simultaneity of two speakers?

[147] Cf., for instance Chapter II/xvii in which the exact posture of Trim (reading the sermon) is portrayed in great detail.

short" (IV/xiii)? Significance is dependent upon the application of a contingent set of rules which determine what is and what is not worth telling. This is strikingly similar to Nietzsche's analysis of 'mythological thinking' in *Beyond Good and Evil* (1886) discussed above (cf. Chapter 3.1): "One should use "cause" and "effect" only as pure concepts, that is to say, as conventional fictions for the purpose of designation and communication" (1989, 29). Unwilling to think mythologically (in Nietzsche's sense), Tristram may use 'conventional fictions for the purposes of communication' – but he highlights time and again that these fictions structure a metaleptic continuum that does not offer the objectifications 'cause' and 'effect.' Accordingly, the question how and for what reasons Tristram chooses what is worthy of his narration is not answered by the conventional rules of storytelling, which, typically create suspense by introducing instabilities and tensions ('Amandus—east, Amanda—west') to be resolved in an ending towards which the whole narrative is structured ('They drop down dead for joy').[148]

The "picaresque quasi-biographical 'history' books" (Imhof 1986, 123), the novels of sentiment, the Gothic romance *The Castle of Otranto* (first published in 1765, shortly after Volumes VII and VIII of *Tristram Shandy*), as well as the 'female didactic novel'[149], all these contemporaries of Laurence Sterne's novel rely heavily on such formulaic plot structures. *Tristram Shandy*'s singularity[150] is that it refuses to stick to the conventional rules of storytelling: it is marked by a refined shapelessness that foregrounds the constructedness and idiosyncrasy of

---

148 On the very few occasions *Tristram Shandy* displays such structures, these structures are employed to create comic effects. The story of Toby's amours with Widow Wadman, for instance, is a reversal and parody of the love story threatened to be thwarted by a moment of crisis (as in Richardson's amatory novel *Clarissa* where the seducer Lovelace enters through the garden on his way to the heroine's house) before the villains are punished and the heroine and hero are happily married. The Shandean moment of crisis (is uncle Toby impotent?) is endlessly prolonged and does not instigate a change of affairs – uncle Toby remains chaste and no one will ever learn where exactly his wound is located.

149 Nünning has termed the novels of eighteenth-century women writers (which preceded Sterne) such as Sarah Fielding, Eliza Haywood and Charlotte Lennox *weibliche Erziehungsromane* (cf. Nünning 1998, 147–152).

150 Naturally, this does not amount to the contention that *Tristram Shandy* is not in other ways characteristic of literary tendencies in its own time or of the tradition of literary models and sources in which Laurence Sterne places his book (cf. e.g. Richetti 1999, 275–277). Drawing on John Sitter's *Literary Loneliness in Mid-eighteenth-century England*, Richetti argues that Sterne's fiction is typical of the eighteenth century insofar as "fiction at mid-century and after is part of a larger tendency in the literature of the time toward exploration of the personal and away from the representation of meaningful public and historical action" (ibid., 276).

every narrative endeavour and continually reminds the reader of the impossibility of authentic representation – Amandus and Amanda are not real and neither are the Shandys. The claim that the very concept of *mimesis* is challenged by *Tristram Shandy* is not new. Allocating Laurence Sterne's novel a place in the tradition of metafictional texts, Rüdiger Imhof argues that

> Sterne appears to have striven not so much towards emulating reality in the realist manner, but towards demonstrating the impossibility of capturing the life and times of his protagonist through *mimesis* [...]. Whereas the realist, from Defoe onwards to the present, has employed conventions of fiction – and preferably those that best serve their individual ends – to sustain *mimesis* without disruption, [...] metafictionists have created a heightened sense of *mimesis* pre-eminently in order to lay bare its inadequacy as an artistic approach. (Imhof 1986, 62)

Thus, Sterne interweaves novelistic novelties into his 'impossible' amalgamation of narrative positions and situations: he is the first novelist to follow the death of a diegetic character (Yorick [I.xii]) with a black page, the first to print a torn-out chapter (IV.xxv), and the first to offer his position of narrative authority when, overwhelmed by the invention of a story he cannot represent, Tristram, in mock exasperation with his narrative plight, invites his narratees to take over: "[A]ny one is welcome to take my pen, and go on with the story for me that will" (IX.xxiv). Tristram's 'impossible' narration thus continually forces the reader to dissolve, (re-)establish and reinterpret the narrative situation, a process which is potentially accompanied by an awareness of what is always already part of the hermeneutic situation between reader, text, and "the historical experiences and traditions of interpretation which we inherit" (Warnke 2002, 316). Offering his 'pen' implies that these 'inherited' experiences and traditions of interpretation (metaleptically) constitute what they purport (and thus fail) to represent.

4.2 "Get My Father and My Uncle Toby off the Stairs and Put Them to Bed": Metaleptic Transgressions in *Tristram Shandy*

Understanding metalepsis in Laurence Sterne's *Tristram Shandy* is embedded in the understanding of a general intention (or strategy) to narrate 'impossibly.' Metaleptic transgressions in *Tristram Shandy* are cued by narrational acts which are, I maintain, the formal centre of this narrative strategy – and which challenge conventional ways of making sense in a liberating increase of complexity. I have argued that in reading metalepses one potentially encounters what Hans-

Georg Gadamer has termed the 'negativity of hermeneutic experience,' the *experience* of a self-reflexive, dynamic, dialogical structure that results in an oscillating openness. Even though no analysis of metalepses can supply an ultimate sense of closure to the openness instigated by Tristram Shandy's 'impossible' narration, there is nevertheless the interpretive possibility of creating a sense of coherence within the hermeneutic situation in which metalepses emerge. In this sense, the following examination is shaped by three interpretive hypotheses: 1. Figurative metalepses in *Tristram Shandy* foreground the 'impossible' multiplicity of conventional narrative temporality. 2. Ontological first and third person immersive metalepses characteristically raise the question of 'reality' and representation. 3. Ontological second person immersive metalepses potentially enact the hermeneutic dialogue between reader, narrative and tradition. The following analyses of the metaleptic potential of Sterne's novel will focus on the hermeneutic dimension of transgressions that deny the distinction between the domains of the signifier and signified – a construction itself based on contextual assumptions and cued by narrational acts.

Yet, at the same time, some literary-historical findings are relevant from a perspective interested in reducing complexity. *The Life and Opinions of Tristram Shandy, Gentleman* is a 'model' case in the sense that it is one of the few pre-twentieth-century narratives that display extensive metaleptic potential. I will offer a brief outline of two tentative conclusions that can be drawn from a close analysis of this potential. First of all, there are no recursive metalepses in this novel. This is striking, since all other metaleptic types offered in Chapter 2 can be found there (although there are few instances classifiable as epistemological metalepsis [cf. Chapter 4.2.1]). Secondly, the metaleptic transgressions in *Tristram Shandy* focus on a general denial of the distinction between the domains of the signifier/signified rather than on a single entity that moves from one domain to the other across a 'boundary' instigated by narrational acts. Thus, it seems that recursive metalepsis and the immersive metalepsis in which a single entity moves from one diegetic level to another are phenomena that only systematically emerge in fictional narratives of the twentieth century.

4.2.1 Figurative Metalepses in *Tristram Shandy* and the Uncontrollability of Time

In Chapter I/xxi, Uncle Toby, striking the head of his pipe on the nail of his thumb, begins to say something and is interrupted in mid-sentence by the narrator in the following manner: "I think, says he:––But to enter rightly into my uncle *Toby*'s sentiments upon this matter, you must be made to enter first a little into his character, the out-lines of which I shall just give you, and then the dialogue between him and my father will go on as well again" (I/xxi). The narrator Tristram then digresses on the relationship between the climate and the irregular characters in England and on the progress of knowledge ("this great harvest of our learning, now ripening before our eyes") which approaches perfection and is about to make all further writing and reading superfluous, when he suddenly remembers his uncle: "But I forget my uncle *Toby*, whom all this while we have left knocking the ashes out of his tobacco pipe" (I/xxi). This is one of the many examples that can be interpreted as rhetorical metalepsis in *Tristram Shandy*. The 'projected simultaneity' of narrational act and storyworld temporality implies a move across diegetic levels, most likely on the part of the narrator. It is as though the narrator usurps the stage on which the events of the storyworld unfold according to his directions, and then interrupts those events to start a digression, in the course of which he inadvertently becomes oblivious to his role as a narrator in charge of his diegesis – while the actors do his bidding behind his back without acknowledging his existence.

The reader can interpret the passage in this way only retrospectively, only after Tristram's sudden realization that his uncle is still "knocking the ashes out of his tobacco pipe." One of the reasons for this is that, usually, "the fictive narrating [...] is considered to have no duration; or, more exactly, everything takes place as if the question of its duration had no relevance"[151] (Genette 1980, 222). Yet even if the act of narration is conceived of as extending over time, this is equally irrelevant for the temporality of the storyworld. Since the duration or lack of duration of the fictive narrating conventionally has no relevance for the duration of the events of the diegesis, any reader will accept the interruption of Uncle Toby without assuming that time lapses (or is frozen) in the storyworld while the narrator relates something else. As the reader learns that Tristram Shandy synchronizes story time and discourse time, he is forced to reconstruct the narrative situation and – presumably – the diegetic status of the narrator Tristram Shandy. The temporal deixis which simultaneously refers to the worlds in which and of which the narrator tells collapses the distinction between the diegetic and extradiegetic levels insofar as the diegetic and extradiegetic relations of temporality are arrayed relatively to a *single* frame of reference. As the reader is confronted in this manner with the problem of multiple duration in Tristram's narrative situation, he or she becomes aware of the conventional

---

[151] Gérard Genette cites *Tristram Shandy* as one of the very few exceptions to this general rule (cf. 1980, 222).

assumptions guiding the hermeneutic dialogue between author, reader, text, and traditions of writing and reading. Rhetorical metalepsis subjects the narrational act and what is narrated to a single temporality.

Conventionally, time in the novel is exclusively a phenomenon of the diegesis, whereas the arrangement of the events in or out of the order of their diegetic occurrence is instigated by the extradiegetic narrating act. The arrangement itself, the duration of the *récit*, is usually measured in words, lines, or pages and not in minutes, hours, and days. In his essay "A Parodying Novel: Sterne's *Tristram Shandy*," originally published in 1921, Victor Shklovsky argued that most narratives in which the chronology of the story told is presented out of sequence display a "motivation for the 'time shift'" (1968 [first Russian ed. 1921], 68) that can be traced back to the logic of the narrated plot:

> In Pushkin's "The Shot" the device of the "time-shift" is also freely used but it is motivated in terms of the narrative. First, we see Silvio practicing marksmanship, then we hear about the unfinished duel; then we meet the Count, Silvio's enemy, and learn about the outcome of events. The chronology of the story is presented out of sequence – II-I-III. But we see the motivation for the "time-shift". Sterne, however, simply lays bare this "time-shift" with no pretense of motivation from the story-line. (Ibid., 68–69)

The "pretense of motivation from the story-line" in *Tristram Shandy* results from the metaleptic introduction of the problem of simultaneity into the narrative situation. In an instance of rhetorical metalepsis similar to the one above (Uncle Toby strikes his pipe on the nail of his thumb for eleven chapters until he finally finishes his sentence in Chapter II/vi), Tristram's mother listens at the parlour door in the pose of the classical statue *Arrotino* as the narrator introduces another set of digressions: "In this attitude I am determined to let her stand for five minutes: till I bring up the affairs of the kitchen (as *Rapin* does those of the church) to the same period" (V.v). After relating the affairs of the kitchen, which include Trim's oration upon death, Tristram offers a short chapter on what sort of chapters he owes the world, and then interrupts Trim before he can begin the story of *Le Fever* in the following manner: "I am a Turk if I had not forgot my mother, as if Nature had plaistered me up, and set me down naked upon the banks of the river *Nile* without one" (V.xi). Here, the simultaneity (potentially) includes not only the perspective of Tristram's mother and the narrating instance but also the storyworld perspectives of the kitchen and the parlour before it possibly extends to the reader in Chapter V/xii[152] and, absurdly, even to

---

[152] The reader is directly addressed and could be argued to be wearing a Gygean ring that allows her or him to be present (and unseen) on the scene, right next to Tristram's mother:

the *récit* in Chapter V/xiii: "She [Tristram's mother] listened to it with composed intelligence, and would have done so to the end of the *chapter*" (emphasis added). The multiple temporal deixis of perspectives belonging to different diegetic levels, as well as the temporality of the *récit*, which comes into being in the duration of writing and reading, are not usually considered problematic either by writers or readers. Rhetorical metalepses in Laurence Sterne's novel foreground the temporal multiplicity that is concealed in the conventional if mostly implicit notion of the "atemporal space of the narrative as text" (Genette 1980, 223). In *Tristram Shandy*, the conventional atemporality of the "narrative as text" is not only given up and replaced by the inescapable duration of narration, of writing and reading, but that duration is also frequently 'subjected' to a temporal multiplicity which cannot be turned into an orderly progression of causally connected events controlled by the narrator. All the possible perspectives Tristram's metaleptic narration offers seem to 'look in on' something that is already going on.

The uncontrollability of time is a recurring motif often expressed by the metaleptic presumption that the events of the storyworld 'crowd in on'[153] the narrator. This is often achieved by highlighting the various possible contexts of the deictic references employed. Thus Tristram, fleeing from death across France, demonstrates in typical fashion the 'projected simultaneity' that unites the multiple temporalities of the diegesis and the 'now' of the extradiegetic narrator with a single 'dash of the pen':

> ——Now this is the puzzled skein of all——for in this last chapter, as far at least as it help'd me through *Auxerre*, I have been getting forwards in two different journies together, and with the same dash of the pen—for I have got entirely out of Auxerre in this journey which I am writing now, and I am got halfway out of Auxerre in that which I shall write hereafter——There is but a certain degree of perfection in every thing; and by pushing at something beyond that, I have brought myself into such a situation, as no traveller ever stood before me; for I am this moment walking across the market-place of Auxerre with my father and my uncle Toby, in our way back to dinner——and I am this moment also entering Lyons with my post-chaise broke into a thousand pieces—and I am moreover this moment

---

"[S]he instantly concluded herself the subject of the conversation, and with that prepossession upon her fancy, you will readily conceive every word my father said, was accommodated either to herself, or her family concerns" (V.xii).

153 Cf. Chapter xxxii of Volume IV ("The thing I lament is, that things have crowded in so thick upon me, that I have not been able to get into that part of my work, towards which, I have all the way, looked forwards […].") or Chapter xxxviii of Volume III ("I have a hundred difficulties which I have promised to clear up, and a thousand […] domestic misadventures crowding in upon me thick and three-fold, one upon the neck of another […].").

> in a handsome pavilion built by Pringello, upon the banks of the Garonne, which Mons. Sligniac has lent me, and where I now sit rhapsodizing all these affairs.
> ——Let me collect myself, and pursue my journey. (VII.xxviii)[154]

This often quoted excerpt could be taken as a paradigmatic example of rhetorical metalepsis. The deictic reference "this moment" refers to the diegetic events in Auxerre and Lyons as well as to the pavilion on the Garonne, which is the (extradiegetic) scene of the act of narration. Thus, the final sentence ("Let me collect myself, and pursue my journey") could be taken to refer to any of the three perspectives or to all of them simultaneously. Robert Gorham Davis has argued that, from the point of view of the reader,

> [t]hese three experiences [...] have the same availability. Real time for the reader is the present time of reading and imagining, and in relation to that real time, all past events have the same status, in that their imaginative availability is not affected by their relative distance in a suppositious chronological past. (1971, 33)

Yet rhetorical metalepsis questions the very notion that there is a 'real time' in relation to which there is such a thing as stable and continuous 'imaginative availability.' Such availability presupposes the combination of the 'present time' of an experience (of reading or writing and imagining) with the imagined past of an experience. However, as the simultaneity of Lyons, Auxerre and the narrating instance demonstrates, they can only be experienced one after the other. The last sentence of Chapter VII/xxviii ("Let me collect myself, and pursue my journey") might refer to all three 'experiences,' but the reader can only imagine them one at a time.[155] Thus, while the 'real time' of reading adds another temporal perspective, it does not alter the predicament: that simultaneity of perspectives is ultimately a paradox which always disintegrates into the singularity of the perspectives involved. That is why Davis' conclusion that "the treatment of time in *Tristram Shandy* [...] is not as difficult or paradoxical as it is sometimes made to be" (1971, 33) is not convincing. On the contrary, it may be argued that the treatment of time in more conventional fiction (as in Shklov-

---

154 For a further analysis of the metaleptic potential of this passage with reference to the conflation of what can be seen as (the analogues of) 'object language' and 'metalanguage,' see Chapter 3.1.4 above.
155 Any reader can, of course, imagine the simultaneity of various Tristrams from the outside. These Tristrams, however, would necessarily be part of one (diegetic) universe, as if they were standing next to each other. What has been termed 'simultaneity of perspectives' above would entail two spatiotemporal positions from which one perceives at the same time – which is clearly impossible.

sky's example above) is not as logical and consistent as it is sometimes made to be – since it withholds a paradox that *Tristram Shandy* exposes. For even though it is conventionally denied, every act of reading or writing necessitates the double temporality of story and discourse. While the temporal dimensions of the story and the discourse are necessarily 'present' in each act of reading and writing, neither the author nor the reader can focus their attention on both temporalities at the same time. This phenomenon is similar to the famous "duck-rabbit" figure[156]: the author cannot simultaneously adopt the perspective(s) of the storyworld and his narratorial perspective at the same time and the reader cannot simultaneously focus on the experience of reading (the time it takes to read) and the experience of imaginative time passing in the storyworld. Mysteriously enough, both temporalities are always included in the *récit*. The objection that there is a difference in quality between the "real time" (Davis 1971, 33) of reading and the construction of a storyworld temporality rests on an assumption questioned by *Tristram Shandy*'s rhetorical metalepses: namely, that storyworld temporality is in a certain sense independent of the 'real' time needed to construct it.

This instance of metalepsis can also be argued to highlight the inescapable structure of self-reference as a logical duality, precisely by the very narrational act that denies this logical duality. In the attempt to 'collect himself,' the narrator Tristram refers to himself as the writing subject and as the object of writing at the same time. This humorous self-reference seemingly collapses the temporal and logical distance between subject and object of reference. In this manner, Tristram demonstrates that in the attempt to know, describe or refer to oneself, that very self 'vanishes' behind the object it invariably turns into. Thus, the noumenal 'I' always bifurcates into the vanishing self and its object. Impossibly, the metaleptic speech act implies that indeed there can be loci where the 'I' as object and the 'I' as subject coincide. Metalepsis demonstrates *ex negativo* that the noumenal 'I' is the unattainable vanishing point whose impossible self-reference generates a hierarchy of levels.

This passage can also be interpreted as an epistemological metalepsis (even though it only offers a limited potential for such an analysis). Epistemological metalepsis is categorized by a character's knowledge of the narrational act that creates the world (including that character) in which he or she 'lives.' When the narrator Tristram describes the diegetic events in Auxerre and Lyons, he adopts

---

[156] Although often attributed to Wittgenstein, it was probably the American psychologist Joseph Jastrow who first mentioned the "duck-rabbit" figure in his article "The Mind's Eye" (1899).

the perspectives of his narrated selves ("I am this moment walking across the market-place of Auxerre with my father and my uncle Toby, in our way back to dinner——and I am this moment also entering Lyons with my post-chaise broke into a thousand pieces"). Here, the characters (Tristram in Auxerre and Tristram in Lyons) seemingly have attained a narratorial knowledge of their diegetic status. Typically, this does not violate the spatial or semantic parameters of diegetic levels, but only their hierarchical relation. Interpreting this instance as an epistemological metalepsis foregrounds how readers may construct Tristram's metaleptic continuity of consciousness, a continuity that transcends diegetic levels.

One of the functions of rhetorical metalepsis in *Tristram Shandy* is, I would maintain, to make impossible the notion that the time of the narrated events can be conceived as a pre-existent structure belonging to "some abstract story which subtends all the possible discursive manifestations of a given narrative" (Herman 2002, 214), and hence can conveniently be segmented into an orderly progression of objectively measurable events.[157] The time of the storyworld is realized by Tristram's act of narration and is, therefore, unstable and dependent on the *experience* of narrating and reading (or listening); accordingly, it cannot be successfully subjected to or harmonized with the chronological succession measured with the 'stop-watch' of the critic in Chapter III/xii. In this sense the experiences of the characters in the diegesis are similar to the experience of their telling. They cannot be presented within what Dorothy van Ghent has termed the "'timeless time' [...] of the imagination" (1987, 15), but only as an experience *in time* that is subject to time's uncontrollability:

> No matter how, or in what mood—but I flew from the tomb of the lovers—[...] and just got time enough to the boat to save my passage;—and e'er I had sailed a hundred yards, the Rhône and the Sâon met together, and carried me down merrily betwixt them.
> But I have described this voyage down the Rhône, before I made it———

---

[157] Classical narratology has on the whole described time and temporal relations in the novel as such chronological structures. Typically, these structures are represented by sequences of numbers or letters or a combination of both, as in Mieke Bal's account of the beginning of the *Iliad* whose "anachronies can be represented by the formula A4-B5-C3-D2-E1" (1985, 55). Andrew Gibson has dismissed such analyses as a "spatialisation" (cf. 1996, 181–183) of time. Richard Walsh has argued that the very basis of such chronologies, the event, cannot function as a structural unit: "There is never an absolute chronology of events, not because they cannot be put into a temporal sequence, but because such a sequence always remains contingent upon interpretive choices, most fundamentally, the determination of what shall count as the events" (2007, 58).

>―――So now I am at Avignon―and as there is nothing to see but the old house, in which the duke of Ormond resided, and nothing to stop me but a short remark upon the place, in three minutes you will see me crossing the bridge upon a mule, with Francois upon a horse with my portmanteau behind him, and the owner of both, striding the way before us with a long gun upon his shoulder, and a sword under his arm, least peradventure we should run away with his cattle. (VII.xli)

In this possible instance of rhetorical metalepsis, Tristram's narrative act has 'overtaken' his diegesis and, accordingly, Tristram has to wait for some time until the diegetic characters appear. Again, the narrator seems to have carried out the characteristic move into the diegetic universe along with his reader, both of whom are present but invisible on the scene. However, although the scene is not yet there, its description is nevertheless given. This is not a typical prolepsis, because the temporality of the narrational act is synchronized with the diegetic 'now.' Waiting for the recounted events to unfold, the reader is confronted with a humorous paradox: in three minutes the reader will "see" the diegetic event. However, all a reader can ever 'see' is the recounting – which is in the present case subordinated to the temporality of the diegesis, which, in turn, is created in the temporality of the experience of writing and reading. This unstable simultaneity of the 'recounted' happenings that have not yet arrived and the 'recounting' that presents them nevertheless highlights the idiosyncratically temporal character of all experience.

This temporal character is jocularly illustrated with Locke's 'succession of ideas' in Chapter III/xviii. At the beginning of that chapter, Walter exclaims that, although two hours and ten minutes had passed since Dr. Slop arrived (according to his watch), "to [his] imagination it seems almost an age" (III.xviii). With that exclamation, Walter intends to prepare a "metaphysical dissertation on the subject of *duration and its simple modes*[158]" (ibid.). It is, nevertheless, Uncle Toby, who, much to Walter's chagrin, is able to introduce the thought that the reason these two hours seem an age is "owing to [...] the succession of our ideas" (ibid.). Walter's exposition of this 'succession of ideas' is then accompanied by Uncle Toby's exclamatory interruptions ("What is that to any body?"; "You puzzle me to death") until, in the final paragraph of Chapter III/xviii, Toby introduces a 'succession of ideas' of his own:

---

[158] This is the precise title of Chapter 14 of Book II of Locke's *An Essay Concerning Human Understanding*. In Chapter III/xviii, Sterne borrows most extensively from Locke – a whole paragraph of Walter's dissertation is an almost verbatim quote out of the chapter 'Of Duration, and its simple Modes.'

> Now, whether we observe it or no, continued my father, in every sound man's head, there is a regular succession of ideas of one sort or other, which follow each other in train just like——A train of artillery? said my uncle *Toby*.—A train of a fiddle stick!—quoth my father,—which follow and succeed one another in our minds at certain distances, just like the images in the inside of a lanthorn turned round by the heat of a candle.—I declare, quoth my uncle *Toby*, mine are more like a smoak-jack.——Then, brother *Toby*, I have nothing more to say to you upon the subject, said my father. (III.xviii)

Walter's 'succession of ideas' is in turn succeeded and altered by Toby's associative reflections, which are decidedly unlike the orderly and even-paced progression of the lanthorn: Uncle Toby's head was "like a smoak-jack;——the funnel unswept, and the ideas whirling round and round about in it, all obfuscated and darkened over with fuliginous matter!" (III.xix). When Walter ends in exasperation what was intended to be a monologue (to which Uncle Toby was supposed to supply some cues), he does it because of Toby's dialogical interference, which is antithetical to his dissertation. The metaphor of the smoke-jack implies that there is no sequence of mental events in Toby's head but a confused state of mind that knows no chronology and no causal connections, an implication that has a profound effect on Walter:

> Tho' my father persisted in not going on with the discourse,—yet he could not get my uncle *Toby*'s smoak-jack out of his head,—piqued as he was at first with it;——there was something in the comparison at the bottom, which hit his fancy; for which purpose [...] he began to commune with himself and philosophize about it: but his spirits being wore out with the fatigues of investigating new tracts, and the constant exertion of his faculties upon that variety of subjects which had taken their turn in the discourse,—the idea of the smoak-jack soon turned all his ideas upside down,—so that he fell asleep almost before he knew what he was about.
> As for my uncle *Toby*, his smoak-jack had not made a dozen revolutions, before he fell asleep also.—Peace be with them both. (III.xx)

When Walter's explication of Locke's 'succession of ideas' is succeeded by – or rather confronted with – Uncle Toby's idiosyncratic associations, the result is a curious impasse. The smoak-jack metaphor could, for instance, be taken to describe the 'timeless' (and coincidentally associative) 'confusion' of a man asleep and dreaming, which, of course, contradicts Walter's dissertation. The moment Walter considers Uncle Toby's way of thinking, he can no longer appropriate Toby's perspective (according to his own rendition of Locke's philosophy) but is forced to acknowledge (by falling asleep) what is "alien and refractory" (Bruns 1992, 210) to his categories.

The use of what may be interpreted as rhetorical metalepses puts the narrator, Tristram, in a similar position with regard to his diegesis. His fictions cannot be contained by his 'succession of ideas' but confront him with another temporality, another position and other meanings – this is the 'reality' of his diegesis that refuses to be appropriated: Tristram's diegetic events and perspectives do not 'follow and succeed one another at certain distances, like the images on the inside of an extradiegetic lanthorn turned round by the heat of a candle.' Tristram's narration grapples with a chaotic diegesis of floating events that resists the extradiegetic 'order' imposed upon it. Rhetorical metalepses are the smoakjack of narration: everything is going on all the time. It may be argued, accordingly, that rhetorical metalepsis supply characters with a quality of 'realness' from the point of view of the narrator. Dealing with an example of what I would call rhetorical metalepsis in Chapter III/xx[159], Rüdiger Imhof maintains that it "implies that the characters are real people with individual interests to be accounted for and therefore with a certain amount of control over their author" (1986, 110). In a similar vein, Jean-Jacques Mayoux contends that "[i]n a remarkable manner, Sterne's world is a world of bodies alive" (1971, 11). It is clearly among the interpretive possibilities to read rhetorical metalepses in *Tristram Shandy* as instances in which the diegetic characters have attained – albeit without acknowledging it – an extradiegetic 'quality' from the perspective of the narrator. Read in this manner, the temporal (and sometimes spatial) synchronization of diegetic levels typical of rhetorical metalepses creates the effect that characters seem to be 'uncontrollably' real, since they cannot be contained on a diegetic level conventionally subordinated to the extradiegesis. Chapter III/xx, in which Tristram is able to write his preface only after his characters are asleep or otherwise occupied, and Chapter VI/v might serve as examples allowing such an interpretation. In this chapter, Toby and Trim each cry "a tear of joy of the first water" (VI.v) after Uncle Toby has suggested *Le Fever*'s son as the governor of the young Tristram to Walter – which prompts the narrator to go on thus:

> [Y]ou will see why when you read *Le Fever*'s story:––fool that I was! nor can I recollect, (nor perhaps you) without turning back to the place, what it was that hindered me from letting the corporal tell it in his own words;—but the occasion is lost,—I must tell it now in my own. (VI.v)

This rarely commented-on quote is a rather intricate example of rhetorical metalepsis. Turning back to Chapters x and xi of the preceding Volume V, the reason for the 'omission' emerges: the last paragraph of Chapter V/x narrates how the scullion, Susannah, Jonathan and Obadiah form a circle around the fire in

---

[159] "All my heroes are off my hands;––'tis the first time I have had a moment to spare,–and I'll make use of it, and write my preface" (III.xx).

the kitchen to listen to Trim's rendition of the story of *Le Fever*. The last sentence of that chapter states that "as soon as the scullion had shut the kitchen door,—the corporal begun" (V.x). In the very first sentence of the following Chapter V/xi Tristram does not begin to narrate Trim's rendition of *Le Fever*'s story but impulsively recollects his mother, which he pretends to have forgotten. This instigates another set of 'digressions and progressions' which is so typical of *Tristram Shandy* and the story of *Le Fever* is not mentioned again until Chapter VI/v (as quoted above). This may be interpreted as another instance of the comical oscillation between incompatible narrative positions on the part of Tristram. Here, Tristram is of necessity an omniscient narrator: this can be seen by the fact that he can relate *Le Fever*'s story (including much dialogue) 'in his own words,' although he was not even born when the events took place. Yet, mysteriously, he is unable to perform the same kind of 'extended ventriloquism' with regard to Trim's narration of that story at a particular moment in the kitchen.

It may be argued that in this instance the diegetic character Trim is indeed 'real' insofar as his temporality is uncontrollable in the same way the extradiegetic narrator's temporality is uncontrollable. Trim's diegetic time passes and is irretrievably lost if the narrator does not record it. Accordingly, since Tristram ostensibly lacks control over Trim, that character could be argued to have – at least temporarily – attained an extradiegetic 'quality' from the perspective of the narrator. The paradoxical humour of this lies in the fact that this 'metaleptic realism' is contrasted in the ostentatiously fictional character of both extradiegesis and diegesis. Moreover, the curious kind of 'realism' instigated by rhetorical metalepses is additionally qualified by the fact that rhetorical metalepsis is also one of the novel's central literary devices for characterizing the diegesis as fictional. This is self-evident, since the synchronization of story time and discourse time is impossible for the "historiographer" (I.xiv) in the historical and non-fictional narrative situation. What becomes apparent here is the manner in which various contradictory interpretive possibilities that emerge in the hermeneutic dialogue applying the concept of 'rhetorical metalepsis' to *Tristram Shandy* refuse any interpretive 'finalization' of the novel's structure. From the perspective of the extradiegesis, the diegetic world of which Tristram tells is uncontrollably 'real,' and at the same time fleetingly unreal. In other words, it both is and is not categorically distinguishable from the extradiegesis in which it supposedly comes into being.

This is connected to fundamental human sense-making capabilities. Since the rhetorical metalepses employed in *Tristram Shandy* frequently foreground the 'now' of the extradiegetic narrative act (and since that 'now' belongs to the life told, to the world of the diegesis), the synchronization of story time and discourse time approximates the simultaneity of telling and told, which is the logically impossible negation of the self-reflexive paradox defined above. "I have a strong propensity in me to begin this chapter very nonsensically, and I will not balk my fancy.—Accordingly, I set off thus" (I.xxiii). Here, the temporal hiatus between the self-reflexive narrative comment and the narration to which it refers is minimal. It seems to be even shorter when Tristram complains that "every letter I trace tells me with what rapidity Life follows the pen" (IX.viii). And there are instances in which there seems to be no hiatus at all. Interrupting himself in Chapter VI/xxxiii, Tristram comments on his own writing in typical fashion: events of the diegesis seem to 'crowd in on' the extradiegesis, and the narrator is seemingly unable to bring order into the temporally intricate storyworld:

> I told him, Sir——for in good truth, when a man is telling a story in the strange way I do mine, he is obliged continually to be going backwards and forwards to keep all tight together in the reader's fancy——which, for my own part, if I did not take heed to do more than at first, there is so much unfixed and equivocal matter starting up, with so many breaks and gaps in it,—and so little service do the stars afford, which, nevertheless, I hang up in some of the darkest passages, knowing that the world is apt to lose its way, with all the lights the sun itself at noon day can give it——and now, you see, I am lost myself! (VI.xxxiii)

While at the beginning of this paragraph there remains a temporal gap between the narrating instance and the narration on which it is commenting, towards the end they seem to coincide. Here, Tristram could be taken to be the observed (belonging to the diegesis) and the observer (belonging to the extradiegesis) simultaneously – a metaleptic 'impossibility,' despite the fact that such self-reflexive comments are highly conventional and seem to lack any transgressive element.

Although the question of a metaleptic tendency in these instances is certainly debatable, the narrative strategy used to synchronize the temporality of different diegetic levels ties in with the sense that time can neither be controlled nor objectively represented by Tristram – despite the fact that "all of the story-time is his to play with *from the start*" (Mayoux 1971, 11). In his influential article "Variations on the Time-sense in *Tristram Shandy*," Jean-Jacques Mayoux has called attention to Tristram's "fear that time was prevailing against him, irresistibly, and that the recovery of lost time was doomed" (1971, 17) which underlies the construction of time and the time-sense in *Tristram Shandy*. Emblematic of this fear are, according to Mayoux, the allegorical Volume VII in which Tristram (the narrating adult) flees from Death across France after a conversation with

Eugenius, and the famous quote in which the mysterious Jenny is addressed thus: "Time wastes too fast: [...] the days and hours of it [...] are flying over our heads like light clouds of a windy day, never to return more——every thing presses on——whilst thou art twisting that lock,——see! It grows grey" (IX.viii). However, the more serious and more sentimental moments in *Tristram Shandy*, which often lament the passing of time, are never accompanied by possible instances of metalepsis. While rhetorical metalepsis is the central literary device in *Tristram Shandy* in connection with the novel's temporality, this device is only employed 'cheerfully.' This observation corroborates Genette's assumption that metalepses rather produce "an effect of strangeness that is either comical [...] or fantastic" (1980, 235).

Despite such humorous effects, rhetorical metalepses offer radical interpretive possibilities. Rhetorical metalepses contribute to what Mendilow, in connection with *Tristram Shandy*, has termed "the effect of an all-pervading present of which past and future are a part, in preference to an orderly progression in time of separated discontinuous events" (Mendilow, qtd. in Moglen 1975, 64). The employment of rhetorical metalepses in *Tristram Shandy* in a certain sense denies that there is a qualitative difference between the past of the life told and the present of its telling. Consequently, the lanthorn of evenly temporal progression in a causal chain is given up for Uncle Toby's smoak-jack. Past, present and future events, thoughts and ideas swirl about in randomly associative confusion, where each can be synchronized with any of the others since all are equivalent with regard to time. The curious kind of 'realism' rhetorical metalepses potentially create, wrestles with the problem that while various diegetic levels in a sense become part of an "all-pervading present," this "all-pervading present" does not alter the fact that each perspective and temporality is necessarily unique and *irretrievable* once its moment has passed. In other words, time in *Tristram Shandy* is an ever-changing phantom that continually turns into the diegetic past ("every letter I trace tells me with what rapidity Life follows the pen" [IX.viii]), which might at any time become uncontrollably 'present' again in the metaleptic telling.

Thus, rhetorical metalepses in *Tristram Shandy* show that the confusion of the smoak-jack cannot authentically portray another perspective. Yet neither can the orderly progression of the lanthorn – the regular 'one after the other.' Tristram Shandy describes the dilemma of such a 'succession' of ideas thus: "[I]f [the author] begins a digression, from that moment, I observe, his whole work stands stock-still;—and if he goes on with his main work, then there is an end of his digression" (I.xxii). This is the narrative situation of the omniscient narrator who subjects the time of the universe *of which* he tells to an assumed absolute atemporality of its telling. Yet Tristram claims that this is "vile work" (I.xxii). In the world(s) of Tristram nothing ever stands still:

> By this contrivance the machinery of my work is of a species by itself; two contrary motions are introduced into it, and reconciled, which were thought to be at variance with each other. In a word, my work is digressive, and it is progressive, too,—and at the same time. (I.xxii)

'Impossibly,' Tristram reconciles elements that are "at variance with each other." 'The timeless time of the imagination' can be irretrievably lost and what is irretrievably past can become part of the 'timeless time of the imagination.' Just as Uncle Toby's and Walter's variations of Locke's 'succession of ideas' become peacefully reconciled, so do *Tristram Shandy*'s rhetorical metalepses offer interpretive possibilities for a reconciliation of the fictional with the uncontrollably 'real.'

The experience of time, it could be argued – following Paul Ricœur's analysis of the order established by the narrative prefiguration, configuration and refiguration of experience – always consists in the relation between 'ordering' structure and the aporetic presence of 'now.' Thus, it could be argued with Ricœur that narrative structuring supplies the necessary frame for any subjective experience of time. The experience of time is always narratively mediated, and narrative structure can only be experienced as temporality. In *Time and Narrative* (1984–1988 [first French ed. 1983–1985), Ricœur's project is to demonstrate "that the circle of narrativity and temporality is not a vicious but a healthy circle, whose two halves mutually reinforce one another" (ibid., 3). This dialectical balance of narrative and temporality, however, cannot ultimately 'dissolve' or 'contain' the aporias of (human) time. As the preceding analysis has demonstrated, metalepses in *Tristram Shandy* playfully engage with the most fundamental of these: that time is inscrutable, unknowable and aporetic. Rhetorical metalepses in *Tristram Shandy* may remind readers that the inevitable multiplicity of 'temporalities' (which emerges in the event of understanding a conventional narrative situation) potentially collapses into the 'here and now' of the hermeneutic situation in which that narrative is understood – and that this 'here and now' presupposes a distinctively narrative conceptualization of experience. "[E]very thing presses on——whilst thou art twisting that lock,——see! It grows grey" (IX.viii).

4.2.2 Ontological Metalepsis: Immersive Metalepsis and the Question of Reality

In Chapter IV/xiii, the extradiegetic narrator Tristram addresses a presumably equally extradiegetic chairman in the following manner:

> Holla!—you chairman!—here's sixpence—do step into that bookseller's shop, and call me a *day-tall* critick. I am very willing to give any one of 'em a crown to help me with this tackling, to get my father and my uncle *Toby* off the stairs, and to put them to bed.—
> —'Tis even high time; for except a short nap, which they both got whilst *Trim* was boring the jack-boots—and which, by the bye, did my father no sort of good upon the score of the bad hinge—they have not else shut their eyes, since nine hours before the time that doctor *Slop* was led into the back parlour in that dirty pickle by *Obadiah*. (IV.xiii)

Acting in compliance with this request would indeed result in what may be interpreted as a typical example of metalepsis. In order to be able to literally send Walter and Uncle Toby to bed, the "critick" would have to move from the extradiegetic 'present' of the world in which Tristram narrates (domain of the signifier) to the 'past' of the diegesis (domain of the signified). Since he is supposed to effect a change in the diegesis, this indeed would amount to a 'mutual contamination' and violation of diegetic levels as outlined above. Complicating matters, the past of the storyworld is portrayed as urgently in need of narratorial 'correction' in the second paragraph quoted above. Walter and Uncle Toby are growing more and more tired as the discourse progresses, since their temporality cannot be brought to a close. Foregrounding the double temporality of diegesis and extradiegesis, this potentially metaleptic example is paradigmatic for Laurence Sterne's 'method' of narrating 'impossibly.' On the one hand, the diegetic characters are presented as fictive (they cannot retire to bed until the Tristram narrates that they retire to bed), on the other hand, their temporality is in a sense uncontrollably real (if Tristram does not narrate that they retire, they grow more and more tired).

It is precisely the character's status (as fictive or 'real') that becomes unstable in this instance of metalepsis. After a digression that follows the quotation above, Walter's and Uncle Toby's status is put into question by the possibly metaleptic 'solution' of the "critick" at the end of Chapter IV/xiii: "—So then, friend! you have got my father and my uncle *Toby* off the stairs, and seen them?—and how did you manage it?—You dropp'd a curtain at the stairs foot—I thought you had no other way for it—Here's a crown for your trouble" (IV.xiii). Among other things, this passage jokingly presents the 'reality' of Walter and Uncle Toby as literally dependent on the world of the telling. The linguistic constitution of the diegesis is foregrounded since readers cannot literally see the curtain, which, as linguistic, is just as 'invisible' as diegetic events. The curtain's 'invisibility' is highlighted precisely because it refuses a 'narrative' solution and amounts to the critick's refusal or inability to *narrate*. The falling curtain ends the scene of the play, the diegesis 'vanishes' and the illusion is broken. But the extradiegetic drawing of a curtain is, and this is part of the humour of this passage, just as illusory as the diegetic events it 'covers' – both the events and the curtain have to be constructed as the 'story' narrated. Even though the complex problematic of this passage has at best been touched upon, it is evident that elemental conditions of understanding (literary) narrative become questionable in this instance of metaleptic narration – conditions that generate the divergent and interminable plurality of meanings that emerges in the dialogical encounter with (this) metaleptic narrative.

Werner Wolf (2005, 89) cites this text as the "prototypical instance" of metalepsis from which its "characteristic traits" can be deduced (ibid., 88–91). Moreover, it is just as prototypical with regard to the interpretive possibilities that emerge in the hermeneutic encounter between reader and (possibly) metaleptic text. Wolf's analysis of the metaleptic transgression in Chapter IV/xiii is presented as a description of the passage's inherent structure (cf. ibid.). Yet the implications of this structure question such descriptions. If one reads this paragraph as metaleptic, then the passage calls for the reinterpretation of the narrative situation it has disrupted: the reader is forced to consider what is implicit in the conventional telling of a story; or, more precisely, with what assumptions and constructions the reader has contributed to the narrative situation up to the metaleptic violation.

Irrespective of the particular interpretive choices of readers, this excerpt instigates the awareness of a meta-level in which the constructedness of diegetic levels comes into view – within the hermeneutic encounter embracing reader, text and tradition. In this encounter, the diegetic levels remain open to *other* (and possibly non-metaleptic) interpretive possibilities. For instance, it could be argued that the extradiegetic "critick" called for in the passage has written a chapter or a scene he (or she) shows to the narrator, a scene which ends with curtains, thus instigating the remarks cited above. Accordingly, this would not be a metaleptic transgression but a multiplication of diegetic levels (the narrator Tristram narrates the narration of the critick). Such an interpretation presupposes that the diegesis is fictive from the perspective of the ostensibly homo- and autodiegetic narrator Tristram Shandy. This is typical insofar as all the interpretive possibilities instigated by a possibly metaleptic text of this kind are connected to the question of the *status* of the diegesis. To interpret the passage above as non-metaleptic, means that the "truth-related narrative illusion"

(Fludernik 2003b, 384) of the novel – the conventional pretence that what the discourse is relating is the literal truth (at least from the perspective of the autodiegetic narrator) – has been violated. Reading the chapter as metaleptic presupposes that the diegesis is, according to representational logic, absolutely inaccessible to the extradiegetic "critick" and must be the 'past' of the world in which Tristram narrates. In the metaleptic dynamic which ensues, such presuppositions become unstable. Among other things, these unstable meanings and boundaries demonstrate that there is no *conclusive* answer to the oscillating openness once metalepsis has radically questioned what one knows. Or in other words the oscillating openness is the answer to that questioning.

"Let love therefore be what it will,—my uncle *Toby* fell into it.——And possibly, gentle reader, with such a temptation—so wouldst thou: For never did thy eyes behold, or thy concupiscence covet any thing in this world, more concupiscible than widow *Wadman*" (VI/xxxvii). I would like to return to the last paragraph of Chapter xxxvii (Volume VI) in *Tristram Shandy*, a chapter analysed above (Chapter 3.1) with regard to what Gadamer terms 'the original mimetic relation.' As mentioned above, the ensuing Chapter xxxviii of Volume VI consists in the following (potentially metaleptic) request: "To conceive this right,— call for pen and ink—here's paper ready to your hand.——Sit down, Sir, paint her to your own mind——as like your mistress as you can——as unlike your wife as your conscience will let you—'tis all one to me——please but your own fancy in it." Should any extratextual reader comply with this and draw widow Wadman on the blank page which follows that request, the result could be argued to constitute an example of ontological metalepsis.

Such an analysis rests on certain presuppositions that guide the establishment of the domains of the signifier and the domains of the signified cued by representational acts: the metaleptic representational acts in *Tristram Shandy* cue the construction of conflicting spatiotemporal bifurcations and their denial. If the narrator is conceived of as having left the extradiegetic world in which he tells, and as being able to direct the actions of an extra-extradiegetic reader, the metalepsis would arguably, in Fludernik's terms, be narratorial: an ascending first person immersive metalepsis. If the directions are understood as an address to the extratextual reader, such directions seem to *imply* a transgression of narrative logic rather than to constitute a 'physical' entering. Accordingly, this could be conceptualized as a figurative metalepsis. If the drawing of the extratextual reader (addressed by narrative *you*) is conceived of as having 'physically' entered the fictional extradiegesis, however, that move could be described as an instance of descending second person (lectorial) metalepsis. This passage is in many ways a borderline case: it is, for instance, questionable whether it instigates a metaleptic dynamic at all, and whether such a dynamic connects and involves the 'real' world and the world of the fictive narrator Tristram – and, finally, whether such a dynamic can be 'realized' by the possibility of a painting that is 'present' in the extratextual *and* the (extra-)diegetic worlds involved.

The dialogue with the narrate, who is addressed as "Sir," the paper and ink, and the drawing of widow Wadman could all be interpreted as belonging to the fictionalized extradiegetic level. Then, the blank page would be merely an invitation (by the – implied? – author or any other conceptualization of a narrative instance above the extradiegesis) to the extratextual reader to 'mirror' the extradiegetic happenings on the extratextual 'level'; there would consequently be no metaleptic transgression. In this case, the drawing of an extratextual reader would have to be interpreted as belonging to the extratextual level (the world in which the real reader reads) and cannot, therefore, penetrate into the extradiegesis. The comments following the blank page which can be attributed to one of the fictional and extradiegetic narratees ("——Was ever anything in Nature so sweet!—so exquisite!") and the narrator ("—Then, dear Sir, how could my uncle *Toby* resist it?") would then not be comments on the drawing of a possible extratextual reader. The metaleptic *potential* of the request to draw widow Wadman (as well as the comment afterwards) is nevertheless clearly evident. As maintained above, such conflicting interpretive possibilities are typical of the many passages in *Tristram Shandy* which display metaleptic potential, a potential that destabilizes the conventional assumptions that guide the hermeneutic encounter in which they come into being.

In this manner, ontological metalepses in *Tristram Shandy* generally present themselves as interpretive possibilities to be 'realized' by the reader. The realization in this case, however, places a unique emphasis on the materiality of the book page on which a reader (extradiegetic, extratextual, etc.) can inscribe the outline of a fictive character. Thus, this passage not only foregrounds the material basis that supports the construction of the domains of the signifier/signified (represented entities presuppose a material combination of signs), but also demonstrates that the materiality of the 'text' is very much a dialogical effort to which readers ontologically *belong*. Making sense of narrative, this potential instance of immersive metalepsis seems to imply, is dependent on a hermeneutics of belonging, insofar as readers always create in *their* world what is supposedly the reconstruction of another. The fact that readers are invited to 'draw' the fictional character 'as like their mistress as they can' jokingly highlights that the text *belongs* to us as we belong to the text. In drawing widow Wadman, the analytic distance conceptualizing *Tristram Shandy* in terms of static results is given up: widow Wadman is a complex experiential process that is actively shaped by the one who understands.

Other passages that supply the possibility of a descending (narratorial) first person immersive metalepsis are the thought shared by the narrator and Dr. Slop (cf. III.ix), or Uncle Toby's sentence interrupting the narratorial digression in mid-sentence in Chapter xv of Volume VIII (which could, from the diegetic character's perspective, be conceptualized as an ascending third person immersive metalepsis). Both examples have limited metaleptic potential and do not radically invalidate the properties of the 'diegetic universes' involved in the metaleptic transgression. With the help of the scalar model proposed above, one could accordingly visualize these transgressions as located between minimal and conspicuous transgressions of what I take to be the properties of diegetic universes. These instances are typical for Laurence Sterne's novel inasmuch as they do not place an emphasis on a single metaleptic entity but rather fundamentally question the representational logic of narrative structure.

As maintained above, the possible collapse of diegetic levels potentially raises the problem of the ontological status of the characters and state(s) of affairs represented. Thus, when Uncle Toby's diegetic whistling disturbs the extradiegetic narrating act in Chapter IX/xvii, the state of affairs represented (Toby's whistling) becomes urgently 'real' from the perspective of the narrator: "True philosophy——but there is no treating the subject whilst my uncle is whistling Lillabullero.——Let us go into the house"[160] (IX.xvii). Yet at the same time, it may also be argued that the narrational act has become as fictional as the diegesis – it is here foregrounded as "being represented only" (Schmid 2010, 30): "The most troubling thing about metalepsis indeed lies in this unacceptable and insistent hypothesis, that the extradiegetic is perhaps always diegetic, and that the narrator and his narratees – you and I – perhaps belong to some narrative" (Genette 1980, 236). The fictive extradiegesis must, of course, be distinguished from the extratextual world, the world in which any flesh-and-blood reader reads. Yet the insight that metalepsis questions categorical differentiations such as 'fictional' and 'real' not only potentially destabilizes the differentiation between understanding 'subject' and 'object'; in seeking to understand *Tristram Shandy*, we are confronted with many metaleptic examples that play with the fact that, in a certain sense, the 'real' can be fictionalized and a fiction can be 'realized.'

The following short example demonstrates, on the one hand, that the delineation of narrational acts and the concomitant worlds in which they take place

---

160 Incidentally and typically, this excerpt could also be interpreted as a rhetorical metalepsis.

and of which they tell (as well as their fictional nature) is dependent on the establishment of the context and does not solely rely on the semantic aspects of a narrative. On the other hand, it shows that the 'realization' of the metaleptic potential that involves the real world relies, as I have argued in Chapter 2.2.2, on certain pragmatic conventions and rules: there can be any number of constative utterances in a fictional narrative without triggering the construction of a metalepsis, because readers approach fiction with the pragmatic rule that qua representation, the represented (domain of the signified) is ontologically distinct from the world of the narration or representation (domain of the signifier) – even if non-fictional 'reality' and narrative fiction resemble each other in many ways. This is the case unless – as the following example indicates – the 'reality' involved in the potential metaleptic transgression consists of signs from a semiotic system dependent on a narrational act. Since 'extratextual' or 'extradiegetic' (etc.) signs can only be distinguished by the contexts in which they appear, they offer radical metaleptic potential.

In Chapter II/xv, as Walter, Dr. Slop and Uncle Toby await Tristram's birth in the parlour, Corporal Trim finds a copy of a sermon in a book by "*Stevinus*, that great mathematician and engineer" (II.xiv) owned, of course, by Uncle Toby. Delighting in the occasion, Walter calls upon Trim to "give us a page or two of it" (II.xv), with which request Trim readily complies. In Chapter II/vvii, the whole sermon is read by the diegetic characters Trim and Walter Shandy and is interrupted and commented on 27 times by the four diegetic characters present. The description of certain practices of the inquisition (which Trim misunderstands as a literal rendering of his brother's fate) arguably creates a metadiegesis, but, since the sermon is not fictional, it does not imply a diegetic exegesis.

The metaleptic quality of this is due to the fact that the sermon in *Tristram Shandy* is the fictional homologue of the *Abuses of Conscience* sermon Laurence Sterne first preached in York Minster on 29 July 1750 at the close of the summer assizes. The "assembled audience of judges and lawyers thought well enough of it to encourage its publication as a sixpenny pamphlet" (Ross 2001, 180–181), a plan which was executed less than two weeks later. The diegetic sermon in Chapter II/xvii of *Tristram Shandy* is an almost word-for-word reproduction of that earlier publication. Accordingly, it can be safely ascertained that there were readers (albeit very few) as early as 1759 who would be aware of that similarity and pick up the metaleptic joke. That Laurence Sterne certainly encouraged his readers to do so can be seen at the end of Chapter II/xvii, where the diegetic author (Yorick) and the fate of the sermon are revealed:

> It seems that *Yorick*, who was inquisitive after all kinds of knowledge, had borrowed *Stevinus* of my uncle *Toby*, and had carelessly popp'd his sermon [...] into the middle of *Stevinus* [...]
> Ill fated sermon! Thou was lost, after this recovery of thee, a second time, dropp'd thro' an unsuspected fissure in thy master's pocket [...]—buried ten days in the mire,—raised up out of it by a beggar, sold for a halfpenny to a parish-clerk,—transferred to his parson,—lost for ever to thy own, the remainder of his days,—nor restored to his restless Manes till this very moment, that I tell the world the story.
> Can the reader believe, that this sermon of *Yorick*'s was preach'd at an assize, in the cathedral of *York*, before a thousand witnesses, ready to give oath of it, by a certain prebendary of that church, and actually printed by him when he had done,——and within so short a space as two years and three months after *Yorick*'s death.—*Yorick*, indeed, was never better served in his life!——but it was a little hard to male-treat him before, and plunder him after he was laid in his grave. (II.xvii)

The fact that Yorick's sermon ends up with a 'certain prebendary of the cathedral of York,' who is obviously Laurence Sterne himself, clearly supplies the last paragraph with a metaleptic quality. From the perspective of any flesh and blood reader who is aware that Laurence Sterne had obtained a prebend in York cathedral (in 1738), the real author and his *Abuses of Conscience* sermon (both extratextual) have both become diegetic in a metaleptic move across diegetic levels and across the boundary that divides the 'fictional' and the 'real.' Or, to be more precise, the sermon foregrounds the contextual assumption that each narrational act, represented or not, prompts the construction of the domain of the signifier and the domain of the signified. The domains of signifier and signified with respect to the sermon are twofold: they can be construed as the 'real' world of Laurence Sterne and the 'world' that sermon represents. Or, they can be construed as diegesis and metadiegesis in a fictional narrative. According to the logic of the storyworld quoted above, Yorick's sermon has by a succession of accidental circumstances reached Laurence Sterne, who preached and published, and thus plagiarized[161] a fiction. Whether the fiction had become (uncontrollably) 'real' or the reality had become 'fictional,' the ensuing paragraph in

---

[161] Scolding himself for lifting from his character Yorick, Sterne adds an interesting twist to the question of plagiarism. It is well known that Sterne attacks plagiarism in a plagiarism in Chapter V/i: "Shall we for ever be adding so much to the *bulk*—so little to the *stock*? Shall we for ever make new books, as apothecaries make new mixtures, by pouring only out of one vessel into another?" (V.i). In 1798, John Ferriar was probably the first to have noted that this is plagiarized from Burton (cf. Swearingen 1977, 156). Plagiarism usually relies on an extratextual source that enters a fictive world. In this case, a fictive source seemingly enters the extratextual world.

Chapter II/xvii defends the "gentleman who did it" and takes the metaleptic game even further:

> However, since the gentleman who did it, was in perfect charity with *Yorick*,—and, in conscious justice, printed but a few copies to give away;—and that, I am told, he could moreover have made as good a one himself, had he thought fit,—I declare I would not have published this anecdote to the world;—nor do I publish it with an intent to hurt his character and advancement in the church;——I leave that to others;——but I find myself impell'd by two reasons, which I cannot withstand. (II.xvii)

The fact that the diegetic 'Laurence Sterne' was, 'as Tristram was told,' able to write a sermon of such quality and remain on good terms with its diegetic author Yorick, is another fine illustration of the humorous potential of metaleptic transgressions. As for the wry comment implying the existence of others who may cherish "an intent to hurt his character and advancement in the church," those could include Laurence Sterne's uncle Jacques Sterne and, possibly Revd. John Fountayne.[162] This ties in with Laurence Sterne's general tendency in *Tristram Shandy* to fictionalize acquaintances, adversaries and his own situation as part of Tristram's (extra)diegesis.[163] It has been claimed that in such instances, the "distinction between Tristram and Laurence Sterne breaks down" (Howes 1958, 5). This case may convincingly be argued and can be aligned with the reading that ontological metalepses playfully deny the distinction between what one *imagines* to be the 'real' world and what one *imagines* as an opposed 'imaginary' world. The two reasons for slandering 'a certain prebendary of York cathedral' announced in the passage above highlight how far Sterne took that metaleptic game. The first of the reasons is to do justice and give rest to Yorick's

---

162 A detailed account of 'others' who helped and thwarted Laurence Sterne's 'advancement in the church,' can be found in the chapter "Ecclesiastical Politics" of *Laurence Sterne: A Life* (2001) by Ian C. Ross. The assessment that Jacques Sterne and Revd. Fountayne were among those who, at least temporarily, hindered his career relies on that chapter, too.
163 Fictionalized acquaintances populating the extradiegesis are for instance the famous actor Garrick (cf. Chapter IV/vii) or the painter Reynolds (cf. III.ii) who painted a portrait of Sterne in 1760. The most famous adversary directly addressed or implied by Tristram is Bishop Warburton (cf. Chapters IV/xx, V/xx and IX/viii). This is part of the game in which the narrator refers to those who objected and will object to *Tristram Shandy* with collective terms such as 'criticks' or "dear Anti-Shandeans" (III.xx). Sterne's own situation is alluded to in Chapter VIII/vi in which Tristram asks himself: "Is it not enough that thou art in debt, and that thou hast ten cart-loads of thy fifth and sixth volumes still—still unsold, and art almost at thy wit's ends, how to get them off thy hands." There were, in fact, over a thousand copies of Volumes V and VI unsold at the time Sterne was writing Volume VIII (cf. Cash 1986, 149–150).

ghost, to restore the sermon to Yorick's restless "Manes." The other reason reads like a marketing ploy:

> The second reason is, That, by laying open this story to the world, I gain an opportunity of informing it,—–That in case the character of parson *Yorick*, and this sample of his sermons is liked,—that there are now in the possession of the *Shandy* family, as many as will make a handsome volume, at the world's service,—and much good may they do it. (II.xvii)

On 22 May 1760, Laurence Sterne's sermons were published in two volumes, each of which bore two title pages. Daringly, the first title page read *The Sermons of Mr Yorick*[164]. In the preface to the first volume, Sterne wrote the following explanatory and apologetic lines: "The sermon which gave rise to the publication of these, having been offered to the world as a sermon of Yorick's, I hope the most serious reader will find nothing to offend him, in my continuing these two volumes under the same title" (Sterne, qtd. in Ross 2001, 244). The second title page reads *Sermons by Laurence Sterne, A.M. Prebendary of York, and Vicar of Sutton on the Forest, and of Stillington near York.* Despite the outrage this caused, Sterne's metaleptic game proved effective as a commercial strategy (cf. Ross 2001, 245). One could argue, in agreement with the model above, that the published sermons have attained a fictive exegesis. For the exegesis that the name Yorick implies for the publication of the sermons written by the clergyman Sterne, metaleptically destabilizes the distinction between a discursively represented 'reality' and a fictive representation 'that is representation only.' Here, the realization of the metaleptic potential of this sermon (if it is construed as having any) relies on the narrational acts and the construction of the contexts in which they are situated. The 'worlds' of the (meta)diegetic or extratextual sermon are evoked by narrative acts in different contexts – the combination of signs that constitutes the sermon remains exactly the same.

Moreover, the title page of *The Sermons of Mr Yorick* greatly contributed to the fact that "Yorick, Tristram Shandy, and Laurence Sterne became hopelessly entangled in the public mind" (Howes 1958, 5). Sterne, it seems, did everything he could to add to the confusion.[165] A newspaper account of 1760 that refers to Sterne as "the rev. Laurence Sterne, editor of Yorick's sermons" (qtd. in Ross

---

164 Sterne's original intention was to call his volumes *The Dramatic Sermons of Mr Yorick. By Tristram Shandy, Gentleman.* Fearing the reception such a title might provoke, he refrained from executing this plan (cf. Ross 2001, 226–230).

165 Sterne "had already signed himself 'Yorick' in a letter in 1759 [...], and in subsequent letters he refers to himself as 'Tristram,' 'Shandy,' or 'Yorick.' Mrs. Sterne's relatives referred to him as 'Tristram' [...]" (Howes 1958, 5).

2001, 226–227) demonstrates how 'successful' he was in taking the metaleptic game into the extratextual reality of his day. Borderline cases, such as this example by Laurence Sterne, not only show how difficult it is to translate the dynamic act of narration into static and stable worlds (which are connected by representational logic), but also highlight the question how metaleptic transgressions can imply the 'real' world. While a diegetic character (say, for instance, Uncle Toby) is evoked by a combination of signs, and there is a distinction between the representation of a human being and the direct experience of a human being, a represented combination of signs is different: if a 'real' combination of signs is reproduced word-for-word in a fictional narrative, it is (as a combination of signs) indistinguishable from 'real' signs. As Sterne's sermon demonstrates, the construction of a diegetic or 'real' domain of the signifier (in which that combination was created) is dependent on a dynamic act of understanding that relies on contextual factors. More precisely, the context of the sermon decides whether it is understood as belonging to *Tristram Shandy*'s diegesis (and whether it creates a metadiegesis) or to the 'real' world of Sterne's contemporaries.

Accordingly, there are many ways in which the sermon can be construed as 'reality' and/or fiction: it could be argued to 'imply' (with little or no metaleptic potential) the extratextual world of its original creation, while it is at the same time 'situated in' the diegesis of *Tristram Shandy*. Alternatively, the sermon could have metaleptically and literally entered the diegesis (and crossed the 'boundary' whose construction is cued by the extratextual narrational act that created *Tristram Shandy*); or, it could be concluded that there is no narrative transgression because, even though the fictional sermon may consist of exactly the same semiotic signs as the 'real' sermon, the fictional sermon and the 'real' sermon are not identical: they are created by different acts of narration (each presupposed by the context in which the sermon is encountered).

Debra Malina has tentatively suggested that metalepsis may not only have "a *rhetorical* effect" on extratextual readers, but may also affect these readers' "construction as subjects, at least in some small way" (2002, 9). In accordance with Genette's "unacceptable and insistent hypothesis, that [...] the narrator and his narratees – you and I – perhaps belong to some narrative" (1980, 236), critics have often attempted to come to terms with the way in which metalepses 'work their way through' to the extratextual reality of real readers. In the case of the fictional narrative *Tristram Shandy*, it may be argued that its metaleptic tendency has not only 'contaminated' various diegetic levels, but also affected the "interconnected and dynamic structure" (Malpas 2002, 212) of its effective history (*Wirkungsgeschichte*) in remarkable ways. The fact that it is possible for a diegetic character to attain a status similar to Laurence Sterne in a newspaper article demonstrates (to a certain extent) the narrativity of the 'reality' which is supposedly ontologically distinct from any fictional narrative world. Jan Christoph Meister has supplied a reading of metalepsis that corroborates this assumption:

> [M]etaleptic constructs prove a possible world impossible not because that world is shown to have some *immanent* logical defect. Rather, they do so because they imply that there is, indeed, only *one* world. In other words, they don't just negate the plausibility of a possible world. They negate *the very idea of a possible world* indexically distinguishable from the observer's reality. (Meister 2003, no pagination)

This thought is related to 'the paradox of transparency': the notion that there can be no 'transparent' representation of a content that is distinguishable from the representational materiality. In other words, another world is only 'present' in the now of its representation and that representation's materiality. There is, strictly speaking, no second or other world existing beyond the telling of it. This potential ontological metalepsis thus arguably foregrounds the complex process in which the aporetic *presence* of the represented disrupts and engenders 'mimesis.' I have argued above (3.1.2) that the 'original mimetic relation' is metaleptic and that metalepsis potentially enacts the original mimetic relation (in Gadamer's sense). Yet the metaleptic dynamic of Yorick's sermon also presents an anti-mimetic movement, for the metaleptic act of introducing a sermon into a fictional work (and a 'fictive' sermon into the 'real' world) *points to* the ontological distance which is bracketed by what Gadamer terms the 'original mimetic relation.' At the same time, however, this ontological distance becomes radically unstable. Malina concludes with Lyotard that, after metalepsis, "the resultant world, everything heretofore considered real can now be seen to be constructed by intersecting, commingling discourses. In such a fluid, discursive universe, Lyotard notes, 'the social subject itself seems to dissolve in the dissemination of language games'" (qtd. in Malina 2002, 8).

However, it is my contention that metalepsis in *Tristram Shandy* is more than just "another thief in the postmodern night" (Bruns 1992, 247) turning the narratological grid of reality and language, "whose wall-to-wall uncontrollability has become an axiomatic given" (O'Neill 1994, 110), into a meaningless aporia. Metalepsis is not the place where the hermeneutic dialogue comes to an end but is always open to further questions. The "reconstructive effects" (Malina 2002, 133) of metalepsis in *Tristram Shandy* call attention to the inescapability of diegetic levels and the boundary separating them. After all, Tristram, we are told, 'must go along with us to the end of the work' (cf. *Tristram Shandy* VI.xx;

cf. Chapter 3.1.1 above). Paradoxically, metalepsis is only 'possible' against a background of stable meanings, recognizable diegetic levels, and hierarchical relations. The moment diegetic levels are done away with, metaleptic narration becomes impossible. Accordingly, in the case of Laurence Sterne's novel, the contention that, as Malina puts it, diegetic and 'real' worlds "are [...] equally discursive" (2002, 9) cannot provide a conclusive reading of metaleptic effects in *Tristram Shandy*.

The tendency of ontological metalepses to conflate the "discursive" elements in the hermeneutic dialogue has, of course, certain limits: "The world has imagined, because I wrote *Tristram Shandy*, that I was myself more Shandean than I ever really was—'tis a good-natured world we live in, and we are often painted in divers colours according to the ideas each one frames in his head" (Sterne, qtd. in Ross 2002, 406). Despite the metaleptic 'ideas each one frames in his head,' readers have little problem distinguishing the world in which Laurence Sterne lived from the diegetic worlds he created (and vice versa). Even if those worlds are "equally discursive," Tristram as a narrator cannot destroy diegetic levels once and for all without ending his story. Thus, as maintained above, ontological metalepsis in *Tristram Shandy* denies *playfully what cannot be denied*. In order to go on with his narration, the diegetic boundaries have to be at least partly reconstructed and reinstated – even if they embed the ontological anomaly of the *Abuses of Conscience* sermon.

The transgression or collapse of diegetic levels in the metaleptic move necessitates the reconstruction of the narrative situation, which has to take into account its (temporary) disruption. Ontological metalepsis is antithetical to the stable meanings it disrupts and thus antithetical to its own prerequisites. Since, according to narrative and representational logic, the meaningful application of the term metalepsis presupposes the allocation of existents, events, utterances and characters to distinct diegetic levels, and since the disruption of these levels in the metaleptic move seemingly implies that structure's dissolution, metalepsis potentially enacts what Gadamer termed the negativity of the hermeneutic experience. In the chapter "Der Begriff der Erfahrung und das Wesen der Hermeneutischen Erfahrung," Gadamer claims that *Erfahrung* throws what one knows into question. Bruns has characterized this understanding of experience as

> a sort of emancipation or releasement. [...] A releasement, say, from some prior certainty or ground, some vocabulary or framework or settled self-understanding; or say that the hermeneutic experience always entails an 'epistemological crisis' that calls for the reinterpretation of our situation, or ourselves, a critical dismantling of what had been decided. (1992, 184)

Ontological metalepses constitute such a 'dismantling of what had been decided' and demonstrate the constructedness and changeability of what was supposedly the stable (diegetic) ground of the narrative situation. This 'releasement from a settled framework' results in the *openness* characteristic of the negativity of the hermeneutic experience. While the characteristic 'openness' instigated by ontological metalepses refuses transhistorical and conclusive knowledge, this does not mean that it makes impossible (the evaluation of) new configurations of meaning. Immersive metalepses in *Tristram Shandy* foreground how immersion is narratively constructed and play with the fact that fictionality and reference can become a matter of degree. The question of reality, fictionality and representation, the question of the status of the 'worlds' in which and of which narrational acts in *Tristram Shandy* tell, must be answered time and again against the unstable background of the awareness that one's answers and constructions, as well as the conceptual frameworks with which one encounters the text, always remain open to further questions.

4.2.3 Ontological Metalepsis: Immersive (Second Person) Metalepsis and Hermeneutic Experience

In a sense, the metaleptic dynamic has an element of (vicious) circularity as it moves from its prerequisites to the denial of those prerequisites before it returns again to what was originally denied/destabilized/destroyed. This ties in with Tristram Shandy's narration, which, for lack of alternatives, always falls back on the 'impossibilities' it has exposed. In this manner, one 'impossibility' opens onto another as the expectations of readers are playfully subverted *and* met time and again. Consequently, as the novel progresses, the reader becomes less and less likely to align his or her understanding of the narrative situation with the novelistic 'rules' implicit in the respective narrative positions evoked. The narrative situation becomes a game the reader is asked to temporarily engage in and is no longer the novel's implicit (and unquestioned) conceptual groundwork. Characteristic of the novel as a whole is that these games present the reader in a parodistic manner with the general problem of narrative representation – and with the fact that this problem is inextricably linked with the singular nature and eccentricity of Tristram's perspective. "[T]he formal reflexivity" (Watt 1969, 21) of *Tristram Shandy* humorously foregrounds what is always implicit in the hermeneutic situation in which the autodiegetic novel is encountered and understood. Without the pretence that the individual perspectives of the life narrated, of the narrator and of the reader can in a certain sense become congruent, that another perspective can be authentically portrayed and experienced, the telling of one's life is doomed to failure.

Tristram characteristically exacerbates that inherent problem of narrative representation by highlighting the insurmountable singularity of each perspective involved. On the level of the diegesis, this is exemplified, for instance, by Toby's predilection for understanding almost anything exclusively within the context of fortification. The self-reflexive comments of the narrator Tristram Shandy keep interrupting the events and the perspectives (such as Uncle Toby's) in the storyworld, and highlight that fact that there are always more and other perspectives involved in the narrative situation of *Tristram Shandy*: the oscillating perspectives of the (fictionalized) narrating instance as well as the perspective(s) of the narratees. Here, when the narrator Tristram is seemingly talking to fictive readers (who sometimes talk back), the metaleptic potential questions the flesh-and-blood reader's establishment of the domains of the signified and signifier of his narrational act. Which domain, which diegetic level, which temporal and spatial locus contains the fictive readers or narratees dialogically addressed by Tristram, who often supply questions and answers of their own? What kind of representational logic is decisive in the construction of the spatiotemporal conditions that make these dialogues possible? I maintain that the narrator's encounters with the fictive narratees enact a hermeneutic dialogue that involves and humorously questions every element of the narrative situation – story and discourse, the multiple perspectives of characters, writer and reader and their respective situatedness. The extratextual reader finds a model for her own narrative sense-making in this unstable dialogue: the dialogue that unites all these elements can never be final but must always be open to further questions. One of the reasons for the openness of these dialogues is simply that each particular context, each situatedness, each perspective involved in the narrative situation – as well as each historical situatedness that shapes the perspective through which any reader must ground his understanding – is singular and irretrievable. This conception of hermeneutic experience is decidedly unlike Dilthey's theory of hermeneutics, with its central notion of the re-experiencing of another's lived experience (*Erlebnis*):

> This reexperiencing – Dilthey's *Nacherleben* – is the task of [...] the hermeneutical disciplines that Dilthey called the *Geisteswissenschaften*. In Dilthey's theory what distinguishes hermeneutical understanding from scientific explanation is that understanding can never occur at an analytical distance; it always means living through what is understood. [...] The point is that in the romantic view what calls for understanding is never just a text but another subject. The text is always understood as a mediation between subjects of historical experience. The thought that one can never work through these mediations to

relive the experience that produced them [...] is what separates us from Dilthey. (Bruns 1992, 181)

The diegetic characters in *Tristram Shandy* often fail to work through each others' linguistic mediations and thus cannot relive the experience that produced them. Instead, they produce new mediations and new experiences as singular as their characters and their contexts. The description of Walter Shandy's peculiar angle of perception marks him as a character whose perception can indeed be termed singular:

> The truth was, his road lay so very far on one side, from that wherein most men travelled,——that every object before him presented a face and section of itself to his eye, altogether different from the plan and elevation of it seen by the rest of mankind.—In other words, 'twas a different object,—and in course was differently considered. (V.xxiv)

However, this singularity seems not to be restricted to the "singularity of [Tristram's] father's notions," (V.xxiv) but extends to all the other inhabitants of the Shandean universe – where every object as well as every encounter is unique. One of the most famous misunderstandings in *Tristram Shandy* humorously demonstrates how far the singular contexts in which something is understood guide that understanding. Uncle Toby and Mrs Wadman each understand a single sentence (concerning the locality where Uncle Toby was wounded) idiosyncratically: "You shall lay your finger upon the place—said my uncle Toby.——I will not touch it, however, quoth Mrs Wadman to herself" (IX.xx). Widow Wadman thinks of Uncle Toby's groin, whereas Toby thinks of the geographical place on a map. Understanding in *Tristram Shandy* is indeed 'understanding differently' – or, rather, 'misunderstanding differently' since the characters seem incapable of understanding each other and avoid, willingly or unwillingly, any dialogue that would entail the moment of crisis in which their expectations, designs and/or knowledge would be questioned.[166]

---

[166] The hobby-horsical 'situatedness' of the diegetic characters' understanding is only 'given up on' on rare occasions. In the few instances in which a dialogue instigates a change of perspective (and a "releasement [...] from some prior certainty or ground" [Bruns 1992, 184]), the result is, characteristically, silence. When uncle Toby learns why widow Wadman has so compassionately inquired about his wound, he acknowledges a change of perspective with a silent gesture and by breaking off the dialogue (with Trim): "My uncle Toby laid down his pipe as gently upon the fender, as if it had been spun from the unravellings of a spider's web——Let us go to my brother Shandy's, said he" (IX.xxxi). Uncle Toby's release from the 'prior ground' of what he considered widow Wadman's motivation (compassion) possibly yields a new perspective (she wanted to know whether he was impotent) – but this does not instigate a dialogical struggle for understanding or a fundamental change in Uncle Toby. His return to Shandy Hall

The dialogues between the narrator and the fictive narratees/readers mirror this diegetic struggle to understand from a singular perspective and the constraints it implies – and mirror the ways in which the understanding of any extratextual reader is equally shaped by the inescapable situatedness of his or her encounter with *Tristram Shandy*. The *enactment* of the process of narrative sense-making has radical metaleptic potential. These encounters attain an additional complexity by one of the effects the narrative *you* can produce – which has been described by Herman as "ontological hesitation" (2002, 338): Narrative *you* "can induce hesitation between reference to entities, situations, and events internal to the storyworld and events external to the storyworld" (ibid.). In *Tristram Shandy*, this effect is exploited from the very beginning of the novel. The narrative *you* in the middle of Chapter I/i is most likely to be read as addressing extratextual readers: "Believe me, good folks, this is not so inconsiderable a thing as many of you may think;—you have all, I dare say, heard of the animal spirits [...]" (I.i). At the very end of the same chapter, the reader learns of the existence of at least one fictional narratee who is able to talk back, as a short extradiegetic dialogue extends into Chapter II:

> Did ever woman, since the creation of the world, interrupt a man with such a silly question? Pray, what was your father saying?——Nothing.
> CHAP. II.
> ——Then, positively, there is nothing in the question, that I can see, either good or bad.—
> —Then let me tell you, Sir, it was a very unseasonable question at least,—because it scattered and dispersed the animal spirits [...].

This instance of narrative *you* is undoubtedly directed at a fictional narratee who is listening to the story told by the narrator and who is referred to as "Sir." The (extratextual) reader has to reconstruct the narrative situation and concomitant narrative personalia in such a way that it can accommodate this fictional narratee (who is capable of 'answering' the narrator Tristram). In the course of the novel, what is taken to be the narrative situation must be aligned with many more addressees, plural and singular, such as 'Madam,' 'your reverences,' or 'lads.' Strikingly, the construction of the narrative situation of *Tristram Shandy* seemingly requires the construction of a locus or 'world' in which these narratees understand and in which they (at least from time to time) interact with the narrator Tristram, as well as a narrational act relating to them.

---

signifies that the idiosyncratic 'situatedness' shaping the 'objects' of his understanding in a particularly Shandean universe remains.

This can be a rather complicated (and potentially metaleptic) matter, as in Chapter I/xx, for instance, when 'Madam' is scolded for being inattentive "in reading the last chapter" and told to "turn back [...] and read the whole chapter over again." The narrator then proceeds to complain about certain reading habits until he acknowledges her return: "But here comes my fair Lady. Have you read the chapter over again, Madam, as I desired you?—You have: And did you not observe the passage [...] which admits the inference?——Not a word like it!" (I.xx). 'Madam' is at once a fictive narratee enjoined to reread the preceding chapter and a character who is able to answer the narrator's discourse with her own in direct conversation. Here, the narration prompts the construction of a further subdivision of the domain of the signifier. These conversations might be construed as being represented by a narrating instance above (or below, according to taste) Tristram Shandy in what could be termed the extra-extradiegesis[167]. This is connected to the question whether the fictional narratees can be conceptualized as belonging to the same diegetic level as the narrator. On the one hand, they seem to be in Tristram's study, arguing over the story as told. On the other hand, they are referred to as *readers* whose discourse – and, indeed, very existence – could be argued to be Tristram's (and not Sterne's or an implied author's) creation. Thus, the ambiguous narrative situation creates a metaleptic quality that suggests that the narratees/readers have, in a descending second person immersive metalepsis, left the domain of the signified (the domain in which they understand Tristram's narration) and entered the domain of the signifier (whatever is represented by Tristram's narration). Part of the humour of this passage is that Tristram sends 'Madam' from one domain to the other.

Yet this is just one way of interpreting one example of the general spatio-temporal make-up and representational logic of Tristram's narrative situation. In other words, the number of narrational acts needed (alongside the construction of the domains of the signifier/signified) to account for Tristram's conversations with readers potentially multiplies, especially when the "ontological hesitation" (Herman 2002, 338) induced by a narrative *you* implies actual readers. In Chapter iv of Volume VII, the narrator considers giving an account of Calais in the following manner:

> For my own part, as heaven is my judge, and to which I shall ever make my last appeal -- I know no more of Calais, (except the little my barber told me of it, as he was whetting his razor) than I do this moment of Grand Cairo; for it was dusky in the evening when I landed, and dark as pitch in the morning when I set out, and yet by merely knowing what is

---

[167] The instance narrating Tristram's narration could, of course, be labelled extradiegetic. This would mean that Tristram's narrative act is diegetic and the story he tells metadiegetic.

what, and by drawing this from that in one part of the town, and by spelling and putting this and that together in another -- I would lay any travelling odds, that I this moment write a chapter upon Calais as long as my arm; and with so distinct and satisfactory a detail of every item, which is worth a stranger's curiosity in the town -- that you would take me for the town clerk of Calais itself -- and where, sir, would be the wonder? was not Democritus, who laughed ten times more than I -- town-clerk of Abdera? and was not (I forget his name) who had more discretion than us both, town clerk of Ephesus? ---- it should be penn'd moreover, Sir, with so much knowledge and good sense, and truth, and precision ----
-- Nay -- if you don't believe me, you may read the chapter for your pains.

This passage potentially instigates the construction of the following subdivisions of the domain of the signifier: the signs can be situated in the 'world' in which Tristram narrates, the 'world' in which a narratee referred to as 'Sir' listens (which may be the same world), the 'world' in which the narratee referred to as 'Sir' reads (which is unlikely to be the world in which Tristram narrates), the world in which these signs are received by other fictive narratees/readers (who may or may not share the world in which 'Sir' listens or reads, 'Madam' being a likely candidate), and the world in which extratextual readers read. The abrupt ending of the penultimate sentence ("---- it should be penn'd moreover, Sir, with so much knowledge and good sense, and truth, and precision"), the gap and the new paragraph ("-- Nay -- if you don't believe me, you may read the chapter for your pains.") suggest an unnarrated reaction (laughter, a reply, yawning, etc.) of either of the narratees. This passage (and many similar ones) have the potential for a descending second person metalepsis in which the narratees/readers share the domain of Tristram's narration by entering the domain of the signified – because Tristram represents their encounter, a representation which itself suggests a new narrational act with new narratees. These unstable and highly complex constructions are instigated by the combination of signs directly accessible to analysis. The more any flesh-and-blood reader aligns the world in which she reads with the world addressed by a narrative *you*, the more metaleptic the last sentence of the chapter in question becomes. Tristram, it could be argued, playfully reacts to the extratextual reader's reaction (the face readers make when they read the chapter, laughter, etc.).

In the many instances in which the narrator addresses his narratees without specifying their gender, number or social station, the narrative *you* forces the extratextual reader to decide on the ontological status of narratees in relation to readers. In this respect *Tristram Shandy* resembles modern second person fictions, "one of whose most characteristic formal gambits is 'to try to put the reader in the text' [...] and thereby abolish the boundary between the textual and extra-textual, the fictive and the real, the virtual and the actual" (Herman

2002, 345). The metaleptic potential of this strategy becomes more conspicuous if the narrative *you* is *read* as addressing the extratextual reader. A similar instance can be found in Chapter II/xvii:

> But before the corporal begins, I must first give you a description of his attitude;—— otherwise he will naturally stand represented, by your imagination, in an uneasy posture,— stiff,—perpendicular,—dividing the weight of his body equally upon both legs;—his eye fix'd, as if on duty;—his look determined,—clinching the sermon in his left hand, like his firelock:—In a word, you would be apt to paint *Trim*, as if he was standing in his platoon ready for action:——His attitude was as unlike all this as you can conceive. (II.xvii)

Much of the humour of this passage depends on the possibility that the phrase "by your imagination" is understood as a direct reference to the extratextual reader's imagination which has thus become fictive and extradiegetic (or has Tristram's/Sterne's narrational act become extratextual?) in what may be argued to imply an instance of ontological metalepsis. In this manner, immersive second person metalepsis (i.e. the structure cued by the narrational act as well as its metaleptic disruption) in *Tristram Shandy* is dependent on the constructive efforts of the reader – who may or may not identify with the narrative *you*, who, in turn, may or may not conceptualize a movement across diegetic levels.

In whichever way a reader interprets the changing narrative situations of *Tristram Shandy*, the hermeneutic encounter within which any interpretation must emerge is mirrored by the narrator's dialogical encounters with what could be termed his *extra-extradiegetic* fictive narratees. The reader is compelled to align his own act of understanding more or less with any of these encounters[168]. In other words, what readers may or may not conceptualize is possibly enacted and anticipated by the narrator's confrontation with the fictive narratees/readers in the passages in which they unambiguously emerge. A certain conventional pomposity is deflated as Tristram "showers his mighty and fashionable readers, whether secular or clerical – your worships and your reverences – with genial contempt" (Ostovich 1992, 156). The "criticks and gentry of refined taste" (II.ii) are (as in Chapter ii of Volume II) presented most often as dim-witted and self-opinionated, and Tristram wrestles dialogically with their pigeon-holing objections and attacks throughout the book. The question of propriety, which the picaresque bawdiness of the work must have raised in

---

[168] Many critics have interpreted these encounters, claiming that they anticipate certain 'reception positions' or habitual responses of Sterne's contemporaries: "Evidently the [...] narrator is to be conceived here as addressing a (fictional) cross-section of society, 'both male and female, of what age, complexion, and condition soever'" (Nelles 1997, 63).

Sterne's contemporaries, is equally anticipated in short conversations: "Surely, Madam, a friendship between the two sexes may subsist, and be supported without———Fy! Mr. *Shandy*:—Without any thing, Madam, but that tender and delicious sentiment, which ever mixes in friendship, where there is a difference of sex" (IX.viii). What is anticipated in these dialogues and encounters is a possible reaction by the reader, who becomes aware of "Tristram's awareness of his reader as a physical being" (Ostovich 1992, 158) – which is (as the foregoing analysis of the narrative *you* demonstrates) possibly metaleptic. Central to all these fictional dialogues and encounters is of course (narrative) understanding and the situatedness governing that understanding. The singularity of some of the retorts by the extradiegetic narratees struggling for understanding demonstrates that this is inevitably unstable:

> ——Grant me patience!——What has *con furia,–con strepito,*——or any other hurlyburly word whatever to do with harmony? (III.v)
> ——How, in the name of wonder! could your uncle *Toby*, who, it seems, was a military man, and whom you have represented as no fool,----be at the same time such a confused, pudding-headed, muddle-headed fellow [...]. (II.ii)
> ——But pray, Sir, What was your father doing all *December*, *January*, and *February*? (I.iv)

Arguably, the extratextual reader's understanding is similarly unstable – especially since there are many instances in which it cannot even be unambiguously established who is listening or reading where and when and who is talking back. Thus, while the fictive readers have been read as a ploy to direct the responses of real readers[169], they nevertheless also demonstrate the inescapable singularity of understanding – which makes a futile endeavour of the ambition to be unquestionably and univocally understood. As the Shandean characters often fail to 'work through the linguistic mediations of each other,' so do the fictive narratees fail to 'work through the linguistic mediations of Tristram Shandy.' They cannot simply relive the experience that 'produced' or 'caused' these mediations, but continually create new mediations in their struggle for understanding. Faced with second-person metalepses in *Tristram Shandy*, the extratextual reader faces the same dilemma. The "unsteady uses of words which have perplexed the clearest and most exalted understandings" (II.ii), which have perplexed Uncle Toby as well as the fictional narratees (—I did not apprehend your uncle *Toby* was o'horseback. [III.iii]), are bound to perplex the flesh

---

[169] Cf., for example, Christian Schuldt: "Der fiktive Leser erfüllt [...] die kommunikative Funktion, dem Erzähler Einflussmöglichkeiten auf die Reaktionen des realen Lesers zu gewährleisten und dessen Aufmerksamkeiten zu steuern" (2005, 33).

and blood reader, too, who has to align all the elements of the particular hermeneutic experience of reading *Tristram Shandy* with the possibility that this experience is to a certain degree fictionalized by a metaleptic awareness of readers' reactions.

The status of the world in which *Tristram Shandy* is read becomes unstable in the dialogical struggle to understand the 'openness' instigated by second person metalepsis. The interpretive possibilities metalepsis offers demonstrate literally "the idea that there is no making sense at a distance; one must always work out some internal connection with what one seeks to understand" (Bruns 1992, 252). The internal connection with what is understood can never result in formulaic and decisive stasis but consists in a process of narrative sense-making that is inextricably linked to the narrative 'object' foregrounding this very process. This process always contains within it the possibility of another encounter, another connection, another hermeneutic experience. The object of metaleptic narrative thus resolves into an experience that is manifold and that cannot occur at an analytic distance. The construction of a potentially metaleptic narrative *you* constitutes the narrative as much as the signs that cue this construction. This ties in with Robert Alter's beautiful observation that "one of the general aims of Sterne's method [...] is to make us repeatedly aware of the infinite horizon of the imagination" (1987, 104) – which, it may be added, becomes evident in each new reading of *Tristram Shandy* and which continually creates new mediations that answer the 'openness' instigated by second person metalepsis.

4.3 "And Now, You See, I Am Lost Myself!———": Instead of a Conclusion on Metalepsis and Laurence Sterne

Chapters 4.1 and 4.2 present analyses of metaleptic transgressions in *Tristram Shandy* and offer the contention that these devices are part of that ostentatiously 'impossible' narration of Tristram's which continually attempts to reconcile elements that are incorrigibly "at variance with each other" (Sterne, *Tristram Shandy* I.xxii) – and which consequently impedes any interpretation that attempts to 'solve' its contradictions. The way metalepsis allows for diverging interpretive possibilities (which are often incompatible with each other) is paradigmatic of this impossible narration. While my reading of figurative metalepses (4.2.1) concentrates on the problematic nature of the 'temporalities' of diegetic levels, the sections on ontological metalepsis (4.2.2 and 4.2.3) consider questions of the representation of the 'real' and of the hermeneutic dialogue in which metalepsis emerges as an interpretive possibility. What has become evident in such an analysis is how the metaleptic dynamic challenges the very boundaries that distinguish metalepsis into types – figurative and ontological, first, second and third-person, epistemological and immersive. For the hermeneutics of distanciation which underlies the narratological category and its typology itself posits an analysis that questions and moves beyond the hermeneutics of distanciation, while the hermeneutics of belonging can be seen to more adequately characterize the metaleptic dynamic, throwing into relief as it does so the conceptual frameworks with which we understand narrative. This may be seen as the resolution of a linear logical system into its circular matrix or counterpart.'

In this manner, the preceding chapters have traced many interpretive possibilities that emerge in the hermeneutic dialogue which approaches *Tristram Shandy* with the narratological concept of metalepsis. Metalepsis in *Tristram Shandy*, I would conclude, is always an application in the Gadamerian sense – unstable, manifold and self-referential, forcing the concepts that make the category possible into a dialogical openness that resists all attempts at final interpretation. Metalepsis is neither some deep-structure logic which precedes – and may become manifest in – the structural analysis of the novel, nor is it a place of stable meanings that transcends the hermeneutic situation in which it comes into being. The construction (and constructedness) of the domains of the signifier and the domains signified is foregrounded in the metaleptic narrational act which, in *Tristram Shandy*, is always followed by the suggestion of a renewed build-up of such domains (without which Tristram's story could not continue). Yet these 'reconstructions' can never be identical with the 'constructions' that preceded the 'realized' metalepsis. Tristram Shandy's 'impossible' narration always presents a new beginning, a new angle that invites diverse readings and conceptualizations as it continually questions itself. Unlike his father Walter, unlike "all systematick reasoners" (I.xix), Tristram seemingly relishes the 'impossible' conclusions that follow logically from the premises of the 'Shandean hypotheses,' and the paradoxes that follow from his narrative situations and positions. In this manner, Sterne's method resists conclusive readings as much as it resists the 'Shandean hypotheses' of Walter. *Tristram Shandy* will always present possibilities of meaning that contradict any attempt to supply a 'closure' excluding antithetical readings.

The following observation by Stuart Sim may be argued to constitute such a 'conclusive' reading: "Sterne [...] prefigures the world of postmodern physics, where individuals are unable to find a basis for free will and some measure of control over their destinies, thanks to the unholy alliance of chance and determinism facing them" (Sim 1996, 121).[170] Nietzsche branded such criticism of Sterne, the "most liberated spirit of his century" (Nietzsche 1986 [first German ed. 1878], 238), whose writing he characterized as an

> artistic style in which the fixed form is constantly being broken up, displaced, transposed back into indefiniteness, so that it signifies one thing and at the same time another. Sterne is the great master of *ambiguity* – this word taken in a far wider sense than is usually done [...]. The reader who demands to know exactly what Sterne really thinks of a thing, whether he is making a serious or a laughing face, must be given up for lost: for he knows how to encompass both in a *single* facial expression; he likewise knows how, and even wants to be in the right and in the wrong at the same time, to knot together profundity and farce. His digressions are at the same time continuations and further developments of the story; [...] his antipathy to seriousness is united with a tendency to be unable to regard anything merely superficially. Thus, he produces in the right reader a feeling of uncertainty as to whether one is walking, standing or lying: a feeling that is closely related to floating. (Ibid., 238–239)

In a sense, this passage supplies the perfect postscript to my chapter. Yet, read as a metacritical comment, it applies, too, to its own reading of *Tristram Shandy*, which is thus "in the right and in the wrong at the same time". Paradoxically, it provides the conclusive reading against which it argues. Nietzsche cannot supply the vantage point from which the right and wrong readers of *Tristram Shandy* can be distinguished. Rather, what he uncovers is that *Tristram Shandy* will always be subject to another reading, 'signifying one thing and at the same time another.' Nietzsche's reading cannot once and for all describe the "artistic style" of the work. *Tristram Shandy* will yield to a reading that deals with the intentionality of the author instead of the "feeling it produces in the right reader" (Nietzsche ibid., 239) in another hermeneutic dialogue in much the same way as it yields (or refuses to yield) to Nietzsche's own reading. Laurence Sterne remarked in a letter that *Tristram Shandy* "was made and formed to baffle all criticism," (Sterne, qtd. in Cash 1986, 24) which, if we take the 'intentions' of its author seriously, includes Nietzsche's – and my own – too.

Tristram Shandy's 'impossible' narration will never completely yield to the principles, vocabularies, concepts, rules and procedures it is confronted with

---

[170] The antithesis to this reading is supplied by Robert Alter, who finds 'a basis for free will and some measure of control' in the "infinite horizon of the imagination" (1987, 104): "Shandean man is everywhere in fetters of circumstance but everywhere his imagination is free; the blind forceps of reality may crush one's nose, or whatever, to a pulp, but the mind can still spin Slawkenbergian fantasies of a man with a proboscis so enormous that it mesmerizes an entire city" (ibid.).

(an insight which does not contradict the statement that there are, from a narratological perspective, no recursive metalepses in *Tristram Shandy*). The present study thus represents, in a certain sense, a 'release from a settled framework,' resulting in the *openness* characteristic of the negativity of hermeneutic experience. But this *openness* (which can only be followed by the dialectic of question and answer) not only questions the narratological concepts applied but also the hermeneutics that applies them. If neither *Tristram Shandy*'s characters nor its readers can transcend their hermeneutic situations to arrive at the (unattainable) final interpretation, how can ontological hermeneutics supply that shortfall? If understanding (*Verstehen*) in Gadamer's sense is the most fundamental way of being-in-the-world, the universal ontology manifest in all acts of cognition, how can this be reconciled with the hermeneutic situation in which ontological hermeneutics emerged, and which, we are told, must always be open to further question? In other words, how can ontological hermeneutics as a theory transcend its own hermeneutic situation – a situation which would necessitate the concession that ontological hermeneutics cannot be universal?

Tristram Shandy demonstrates that the frameworks governing the tradition of criticism to which the present study belongs are much more like 'Shandean hypotheses' than we would like to think. Neither Nietzsche's reading, nor an applied narratological concept, nor ontological hermeneutics can supply the last word on *Tristram Shandy*'s structure, (possibilities of) meaning, style or 'method' – the openness that emerges in every reading remains as an untheorizable place and will always call for another reading. For the 'rules and compasses' of the "Excellent critic!" (III.xii) will forever fail to measure the elusive art of Tristram's narration. This follows – and can only be 'followed' or 'understood' – by its own rules (cf. IV.x), and ideally, therefore, by the reader "whose generous heart will give up the reins of his imagination into his author's hands,——be pleased he knows not why, and cares not wherefore" (III.xii). It is in this sense that Meister Eckhart's paradoxical principle may be a fitting 'conclusion' to *Tristram Shandy*: "Only that which is without a principle properly lives" (qtd. in Bruns 1992, 266).

Yet *Tristram Shandy* forever resists last words. Tristram's 'impossible' narration always presents another answer, another angle, another beginning with endless possibilities. In this sense, the dialogue with Laurence Sterne's work can never come to a conclusion. In Chapter VI/xi, Tristram reveals how Yorick disparages his own self-commendation written in praise of one of his sermons – which may more fittingly answer and 'end' the present dialogical encounter:

~~BRAVO~~

5 Beyond Sterne: The Potential of Metaleptic Experience

> Colonel Sandurz: Try here. Stop.
> Dark Helmet: What the hell am I looking at?
> When does this happen in the movie?
> Colonel Sandurz: Now. You're looking at now, sir.
> Everything that happens now, is happening now.
> Dark Helmet: What happened to then?
> Colonel Sandurz: We passed then.
> Dark Helmet: When?
> Colonel Sandurz: Just now. We're at now now.
> Dark Helmet: Go back to then.
> Colonel Sandurz: When?
> Dark Helmet: Now.
> Colonel Sandurz: Now?
> Dark Helmet: Now.
> Colonel Sandurz: I can't.
> Dark Helmet: Why?
> Colonel Sandurz: We missed it.
> Dark Helmet: When?
> Colonel Sandurz: Just now.
> — Mel Brooks, *Spaceballs*

One of the aims of this book has been to trace metalepsis back to the conditions and possibilities of the hermeneutic situation in which metaleptic transgressions come into being. As the preceding analyses have demonstrated, such an endeavour yields two different approaches, which are mutually dependent. Considering the hermeneutic dimensions of metalepsis presupposes a structuralist account of narrative: without a conceptual model of the representational logic of narrative, there can be no metaleptic transgression. A detailed analysis of the metaleptic dynamic, however, demonstrates the limitations of narratological categories and foregrounds the hermeneutics which makes them possible. The complexity of the event of understanding metalepsis ultimately contradicts the rigid conceptual geometry of (structuralist) narratology on which it relies. The contextual assumption that narrational acts cue the construction of a spatiotemporal and logical bifurcation (the domains of the signified/signifier), a prerequisite of a structuralist account, is a necessary element of the complex reality of understanding metaleptic narrative, a reality which presupposes, embeds, and denies this element. In other words, the process of understanding metalepsis relies on a moment of (textual) objectification which is denied – or at least relativized.

This chapter offers an outline of the 'state of the art' of metalepsis along this 'impossible' trajectory. It does not describe the most recent or, in terms of media technology, most sophisticated metalepses – but offers the outline of a movement towards the most radical metaleptic potential of narrative. It begins with a description of what may happen in the process of understanding contemporary metaleptic transgressions in some Mel Brooks films from the 1970s and 1980s and a contemporary comic book, Cullen Bunn's *Deadpool Kills the Marvel Universe* (2011). Instead of placing these metalepses in a recent 'stage' of a long historical development that began long before Laurence Sterne's *Tristram Shandy*, [171] I will establish a connection between the metaleptic potential displayed in these narratives and what I take to be this potential's most potent realization: *The Tibetan Book of the Dead*. This religious text has arguably more radical metaleptic potential than any of the numerous instances of metaleptic transgressions in the twentieth and twenty-first centuries – here I find a profound enactment of metaleptic experience, an experience which not only demonstrates how the frameworks of understanding narrative belong to the historical contingency of an understanding subjectivity, but which transcends how we make sense of the world. This metaleptic potential resists *bon mots* concerning the historical development of metalepsis and its place in contemporary culture and history of ideas.

At the centre of the narratological framework enabling investigation of metaleptic potential stands the notion of the diegesis. The notion of diegetic levels (or, more generally, any model of the sense-making capabilities they represent) is the point of origin of the metaleptic dynamic. I have argued that diegetic geometry is a model of the representational logic of narrating lived experience, a narration which presupposes a non-linguistic *conceptualization* of a spatiotemporal frame of reference distinct from the 'unmediated' spatiotemporal conditions of the 'world' in which that experience is represented. The inevitable relatedness of every experience that unfolds in this spatiotemporal dichotomy can be explored from a Heideggerian perspective with the notion of '*being-in-the-world*':

> Being-in is not a 'property' which Dasein sometimes has and sometimes does not have, and without which it could just be just as well as it could be with it. It is not the case that man 'is' and then has, by way of an extra, a relationship-of-Being towards the 'world' – a

---

[171] Ute E. Eisen and Peter von Möllendorff maintain in the introduction to the collection *Über die Grenze: Metalepse in Text- und Bildmedien des Altertums* (2013) that narrative metalepsis belongs to the generic make-up of a wide variety of works from classical antiquity (cf. Eisen and von Möllendorff 2013, 8).

> world with which he provides himself occasionally. Dasein is never 'proximally' an entity which is, so to speak, free from Being-in, but which sometimes has the inclination to take up a 'relationship' towards the world. Taking up relationships towards the world is possible only because Dasein, as Being-in-the-world, is as it is. This state of Being does not arise just because some entity is present-at-hand outside of Dasein and meets up with it. Such an entity can 'meet up with' Dasein only in so far as it can, of its own accord, show itself within a world. (Heidegger 1967 [first German ed. 1927], 84; emphasis in the original)

Narrative in this sense relies on the inescapable condition of 'being-in': for lived experience and the relation or representation of lived experience are, on the one hand, inextricably linked to the spatiotemporal conditions in which that particular experience has arisen; and on the other hand, lived experience is always already embedded in a network of meaning, relatedness and involvement that characterizes human understanding generally. This can never, even as a past experience, be in any sense external to Heidegger's notion of *Dasein*. The most radical potential of metalepsis questions not only the structural element of the metaleptic dynamic (where the notion of diegetic levels basically amounts to the insight that narrative locates binary structures within the event in which narrative comes into being); it also questions what could, from a philosophical perspective, be considered the network of meaning and relatedness presupposed by human understanding (which cuts across the distinctions of representational logic). Thus the most radical metalepses challenge the *a priori* conditions of human understanding – and present a movement towards what does *not* 'show itself within a world.'

Before I explore this metaleptic potential, I would like to offer a hermeneutic *caveat*. This chapter offers a narratological practice: from a hermeneutic perspective, the following analyses draw the boundaries of what I take to be narratology; they trace the dialectic between the hermeneutics of distanciation and that of belonging; they rely, that is, on a hermeneutics that (temporarily) situates itself analytically outside of what it belongs to ontologically. For in practice, understanding metalepsis potentially involves an elusively circular hermeneutic understanding of the rigid conceptual order that governs tradition, and hence too the interpreter and the narrative itself. In this sense metalepsis is indeed, as John Pier puts it, "a threshold of discovery" (2011, 275). This chapter, then, characterizes the experience of understanding narrative in terms of the telos of 'the unity of experiencing narrative' (cf. Chapter 3.1.1) *and* in terms of the unique process that moves understanding beyond such unity. Paradoxically, this is at the same time the hermeneutic ground that moves understanding beyond the metaleptic games of Laurence Sterne.

Mel Brooks' films have often been cited in discussions of self-reference and metalepsis[172] in movies. One of Brooks' favourite games with the medium-specific conditions of film is the playful interaction of extradiegetic[173] fictional production contexts and diegetic characters. In *Spaceballs* (1987), for instance, Dark Helmet (the spoof of Darth Vader) accidentally kills a member of the filmmaking crew with his light-sabre in the final battle against Lone Starr (the spoof of Luke Skywalker), at which point they both stop fighting, looking at the man who went down. After a short pause, Dark Helmet points at Lone Starr and says: "Um, he did it!" This enrages Lone Starr (or the actor playing Lone Starr), and they continue to fight as the extradiegetic production context moves out of the frame to the left.[174] Much of the scene's humour is indebted to a metaleptic blurring of the diegetic 'world' in which the fight takes place and the extradiegetic 'world' in which this fight is staged and filmed. Assuming that the spectators see the 'real' (extrafictional) cameras with which the movie is shot (and real crew members) implies a peculiar metaleptic violation. Since the light-sabre with which Dark Helmet slays the crew member is literally and exclusively part of the diegesis (in the extrafictional 'reality,' the actors Rick Moranis and Bill Pullman use props which have to be turned into light-sabres in postproduction by special effects artists), its appearance and usage defies representational logic. The supposedly 'real' crew member is killed by a fictive weapon (a fact which may be taken to argue that this is a fictive and extradiegetic production context). Moreover, and this is one of the reasons for the quirky humour of this scene, the actors could be argued to never 'emerge' in this scene – neither Dark Helmet nor Lone Starr fall out of character. As diegetic beings, both know and accept the fact that they are being filmed, and they accept the extradiegetic

---

172 Among the critics who have discussed metaleptic passages in Mel Brooks' films are Meister (2003, 2005), Limoges (2008), Sarkhosh (2011), Limoges (2011), who calls Brooks "another metalepsis master" (2011, 205), and Thoss (2015). There is even a very brief discussion of an instance of the rhetorical trope *metalepsis* in connection with Mel Brooks' *High Anxiety* in a footnote by Lee Edelman in his *No Future: Queer Theory and the Death Drive* (cf. 2004, 175).

173 There are no doubt minor medium-specific peculiarities of the "possible worlds within the larger filmic universe" (cf. Sarkhosh 2011, 172–173). Yet I basically agree with the model used in the accounts of filmic metalepsis by Sarkhosh (2011) and Limoges (2011), which can easily be correlated with Genette. There is a world in which a story takes place (diegetic universe) and a world in which that story is filmed, enacted, made. If the semiotic signs of the filmic narrative cue the construction of a fictive domain of the signifier, a fictive context of production, I here and in the following refer to that context as extradiegetic.

174 This scene has also been briefly described by Sarkhosh (2011, 181–182) as a metalepsis that breaches the boundaries of production and by Thoss (2015, 119–120) as what he terms a 'story-world-reality transgression.'

production that is needed to mediate their story. Seemingly, the diegetic Dark Helmet and Lone Starr have for a moment metaleptically spilled over[175] into a fictive context of production; an extradiegesis that is at least partly indebted to the logic of the diegesis.

This metaleptic spillover that destabilizes the logical distinction between diegetic story (domain of the signified) and extradiegetic and fictive production context (domain of the signifier) is one of Mel Brooks' trademarks. Many further instances of this can be found in *Spaceballs*, for instance when the villains accidentally catch the stunt doubles of the characters they were chasing or the often discussed scene (cf. Limoges 2008, 38; Sarkhosh 2011, 180; Thoss 2015, 120–122) in which Dark Helmet and Colonel Sandurz watch the movie *Spaceballs* on video. When Sandurz suggests that they should watch the "instant cassette" of this movie to find out the location of the heroes, Dark Helmet asks: "How can there be a cassette of *Spaceballs: The Movie*? We're still in the middle of making it!" Uttering this sentence, Helmet takes a confused look at the camera, thus acknowledging its existence. Sarkhosh argues that "[s]uch direct glimpses into the camera open a rupture between the diegetic world of the characters and the spectatorial world of the audience. Thus any direct glimpse into the camera is metaleptic: its effect is to interrupt the filmic illusion" (2011, 175).

Yet what is the 'spectatorial world'? Who is addressed by this look into the camera? Potentially, such a look induces effects that can be compared to the effects the narrative *you* can produce. Herman has argued that a narrative *you* "can induce hesitation between reference to entities, situations, and events internal to the storyworld and events external" (2002, 338). The question who or what is focused by a look into the camera may result in an even more complex variety of answers: the 'real' audience, the 'real' filming crew, the extradiegetic (and fictional) cameraman, the extradiegetic director, a diegetic location or person?[176] It is not only the production context of the movie that is in this man-

---

[175] The metaphor of a 'spillover' has at times been used to non-specifically describe a variety of metalepses (cf. for instance, Huber 2014, 217; de Bourcier 2012, 27; Pier 2009, 271; Rubik 2007, 174, Ryan 2006, 225), thus highlighting the transgression of generic and other conventional rules. I employ the metaphor mainly because it questions the notion of agency: the metaleptic 'spillovers' in this chapter radically challenge and deny the (narratively constituted) subjectivities involved.

[176] In the movie *Being John Malkovich* (1999), for instance, the diegetic character Maxine looks directly into the camera – and clearly looks at the equally diegetic Malkovich (or Lotte inside Malkovich). Thus, even though she is looking into the camera, most viewers presumably construct a diegetic subject position that is seen by Maxine. Accordingly, most viewers would agree that such a look into the camera does not necessarily undermine the filmic illusion. At

ner 'laid bare,' but also the way in which viewers construct the structural and logical relations which understanding narrative requires. Generic conventions, cultural knowledge, the particular individual conditions of each (group of) viewer(s), all contribute to the complex hermeneutic situation in which the 'worlds' emerge that are part of the experience of watching *Spaceballs*. Here, the metaleptic possibilities of meaning foreground the fact that the situatedness of the combination of signs resulting from the narrational act that created *Spaceballs* is constructed according to certain rules (logical, generic, etc.).

Later in this hilarious scene, the diegetic Colonel Sandurz and Dark Helmet fast forward the movie (which exists in the diegesis because these "instant cassettes," as Sandurz explains, are available before the production of the movie is finished) up to the point where the metadiegetic Sandurz and Helmet in the video are viewing the movie. Watching the moment that shows them watching this very moment (aptly described by Jeff Thoss as "an infinite regress, an aporetic mise en abyme" [2015, 121]) leaves Dark Helmet flabbergasted: "What the hell am I looking at? When does this happen in the movie?" "Now, you are looking at now, Sir. Everything that happens now is happening now, Sir," answers Sandurz, pointing towards the monitor showing the video. Here, as they discuss the finished product of the film they are in the middle of making, the spatiotemporal conditions of their dialogue become ambiguous. The illogical contemporaneity of diegesis and metadiegetic representation makes the temporal and spatial 'boundaries' of human understanding visible. It is 'impossible' to fast forward the finished product of the filmic representation you are in the middle of making to 'now.' Helmet is confused by the metaleptic presence of the present moment in the representation ("We're at now now"), recognizing that what in the beginning may appear as the object analyzed from a safe distance (watching a cassette) turns out to be inextricably linked to the present attempt to make sense of it. This denial of representational logic highlights that understanding

---

the same time, however, the movie *Being John Malkovich* invites diegetic characters (and the audience) to enter into Malkovich's head, and displays metaleptic potential on many levels. The unmediated access to Malkovich's perspective could be argued to metaleptically enhance the immersive quality of this movie. From the perspective of the diegetic characters who travel the portal into Malkovich, the experience of being Malkovich no longer has to be represented or narrated. The characters know/experience Malkovich 'from the inside out,' and, in the case of Craig, are even able to control Malkovich and 'narrate' his diegetic existence (which, once it is controlled by a diegetic character, could be argued to have attained a metadiegetic status). Of course, and this is typical for the interpretive possibilities offered by metalepsis, such knowing 'from the inside out' is an 'impossibility' which at the same time highlights the mediated character of such (fictional) experience.

narrative conventionally depends on a network of relatedness that harmonizes the 'dual now' of the domains of signifier and signified. Moreover – and this is an insight that the audience constructing this duality of 'nows' may mirror – this denial of representational logic highlights that the one who understands potentially moves from the hermeneutics of distanciation to the hermeneutics of belonging.

As characters with knowledge of the filmic production of the scene they are shooting, watching a *mise en abyme* of themselves (of which they are a part), do they belong to the storyworld in the same way as in the scenes before? In other words, are they diegetic, extradiegetic, or hypodiegetic (at the same time), or have these distinctions lost their validity *vis-à-vis* an infinite multiplication of the very same distinction? One way of conceptualizing this narratologically and metaphorically is that in Mel Brooks' films the storyworld (diegesis) has a metaleptic reach that embraces the extradiegesis (and/or, for that matter, the hypodiegesis and the hypo-hypodiegesis and so on and so forth). In other words, the characters seem to stay indebted to the logic of the diegesis – or, more precisely, indebted to the impossible logic of a diegesis that extends to the context of its own mediation.

The violation of such conventions by characters who fall out of the diegesis without falling out of character is explored more thoroughly in an earlier movie by Mel Brooks. *Blazing Saddles* (1974), a satirical Western comedy, takes this metaleptic game to its radical conclusion. In the ending of that movie, there is an epic fight scene between the heroes Bart (Cleavon Little), Jim (Gene Wilder) and the inhabitants of the small town Rock Ridge on the one hand, and the villain Hedley Lamarr (Harvey Corman) and a gang of thugs on the other. This whole fight metaleptically spills into a neighbouring film studio (literally breaking the wall that separated this neighbouring studio from the lot where the fight for Rock Ridge was filmed). In that studio a cast of men in tuxedos is performing the musical number "The French Mistake" under the direction of the effeminate choreographer Buddy Bizarre (Dom DeLuise), a spoof of Busby Berkeley numbers with gay overtones. Buddy Bizarre manages to stop the pandemonium after about ten seconds, when he screams through his megaphone: "Cut! What in the hell do you think you are doing here? This is a closed set." At this point, one of Lamarr's henchmen walks up to Buddy Bizzare, screams ("Piss on you, I'm working for Mel Brooks!") and knocks him out. Absurdly, the ensuing fight between men in tuxedos and cowboys is in some shots framed both by the film crew (who watch the fray without moving) and cameras of the musical film production, thus mirroring the camera and crew that are needed to film the film crew in front of the fighting. Here, the layers of representational logic with which Brooks plays literally meet in the movie's diegesis.

Yet the metaleptic game does not stop at this point. The fight transforms into a pie fight in the studio's canteen that extends to Tarzan and an ape and includes a guided tour through the studio – a hint that this extradiegesis contains more than just people who make movies – and is ultimately taken onto the streets surrounding the studio. Lamarr escapes, calls a taxi, and tells the driver to 'take him off this picture' before visiting Grauman's Chinese Theatre, buying a ticket (showing his student ID to no avail) and watching the movie '*Blazing Saddles*.' If we think of Lamarr as a diegetic figure who has ascended to the extradiegetic context of production and reception of the movie in which he is a character, he has access to the diegetic movie as an extradiegetic spectator. However, since the 'real' audience can see this access, this could also be constructed as a metadiegetic movie created in a diegesis that included its own context of production. In either case (or both together), Lamarr does not find a way 'off this picture' and remains in his diegetic character role even as he watches the movie (in which he is watching the movie). Much to Lamarr's obvious dismay, his enemy Bart appears in front of the cinema (on horseback), an arrival which is also part of the movie within the movie. Lamarr attempts to flee but is stopped by Bart, who guns him down in a final fight in the ambiguous space in front of the movie theatre. After this, it is Bart's and Jim's turn to watch the ending of the movie – which shows Bart and Jim dismounting from the horses they rode into the sunset and climbing into a limousine.

A narratological analysis of these scenes can only begin with the hermeneutics of distanciation and approach the narrative *Blazing Saddles* as if it had an ahistorical structural make-up. The characters metaleptically cross the boundary between diegesis (the world in which the fictive town Rock Ridge and its inhabitants are situated) and extradiegesis (the world in which that fictive town is 'represented,' filmed and viewed), thereby implying "a metastatement on its medial nature as an artefact" (Wolf 2009b, 50). Yet this reading is only the beginning of the metaleptic dynamic. First of all, in Mel Brooks' movies, the distinction between diegesis and extradiegesis is challenged by metaleptic transgressions in particular ways. The mystery of characters who do not fall out of character when they display an awareness of this extradiegesis marks a very fluid boundary. The extradiegesis seems to include a fictive production context (cameras and film crew), a fictive audience (looking directly at the camera, Lamarr asks at one point: "Why am I asking you?" – although this might also be directed at the cameraman), and even a movie theatre that shows '*Blazing Saddles*.' Yet it is not clear whether the theatre showing '*Blazing Saddles*,' the guided tour through the studio canteen, and the pie fight involving studio visitors are all in the same 'universe.' One of the two is seemingly closer to the 'real world' in which flesh-and-blood human beings watch Mel Brooks' *Blazing Saddles*. In other words, what is the spatiotemporal logic of the fictive construction and representation of '*Blazing Saddles*'?

As has already been demonstrated, the concept of metalepsis offers various options for an analysis of this set-up. First of all, it could be argued that it is an instance of ascending metalepsis, where diegetic characters (e.g. Jim, Hedley and Bart) have seemingly moved out of the story as told into the fictive production context of its telling. The humorous potential is indebted to the 'impossibility' that despite Hedley Lamarr's desire to be 'taken off the movie,' the movie just spills over into the streets of the world in which it is to be shown (and is manifestly already being shown) in cinemas. Secondly, since the logic of the world in which that movie is shown (which resembles the 'real' world) influences the movie, this could be interpreted as a descending metalepsis. The audience watching the Western '*Blazing Saddles*' expect the villain(s) to be shot and the heroes to ride off into the sunset, both of which Bart and Jim see 'for real' both in the diegesis and as a fictive representation on the extradiegetic screen. The extradiegetic logic of cinematic convention, shaped by consumer capitalism, thus literally descends on the characters and shapes the diegesis.

This is humorously foregrounded by Count Basie's orchestra, which Bart crosses on horseback earlier in the movie. Before the camera shows the orchestra, any audience will in all likelihood assume that the Big Band music that can be heard while Bart rides across the desert is nondiegetic. Yet as Bart passes a whole orchestra in the desert, the source of the music seems to be diegetic. In a similar way, the film crew and actors of another production could be argued to 'invade' the diegesis of *Blazing Saddles*. The competitive nature of the movie market thus also literally descends on the diegesis which is inevitably shaped by such (extradiegetic/extratextual) forces. In *Spaceballs*, the merchandising has in a similar manner invaded the diegesis, which in turn is designed with the possibility (or rather inevitability) of merchandising in mind. Jogurt (the spoof of Yoda, played by Mel Brooks), introduces the other characters to a wide range of merchandising articles that include a flamethrower ("the kids love this one") and a Jogurt/Yoda doll.

This metaleptic set-up implies that there is ultimately no distinction between diegesis and extradiegesis – that there is, in other words, a spatiotemporal continuum in which actors enact the story that does not require a fiction-internal spatiotemporal bifurcation. Diegesis, production, mediation, audience are all subjected to the same network of relatedness. The fact that the characters do not fall out of character in Mel Brooks' universe corroborates such a reading. There is only one 'world' in *Blazing Saddles*. Even though Hedley Lamarr wants to leave the movie (and thus the diegesis), he nevertheless signs the wet concrete on which he dies with "Hedley Lamarr" (and not with the name of the actor playing Hedley Lamarr).[177]

The metaleptic *tour de force* of the ending of *Blazing Saddles* makes visible that it is impossible to experience narrative from a safe distance: the members of the extradiegetic audience (Hedley Lamarr accidentally sits down on one of them when he visits Grauman's Chinese Theatre) find themselves in the middle of the movie they are watching. This is not a clear-cut case of an ascending or descending metalepsis. The metaleptic spill of Brooks' films not only imposes the represented on the world of the representation, but also suggests the opposite. The expectations of the audience (and the force – or its lack – with which these expectations shape the narratives towards which they are directed) are playfully (re)-enacted by the diegetic characters Jim and Bart. After Bart has shot Hedley Lamarr in front of the cinema on the 'walk of fame,' he wants to see the movie '*Blazing Saddles*' and says to Jim: "Come on, let's check out the end of the flick." Walking beside Bart into the cinema, Jim says: "I sure hope there's a happy ending. I love a happy ending." Then they watch a happy ending – an ending that is shaped (if not created) by the desire of an extrafictional community that is metaleptically mirrored or anticipated by the diegetic characters who have assumed the position of the audience.

Mel Brooks' *Blazing Saddles* destabilizes the conceptual basis of metalepsis; for the spatiotemporal conditions of narrative are conventionally cued by narrational acts and their results, but in Mel Brooks' *Blazing Saddles* the domains of the signifier and signified potentially collapse into each other. As the boundary between diegesis and extradiegesis collapses, the real audience is potentially confronted with the fact that both the world of which the movie tells and the (fictive) world in which it is produced are similarly rule-governed narratives informed by the selfsame narrative logic. Both these 'levels' have a *telos* towards which they are structured: that of the diegesis is the happy end of the

---

[177] Incidentally, Hedy Lamarr's star is not far away. Here, the metaleptic games of the movie imply the 'real' world. It is a curious footnote that Hedy Lamarr filed an invasion of privacy lawsuit for the unauthorized use of her name in *Blazing Saddles* (cf. Barton 2010, 220). In a metaleptic foreshadowing of this, the diegetic Governor William J. Le Petomane advises an exasperated Hedley (who is tired of being called Hedy, one of the running gags in *Blazing Saddles*) to sue Hedy Lamarr. The dialogue runs as follows: "Governor: 'Thank you, Hedy, thank you.' Lamarr: 'It's not *Hedy*, it's *Hedley*. Hedley Lamarr.' Governor: 'What the hell are you worried about? This is 1874. You'll be able to sue *her*.'"

Western genre, and that of the extradiegesis is a successful movie production. The metaleptic spillover highlights how this (dual) narrative logic forms the narrative(s) in the process of making it. The script of the Western genre and that of the movie production in a capitalist society meet in the limousine that takes the heroes (now unhorsed) into the sunset. The insight that narrative scripts shape the diegesis and the extradiegesis to the point where these become indistinguishable may lead to the awareness in extratextual audiences that their reality is also shaped by narrative scripts structured towards a similar *telos*. With such an insight, the hermeneutics of distanciation gives way to the hermeneutics of belonging; for in the language-world we inhabit, the narrative configuration of sense-making shapes narrative and recipients alike.

This insight interprets the laughter evoked by Mel Brooks' movies as a foregrounding of that belonging and a distanciation from the pervasiveness of conventional (generic) narrative logic. Malina (2002) argues that the metaleptic subject construction of fiction may influence and shape nonfictional processes of subject construction: metalepsis "mirrors the process by which our sometimes violent narrative framings, deframings, and reframings of our world, ourselves and others make us what we, for all practical purposes, *are*" (3, emphasis in the original). Mel Brooks' movies offer a parody of the subject construction of successful (and thus generic) narratives within capitalist society. The metaleptic foregrounding of this logic arguably performs a subject deconstruction: characters disintegrate into the agents of generic necessity and cinematic audiences are presented as diegetic, inevitably belonging to the discursive creations of the narrative identities they consume.

Some metaleptic strategies, such as the diegetic hero who does not want to be narrated, pose a more profound challenge to the narrative scripts that structure human experience. A telling example of this can be found in Cullen Bunn's comic book *Deadpool Kills the Marvel Universe* (2011). Deadpool is a slightly unhinged superhero-character from the Marvel Universe who has a 'healing factor.' That means he is practically invincible, because any damaged tissue regrows instantly; so Deadpool cannot die. In the four instalments of this comic book, Deadpool becomes aware of his status as a narrated superhero in an endless cycle of violence and suffering. To end this cycle, Deadpool sets out to kill every superhero and thus the whole universe in which he is trapped. The comic book begins with "the watcher," a member of an extra-terrestrial race who stands outside the panel and offers the following introduction to the plot:

> I am the watcher. Like the others of my ageless race, I wander the multiverse in observation of countless worlds and countless realities! Yes! Countless worlds ... and upon each of these worlds countless stories unfold ... I have witnessed the ascension of gods and the

destruction of celestial bodies … the birth of entire worlds and apocalyptic endings of civilizations. To all things must come an ending … But such cessations may be quiet and peaceful … the passing of one existence to make way for the next … while others are filled with naught but pain and terror. (Bunn and Talajic 2011, no pagination)

Figure 27: Bunn and Talajic 2011, no pagination

Beyond Sterne: The Potential of Metaleptic Experience —— 255

The watcher assumes a godlike position from which the storyworld can be seen without danger of becoming involved or threatened by the events that happen. Yet that position (which mirrors the comic book audience) is metaleptically questioned on the very first page. On the one hand, the watcher is some kind of omniscient focalizer and the panels next to which he is placed at the beginning offer his perspective on the storyworld. On the other hand, he is focalized and presented within the confined space of the panels. After Deadpool attacks the (surprised) watcher, Deadpool's inner voice (visible as a red square) demands that Deadpool should ask a question:

Figure 28: Bunn and Talajic 2011, no pagination

Here, the dying watcher seemingly points Deadpool in the direction of a watching audience, and Deadpool looks into the extradiegetic or extratextual 'world' outside the panels. Deadpool's awareness of the 'watchers' who have, as regular comic book readers, indeed 'watched the ascension of gods and the destruction of bodies,' who construct the stories from panels and gutters from a safe distance, marks the beginning of a metaleptic game that offers a counter-narrative to traditional superhero comic books.

Figure 29: Bunn and Talajic 2011, no pagination

Repeatedly violating the fourth wall convention, Deadpool promises his audience a tale of violence and gore. This is very much in agreement with conventional generic expectations. Yet Deadpool's aim is to tell the story that ends all stories about Deadpool – thus paradoxically offering the narrative that does not want to be told; a narrative that not only threatens the narrative contract but also soon literally threatens its audience.

At times, Deadpool's metaleptic game is highly entertaining. In a fine example of epistemological metalepsis, Deadpool displays an awareness of the (extradiegetic or extratextual) world of production and reception in which superhero stories are drawn, manufactured and read. In his fight with Spiderman (Spiderman wants to stop Deadpool's random killings, Deadpool wants to kill Spiderman as part of the world he wants to escape). Deadpool is then pushed to the ground from a great height and badly injured. Spiderman stands above him and says: "You're lucky I am not like you. You're lucky I don't kill you for what you have done." Deadpool answers: "Am I? Do you really think they would let you break character even if you wanted to?" (Bunn and Talajic 2011, no pagination) This short dialogue demonstrates that Deadpool is aware of the narrative logic and generic conventions in superhero comic books; he is, in other words, aware of being a narrated entity. The absurd notion (from a nondiegetic perspective) that Spiderman could want something that those who create him do not allow, endorse, draw, etc., is balanced by the equally absurd notion (from a diegetic perspective) that the actions and thoughts of Spiderman are ultimately not diegetic at all, but emerge in and belong to the world that logically creates the diegesis (of which the diegesis is but a shadow).

Killing Wolverine, Deadpool takes the metaleptic game to another level.

Figure 30: Bunn and Talajic 2011, no pagination

The reason for Wolverine's staying power is not his diegetic healing factor but his extratextual (or extradiegetic) popularity. Since Deadpool offers this nondiegetic perspective from within the diegesis, he has attained the 'impossible' perspective of the panel and of the gutter – he knows about the constructedness of comic book fiction and knows how popularity and the rules of consumer capitalism shape the diegetic worlds of comic books. So he finds himself in the metaleptic position of being able to trace a diegetic character's healing factor to that character's extradiegetic or extratextual popularity.[178]

---

[178] Incidentally, Deadpool's diegetic struggle has not been successful. It was arguably popularity that renewed his cycle of violence and suffering and transported it to a different medium.

In the final pages of the comic book *Deadpool Kills the Marvel Universe* (2011), Deadpool visits the creative team who create, draw, and write him – and who, in their own panel, as he approaches, talk about Deadpool approaching them. They have metaleptically written their own way out: the last panels narrate how they create a metadiegetic world in which they narrate how the meta-metadiegetic character Deadpool prepares to end their narration. This is the last panel before the comic ends; the fictionalized 'world' in which *Deadpool* is made will be unmade by its making. One of the interpretive possibilities is that this ending negates, in Jan Christoph Meister's words, "the very idea of a possible world indexically distinguishable from the observer's reality" (Meister 2003, no pagination). As Deadpool's violence destroys not only superheroines and superheroes but also the universes that hold them, this comic book radically denies its own conventional and generic spatiotemporal make-up. There is, from the perspective of Deadpool, only one world: the world in which he is created. *Deadpool Kills the Marvel Universe* is the story that does not want to be told. Just as readers construct 'worlds' according to representational logic, so Deadpool attempts to deconstruct them. The world that emerges in the panel is threatened by the extinction that is suggested by the gutter. Deadpool's metaleptic moves seem pre-eminently to exemplify this dialectic, as they negate the very basis of storytelling. In *Deadpool Kills the Marvel Universe* metalepsis grounds the diegetic in an extradiegesis that – by inventing Deadpool – cancels itself out.

As readers construct Deadpool's metaleptic movements and configurations, the narrative to end all narratives of the Marvel universe takes this configuration apart and deconstructs readerly constructions. At one point, a group of superheroes and villains decide to commit mass suicide. This diegetic suicide not only points towards the world in which the world is drawn, but also expresses dissatisfaction with the immersion it offers comic book readers. The suicide pact is graphically illustrated (enhancing imaginative immersion) and is the last appearance of those superheroes (destroying imaginative immersion). As has often been argued, the ubiquity of metaleptic transgression belongs to a compendium of strategies that can foster and further imaginative immersion in

---

The third-person action video game *Deadpool* (2013, developed by High Moon Studios) offers a wide range of metaleptic potential. For instance, Deadpool comments on the fact that he repeatedly slaps Wolverine: "That's because the player keeps mashing the button." This (epistemologically) metaleptic game seems to travel without difficulties from one medium to the next. And popularity condemns both Wolverine and Deadpool to an ongoing 'existence' in diegetic stories in various media – the movie *Deadpool* was released in 2016.

the storyworld. In *Deadpool Kills the Marvel Universe*, the imaginative immersion in a 'world' that negates the conventional distinctions cued by narrational acts (the distinction between diegetic and extradiegetic 'worlds') can also be read as an allegory of the limitations and fleetingness of human understanding. Everything we narratively construct, this comic book suggests, potentially disintegrates into the present moment of understanding.

The metaleptic trajectory traced in this chapter moves towards the dissolution of what Marie-Laure Ryan terms "the actual base of the narrative stack, the world of ground zero" (2006, 209), which "remains protected from metaleptic phenomena" (ibid.). This can be found in a religious text that is at least 1200 years old and far removed from the cultural heritage that shapes *Deadpool Kills the Marvel Universe*. The eighth-century Buddhist scriptures usually known in the West as the *Tibetan Book of the Dead* are a cycle of spiritual texts whose original Tibetan title explicitly denotes their purpose: *The Great Liberation by Hearing in the Intermediate States (Bar-do thos-grol chen-mo)*.[179] The purpose of these spiritual texts is to guide human beings on their way through the transitional stages of conscious (human) existence on the path to pristine cognition, the modality of buddha-mind. According to the Buddhist Nyingma tradition, there are six different kinds of intermediate stage: "the intermediate state of living or natural existence, the intermediate state of dreams, the intermediate state of meditative stability or concentration, the intermediate state of the time of death, the intermediate state of reality, and the intermediate state of rebirth" (Padmasaṃbhava and Lingpa 2005, 234–235; emphasis in the original). Many (Buddhist) texts employ the word *bardo* (which literally means 'intermediate state') to exclusively refer to the experience between the moment of death and the time of rebirth. *The Great Liberation by Hearing in the Intermediate States*, however, stresses the essential *bardo*-nature of all the conscious experience of sentient beings that have not realized the ultimate nature of mind and attained Buddhahood. Dreams, everyday activities, meditation, etc., are all transitional insofar as they are the consequence of a misapprehension of the nature of mind, of actual reality. In an introductory commentary to the *Tibetan Book of the Dead* the fourteenth Dalai Lama outlines the perspective of Buddhist philosophy as follows:

---

[179] Gyurme Dorje supplies this translation and the original Tibetan in his "Brief Literary History of the *Tibetan Book of the Dead*" (cf. 2005, xxxviii). He cites the successful publication of three chapters from that cycle of texts under the title *The Tibetan Book of the Dead* by Lama Kazi Dawa Samdup and W. Y. Evans-Wentz in 1927 as the reason for the popularity of the (slightly misleading) title known in the West (cf. ibid.).

> The process through which the external world and the sentient beings within it revolve in a cycle of existence propelled by karmic propensities and their interaction with misapprehension, attraction and aversion and conditions is described in terms of twelve interdependent links. Each cycle of the process begins with a misapprehension of the nature of actual reality. This fundamental ignorance acts as a condition for the arising of the propensities created by our past actions, mental, verbal and physical, which condition our dualising consciousness. Our dualising consciousness, in turn, conditions the qualities and mode of interaction of our psycho-physical aggregates, which condition our sensory fields, which generate contact, which generate sensations, and then in turn, attachment, grasping, and maturation towards rebirth. (His Holiness the Dalai Lama 2005, xvi–xvii)

This, in Buddhist terms, is the beginning of narration. The misapprehension of awareness instigates the cyclic existence of (human) consciousness. It is this misapprehension that conditions the 'dualising consciousness' that in a very literal sense places itself as an ego in a spatiotemporal surrounding distinct from that ego. Everyday conscious awareness is, according to Buddhist philosophy, in turn conditioned by 'dualising consciousness,' inasmuch as conscious experience relies on the ego (that is distinct from its surroundings), the body that carries it (that is distinct from all other bodies), and the dichotomy of subject and object. This is the logical basis of narration that Buddhist philosophy declares as transitional. The mind, in its non-transitional state, is beyond the ego. This Buddhist view of conscious (human) existence entails the existence of a continuity of consciousness that moves through cycles of transitional states and stages, a movement that only comes to an end when complete Buddhahood is attained.

The Buddhist notion that human beings can be guided after death in one of the transitional realms known as *bardo* has a distinct metaleptic quality. Human beings that find themselves after death in the intermediate state of reality (neither incarnated, and thus part of our material world, nor part of the nirvana) can still be directed by a spiritual teacher or lama who, in our physical world, addresses the dead body and recites parts of the *Bardo Thodol*, which, in turn, depicts the very things the human being encounters in that *bardo*:

> If, upon hearing these words, [the deceased] recognizes the meditational deities, he or she will dissolve indivisibly [with them] and thereby attain Buddhahood [in the Buddha-body of Perfect Resource].
> Yet, even after receiving this instruction, there are those who are held back by their negative habitual tendencies and there are those who will not recognize their meditational deities because they have fled in awe and terror. The recognition not having been attained, so it is that, on the twelfth day, the assembled deities of the Karma family of blood-drinking deities […] will come to escort the deceased. Since an even greater fear and terror will arise if these are not recognized, again, call the deceased by name, and offer the introduction in the following words:

> O, Child of Buddha Nature, listen without distraction. When the twelfth day comes, he who is called the transcendent lord Karma Heruka, of the karma family of blood-drinking deities, will arise from the northern direction of your brain, in union with his consort and appear vividly before you. [...] Do not be afraid! Do not be terrified! And do not be awed! Recognize this to be the buddha-body of your own awareness. These are your own meditational deities, so do not be terrified. This, in reality, is the transcendent lord Amoghasiddhi and his consort, so regard them with intense devotion! Recognition and Liberation will occur simultaneously!
> If, upon hearing these words, [the deceased] recognizes the meditational deities, he or she will dissolve indivisibly [with them] and thereby attain buddhahood [in the Buddha-body of Perfect Resource]. (Padmasaṃbhava and Lingpa 2005, 262–263)

The world in which *The Great Liberation upon Hearing* is read (the domain of the signifier), and the world in which the deceased listens (the domain of the signified), initially agree with the representational logic of narratological accounts of narrative. If one approaches this narrative as fictional, then the domain of the signified (diegesis or metadiegesis) is the world in which the dead person encounters the wrathful deities, and the domain of the signifier (extradiegesis or diegesis) is the world in which that person is addressed. The denial of the manner in which narrational acts cue the construction of these domains is, in a narratological perspective, highly metaleptic. Either the detailed descriptions of the world in which the deceased find themselves travel metaleptically from the world in which they are narrated to the world in which they are experienced (descending metalepsis), or the states of affairs the deceased encounter have metaleptically entered the world in which they are narrated.

The domains of both signifier and signified are, from a Buddhist perspective, part of a cycle of *bardo*-states which, in the words of the Dalai Lama, begin "with a misapprehension of the nature of actual reality." In other words, this misapprehension ('dualising consciousness') causes a string of intermediate stages that makes possible the distinctions on which metalepsis relies. The fundamental notion of being-in-the-world and the spatiotemporal distinctions it engenders are thus just a misunderstanding of the single nature of mind. Metalepsis, it may be argued, moves towards this single nature by sidestepping or transcending the effects of 'dualising consciousness.' From a Buddhist perspective, the metaleptic denial of conventional sense-making runs counter to cyclic existence – or, perhaps more precisely, runs counter to how we construct cyclic existence – and questions the habitual tendencies that we accumulate.

This most radical form of metalepsis negates the hermeneutic prerequisites of understanding (metaleptic) narrative more thoroughly and fundamentally than any other metaleptic transgression. In a sense, then, it is the radical conclusion of the metaleptic dynamic that questions the present account of metalepsis.

Metalepsis, I have argued in agreement with most narratologists, is a fiction-internal phenomenon (which can *imply* the 'real' world). From the perspective of Buddhist monks, this metalepsis is neither fictional, nor a transgression. Here, we encounter a radical questioning of our prerequisites, for *The Great Liberation by Hearing in the Intermediate States* negates not only "*the very idea of a possible world* indexically distinguishable from the observer's reality" (Meister 2003, no pagination), but also the very idea of the observer's reality as we know it – alongside the 'I' that forms the perspectival centre of that world (cf. xvi). The representational *aporias* inherent to the hermeneutic situation in which narrative is understood are corollaries of the distanciation in which alone an object can (safely) be known as such. In contrast, *The Great Liberation by Hearing in the Intermediate States* introduces a hermeneutics of ultimate belonging; for ultimate dissolution with (and into) the meditational deities entails an awareness that is no longer spatiotemporal and no longer, therefore, relies on the dichotomy between self and world, self and other. In this sense the *Bardo Thodol* tells the narrative that ends all narratives. It is fitting that the present book should end with an introduction to an experience that metaleptically transcends the many ways in which we make sense of the world in narrative:

> [First, recognize that] past thoughts are traceless, velar, and empty,
> [Second, recognize that] future thoughts are unproduced and fresh,
> And [third recognize that] the present moment abides naturally and unconstructed.
> When this ordinary, momentary consciousness is examined nakedly [and directly] by oneself,
> Upon examination it is radiant awareness,
> Which is free from the presence of an observer,
> Manifestly stark and clear,
> Completely empty and uncreated in all respects,
> Lucid, without duality of radiance and emptiness,
> Not permanent, for it is lacking inherent existence in all respects,
> Not a mere nothingness, for it is radiant and clear,
> Not a single entity, for it is clearly perceptible as a multiplicity,
> Yet not existing inherently as a multiplicity, for it is indivisible and of a single savour.
> (2005, 41–42)

References

Abbott, H. P. 2005. "The Future of All Narrative Futures." In *A Companion to Narrative Theory*, edited by James Phelan and Peter J. Rabinowitz, 529–541. Malden, MA: Blackwell.
Abbott, H. P. 2006. "Cognitive Literary Studies: The 'Second Generation'." *Poetics Today* 27 (4): 711–722.
Abbott, H. P. 2008 [2002]. *The Cambridge Introduction to Narrative*. Cambridge: Cambridge University Press.
Abel, Günter. 1995. "Sprache, Zeichen und Interpretation." In *Sprache Denken: Positionen aktueller Sprachphilosophie*, edited by Jürgen Trabant and Günter Abel, 165–190. Frankfurt am Main: Fischer.
Abish, Walter. 1974. *Alphabetical Africa*. New York: New Directions.
Adamson, Sylvia, Gavin Alexander, and Katrin Ettenhuber, eds. 2007. *Renaissance Figures of Speech*. Cambridge: Cambridge University Press.
Alber, Jan, and Alice Bell. 2012. "Ontological Metalepsis and Unnatural Narratology." *Journal of Narrative Theory* 42 (2): 166–192.
Alber, Jan, and Monika Fludernik, eds. 2010. *Postclassical Narratology: Approaches and Analyses*. Columbus: Ohio State University Press.
Alber, Jan, and Rüdiger Heinze, eds. 2011. *Unnatural Narratives: Unnatural Narratology*. Berlin, Boston: De Gruyter.
Alber, Jan, Henrik Skov Nielsen, and Brian Richardson, eds. 2013. *A Poetics of Unnatural Narrative*. Columbus: Ohio State University Press.
Allen, Woody. 1997. *The Complete Prose of Woody Allen*. London: Picador.
Allen, Woody. 1997. "The Kugelmass Episode." In *The Complete Prose of Woody Allen*, 347–360. London: Picador.
Alter, Robert. 1975. *Partial Magic: The Novel as a Self-Conscious Genre*. Berkeley: University of California Press.
Alter, Robert. 1987. "Sterne and the Nostalgia for Reality." In *Laurence Sterne's Tristram Shandy*, edited by Harold Bloom, 87–105. New York: Chelsea House.
Amis, Martin. 1984. *Money: A Suicide Note*. London: Penguin Books.
Aristotle. 1996. *Poetics*. Edited and translated by Malcom Heath. London: Penguin.
Attridge, Derek, ed. 1992. *Acts of Literature*. New York, NY: Routledge.
Audet, René, and Richard St-Gelais, eds. 2007. *La fiction, suites et variations*. Québec: Nota Bene.
Austin, John. 1962. *How to Do Things with Words*. Oxford: Clarendon.
Baird, Theodore. 1936. "The Time-Scheme in Tristram Shandy and a Source." *PMLA* 51 (3): 803–822.
Bakhtin, Mikhail M. 1984 [first Russian ed. 1929/1963]. *Problems of Dostoevsky's Poetics*. Edited by Caryl Emerson and Wayne C. Booth. Minneapolis: University of Minnesota Press.
Bal, Mieke. 1985. *Narratology: Introduction to the Theory of Narrative*. Toronto: University of Toronto Press.
Balzac, Honoré de. 1971 [first French ed. 1837–1843]. *Lost Illusions*. Edited and translated by Herbert James Hunt. Harmondsworth: Penguin.
Banfield, Ann. 1982. *Unspeakable Sentences: Narration and Representation in the Language of Fiction*. Boston: Routledge.

Bareis, J. Alexander. 2008. *Fiktionales Erzählen: Zur Theorie der literarischen Fiktion als Make-Believe*. Gothenburg: Acta Universitatis Gothoburgensis.
Baron, Christine. 2005. "Effet métaleptique et statut des discours fictionnels." In *Métalepses: Entorses au pacte de la représentation*, edited by John Pier and Jean-Marie Schaeffer, 295–310. Paris: Éd. de l'EHESS.
Barthes, Roland. 1968. "L'Effet de réel." *Communications* (11): 84–89.
Bartlett, Steven J., and Peter Suber, eds. 1987. *Self-Reference: Reflections on Reflexivity*. Dordrecht: Springer Netherlands.
Barton, Ruth. 2010. *Hedy Lamarr: The Most Beautiful Woman in Film*. Lexington, KY: University Press of Kentucky.
Beardsworth, Richard. 1996. *Derrida & the Political*. London, New York: Routledge.
Beck, Hamilton H. H. 1987. *The Elusive "I" in the Novel: Hippel, Sterne, Diderot, Kant*. New York, NY: Lang.
Beckett, Samuel. 1970 [1953, first English ed. 1958]. *The Unnamable: Translated from the French by the Author*. New York: Grove.
Bell, Alice. 2016. "Interactional Metalepsis and Unnatural Narratology." *Narrative* 24 (3): 294–310.
Bell, Alice, and Astrid Ensslin. 2011. "'I Know What It Was. You Know What It Was': Second-Person Narration In Hypertext Fiction." *Narrative* 19 (3): 311–329.
Ben-Merre, David. 2011. "'I'm So Vain I Bet I Think This Song Is About Myself': Carly Simon, Pop Music and the Problematic 'I' of Lyric Poetry." In *Metalepsis in Popular Culture*, edited by Karin Kukkonen and Sonja Klimek, 65–82. Berlin, New York: De Gruyter.
Bennett, Tony. 1979. *Formalism and Marxism*. New York, NY: Methuen.
Benveniste, Emile. 1971. *Problems in General Linguistics*. Translated by Mary Elizabeth Meek. Coral Gables: University of Miami Press.
Bergson, Henri. 1980 [first French ed. 1900]. "Laughter." In *Comedy*, edited by Wylie Sypher, 61–190. Baltimore, MD: Johns Hopkins University Press.
Berkeley, George. 1957 [1710]. *A Treatise Concerning the Principles of Human Knowledge*. Indianapolis, IN: Bobbs-Merrill.
Bessière, Jean. 2005. "Récit de fiction, transition discursive, présentation actuelle du récit, ou que le récit de fiction est toujours métaleptique." In *Métalepses: Entorses au pacte de la représentation*, edited by John Pier and Jean-Marie Schaeffer, 279–294. Paris: Éd. de l'EHESS.
Bloom, Harold. 1975. *A Map of Misreading*. New York: Oxford University Press.
Bloom, Harold, ed. 1987. *Laurence Sterne's Tristram Shandy*. New York: Chelsea House.
Blum, Joachim. 2001. *Things and Opinions in Tristram Shandy*. Trier: WVT.
Bolter, Jay D., and Richard Grusin. 1999. *Remediation: Understanding New Media*. Cambridge, MA: MIT Press.
Booth, Wayne. 1952. "The Self-Conscious Narrator in Comic Fiction before Tristram Shandy." *PMLA* 67 (2): 163–185.
Bordwell, David. 1985. *Narration in the Fiction Film*. Madison: University of Wisconsin Press.
Borges, Jorge L. 1964 [1962]. *Labyrinths: Selected Stories & Other Writings*. Edited by Donald A. Yates and James East Irby. New York: New Directions.
Brontë, Charlotte. 1996 [1847]. *Jane Eyre*. Edited by Beth Newman. Boston, MA: Bedford Books of St. Martin's Press.
Brontë, Emily. 1992 [1847]. *Wuthering Heights*. Edited by Linda H. Peterson. Boston, MA: Bedford Books of St. Martin's Press.

Brook, Andrew. 2001. "Kant, Self-Awareness and Self-Reference." In *Self-Reference and Self-Awareness*, edited by Andrew Brook and Richard C. DeVidi, 9–30. Amsterdam, Philadelphia: John Benjamins.

Brook, Andrew. 2006. "Kant: A Unified Representational Base for All Consciousness." In *Self-Representational Approaches to Consciousness*, edited by Uriah Kriegel and Kenneth Williford, 89–110. Cambridge, MA: MIT Press.

Brook, Andrew, and Richard C. DeVidi, eds. 2001. *Self-Reference and Self-Awareness*. Amsterdam, Philadelphia: John Benjamins.

Brooke-Rose, Christine. 1975. *Thru*. London: H. Hamilton.

Brooks, Mel. *Blazing Saddles*. USA: Warner Bros, 1974.

Brooks, Mel. *Spaceballs*. USA: Metro-Goldwyn-Mayer, 1987.

Brooks, Mel. *Robin Hood*: Men in Tights. USA: Columbia, 1993.

Bruns, Gerald L. 1992. *Hermeneutics, Ancient and Modern*. New Haven: Yale University Press.

Bunn, Cullen, and Dalibor Talajic. 2012. *Deadpool Kills the Marvel Universe*. New York: Marvel Enterprises.

Burkhardt, Armin. 1992. "Metalepsis." In *Historisches Wörterbuch der Rhetorik*, edited by Gert Ueding, Gregor Kalivoda, Franz-Hubert Robling, and Heike Mayer, 1087–1099. Tübingen: Niemeyer.

Butler, Judith. 1990. *Gender Trouble: Feminism and the Subversion of Identity*. New York: Routledge.

Butler, Judith. 1993. *Bodies that Matter: On the Discursive Limits of "Sex"*. New York: Routledge.

Butler, Judith. 1997. *Excitable Speech: A Politics of the Performative*. New York: Routledge.

Byron, George Gordon Byron. 1875. *The Works of Lord Byron: In Verse and Prose*. Edited by Fitz-Greene Halleck. New York: World Publishing House.

Call of Duty: Black Ops. 2010. Xbox 360. Los Angeles, CA: Activision.

Carnap, Rudolf. 1958. *Introduction to Symbolic Logic and its Applications*. New York, NY: Dover.

Carroll, Jonathan. 2000. *The Land of Laughs*. London: Millenium.

Carter, Angela. 1987 [1974]. *Fireworks: Nine Profane Pieces*. London: Virago Modern Classics.

Carter, Angela. 1987 [1974]. "The Loves of Lady Purple." In *Fireworks: Nine Profane Pieces*, 23–38. London: Virago Modern Classics.

Carter, Angela. 2011 [1972]. *The Infernal Desire Machines of Doctor Hoffman*. London: Penguin.

Cash, Arthur H. 1986. *Laurence Sterne: The Later Years*. London: Methuen.

Cash, Arthur H., and John M. Stedmond, eds. 1971. *The Winged Skull: Papers from the Laurence Sterne Bicentenary Conference*. London: Methuen.

Castañeda, Hector-Neri. 1966. "'He': A Study on the Logic of Self-Consciousness." *Ratio* (8): 130–157.

Cervantes Saavedra, Miguel de. 1963 [first Spanish ed. 1605/1615]. *Adventures of Don Quixote de la Mancha*. Baltimore: Penguin Books.

Chaplin, Charlie. *The Great Dictator*. USA: United Artists, 1940.

Chatman, Seymour. 1978. *Story and Discourse: Narrative Structure in Fiction and Film*. Ithaca, NY: Cornell Univ. Press.

Chatman, Seymour. 1990. *Coming to Terms: The Rhetoric of Narrative in Fiction and Film*. Ithaca, NY: Cornell University Press.

Chihaia, Matei. 2011. *Der Golem-Effekt: Orientierung und phantastische Immersion im Zeitalter des Kinos*. Bielefeld: Transcript.

Chopin, Kate. 2008. *The Awakening & Other Short Stories*. Edited by Philip M. Parker. San Diego, CA: Icon Classics.

Cohn, Dorrit. 2005. "Métalepse et mise en abyme." In *Métalepses: Entorses au pacte de la représentation*, edited by John Pier and Jean-Marie Schaeffer, 121–130. Paris: Éd. de l'EHESS.

Cohn, Dorrit. 2012 [2005]. "Metalepsis and Mise en Abyme." Translated by Lewis S. Gleich. *Narrative* 20 (1): 105–114.

Coleridge, Samuel T. 1983 [1817]. *Biographia Literaria, Or, Biographical Sketches of My Literary Life and Opinions*. Ed. James Engell and Walter Jackson Bate. London, Princeton: Routledge & Princeton University Press.

Conrad, Joseph. 1995 [1899]. *Heart of Darkness: With the Congo Diary*. Edited by Robert Hampson. London, New York: Penguin Books.

Cortázar, Julio. 1967 [first Spanish ed. 1964]. "Continuity of Parks." In *End of the Game and Other Stories*, edited by Paul Blackburn, 63–65. New York: Pantheon Books.

Cortázar, Julio. 1967. *End of the Game and Other Stories*. Edited by Paul Blackburn. New York: Pantheon Books.

Coste, Didier, and John Pier. 2009. "Narrative Levels." In *Handbook of Narratology*, edited by Peter Hühn, John Pier, Wolf Schmid, and Jörg Schönert, 295–308. Berlin, New York: De Gruyter.

Craven, Wes. *Wes Craven's The Hills Have Eyes*. USA: Blood Relations Co., 1977.

Culler, Jonathan. 1981. "Story and Discourse in the Analysis of Narrative." In *The Pursuit of Signs: Semiotics, Literature, Deconstruction*, edited by Jonathan Culler, 169–187. Ithaca, NY: Cornell Univ. Press.

Culler, Jonathan, ed. 1981. *The Pursuit of Signs: Semiotics, Literature, Deconstruction*. Ithaca, NY: Cornell University Press.

Cummings, Brian. 2007. "Metalepsis: The Boundaries of Metaphor." In *Renaissance Figures of Speech*, edited by Sylvia Adamson, Gavin Alexander, and Katrin Ettenhuber, 217–236. Cambridge: Cambridge University Press.

Currie, Mark, ed. 1995. *Metafiction*. London: Longman.

Currie, Mark. 1998. *Postmodern Narrative Theory*. New York, NY: St. Martin's Press.

Dahlberg, Leif. 2010. "Put a Tiger in Your Text: Metalepsis and Media Discourse." *Nordicom Review* (31): 103–114.

Danielewski, Mark Z. 2000. *House of Leaves*. New York, NY: Pantheon Books.

Darby, David. 2001. "Form and Context: An Essay in the History of Narratology." *Poetics Today* 22 (4): 829–852.

Davis, Robert G. 1971. "Sterne and the Delineation of the Modern Novel." In *The Winged Skull: Papers from the Laurence Sterne Bicentenary Conference*, edited by Arthur H. Cash and John M. Stedmond, 21–40. London: Methuen.

de Bourcier, Simon. 2012. *Pynchon and Relativity: Narrative Time in Thomas Pynchon's Later Novels*. London: Continuum.

de Jong, Irene. 2009. "Metalepsis in Ancient Greek Literature." In *Narratology and Interpretation: The Content of Narrative Form in Ancient Literature*, edited by Jonas Grethlein and Antonios Rengakos, 87–115. Berlin, New York: De Gruyter.

de Man, Paul. 1979. *Allegories of Reading: Figural Language in Rousseau, Nietzsche, Rilke, and Proust*. New Haven, CT: Yale University Press.

de Man, Paul. 1979. "Rhetoric of Tropes." In *Allegories of Reading: Figural Language in Rousseau, Nietzsche, Rilke, and Proust*, 103–118. New Haven, CT: Yale University Press.

Defoe, Daniel. 2001. *Robinson Crusoe*. Edited by John Richetti. Penguin Classics. London: Penguin.
Derrida, Jacques. 1977. "Signature, Event, Context." *Glyph* (1): 172–197.
Derrida, Jacques. 1992 [first French ed. 1984]. "Before the Law." In *Acts of Literature*, edited by Derek Attridge, 183–220. New York, NY: Routledge.
Devitt, M. 1991. *Realism and Truth*. Princeton, NJ: Princeton University Press.
Dilthey, Wilhelm. 1976. *Selected Writings*. Edited by H. P. Rickman. Cambridge: Cambridge University Press.
Dorje, Gyurme. 2005. "Brief Literary History of the *Tibetan Book of the Dead*." In *The Tibetan Book of the Dead [English Title]: The Great Liberation by Hearing in the Intermediate States [Tibetan Title]*, edited by Graham Coleman and Thupten Jinpa, xl-li. London: Penguin.
Dutt, Carsten. 1995. *Hans-Georg Gadamer im Gespräch*. Heidelberg: Universitätsverlag C. Winter.
Eco, Umberto. 1983 [first Italian ed. 1980]. *The Name of the Rose*. Translated by William Weaver. New York NY: Harcourt Brace Jovanovich.
Edelman, Lee. 2004. *No Future: Queer Theory and the Death Drive*. Durham: Duke University Press.
Eisner, Will. 1980. *The Spirit*. Park Forest, IL: Ken Pierce.
Else, Gerald F. 1957. *Aristotle's Poetics*. Leiden: BRILL.
Evans, Gareth. 1982. *The Varieties of Reference*. Edited by John McDowell. Oxford: Clarendon.
Faris, J. A. 1996. *The Paradoxes of Zeno*. Aldershot: Avebury.
Fauconnier, Gilles. 1994. *Mental Spaces: Aspects of Meaning Construction in Natural Language*. Cambridge: Cambridge University Press.
Fauconnier, Gilles. 1997. *Mappings in Thought and Language*. Cambridge: Cambridge University Press.
Federman, Raymond. 1976. *Take It or Leave It: An Exaggerated Second-Hand Tale to Be Read Aloud Either Standing or Sitting*. Tuscaloosa, AL: University of Alabama Press.
Feyersinger, Erwin. 2011. "Metaleptic TV Crossovers." In *Metalepsis in Popular Culture*, edited by Karin Kukkonen and Sonja Klimek, 127–157. Berlin, New York: De Gruyter.
Feyersinger, Erwin 2012. "The Conceptual Integration Network of Metalepsis." In *Blending and the Study of Narrative: Approaches and Applications*, edited by Marcus Hartner and Ralf Schneider, 173–198. Berlin, Boston: De Gruyter.
Fforde, Jasper. 2001. *The Eyre Affair*. London: Hodder and Stoughton.
Fielding, Henry. 1999 [1741/1742]. *Joseph Andrews and Shamela*. Edited by Judith Hawley. London: Penguin Books.
Fielding, Henry. 2011 [1749]. *The History of Tom Jones, a Foundling*. Edited by Thomas Keymer and Alice Wakely. Cambridge: Proquest.
Figal, Günter, ed. 2007. *Hans-Georg Gadamer: Wahrheit und Methode*. Berlin: Akad.-Verlag.
Flaubert, Gustave. 2003 [first French ed. 1857]. *Madame Bovary*. Edited by Geoffrey Wall. London, New York: Penguin Books.
Fletcher, Angus, and John Hollander. 1993. "Metalepsis or Transumption." In *The New Princeton Encyclopedia of Poetry and Poetics*, edited by Alex Preminger, 759–760. Princeton, NJ: Princeton University Press.
Fludernik, Monika. 1996. *Towards a "Natural" Narratology*. London: Routledge.
Fludernik, Monika. 2000. "Beyond Structuralism in Narratology: Recent Developments and New Horizons in Narrative Theory." *Anglistik* 11 (1): 83–96.

Fludernik, Monika. 2003a. "Metanarrative and Metafictional Commentary: From Metadiscursivity to Metanarration and Metafiction." *Poetica: Zeitschrift für Sprach- und Literaturwissenschaft* 35 (1–2): 1–39.
Fludernik, Monika. 2003b. "Scene Shift, Metalepsis, and the Metaleptic Mode." *Style* 37 (4): 382–400.
Fludernik, Monika. 2005. "Histories of Narrative Theory (II): From Structuralism to the Present." In *A Companion to Narrative Theory*, edited by James Phelan and Peter J. Rabinowitz, 36–59. Malden, MA: Blackwell.
Fowles, John. 1987 [1969]. *The French Lieutenant's Woman*. London: Pan Books.
Fricke, Harald. 2003. "Potenzierung." In *Reallexikon der Deutschen Literaturwissenschaft*, edited by Jan-Dirk Müller, 144–147. Berlin, New York: De Gruyter.
Gadamer, Hans-Georg. 1986a [first German ed. 1972]. "Poetry and Mimesis." In *The Relevance of the Beautiful and Other Essays*, edited by Robert Bernasconi and translated by Nicholas Walker, 116–122. Cambridge: Cambridge University Press.
Gadamer, Hans-Georg. 1986b [first German ed. 1977]. "The Play of Art." In *The Relevance of the Beautiful and Other Essays*, edited by Robert Bernasconi and translated by Nicholas Walker, 123–130. Cambridge: Cambridge University Press.
Gadamer, Hans-Georg. 1999a. *Gesammelte Werke Band 1: Wahrheit und Methode*. Tübingen: Mohr.
Gadamer, Hans-Georg. 1999b. *Gesammelte Werke Band 2: Wahrheit und Methode*: Ergänzungen, Register. Tübingen: Mohr.
Gadamer, Hans-Georg. 2013 [first German ed. 1960]. *Truth and Method*. London: Bloomsbury.
Gass, William H. 1970. *Fiction and the Figures of Life*. New York: Knopf.
Gavins, Joanna. 2007. *Text World Theory: An Introduction*. Edinburgh: Edinburgh University Press.
Gebauer, Gunter, and Christoph Wulf. 1995. *Mimesis: Culture, Art, Society*. Berkeley: University of California Press.
Genette, Gérard. 1980. *Narrative Discourse: An Essay in Method*. Translated by Jane E. Lewin. Ithaca, NY: Cornell University Press.
Genette, Gérard. 1988. *Narrative Discourse Revisited*. Translated by Jane E. Lewin. Ithaca, NY: Cornell University Press.
Genette, Gérard. 2004. *Métalepse: De la figure à la fiction*. Poétique. Paris: Seuil.
Gibson, Andrew. 1996. *Towards a Postmodern Theory of Narrative*. Edinburgh: Edinburgh University Press.
Gide, André. 1966 [first French ed. 1925]. *The Counterfeiters*. Translated by Dorothy Bussy. London: Penguin Books.
Goodman, Nelson. 1978. *Ways of Worldmaking*. Hassocks, UK: Harvester Press.
Grethlein, Jonas, and Antonios Rengakos, eds. 2009. *Narratology and Interpretation: The Content of Narrative Form in Ancient Literature*. Berlin, New York: Walter de Gruyter.
Hamburger, Käte. 1977 [1957]. *Die Logik der Dichtung*. Stuttgart: Klett-Cotta.
Hanebeck, Julian. 2011. "Der ontologische Rahmen von (Re-)Medialisierungen: Metaleptische Echos in Mark Z. Danielewskis House of Leaves." In *Medialisierung des Erzählens im englischsprachigen Roman der Gegenwart: Theoretischer Bezugsrahmen, Genres und Modellinterpretationen*, edited by Ansgar Nünning, 203–218. Trier: WVT.
Harpold, Terry. 2008. "Screw the Grue: Mediality, Metalepsis, Recapture." In *Playing the Past: History and Nostalgia in Video Games*, edited by Laurie N. Taylor and Zach Whalen, 91–108. Nashville, TN: Vanderbilt University Press.

Hartner, Marcus, and Ralf Schneider, eds. 2012. *Blending and the Study of Narrative: Approaches and Applications*. Berlin, Boston: De Gruyter.
Häsner, Bernd. 2005. "Metalepsen: Zur Genese, Systematik und Funktion transgressiver Erzählweisen." http://www.diss.fu-berlin.de/diss/receive/FUDISS_thesis_000000001782. Accessed September 15, 2014.
Hauthal, Janine, Julijana Nadj, Ansgar Nünning, and Henning Peters. 2007. "Metaisierung in Literatur und anderen Medien: Begriffsklärungen, Typologien, Funktionspotentiale und Forschungsdesiderate." In *Metaisierung in Literatur und anderen Medien: Theoretische Grundlagen, historische Perspektiven, Metagattungen, Funktionen*, edited by Janine Hauthal, Julijana Nadj, Ansgar Nünning, and Henning Peters, 1–24. Berlin, New York: De Gruyter.
Hawes, Clement. 2005. *The British Eighteenth Century and Global Critique*. New York, NY: Palgrave Macmillan.
Heidegger, Martin. 1967 [first German ed. 1927]. *Being and Time*. Edited and translated by John Macquarrie & Edward Robinson. Oxford: Blackwell.
Heinen, Sandra. 2002. "Postmoderne und poststrukturalistische (Dekonstruktionen) der Narratologie." In *Neue Ansätze in der Erzähltheorie*, edited by Ansgar Nünning, 243–264. Trier: WVT.
Heinen, Sandra, and Roy Sommer, eds. 2009. *Narratology in the Age of Cross-Disciplinary Narrative Research*. Berlin: De Gruyter.
Heise, Ursula K. 1993. *Chronoschisms: Temporality and Contingency in Postmodern Narrative*. Cambridge: Cambridge University Press.
Hempfer, Klaus W. 1982. "Die potentielle Autoreflexivität des narrativen Diskurses und Ariosts Orlando Furioso." In *Erzählforschung: Ein Symposion*, edited by Eberhard Lämmert, 130–156. Stuttgart: Metzler.
Hempfer, Klaus W. 1999. "(Pseudo-)Performatives Erzählen im zeitgenössischen französischen und italienischen Roman." In *Romanistisches Jahrbuch 50*, 158–182
Herman, David. 1997. "Toward a Formal Description of Narrative Metalepsis." *Journal of Literary Semantics* (26): 132–152.
Herman, David, ed. 1999. *Narratologies: New Perspectives on Narrative Analysis*. Columbus, OH: Ohio State University Press.
Herman, David. 1999. "Narratologies: An Introduction." In *Narratologies: New Perspectives on Narrative Analysis*, edited by David Herman, 1–30. Columbus, OH: Ohio State University Press.
Herman, David. 2002. *Story Logic: Problems and Possibilities of Narrative*. Lincoln, NE: University of Nebraska Press.
Herman, David. 2005a. "Histories of Narrative Theory (I): A Genealogy of Early Developments." In *A Companion to Narrative Theory*, edited by James Phelan and Peter J. Rabinowitz, 19–35. Malden, MA: Blackwell.
Herman, David. 2005b. "Structuralist Narratology." In *Routledge Encyclopedia of Narrative Theory*, edited by David Herman, Manfred Jahn, and Marie-Laure Ryan, 571–576. London, New York: Routledge.
Herman, David. 2009. *Basic Elements of Narrative*. Chichester, UK: Wiley-Blackwell.
Herman, David. 2011. "Introduction." In *The Emergence of Mind: Representations of Consciousness in Narrative Discourse in English*, edited by David Herman, 1–42. Lincoln: University of Nebraska Press.

Herman, David, ed. 2012. *Narrative Theory: Core Concepts and Critical Debates.* Columbus, OH: Ohio State University Press.
Herman, David. 2013. *Storytelling and the Sciences of Mind.* Cambridge, MA: MIT Press.
Herman, David, Manfred Jahn, and Marie-Laure Ryan, eds. 2005. *Routledge Encyclopedia of Narrative Theory.* London, New York: Routledge.
His Holiness the Dalai Lama. 2005. "Introductory Commentary." In *The Tibetan Book of the Dead [English Title]: The Great Liberation by Hearing in the Intermediate States [Tibetan Title]*, edited by Graham Coleman and Thupten Jinpa, xv–xxix. London: Penguin.
Hofer, Roberta. 2011. "Metalepsis in Live Performance: Holographic Projections of the Cartoon Band 'Gorillaz' as a Means of Metalepsis." In *Metalepsis in Popular Culture*, edited by Karin Kukkonen and Sonja Klimek, 232–251. Berlin, New York: De Gruyter.
Hofstadter, Douglas R. 1979. *Gödel, Escher, Bach: An Eternal Golden Braid.* Hassocks: Harvester Press.
Hollander, John. 1981. *The Figure of Echo: A Mode of Allusion in Milton and After.* Berkeley: University of California Press.
Holub, Robert. 2005. "Hermeneutics." In *The Cambridge History of Literary Criticism*, edited by Raman Selden, Peter Brooks, Hugh B. Nisbet, and Claude J. Rawson. Cambridge: Cambridge University Press.
Horstkotte, Silke. 2009. "Seeing or Speaking: Visual Narratology and Focalization, Literature To Film." In *Narratology in the Age of Cross-Disciplinary Narrative Research*, edited by Sandra Heinen and Roy Sommer, 170–192. Berlin: De Gruyter.
Howes, Alan B. 1958. *Yorick and the Critics: Sterne's Reputation in England, 1760–1868.* New Haven: Yale University Press.
Huber, Irmtraud. 2014. *Literature after Postmodernism: Reconstructive Fantasies.* New York, NY: Palgrave Macmillan.
Huber, Werner, Martin Middeke, and Hubert Zapf, eds. 2005. *Self-Reflexivity in Literature.* Würzburg: Königshausen & Neumann.
Hühn, Peter, John Pier, Wolf Schmid, and Jörg Schönert, eds. 2009. *Handbook of Narratology.* Berlin, New York: De Gruyter.
Hühn, Peter, Wolf Schmid, and Jörg Schönert, eds. 2009. *Point of View, Perspective, and Focalization: Modeling Mediation in Narrative.* Berlin, New York: De Gruyter.
Hume, David. 1978 [1739–1740]. *A Treatise of Human Nature.* Edited by Lewis A. Selby-Bigge. Oxford: Clarendon Press.
Hutcheon, Linda. 1980. *Narcissistic Narrative: The Metafictional Paradox.* New York: Methuen.
Hutcheon, Linda. 2005. "Reflexivity." In *Routledge Encyclopedia of Narrative Theory*, edited by David Herman, Manfred Jahn, and Marie-Laure Ryan, 494–495. London, New York: Routledge.
Hyams, Peter. *Stay Tuned.* USA: Warner Bros. Pictures, 1992.
Imhof, Rüdiger. 1986. *Contemporary Metafiction: A Poetological Study of Metafiction in English Since 1939.* Heidelberg: Winter.
Iser, Wolfgang. 1988. *Laurence Sterne: Tristram Shandy.* Cambridge, New York: Cambridge University Press.
Jahn, Manfred. 2005. "Cognitive Narratology." In *Routledge Encyclopedia of Narrative Theory*, edited by David Herman, Manfred Jahn, and Marie-Laure Ryan, 67–71. London, New York: Routledge.

Jefferson, D. W. 1992. "Tristram Shandy and the Tradition of Learned Wit." In *New Casebooks: The Life and Opinions of Tristram Shandy, Gentleman: Contemporary Critical Essays*, edited by Melvyn New, 17–35. London: Macmillan.
Jonze, Spike. *Being John Malkovich*. USA: Propaganda Films, 1999.
Kalish, Donald, Richard Montague, Gary Mar, and Robert J. Fogelin, eds. 1992. *Logic: Techniques of Formal Reasoning*. 2nd ed. New York, NY: Oxford Univ. Press.
Kane, Sarah. 2000. *Cleansed*. London: Methuen Publishing.
Kant, Immanuel. 1996 [first German ed. 1781]. *Critique of Pure Reason*. Translated by Werner Pluhar. Indianapolis, IN. Hackett.
Kant, Immanuel. 2007 [first German ed. 1790]. *Critique of Judgement*. Edited by James Meredith and translated by Nicholas Walker. Oxford, New York: Oxford University Press.
Kertscher, Jens. 2002. "'We Understand Differently, If We Understand at All': Gadamer's Ontology of Language Reconsidered." In *Gadamer's Century: Essays in Honor of Hans-Georg Gadamer*, edited by Jeff Malpas, Ulrich Arnswald, and Jens Kertscher, 135–156. Cambridge, MA: MIT Press.
Kindt, Tom, and Hans-Harald Müller. 2003. "Narrative Theory and/or/as Theory of Interpretation." In *What is Narratology? Questions and Answers Regarding the Status of a Theory*, edited by Tom Kindt and Hans-Harald Müller, 205–219. Berlin, New York: De Gruyter.
Kindt, Tom, and Hans-Harald Müller, ed. 2003. *What is Narratology? Questions and Answers Regarding the Status of a Theory*. Berlin, New York: De Gruyter.
Kindt, Tom, and Hans-Harald Müller. 2006. *The Implied Author: Concept and Controversy* Berlin, New York: De Gruyter.
Klaus Meyer-Minnemann. 2005. "Un procédé narratif qui 'produit un effet de bizarrerie': la métalepse littéraire." In *Métalepses: Entorses au pacte de la représentation*, edited by John Pier and Jean-Marie Schaeffer, 133–150. Paris: Éd. de l'EHESS.
Klimek, Sonja. 2009. "Metalepsis and its (Anti-)Illusionist Effects in the Arts, Media and Role-Playing Games." In *Metareference Across Media: Theory and Case Studies*, edited by Werner Wolf, Katharina Bantleon, Jeff Thoss, and Walter Bernhart, 169–182. Amsterdam, New York: Rodopi.
Klimek, Sonja. 2010. *Paradoxes Erzählen: Die Metalepse in der Phantastischen Literatur*. Paderborn: Mentis.
Klimek, Sonja. 2011. "Metalepsis in Fantasy Fiction." In *Metalepsis in Popular Culture*, edited by Karin Kukkonen and Sonja Klimek, 22–40. Berlin: De Gruyter.
Knutsen, Karen P., Sigmund Kvam, and Peter Langemeyer, eds. 2010. *Textsorten und Kulturelle Kompetenz*. Münster: Waxmann.
Koch, Johann S., and Rolf Kloepfer, eds. 2006. *Strukturalismus: Zur Geschichte und Aktualität eines kulturwissenschaftlichen Paradigmas*. Heidelberg: Synchron.
Kockelmans, Joseph. 1991. "Beyond Realism and Idealism: A Response to Patrick A. Heelan." In *Gadamer and Hermeneutics: Science, Culture, Literature; Plato, Heidegger, Barthes, Ricœur, Habermas, Derrida*, edited by Hugh J. Silverman, 229–244. New York, NY: Routledge.
Korthals Altes, Liesbeth. 2014. *Ethos and Narrative Interpretation: The Negotiation of Values in Fiction*. Lincoln, NE: University of Nebraska Press.
Krah, Hans. 2005. "Selbstreferentialität, Selbstbezüglichkeit, Selbstreferenz: Die Begriffe und ihr Bedeutungsspektrum." *Zeitschrift für Semiotik* 27 (1–2): 3–21.
Kriegel, Uriah, and Kenneth Williford, eds. 2006. *Self-Representational Approaches to Consciousness*. Cambridge, MS: MIT Press.

Kuhn, Markus. 2011. *Filmnarratologie: Ein erzähltheoretisches Analysemodell*. Berlin: De Gruyter.
Kukkonen, Karin. 2011a. "Metalepsis in Comics and Graphic Novels." In *Metalepsis in Popular Culture*, edited by Karin Kukkonen and Sonja Klimek, 213–231. Berlin, New York: De Gruyter.
Kukkonen, Karin. 2011b. "Metalepsis in Popular Culture: An Introduction." In *Metalepsis in Popular Culture*, edited by Karin Kukkonen and Sonja Klimek, 1–21. Berlin, New York: De Gruyter.
Kukkonen, Karin, and Sonja Klimek, eds. 2011. *Metalepsis in Popular Culture*. Berlin, New York: De Gruyter.
Lakoff, George, and Mark Johnson. 1980. *Metaphors We Live By*. Chicago, IL: University of Chicago Press.
Lakoff, George, and Mark Turner. 1989. *More than Cool Reason: A Field Guide to Poetic Metaphor*. Chicago, IL: University of Chicago Press.
Lämmert, Eberhard, ed. 1982. *Erzählforschung: Ein Symposion*. Stuttgart: Metzler.
Landfester, Ulrike. 1997. "'… die Zeit selbst ist thöricht geworden …': Ludwig Tiecks Komödie 'Der gestiefelte Kater' (1797) in der Tradition des Spiel im Spiel-Dramas." In *Ludwig Tieck: Literaturprogramm und Lebensinszenierung im Kontext seiner Zeit*, edited by Walter Schmitz, 101–133. Tübingen: Niemeyer.
Langemeyer, Peter. 2010. "Metaleptische Erzählverfahren in Erich Kästners 'Romanen für Kinder'." In *Textsorten und Kulturelle Kompetenz*, edited by Karen P. Knutsen, Sigmund Kvam, and Peter Langemeyer, 297–320. Münster: Waxmann.
Lanham, Richard A. 1968. *A Handlist of Rhetorical Terms: A Guide for Students of English Literature*. Berkeley, CA: University of California Press.
Lanser, Susan S. 1992. *Fictions of Authority: Women Writers and Narrative Voice*. Ithaca, NY: Cornell University Press.
Lanser, Susan S. 2010. "Sapphic Dialogics: Historical Narratology and the Sexuality of Form." In *Postclassical Narratology: Approaches and Analyses*, edited by Jan Alber and Monika Fludernik, 186–205. Columbus, OH: Ohio State University Press.
Laudando, Carla M. 1996. "Deluge of Fragments: Rabelais's 'Fourth book', Sterne's 'Fragment' and Beckett's 'Fizzles'." In *Laurence Sterne in Modernism and Postmodernism*, edited by David Pierce and Peter Jan de Voogd, 157–166. Amsterdam, Atlanta: Rodopi.
Lavocat, Françoise. 2007. "Transfictionnalité, métafiction et métalepse aux XVIe et XVIIe siècles." In *La fiction, suites et variations*, edited by René Audet and Richard St-Gelais, 157–178. Québec: Nota Bene.
Lavocat, Françoise. 2016. *Fait et fiction: Pour une frontière*. Paris: Seuil.
Lawson, Hilary. 1985. *Reflexivity: The Post-Modern Predicament*. La Salle: Open Court.
Leavis, Frank R. 1948. *The Great Tradition: George Eliot, Henry James, Joseph Conrad*. London: Chatto & Windus.
Leitch, Vincent B., ed. 2001. *The Norton Anthology of Theory and Criticism*. New York, NY: Norton.
Lemon, Lee T., Marion J. Reis, and Gary S. Morson, eds. 2012. *Russian Formalist Criticism: Four Essays*. Lincoln, NE: University of Nebraska Press.
Lewis, David K. 1973. *Counterfactuals*. Oxford: Blackwell.
Lewis, David K. 1978. "Truth in Fiction." *American Philosophical Quarterly* (15): 37–46.
Limoges, Jean-Marc. 2008. "Quand Mel dépasse les bornes: d'un usage comique de la métalepse chez Brooks." *Humoresque*. (28): 31–41.

Limoges, Jean-Marc. 2011. "Metalepsis in The Cartoons of Tex Avery: Expanding the Boundaries of Transgression." In *Metalepsis in Popular Culture*, edited by Karin Kukkonen and Sonja Klimek, 196–212. Berlin, New York: De Gruyter.

Luhmann, Niklas. 1995. *Die Kunst der Gesellschaft*. Frankfurt am Main: Suhrkamp.

Lutas Liviu. 2015. "Metalepsis and Participation in Games of Make-Believe." In *How to Make Believe: The Fictional Truths of the Representational Arts*, edited by J. Alexander Bareis and Lene Nordrum, 203–222. Berlin, New York: De Gruyter.

Malick, Terrence. *The Thin Red Line*. USA: Phoenix Pictures, 1998.

Malina, Debra. 2002. *Breaking the Frame: Metalepsis and the Construction of the Subject*. Columbus, OH: Ohio State Univ. Press.

Malpas, Jeff. 2002. "Gadamer, Davidson, and the Ground of Understanding." In *Gadamer's Century: Essays in Honor of Hans-Georg Gadamer*, edited by Jeff Malpas, Ulrich Arnswald, and Jens Kertscher, 195–215. Cambridge, MA: MIT Press.

Malpas, Jeff. 2010. "The Beginning of Understanding: Event, Place, Truth." In *Consequences of Hermeneutics: Fifty Years after Gadamer's Truth and Method*, edited by Jeff Malpas and Santiago Zabala, 261–280. Evanston: Northwestern University Press.

Malpas, Jeff, Ulrich Arnswald, and Jens Kertscher, eds. 2002. *Gadamer's Century: Essays in Honor of Hans-Georg Gadamer*. Cambridge, MA: MIT Press.

Malpas, Jeff, and Santiago Zabala, eds. 2010. *Consequences of Hermeneutics: Fifty Years after Gadamer's Truth and Method*. Evanston: Northwestern University Press.

Martínez, Matías. 2012. "Dos Passos Instead of Goethe! Some Observations on How the History of Narratology is and Ought to be Conceptualized." *DIEGESIS: Interdisciplinary E-Journal for Narrative Research* 1 (1): 134–142. https://www.diegesis.uni-wuppertal.de/index.php/diegesis/article/view/93. Accessed September 14, 2014.

Mayer, Robert. 1997. *History and the Early English Novel: Matters of Fact from Bacon to Defoe*. Cambridge: Cambridge University Press.

Mayoux, Jean-Jacques. 1971. "Variations on the Time-Sense in Tristram Shandy." In *The Winged Skull: Papers from the Laurence Sterne Bicentenary Conference*, edited by Arthur H. Cash and John M. Stedmond, 3–18. London: Methuen.

McHale, Brian. 1987. *Postmodernist Fiction*. New York: Methuen.

McHale, Brian. 2009. "Speech Representation." In *Handbook of Narratology*, edited by Peter Hühn, John Pier, Wolf Schmid, and Jörg Schönert, 434–446. Berlin, New York: De Gruyter.

McQuillan, Martin. 2000. *The Narrative Reader*. London, New York: Routledge.

Meister, Jan Christoph. 2003. "The Metalepticon: A Computational Approach to Metalepsis." Accessed September 08, 2014. http://www.jcmeister.de/downloads/texts/jcm-metalepticon.html.

Meister, Jan Christoph. 2005. "Le Metalepticon: une étude informatique de la métalepse." In *Métalepses: Entorses au pacte de la représentation*, edited by John Pier and Jean-Marie Schaeffer, 225–246. Paris: Éd. de l'EHESS.

Meister, Jan Christoph. 2008. *Computing Action: A Narratological Approach*. Berlin, New York: De Gruyter.

Meister, Jan Christoph. 2009. "Narratology." In *Handbook of Narratology*, edited by Peter Hühn, John Pier, Wolf Schmid, and Jörg Schönert, 329–350. Berlin, New York: De Gruyter.

Meister, Jan Christoph, Tom Kindt, and Wilhelm Schernus, eds. 2005. *Narratology Beyond Literary Criticism: Mediality, Disciplinarity*. Berlin, New York: De Gruyter.

Melanchthon, Philipp. 2001 [1531]. *Elementa Rhetorices*. Edited by Volkhard Wels. Berlin: Weidler.

Melberg, Arne. 1995. *Theories of Mimesis*. Cambridge, New York: Cambridge University Press.
Miller, D. A. 2003. *Jane Austen or the Secret of Style*. Princeton, NJ: Princeton University Press.
Miller, J. H. 1976. "The Linguistic Moment in the 'Wreck of the Deutschland'." In *The New Criticism and After*, edited by Thomas D. Young, 47–60. Charlottesville, VA: University Press of Virginia.
Mitchell, William John Thomas, ed. 1981. *On Narrative*. Chicago, IL: University of Chicago Press.
Moglen, Helene. 1975. *The Philosophical Irony of Laurence Sterne*. Gainesville, FL: University Presses of Florida.
Möllendorff, Peter v., and Ute E. Eisen. 2013. *Über die Grenze: Metalepse in Text- und Bildmedien des Altertums*. Berlin, Boston: De Gruyter.
Mootz, Francis J., and George H. Taylor, eds. 2011. *Gadamer and Ricœur: Critical Horizons for Contemporary Hermeneutics*. London, New York: Continuum.
Morreall, John. 2009. *Comic Relief: A Comprehensive Philosophy of Humor*. Malden, MA: Wiley-Blackwell.
Morrison, Grant. 2003. *Animal Man: Deus Ex Machina*. New York: DC Comics.
Morsch, Thomas. 2012. "Permanent Metalepsis: Pushing the Boundaries of Narrative Space." In *Screen Dynamics: Mapping the Borders of Cinema*, edited by Gertrud Koch, Volker Pantenburg and Simon Rothöhler, 108–125. Wien: Synema.
Müller, Jan-Dirk, ed. 2003. *Reallexikon der Deutschen Literaturwissenschaft*. Berlin, New York: De Gruyter.
Nelles, William. 1992. "Stories within Stories: Narrative Levels and Embedded Narrative." *Studies in the Literary Imagination* 25 (1): 79–96.
Nelles, William. 1997. *Frameworks: Narrative Levels and Embedded Narrative*. New York: P. Lang.
Neumann, Birgit, and Ansgar Nünning. 2009. "Metanarration and Metafiction." In *Handbook of Narratology*, edited by Peter Hühn, John Pier, Wolf Schmid, and Jörg Schönert, 204–211. Berlin, New York: De Gruyter.
New, Melvyn. 1969. *Laurence Sterne as Satirist: A Reading of Tristram Shandy*. Gainesville, FL: University of Florida Press.
New, Melvyn. 1992. "Introduction." In *The Life and Opinions of Tristram Shandy, Gentleman*, edited by Melvyn New, 1–16. Basingstoke Hampshire, London: Macmillan.
New, Melvyn, ed. 1992. *New Casebooks: The Life and Opinions of Tristram Shandy, Gentleman: Contemporary Critical Essays*. London: Macmillan.
New, Melvyn, ed. 1992. *The Life and Opinions of Tristram Shandy, Gentleman*. Basingstoke Hampshire, London: Macmillan.
Newmeyer, Frederick J. 2000. *Language Form and Language Function*. Cambridge, MA: MIT Press.
Nietzsche, Friedrich W. 1986 [first German ed. 1878]. *Human, all Too Human: A Book for Free Spirits*. Translated by R. J. Hollingdale. Cambridge, New York: Cambridge University Press.
Nietzsche, Friedrich W. 1989 [first German ed. 1886]. *Beyond Good and Evil: Prelude to a Philosophy of the Future*. Edited and translated by Walter Arnold Kaufmann. New York: Vintage Books.
Nietzsche, Friedrich W. 1992 [first German ed. 1896]. "On Truth and Lies in a Nonmoral Sense." In *Philosophy and Truth: Selections from Nietzsche's Notebook of the Early 1870's*, edited by Daniel Breazeale, 79–91. New Jersey: Humanities Press International.
Nietzsche, Friedrich W. 1992. *Philosophy and Truth: Selections from Nietzsche's Notebook of the Early 1870's*. Edited by Daniel Breazeale. New Jersey: Humanities Press International.

Nietzsche, Friedrich W. 2006 [first German ed. 1882]. *The Gay Science*. Mineola, NY: Dover Publications.
Nordlund, Marcus. 2002. "Consilient Literary Interpretation." *Philosophy and Literature* (26.2): 312–333.
Nöth, Winfried. 2009. "Metareference from a Semiotic Perspective." In *Metareference Across Media: Theory and Case Studies*, edited by Werner Wolf, Katharina Bantleon, Jeff Thoss, and Walter Bernhart, 89–120. Amsterdam, New York: Rodopi.
Nünning, Ansgar. 1995. *Von historischer Fiktion zu historiographischer Metafiktion*. Trier: WVT.
Nünning, Ansgar. 2001. "Metanarration als Lakune der Erzähltheorie: Definition, Typologie und Grundriss einer Funktionsgeschichte metanarrativer Erzähleräußerungen." *Arbeiten aus Anglistik und Amerikanistik* 26 (2): 125–164.
Nünning, Ansgar, ed. 2002. *Neue Ansätze in der Erzähltheorie*. Trier: WVT.
Nünning, Ansgar. 2003. "Narratology or Narratologies? Taking Stock of Recent Developments, Critique and Modest Proposals for Future Usages of the Term." In *What is Narratology? Questions and Answers Regarding the Status of a Theory*, edited by Tom Kindt and Hans-Harald Müller, 239–275. Berlin, New York: De Gruyter.
Nünning, Ansgar. 2004. "Towards a Definition, a Typology and an Outline of the Functions of Metanarrative Commentary." In *The Dynamics of Narrative Form: Studies in Anglo-American Narratology*, edited by John Pier, 11–57. Berlin, New York: De Gruyter.
Nünning, Ansgar. 2009. "Surveying Contextualist and Cultural Narratologies: Towards an Outline of Approaches, Concepts and Potentials." In *Narratology in the Age of Cross-Disciplinary Narrative Research*, edited by Sandra Heinen and Roy Sommer, 48–70. Berlin: De Gruyter.
Nünning, Ansgar, ed. 2011. *Medialisierung des Erzählens im englischsprachigen Roman der Gegenwart: Theoretischer Bezugsrahmen, Genres und Modellinterpretationen*. Trier: WVT.
Nünning, Vera, and Ansgar Nünning. 1998. *Englische Literatur des 18. Jahrhunderts*. Stuttgart: Klett.
O'Brien, Flann. 1966 [1939]. *At Swim-Two-Birds*. London: MacGibbon & Kee.
Olson, Greta, ed. 2011. *Current Trends in Narratology*. Berlin: De Gruyter.
O'Neill, Patrick. 1994. *Fictions of Discourse: Reading Narrative Theory*. Toronto: University of Toronto Press.
Ostovich, Helen. 1992. "Reader as Hobby-Horse in Tristram Shandy." In *New Casebooks: The Life and Opinions of Tristram Shandy, Gentleman: Contemporary Critical Essays*, edited by Melvyn New, 155–173. London: Macmillan.
Padmasaṃbhava, and Terton Karma Lingpa. 2005. *The Tibetan Book of the Dead [English Title]: The Great Liberation by Hearing in the Intermediate States [Tibetan Title]*. Edited by Graham Coleman and Thupten Jinpa. London: Penguin.
Patrick, Brian D. 2008. "Metalepsis and Paradoxical Narration in Don Quixote: A Reconsideration." *Letras Hispanas* 5 (2): 116–132.
Perry, John. 1979. "The Problem of the Essential Indexical." *Noûs* (13): 3–21.
Petterson, Bo. 2009. "Narratology and Hermeneutics: Forging the Missing Link." In *Narratology in the Age of Cross-Disciplinary Narrative Research*, edited by Sandra Heinen and Roy Sommer, 11–34. Berlin, New York: De Gruyter.
Phelan, James. 1996. *Narrative as Rhetoric: Technique, Audiences, Ethics, Ideology*. Columbus, OH: Ohio State University Press.
Phelan, James, and Peter J. Rabinowitz, eds. 2005. *A Companion to Narrative Theory*. Malden, MA: Blackwell.

Pier, John, ed. 2004. *The Dynamics of Narrative Form: Studies in Anglo-American Narratology.* Berlin, New York: De Gruyter.
Pier, John. 2009. "Metalepsis." In *Handbook of Narratology*, edited by Peter Hühn, John Pier, Wolf Schmid, and Jörg Schönert, 190–203. Berlin, New York: De Gruyter.
Pier, John. 2011. "Afterword." In *Metalepsis in Popular Culture*, edited by Karin Kukkonen and Sonja Klimek, 268–276. Berlin, New York: De Gruyter.
Pier, John, and Jean-Marie Schaeffer, eds. 2005. *Métalepses: Entorses au pacte de la représentation.* Paris: Éd. de l'EHESS.
Pierce, David, and Voogd, Peter Jan de, eds. 1996. *Laurence Sterne in Modernism and Postmodernism.* Amsterdam, Atlanta: Rodopi.
Plato. 1994. *Republic.* Edited by Robin Waterfield. Oxford, New York: Oxford University Press.
Preminger, Alex, ed. 1993. *The New Princeton Encyclopedia of Poetry and Poetics.* Princeton, NJ: Princeton University Press.
Prince, Gerald. 1990. "On Narratology (Past, Present, Future)." *French Literature Series* (17): 1–14.
Prince, Gerald. 1995. "Narratology." In *The Cambridge History of Literary Criticism*, edited by Raman Selden, Peter Brooks, Hugh B. Nisbet, and Claude J. Rawson, 110–130. Cambridge: Cambridge University Press.
Prince, Gerald. 2003. *A Dictionary of Narratology: Revised Edition.* Lincoln, NE: University of Nebraska Press.
Prince, Gerald. 2003. "Surveying Narratology." In *What is Narratology? Questions and Answers Regarding the Status of a Theory*, edited by Tom Kindt and Hans-Harald Müller, 205–219. Berlin, New York: De Gruyter.
Prince, Gerald. 2005. "On a Postcolonial Narratology." In *A Companion to Narrative Theory*, edited by James Phelan and Peter J. Rabinowitz, 372–381. Malden, MA: Blackwell.
Prince, Gerald. 2006. "Disturbing Frames." *Poetics Today* (27): 625–630.
Puntel, Lorenz B., and Alan White. 2008. *Structure and Being: A Theoretical Framework for a Systematic Philosophy.* University Park: Pennsylvania State University Press.
Putnam, Hilary. 1981. *Reason, Truth and History.* Cambridge: Cambridge University Press.
Quintilian. 2001. *The Orator's Education.* 5 vols. Translated by D. A. Russell. Cambridge, Mass. Harvard University Press.
Rabinowitz, Peter. 1977. "Truth in Fiction: A Reexamination of Audiences." *Critical Inquiry* (4): 121–141.
Rhys, Jean. 1998 [1966]. *Wide Sargasso Sea.* Edited by Judith L. Raiskin. London, New York: W.W. Norton.
Richardson, Brian. 2006. *Unnatural Voices: Extreme Narration in Modern and Contemporary Fiction.* Columbus, OH: Ohio State University Press.
Richardson, Samuel. 1985. *Pamela, or Virtue Rewarded.* Edited by Peter Sabor. London: Penguin Books.
Richardson, Brian, et al. 2010. "Unnatural Narratives, Unnatural Narratology: Beyond Mimetic Models." *Narrative* (18.2): 113–136.
Richetti, John J. 1999. *The English Novel in History: 1700–1780.* London, New York: Routledge.
Ricks, Christopher. 1997. "Introductory Essay." In *The Life and Opinions of Tristram Shandy, Gentleman*, edited by Melvyn New and Joan New, vii–xxv. London, New York: Penguin Books.
Ricœur, Paul. 1963. "Structure et herméneutique." *Esprit* (322): 596–635.

Ricœur, Paul. 1981a [1980]. "Narrative Time." In *On Narrative*, edited by William John Thomas Mitchell, 165–186. Chicago, IL: University of Chicago Press.

Ricœur, Paul. 1981b [first French ed. 1973]. "Hermeneutics and the Critique of Ideology." In *Hermeneutics and the Human Sciences: Essays on Language, Action and Interpretation*, edited and translated by John B. Thompson, 61–100. Cambridge: Cambridge University Press.

Ricœur, Paul. 1984–1988 [first French ed. 1983–1985]. Vols. 1–3. *Time and Narrative*. Translated by Kathleen McLaughlin and David Pellauer. Chicago: University of Chicago Press.

Ricœur, Paul. 1991 [first French ed. 1986]. *From Text to Action: Essays in Hermeneutics, II*. Edited by Kathleen Blamey and John B. Thompson. London: Continuum.

Ricœur, Paul. 2002. "Temporal Distance and Death in History." In *Gadamer's Century: Essays in Honor of Hans-Georg Gadamer*, edited by Jeff Malpas, Ulrich Arnswald, and Jens Kertscher, 239–256. Cambridge, MA: MIT Press.

Rimmon-Kenan, Shlomith. 1983. *Narrative Fiction: Contemporary Poetics*. London, New York: Methuen.

Risser, James. 1997. *Hermeneutics and the Voice of the Other: Re-Reading Gadamer's Philosophical Hermeneutics*. Albany, NY: State University of New York Press.

Robbe-Grillet, Alain. 1957. *La Jalousie: Roman*. Paris: Les Éd. de Minuit.

Robertson, Scott. 2010. *Henry Fielding: Literary and Theological Misplacement*. Oxford: Peter Lang.

Römer, Inga. 2010. *Das Zeitdenken bei Husserl, Heidegger und Ricœur*. Dordrecht: Springer.

Ronen, Ruth. 2005. "Theories of Realism." In *Routledge Encyclopedia of Narrative Theory*, edited by David Herman, Manfred Jahn, and Marie-Laure Ryan, 486–491. London, New York: Routledge.

Ross, Ian C. 2001. *Laurence Sterne: A Life*. Oxford: Oxford University Press.

Roth, Eli. *Hostel*. USA: Next Entertainment, 2005.

Roussin, Philippe. 2005. "Rhétorique de la métalepse, états de cause, typologie, récit." In *Métalepses: Entorses au pacte de la représentation*, edited by John Pier and Jean-Marie Schaeffer, 37–58. Paris: Éd. de l'EHESS.

Rubik, Margarete. 2005. "Provocative and Unforgettable: Peter Carey's Short Fiction. A Cognitive Apporach." *European Journal of English Studies* 9 (2): 169–184.

Rubik, Margarete. 2007. "Invasions into Literary Texts, Re-Plotting and Transfictional Migration in Jasper Fforde's The Eyre Affair." In *A Breath of Fresh Eyre: Intertextual and Intermedial Reworkings of Jane Eyre*, edited by Margarete Rubik & Elke Mettinger-Schartmann, 167–180. Amsterdam und New York: Rodopi.

Russell, Bertrand. 1903. *The Principles of Mathematics*. Cambridge: Cambridge University Press.

Russell, Bertrand. 1908. "Mathematical Logic as Based on the Theory of Types." *American Journal of Mathematics* 30 (3): 222–262.

Ryan, Marie-Laure. 1991. *Possible Worlds, Artificial Intelligence, and Narrative Theory*. Bloomington, IN: Indiana University Press.

Ryan, Marie-Laure. 1997. "Postmodernism and the Doctrine of Panfictionality." *Narrative* 5 (2): 165–188.

Ryan, Marie-Laure. 2004. *Narrative Across Media: The Languages of Storytelling*. Lincoln, NE: University of Nebraska Press.

Ryan, Marie-Laure. 2005. "Logique culturelle de la métalepse, ou la métalepse dans tous ses états." In *Métalepses: Entorses au pacte de la représentation*, edited by John Pier and Jean-Marie Schaeffer, 201–223. Paris: Éd. de l'EHESS.

Ryan, Marie-Laure. 2006. *Avatars of Story*. Minneapolis: University of Minnesota Press.

Sallé, Jean-Claude. 1955. "A Source of Sterne's Conception of Time." *Review of England Studies* (6): 180–182.

Sallis, John. 2007. "The Hermeneutics of the Artwork." In *Hans-Georg Gadamer: Wahrheit und Methode*, edited by Günter Figal, 45–58. Berlin: Akad.-Verlag.

Sarkhosh, Keyvan. 2011. "Metalepsis in Popular Comedy Film." In *Metalepsis in Popular Culture*, edited by Karin Kukkonen and Sonja Klimek, 171–195. Berlin, New York: De Gruyter.

Schaeffer, Jean-Marie. 2005. "Métalepses et immersion fictionnelle." In *Métalepses: Entorses au pacte de la représentation*, edited by John Pier and Jean-Marie Schaeffer, 323–334. Paris: Éd. de l'EHESS.

Schaeffer, Jean-Marie. 2009. "Fictional vs. Factual Narration." In *Handbook of Narratology*, edited by Peter Hühn, John Pier, Wolf Schmid, and Jörg Schönert, 98–114. Berlin: De Gruyter.

Scheffel, Michael. 1997. *Formen selbstreflexiven Erzählens: Eine Typologie und sechs exemplarische Analysen*. Tübingen: Niemeyer.

Scheffel, Michael. 2007. "Metaisierung in der literarischen Narration." In *Metaisierung in Literatur und Anderen Medien: Theoretische Grundlagen, historische Perspektiven, Metagattungen, Funktionen*, edited by Janine Hauthal, Julijana Nadj, Ansgar Nünning, and Henning Peters, 155–171. Berlin, New York: De Gruyter.

Schleiermacher, Friedrich. 1977. *Hermeneutics: The Handwritten Manuscripts*. Edited by Heinz Kimmerle. Missoula: Scholars Press.

Schlickers, Sabine. 2005. "Inversions, transgressions, paradoxes et bizzareries: La métalepse dans les littératures espagnole et française." In *Métalepses: Entorses au pacte de la représentataion*, edited by John Pier and Jean-Marie Schaeffer, 151–166. Paris: Éd. de l'EHESS.

Schmid, Wolf. 2005. *Elemente der Narratologie*. Berlin, New York: De Gruyter.

Schmid, Wolf. 2010. *Narratology: An Introduction*. Berlin, New York: De Gruyter.

Schmidt, Johann N. 2009. "Narration In Film." In *Handbook of Narratology*, edited by Peter Hühn, John Pier, Wolf Schmid, and Jörg Schönert, 212–227. Berlin: De Gruyter.

Schmitz, Walter, ed. 1997. *Ludwig Tieck: Literaturprogramm und Lebensinszenierung im Kontext seiner Zeit*. Tübingen: Niemeyer.

Scholes, Robert. 1970. "Metafiction." *Iowa Review* 1 (4): 100–115.

Schuldt, Christian. 2005. *Selbstbeobachtung und die Evolution des Kunstsystems: Literaturwissenschaftliche Analysen zu Laurence Sternes Tristram Shandy und den frühen Romanen Flann O'Briens*. Bielefeld: Transcript.

Scott-Baumann, Alison. 2009. *Ricœur and the Hermeneutics of Suspicion*. London: Bloomsbury Publishing.

Searle, John R. 1969. *Speech Acts: An Essay in the Philosophy of Language*. London: Cambridge University Press.

Selden, Raman, Peter Brooks, Hugh B. Nisbet, and Claude J. Rawson, eds. 1995. *The Cambridge History of Literary Criticism*. Cambridge: Cambridge University Press.

Shankman, Steven. 1994. "Plato and Postmodernism." In *Plato and Postmodernism*, edited by Steven Shankman, 3–28. Glenside: The Aldine Press.

Shklovsky, Viktor. 1968 [first Russian ed. 1921]. "A Parodying Novel: Sterne's Tristram Shandy." In *Laurence Sterne: A Collection of Critical Essays*, edited by John Traugott, 66–89. Englewood Cliffs, NJ: Prentice Hall.

Shklovsky, Viktor. 2012 [first Russian ed. 1917]. "Art as Technique." In *Russian Formalist Criticism: Four Essays*, edited by Lee T. Lemon, Marion J. Reis, and Gary S. Morson. Lincoln, NE: Univ. of Nebraska Press.

Shoemaker, Sidney. 1968. "Self-Reference and Self-Awareness." *Journal of Philosophy* (65): 555–567.

Silverman, Hugh J., ed. 1991. *Gadamer and Hermeneutics: Science, Culture, Literature; Plato, Heidegger, Barthes, Ricœur, Habermas, Derrida*. New York, NY: Routledge.

Sim, Stuart. 1996. "Shandean Sentiment and Postmodern Physics." In *Laurence Sterne in Modernism and Postmodernism*, edited by David Pierce and Jan Peter de Voogd, 109–122. Amsterdam, Atlanta: Rodopi.

Skinner, John. 2001. *An Introduction to Eighteenth-Century Fiction: Raising the Novel*. Basingstoke: Palgrave.

Smith, Barbara H. 1981. "Narrative Versions, Narrative Theories." In *On Narrative*, edited by William John Thomas Mitchell, 209–232. Chicago, IL: University of Chicago Press.

Sommer, Roy. 2000. "Funktionsgeschichten: Überlegungen zur Verwendung des Funktionsbegriffs in der Literaturwissenschaft und Anregungen zu seiner terminologischen Differenzierung." *Literaturwissenschaftliches Jahrbuch im Auftrage der Görres-Gesellschaft* (41): 319–341.

Sommer, Roy. 2007. "'Contextualism' Revisited: A Survey (and Defence) of Postcolonial and Intercultural Narratologies." *JLT* (1.1): 61–79.

Sommer, Roy. 2009. "Making Narrative Worlds: A Cross-Disciplinary Approach to Literary Storytelling." In *Narratology in the Age of Cross-Disciplinary Narrative Research*, edited by Sandra Heinen and Roy Sommer, 88–108. Berlin, New York: De Gruyter.

Sommer, Roy. 2012. "The Merger of Classical and Postclassical Narratologies and the Consolidated Future of Narrative Theory." *DIEGESIS: Interdisciplinary E-Journal for Narrative Research* 1 (1): 143–157. https://www.diegesis.uni-wuppertal.de/index.php/diegesis/article/ view/96/94. Accessed September 12, 2014.

Sterne, Laurence. 1997 [1759–1767]. *The Life and Opinions of Tristram Shandy, Gentleman*. Edited by Melvyn New and Joan New. London, New York: Penguin Books.

Swearingen, James E. 1977. *Reflexivity in Tristram Shandy: An Essay in Phenomenological Criticism*. New Haven, London: Yale University Press.

Sypher, Wylie, ed. 1980. *Comedy*. Baltimore: Johns Hopkins University Press.

Tatarkiewicz, Władysław. 1980. *A History of Six Ideas: An Essay in Aesthetics*. The Hague, Boston, London: Polish Scientific Publishers Warszawa.

Tate, Daniel L. 2008. "Transforming Mimesis: Gadamer's Retrieval of Aristotle's Poetics." *Epoché: A Journal for the History of Philosophy* 13 (1): 185–208.

Taylor, Laurie N., and Zach Whalen, eds. 2008. *Playing the Past: History and Nostalgia in Video Games*. Nashville, TN: Vanderbilt University Press.

Thoss, Jeff. 2011. "Unnatural Narrative and Metalepsis: Grant Morrison's Animal Man." In *Unnatural Narratives: Unnatural Narratology*, edited by Jan Alber and Rüdiger Heinze, 189–209. Berlin, Boston: De Gruyter.

Thoss, Jeff. 2011. "'Some Weird Kind of Video Feedback Time Warp Zapping Thing': Television, Remote Controls, and Metalepsis." In *Metalepsis in Popular Culture*, edited by Karin Kukkonen and Sonja Klimek, 158–170. Berlin, New York: De Gruyter.

Thoss, Jeff. 2015. *When Storyworlds Collide: Metalepsis in Popular Fiction, Film and Comics*. Leiden: Brill/Rodopi.
Tittle, Peg. 2011. *Critical Thinking: An Appeal to Reason*. New York: Routledge.
Todorov, Tzvetan. 2001 [1969]. "Structural Analysis of Narrative." In *The Norton Anthology of Theory and Criticism*, edited by Vincent B. Leitch, 2099–2106. London, New York: W.W. Norton.
Tolkien, John Ronald Reuel. 2007 [1954/1955]. *The Lord of the Rings*. London: HarperCollins.
Tolstoy, Leo. 1996 [first Russian ed. 1869]. *War and Peace: The Maude Translation, Backgrounds and Sources, Criticism*. Edited by George Gibian. New York: W.W. Norton.
Trabant, Jürgen, and Günter Abel, eds. 1995. *Sprache Denken: Positionen Aktueller Sprachphilosophie*. Frankfurt am Main: Fischer.
Traugott, John. 1954. *Tristram Shandy's World: Sterne's Philosophical Rhetoric*. Berkeley: University of California Press.
Traugott, John, ed. 1968. *Laurence Sterne: A Collection of Critical Essays*. Englewood Cliffs, NJ: Prentice Hall.
Ueding, Gert, Gregor Kalivoda, Franz-Hubert Robling, and Heike Mayer, eds. 1992. *Historisches Wörterbuch der Rhetorik*. Tübingen: Niemeyer.
van Ghent, Dorothy. 1987. "On Tristram Shandy." In *Laurence Sterne's Tristram Shandy*, edited by Harold Bloom, 7–22. New York: Chelsea House.
Volkmann, Richard. 1885. *Die Rhetorik der Griechen und Römer in systematischer Uebersicht*. 2. Auflage. Leipzig: Teubner.
Wagner, Frank. 2002. "Glissements et déphasages: note sur la métalepse narrative." *Poétique* 33 (130): 235–253.
Walsh, Richard. 2007. *The Rhetoric of Fictionality: Narrative Theory and the Idea of Fiction*. Columbus, OH: Ohio State University Press.
Walsh, Richard. 2010. "Person, Level, Voice: A Rhetorical Reconsideration." In *Postclassical Narratology: Approaches and Analyses*, edited by Jan Alber and Monika Fludernik, 35–57. Columbus, OH: Ohio State University Press.
Warhol, Robyn. 1986. "Toward a Theory of the Engaging Narrator: Earnest Interventions in Gaskell, Stowe, and Eliot." *PMLA* (101): 811–818.
Warnke, Georgia. 2002. "Social Identity as Interpretation." In *Gadamer's Century: Essays in Honor of Hans-Georg Gadamer*, edited by Jeff Malpas, Ulrich Arnswald, and Jens Kertscher, 307–329. Cambridge, MA: MIT Press.
Watt, Ian. 1967. *The Rise of the Novel: Studies in Defoe, Richardson and Fielding*. Berkeley and Los Angeles: University of California Press.
Watt, Ian. 1987. "The Comic Syntax of Tristram Shandy." In *Laurence Sterne's Tristram Shandy*, edited by Harold Bloom, 43–58. New York: Chelsea House.
Waugh, Patricia. 1984. *Metafiction: The Theory and Practice of Self-Conscious Fiction*. London: Methuen.
Weinsheimer, Joel C. 1985. *Gadamer's Hermeneutics*. New Haven and London: Yale University Press.
Werler, Tobias, and Christoph Wulf, eds. 2006. *Hidden Dimensions of Education: Rhetoric, Rituals and Anthropology*. Münster: Waxmann.
Westphal, Merold. 2011. "The Dialectic of Belonging and Distanciation in Gadamer and Ricœur." In *Gadamer and Ricœur: Critical Horizons for Contemporary Hermeneutics*, edited by Francis J. Mootz and George H. Taylor, 43–62. London, New York: Continuum.

Whewell, D. A. 1987. "Self-Reference and Meaning in a Natural Language." In *Self-Reference: Reflections on Reflexivity*, edited by Steven J. Bartlett and Peter Suber, 31–40. Dordrecht: Springer Netherlands.

White, Hayden. 1987. *The Content of the Form: Narrative Discourse and Historical Representation*. Baltimore: Johns Hopkins University Press.

Willbergh, Ilmi. 2006. "Mimesis and the Use of Digital Media in Teaching." In *Hidden Dimensions of Education: Rhetoric, Rituals and Anthropology*, edited by Tobias Werler and Christoph Wulf, 50–63. Münster: Waxmann.

Wittgenstein, Ludwig. 1958 [first German ed. 1953]. *Philosophical Investigations*. Oxford: Blackwell.

Wolf, Werner. 1993. *Ästhetische Illusion und Illusionsdurchbrechung in der Erzählkunst: Theorie und Geschichte mit Schwerpunkt auf englischem illusionsstörenden Erzählen*. Tübingen: Niemeyer.

Wolf, Werner. 2005. "Metalepsis as a Transgeneric and Transmedial Phenomenon. A Case Study of the Possibilities of 'Exporting' Narratological Concepts." In *Narratology Beyond Literary Criticism: Mediality, Disciplinarity*, edited by Jan Christoph Meister, Tom Kindt, and Wilhelm Schernus, 83–107. Berlin, New York: Walter de Gruyter.

Wolf, Werner. 2009. "Illusion (Aesthetic)." In *Handbook of Narratology*, edited by Peter Hühn, John Pier, Wolf Schmid, and Jörg Schönert, 144–159. Berlin, New York: De Gruyter.

Wolf, Werner. 2009. "Metareference Across Media: The Concept, Its Transmedial Potentials and Problems, Main Forms and Functions." In *Metareference Across Media: Theory and Case Studies*, edited by Werner Wolf, Katharina Bantleon, Jeff Thoss, and Walter Bernhart, 1–85. Amsterdam, New York: Rodopi.

Wolf, Werner. 2013. "'Unnatural' Metalepsis and Immersion: Necessarily Incompatible?" In *A Poetics of Unnatural Narrative*, edited by Jan Alber, Henrik Skov Nielsen, and Brian Richardson, 113–141. Columbus, OH: Ohio State University Press.

Wolf, Werner, Katharina Bantleon, Jeff Thoss, and Walter Bernhart, eds. 2009. *Metareference Across Media: Theory and Case Studies*. Amsterdam, New York: Rodopi.

Wright, Crispin. 1987. *Realism, Meaning and Truth*. Oxford: Blackwell.

Young, Thomas D., ed. 1976. *The New Criticism and After*. Charlottesville, VA: University Press of Virginia.

Index

Abbott, H. Porter 125, 159
Abish, Walter
- *Alphabetical Africa* 179–180
Alber, Jan 24, 25, 38–39, 47, 69, 72, 97, 112, 127, 128, 130, 154
Allen, Woody
- "The Kugelmass Episode" 23, 25, 26, 43, 60, 94, 95, 97, 172, 173, 174
Alter, Robert 182, 193, 196, 238, 240
Amis, Martin
- *Money* 28–29
Aristotle 133–134, 150, 157, 166–169, 171, 176–177
Austin, John 65, 190

Bakhtin, Mikhail 9
Bal, Mieke 132, 210
Balzac, Honoré de
- *Lost Illusions* 41, 42, 43
Banfield, Ann 156, 185
Bareis, Alexander 39, 70
Barthes, Roland 125, 174
Barton, Ruth 250
Beardsworth, Richard 153, 159, 164
Beck, Hamilton 196
Beckett, Samuel
- *The Unnamable* 154
Bell, Alice 24, 25, 38–39, 47, 69, 72, 79, 97, 112, 119
Ben-Merre, David 7, 72
Bennett, Tony 154, 192
Benveniste, Emile 185
Bergson, Henry 114
Berkeley, George 175
Bloom, Harold 14
Bolter, Jay David 118
Booth, Wayne 191, 192
Bordwell, David 75
Borges, Jorge Luis
- "Tlön, Uqbar, Orbis Tertius" 45, 105–106, 108
Brontë, Charlotte
- *Jane Eyre* 60, 61, 62, 96, 97
Brontë, Emily

- *Wuthering Heights* 119
Brook, Andrew 188
Brooke-Rose, Christine
- *Thru* 111, 154
Brooks, Mel 244, 246, 247, 249, 251, 252, 253
- *Blazing Saddles* 249–253
- *Robin Hood: Men in Tights* 73, 75–78
- *Spaceballs* 243, 246–249, 251
Bruns, Gerald 118–119, 140, 143, 144, 149, 212, 228, 229, 232, 238, 241
Bunn, Cullen, and Dalibor Talajic
- *Deapool Kills the Marvel Universe* 85, 244, 253–259
Burkhardt, Armin 11, 12, 13, 16
Burton, Robert 191, 224
Butler, Judith 14, 66

Carnap, Rudolf 182
Carroll, Jonathan
- *The Land of Laughs* 103, 104
Carter, Angela
- "The Loves of Lady Purple" 1
- *The Infernal Desire Machines of Doctor Hoffman* 177–178
Cash, Arthur H. 225, 240
Castañeda, Hector-Neri 188
Cervantes Saavedra, Miguel de 191
- *Don Quixote* 70, 192, 193
Chambers, Ephraim 191
Chaplin, Charlie
- *The Great Dictator* 79
Chatman, Seymour 18, 75
Chihaia, Matei 24
Chopin, Kate
- *The Awakening* 132
Coleridge, Samuel 189, 190
Conrad, Joseph
- *Heart of Darkness* 57–58, 60
Cortázar, Julio 18, 118
Coste, Didier 18, 53, 163
Craven, Wes
- *Wes Craven's The Hills Have Eyes* 115
Culler, Jonathan 159

Cummings, Brian 11, 12, 13, 14, 16
Currie, Mark 182

Dahlberg, Leif 79
Danielewski, Mark Z.
- *House of Leaves* 158
Darby, David 8, 128
Davis, Robert G. 208, 209
de Bourcier, Simon 245
de Jong, Irene 8, 169
de Man, Paul 14
Defoe, Daniel 191, 194, 203
- *Robinson Crusoe* 57, 160
Derrida, Jacques 66, 156
Desiderius Erasmus 13
Devitt, Michael 175
Dilthey, Wilhelm 120, 137–138, 142, 231–232
Dorje, Gyurme 257
Dummett, Michael 176
Dutt, Carsten 142

Eco, Umberto 185
- *The Name of the Rose* 64
Edelman, Lee 246
Eisen, Ute E. 244
Eisner, Will
- *The Spirit* 73
Else, Gerald F. 168
Evans, Gareth 188

Faris, J. A. 199, 200
Fauconnier, Gilles 141
Federman, Raymond
- *Take It or Leave It* 152, 156–157, 158–159, 160
Ferriar, John 224
Feyersinger, Erwin 24, 25
Fforde, Jasper
- *The Eyre Affair* 59–63, 67, 96–97
Fielding, Henry 117, 191, 195–196, 197, 200, 202
- *An Apology for the Life of Mrs Shamela Andrews* 39, 70
- *Tom Jones* 91–92, 116–117, 177, 193–194
Fielding, Sarah 191, 202

Flaubert, Gustave
- *Madame Bovary* 23, 39, 43, 44, 97, 172
Fletcher, Angus 14
Fludernik, Monika 2–3, 5, 7, 24, 33–35, 38, 40, 72, 81–84, 87–93, 94–97, 98, 106, 107, 116–117, 124, 127, 128, 130, 166, 174, 177, 179, 182, 220
Fontanier, Pierre 12, 14, 15, 16
Fountayne, John 225
Fowles, John 27, 28, 29, 30, 31
- *The French Lieutenant's Woman* 6, 27, 28, 29–31
Fricke, Harald 181

Gadamer, Hans-Georg 6, 7, 9, 123, 131–134, 136–151, 152, 156, 166, 168–174, 204, 220, 228, 229, 241
Gass, William H. 181
Gavins, Joanna 118
Gebauer, Gunter 167, 168
Genette, Gérard 1–3, 7, 8, 11–12, 14–31, 34, 35, 36, 37, 38, 39, 40, 41, 44, 47–48, 51, 53, 55, 56, 59, 64, 66, 67, 69, 70, 72, 75, 78, 81, 87, 88, 89, 92, 93, 94, 95, 98, 106, 107, 110, 113, 126, 128, 134, 135, 139, 152, 155, 157–161, 164, 174, 179, 181, 183, 192, 196, 205, 207, 216, 222, 227
Gibson, Andrew 155, 156, 162, 163, 164
Gide, André
- *The Counterfeiters* 101–102
Goodman, Nelson 70, 167
Grusin, Richard 118

Hamburger, Käte 185
Hanebeck, Julian 158
Harpold, Terry 7, 72, 78–80
Häsner, Bernd 24, 36–38, 81, 91
Hauthal, Janine 181
Hawes, Clement 15, 16
Haywood, Eliza 202
Hegel, Georg Wilhelm Friedrich 147, 148
Heidegger, Martin 131, 133, 142, 144, 244
Heinen, Sandra 156
Hempfer, Klaus W. 24, 181, 182
Herman, David 18, 23, 24, 35, 36, 48, 50, 56, 97, 102, 109–110, 122, 125, 128,

130, 135–136, 143, 160, 161, 162, 210, 233, 234, 235, 247
Hofer, Roberta 23, 72, 80
Hofstadter, Douglas 24, 32, 100–101, 152
Hollander, John 14, 15, 17
Holub, Robert C. 141–142, 151
Howes, Alan B. 191, 225, 226
Huber, Irmtraud 247
Huber, Werner 182
Hühn, Peter 31
Hume, David 187–188
Hutcheon, Linda 181, 182, 185, 186
Hyams, Peter
– *Stay Tuned* 70

Imhof, Rüdiger 182, 202, 203, 213
Immermann, Karl 151
Iversen, Stefan 154

Jahn, Manfred 141
Jakobson, Roman 185
Jaslow, Joseph 209
Jonze, Spike
– *Being John Malkovich* 50, 96, 119, 247, 248
Joyce, James
– *Finnegan's Wake* 38

Kalish, Donald 20
Kane, Sarah
– *Cleansed* 73
Kant, Immanuel 113, 188
Kertscher, Jens 143
Kindt, Tom 124, 126–128, 130, 132, 133, 134
Klimek, Sonja 7, 24, 28–29, 33, 39, 63, 69, 71, 72, 78, 82, 101, 103, 116, 152
Kockelmans, Joseph 140
Korthals Altes, Liesbeth 130–131
Krah, Hans 181
Kuhn, Markus 75
Kukkonen, Karin 7, 15, 27, 72, 98–99, 110, 116

Landfester, Ulrike 7, 72
Lanser, Susan 129
Laudando, Carla M. 192

Lavocat, Françoise 24
Lawson, Hilary 187
Lennox, Charlotte 191, 202
Lewis, David 175
Limoges, Jean-Marc 7, 63, 72, 244, 245
Locke, John 8, 211, 212, 217
Luhmann, Niklas 107
Lutas, Liviu 24
Lyotard, Jean-François 228

Malick, Terence
– *The Thin Red Line* 77
Malina, Debra 7, 24, 26, 36, 45, 64, 65, 68, 97, 111, 115, 128, 163, 227, 228, 229, 253
Malpas, Jeff 3, 142, 227
Mar, Gary 20
Martínez, Matías 125
Mayer, Robert 57
Mayoux, Jean-Jacques 213, 215
McHale, Brian 24, 32, 87, 101, 103, 152, 156, 166
McQuillan, Martin 27
Meister, Jan Christoph 15, 24, 36, 63, 124, 128, 134, 152, 228, 246, 258, 262
Melanchthon, Philipp 12, 13, 14
Mendilow, A. A. 216
Meyer-Minnemann, Klaus 15
Middeke, Martin 182
Miller, D. A. 185
Miller, Hillis 14
Moglen, Helene 216
Montague, Richard 20
Montaigne, Michel de 191
Morreall, John 114
Morrison, Grant
– *Animal Man* 49, 98–99, 100
Morsch, Thomas 24, 72
Mukařovský, Jan 185
Müller, Hans-Harald 124, 126–128, 130, 134

Nadj, Julijana 181
Nelles, William 16, 18, 24, 27, 33, 36, 51, 59, 81–82, 85, 89, 91, 97, 190, 195, 236
Neumann, Birgit 182

Newman, Beth 195
Newmeyer, Frederick J. 109
Nielsen, Henrik Skov 154
Nietzsche, Friedrich 1, 3, 4–5, 49, 139, 202, 240, 241
– "On Truth and Lies in an Extra-Moral Sense" 1
– *Beyond Good and Evil* 4, 202
– *Human, all Too Human* 240
– *The Gay Science* 4
Nordlund, Marcus 140
Nöth, Winfried 190
Nünning, Ansgar 124, 127, 128, 129, 130, 181, 182, 194, 202
Nünning, Vera 194

O'Neill, Patrick 24, 36, 155, 156, 157, 163
O'Brien, Flann
– *At-Swim-Two-Birds* 44
Olsen, Greta 127
Ostovich, Helen 236, 237

Padmasaṃbhava, and Terton Karma Lingpa
– *The Tibetan Book of the Dead* 9, 121, 123, 244, 259–262
Perry, John 188
Petterson, Bo 131–132
Phelan, James 27
Pier, John 3, 7, 15, 16, 18, 23, 24, 39, 40, 53, 81, 84, 88, 122, 152, 163, 166, 181, 245, 247
Plato 55, 119, 167–169, 176, 177, 179
Prince, Gerald 17, 18, 24, 34, 102, 124, 126, 133, 150, 157, 162, 194
Puntel, Lorenz B. 178
Putnam, Hilary 175, 178

Quintilian 12, 13, 15, 16, 17

Rabelais, François 192, 193
– *Gargantua and Pantagruel* 191
Rabinowitz, Peter J. 27
Rhys, Jean
– *Wide Sargasso Sea* 39
Richardson, Brian 154, 166, 180

Richardson, Samuel 160, 191, 194, 196, 202
– *Clarissa* 202
– *Pamela, or Virtue Rewarded* 70
Richetti, John J. 191, 202
Ricks, Christopher 199
Ricœur, Paul 4, 5, 6, 123, 130, 132, 133, 136–137, 142, 144–146, 217
Rilke, Rainer Maria 151
Rimmon-Kenan, Slomith 157
Risser, James 148
Robbe-Grillet, Alain 154
– *La Jalousie* 18, 111
Robertson, Scott 117
Römer, Inga 144
Ronen, Ruth 174
Ross, Ian C. 223, 225, 226, 229
Roth, Eli
– *Hostel* 115
Roussin, Philippe 15
Rubik, Margarete 245
Russell, Bertrand 182, 183
Ryan, Marie-Laure 7, 15, 23, 24, 27, 32, 33, 36, 48–50, 59, 63, 65, 81–84, 87–93, 94, 101, 112, 115, 116, 120, 128, 152, 155, 156, 161, 162, 247, 259

Sallis, John 170
Sarkhosh, Keyvan 7, 72, 246, 247
Schaeffer, Jean-Marie 23, 79, 88, 177
Scheffel, Michael 181, 182, 184–185
Schleiermacher, Friedrich 118
Schlickers, Sabine 15
Schmid, Wolf 31, 49, 56, 60, 66, 184
Schmidt, Johann N. 75
Scholes, Robert 181, 182
Schönert, Jörg 31
Schuldt, Christian 237
Scott-Baumann, Alison 5, 145
Searle, John R. 65, 190
Shankman, Steven 167
Shklovsky, Viktor 192, 197, 206, 209
Shoemaker, Sidney 188
Sim, Stuart 239–240
Sitter, John 202
Smith, Barbara H. 162
Smollett, Tobias 191

Sommer, Roy 77, 108, 109, 122, 128, 129, 130
Stanzel, Franz Karl 154, 194
Sterne, Laurence 1, 2, 8, 12, 18, 19, 24, 56, 67, 80, 191–241, 243, 244
– *The Life and Opinions of Tristram Shandy, Gentleman* 1–3, 8–9, 28, 33–34, 36, 37, 56, 67, 88, 93, 106–107, 159–165, 172–173, 186–187, 188, 189, 190, 191–241, 244
– *The Sermons of Mr Yorick* 67, 80, 226
Swift, Jonathan 191

Tatarkiewicz, Władysław 169
Tate, Daniel L. 171
Thoss, Jeff 3, 7, 24, 27, 38, 39, 49, 68, 69, 70, 72, 98–99, 246, 247, 248
Todorov, Tzvetan 125, 126, 130
Tolkien, J.R.R.
– *The Lord of the Rings* 177
Tolstoy, Leo 21
– *War and Peace* 21, 66, 67
Traugott, John 199
Tryphon 11, 12, 13, 17

van Ghent, Dorothy 210

von Möllendorff, Peter 244

Wagner, Frank 24, 38, 47, 63, 69
Walsh, Richard 22, 25, 26, 49, 50, 55–56, 58, 61, 210
Warhol, Robyn 24, 129
Warnke, Georgia 143, 203
Watt, Ian 34, 160, 194, 230
Waugh, Patricia 106, 182
Weinsheimer, Joel C. 135, 137, 138, 142
Westphal, Merold 136–138, 145, 146
Whewell, D. A. 183
White, Alan 178
White, Hayden 155
Willbergh, Ilmi 167
Wittgenstein, Ludwig 124–125, 133, 143, 209
Wolf, Werner 2–4, 5, 8, 14, 23, 24, 25, 27, 36, 47, 68, 72, 77–78, 85, 93, 101, 112–113, 115, 116, 120, 140, 152, 153, 166, 174, 177, 181, 182, 184, 185, 186, 219, 250
Wright, Crispin 176, 180
Wulf, Christoph 167, 168

Zapf, Hubert 182

www.ingramcontent.com/pod-product-compliance
Lightning Source LLC
Chambersburg PA
CBHW061934220426
43662CB00012B/1905